Inconceivable Effects

signale
modern german letters, cultures, and thought

Series editor: Peter Uwe Hohendahl, Cornell University

Signale: Modern German Letters, Cultures, and Thought publishes new English-language books in literary studies, criticism, cultural studies, and intellectual history pertaining to the German-speaking world, as well as translations of important German-language works. *Signale* construes "modern" in the broadest terms: the series covers topics ranging from the early modern period to the present. *Signale* books are published under a joint imprint of Cornell University Press and Cornell University Library in electronic and print formats. Please see http://signale.cornell.edu/.

INCONCEIVABLE EFFECTS

Ethics through Twentieth-Century German Literature, Thought, and Film

MARTIN BLUMENTHAL-BARBY

A Signale Book

CORNELL UNIVERSITY PRESS AND CORNELL UNIVERSITY LIBRARY
ITHACA, NEW YORK

Cornell University Press and Cornell University Library gratefully acknowledge The Andrew W. Mellon Foundation and the College of Arts & Sciences, Cornell University, for support of the Signale series.

Copyright © 2013 by Cornell University

All rights reserved. Except for brief quotations in a review, this book, or parts thereof, must not be reproduced in any form without permission in writing from the publisher. For information, address Cornell University Press, Sage House, 512 East State Street, Ithaca, New York 14850.

First published 2013 by Cornell University Press and Cornell University Library

Printed in the United States of America

Library of Congress Cataloging-in-Publication Data
Blumenthal-Barby, Martin, author.
  Inconceivable effects : ethics through twentieth-century German literature, thought, and film / Martin Blumenthal-Barby.
      pages cm. — (Signale : modern German letters, cultures, and thought)
   Includes bibliographical references and index.
   ISBN 978-0-8014-7812-3 (pbk. : alk. paper)
  1. German literature—20th century—History and criticism. 2. Ethics—Germany—History—20th century. 3. Ethics in literature. 4. Ethics in motion pictures. I. Title.
   PT405.B5384 2013
   830.9'353—dc23   2013013210

Cornell University Press strives to use environmentally responsible suppliers and materials to the fullest extent possible in the publishing of its books. Such materials include vegetable-based, low-VOC inks and acid-free papers that are recycled, totally chlorine-free, or partly composed of nonwood fibers. For further information, visit our website at www.cornellpress.cornell.edu.

Paperback printing   10 9 8 7 6 5 4 3 2

Contents

Acknowledgments	vii
Prologue. Ethics and Poetics: An Uneasy Affair	ix
Introduction	1
1. "The Odium of Doubtfulness": Or the Vicissitudes of Arendt's Metaphorical Thinking	16
2. Why Does Hannah Arendt Lie? Or the Vicissitudes of Imagination	40
3. "A Peculiar Apparatus": Kafka's Thanatopoetics	56
4. A Strike of Rhetoric: Benjamin's Paradox of Justice	81
5. Pernicious Bastardizations: Benjamin's Ethics of Pure Violence	101
6. The Return of the Human: *Germany in Autumn*	122
7. A Politics of Enmity: Müller's *Germania Death in Berlin*	151
Index	181

Acknowledgments

The writing of this book was possible thanks to the support of three institutions: Yale University, where the project originated; Rice University, where the manuscript gradually turned into a book; and Stanford University, where an External Faculty Fellowship at the Humanities Center in 2011–12 allowed for its completion.

I am grateful to Carol Jacobs, Rainer Nägele, and Henry Sussman; their inspirational teaching and highly discerning attention throughout the early development of this project were invaluable. I am beholden to my colleagues at Rice University, especially Uwe Steiner, Christian J. Emden, and Klaus Weissenberger, for their friendly encouragement, support, and understanding. My thanks to *Signale*'s series editor, Peter Hohendahl, to the editorial board, and to two anonymous reviewers for their unfailing and discriminating feedback. Thanks also to Kizer Walker and Marian Rogers for their help in steering the book through production. I am much indebted to Katie Trumpener for her mentorship, and I wish to thank Kirk Wetters for contributing his analytical acumen to portions of the study. Harriet Bergmann and Marshall Kibbey generously gave time and helped to smooth out stylistic infelicities. Namwali Serpell and Ansgar Mohnkern offered insightful comments. A special word of thanks is owed to Jenny Blumenthal-Barby, whose philosophical attention and responsiveness provided me with a valuable perspective, and whose very presence gives me the feeling of having arrived in the New World. The teaching of Shoshana Felman and Seyla Benhabib has shaped my thinking throughout, in different ways, and I wish to thank both of them. That this book could draw on the expertise of so many fine scholars, whose methodological preferences are far from compatible, cannot go unmentioned. What rates more than a mere mention is how profoundly grateful I am for the opportunity to have benefited from their exceptional erudition.

* * *

An early version of chapter 1, entitled "'The Odium of Doubtfulness,' or the Vicissitudes of Arendt's Metaphorical Thinking," appeared in *New German Critique* 36.1 (2009): 61–81, published by Duke University Press.

An early version of chapter 2, entitled "Why Does Hannah Arendt Lie?, or the Vicissitudes of Imagination," appeared in *Germanic Review* 82.4 (Fall 2007 [de facto 2008]): 369–88, published by Taylor and Francis.

An early version of chapter 5, entitled "Pernicious Bastardizations: Benjamin's Ethics of Pure Violence," appeared in the German issue of *Modern Language Notes* 124.3 (Spring 2009): 728–51, published by Johns Hopkins University Press.

An early version of chapter 6, entitled "'Germany in Autumn': The Return of the Human," appeared in *Discourse: Journal for Theoretical Studies in Media and Culture* 29.1 (Winter 2007 [de facto Winter 2008/2009]): 140–68, published by Wayne State University Press.

The publication of this book was graciously subsidized by the Department of German Studies at Rice University.

Prologue

Ethics and Poetics: An Uneasy Affair

A book including the word "ethics" on its cover invokes, for better or for worse, a certain professional affiliation with the field of philosophy and, more specifically, the philosophical branch of ethics. This book, however, is neither written *by* a philosopher, nor is it, strictly speaking, written *for* philosophers. As a matter of fact, philosophers, especially those who professionally concern themselves with questions of ethics, will likely perceive this book to be a great disappointment. The book will disappoint professional philosophers because it conceives ethics in an extremely flexible sense as it arises out of the reading of individual texts that, in their nuances and particularities, remain defiant to philosophical conceptualization. Moreover, this book is doomed to dissatisfy philosophers, since it is not framed in terms of established philosophical ideas or positions but instead limits itself to a cursory and narrowly focused engagement with such positions, an engagement hardly contributing to the existing philosophical scholarship. Professional ethicists might, finally, experience this book as underwhelming insofar as it does not attend to "ethics," as commonly understood, as the study of moral values and their justification; it deals with ethics in a rather particular way, one we shall later describe as "literary ethics," an approach that seeks to evoke interest in literary circles, but one that can, at best, hope for open-minded skepticism among philosophers. Why then—with so little hope for philosophical dividends—a book on "ethics," and why such a book by a literary critic who lacks any certified expertise on the matter and who, in fact, would not lay claim to such expertise? Precisely what sort of competency might a literary critic, trained in the art of close reading and poetic scrutiny, bring to the table that could be relevant to the issue of "ethics"?

This book—in the course of seven essays—performs readings of theoretical, literary, and cinematic works that appear noteworthy for the ethical questions they raise. Via critical analysis of writers and filmmakers whose projects have changed our ways of viewing the modern world, these essays furnish a cultural base for contemporary discussions on totalitarian domination (chapter 1), lying and politics (chapter 2), the relation between law and body (chapter 3), the relation between law and justice (chapters 4 and 5), our ways of conceptualizing "the human" (chapter 6), and the question of violence (chapter 7). Yet if the "common denominator" is what may be described as "ethics," then ethics is never addressed "in general." It seems that whatever understanding of the ethical one may have, it is always contingent on a particular mode of presentation (*Darstellung*), on particular aesthetic qualities and mediatic specificities. Whatever there is to be said about ethics, it is still bound to certain forms of saying, certain ways of telling, certain modes of narration. That modes of presentation differ across genres and media goes without saying; that such differences are intimately linked with the question of the ethical will emerge with increasing urgency.

To be sure, the relationship between ethics and aesthetics has been subject to scholarly debate for some time. This debate, which could easily be traced back to Plato's and Aristotle's respective reflections on the matter, finds—in its contemporary configuration—perhaps its most significant forerunner in early twentieth-century philosopher Ludwig Wittgenstein. In conversation with his friend Friedrich Waismann, Wittgenstein stated: "In ethics, one constantly tries to say something that does not concern and can never concern the essence of the matter. It is a priori certain that, whatever definition one may give of the Good, it is always a misunderstanding to suppose that the formulation corresponds to what one really means."[1] Such skepticism regarding the possibility of grasping the essence of ethics by dint of propositional language pervades much of the late twentieth-century philosophical literature concerned with the nexus between ethics and language. "If a man," Wittgenstein elaborates in imagistic terms in his 1929–30 "Lecture on Ethics," "could write a book on Ethics which really was a book on Ethics, this book would, with an explosion, destroy all the other books in the world. Our words used as we use them in science, are vessels capable only of containing and conveying meaning and sense, *natural* meaning and sense. Ethics, if it is anything, is supernatural."[2] The purported insufficiency of propositional language in the face of ethics, that is, ethics' resistance to lending itself as "subject matter" to philosophy, indeed leads Wittgenstein to speak of a "characteristic misuse of our language [that] runs through *all* ethical...expressions."[3] He concludes that "to write or talk Ethics [is] to run against the boundaries of language. This running against the walls of our cage is perfectly, absolutely hopeless."[4]

The vexed relationship between ethics and language in general, and ethics and poetic language in particular, lies at the heart of much of the contemporary "literature and ethics" debate as it has evolved over the course of some thirty years now. The profound hopelessness invoked by Wittgenstein did not prevent this debate

---

1. Ludwig Wittgenstein, "Notes on Talks with Wittgenstein," *Philosophical Review* 74.1 (1965): 12–16, here 13.
2. Ludwig Wittgenstein, "A Lecture on Ethics," *Philosophical Review* 74.1 (1965): 3–12, here 7. Wittgenstein translates this contention into the language of yet another image, according to which "a teacup will only hold a teacup full of water" (7), even if one pours out a gallon over it. And as a teacup is confined to the limits of a teacup, so propositional language cannot exceed its own limits, cannot appropriate what lies "*beyond*" itself, namely ethics (11).
3. Wittgenstein, "Lecture on Ethics," 4, 9.
4. Ibid., 11f.

from becoming an academic growth industry, including, in the forefront, such notable philosophers as Alasdair MacIntyre, Richard Rorty, and Martha Nussbaum, as well as eminent literary critics the likes of Wayne Booth, Tobin Siebers, and J. Hillis Miller. "Their combined efforts have signaled what has come to be perceived and referred to as a 'turn to ethics' in literary studies and, conversely, a 'turn to literature' in (moral) philosophy," Michael Eskin writes in the introduction to the 2004 special issue of *Poetics Today*, "The Double 'Turn' to Ethics and Literature."[5] In the subsequent pages I hope to flesh out some of the major positions that have been assumed in this debate, first by three philosophers (namely MacIntyre, Rorty, and Nussbaum) who exemplify moral philosophy's turn to narrative, then by three literary critics (Booth, Siebers, and Miller) who represent literary studies' turn to ethics. What should result from this is a sense of how my own thoughts on the interrelatedness of ethics and poetics correspond with and especially differ from the canonical positions on the subject.

Philosophy's Turn to Narrative

One of the most broadly conceived positions concerned with the relation between ethics and language has been that of Alasdair MacIntyre, who, in his 1981 *After Virtue*, claimed that "the language of morality is in [a] state of grave disorder": "What we possess...are the fragments of a conceptual scheme, parts which now lack those contexts from which their significance derived. We possess indeed simulacra of morality, we continue to use many of the key expressions. But we have—very largely, if not entirely—lost our comprehension, both theoretical and practical, of morality."[6] In response to this state of "grave disorder," MacIntyre brings into play the powerful cultural tradition of *storytelling*. More concretely, he juxtaposes the presumed "liquidation of the self into a set of demarcated areas of role-playing" with his own— distinctly *narrative*—concept of selfhood, "a concept of a self whose unity resides in the unity of a narrative which links birth to life to death as narrative beginning to middle to end."[7] What emerges forcefully here is MacIntyre's underlying postulation according to which "man is in his actions and practice...essentially a storytelling animal."[8] Once the axiomatic assumption of it being "natural...to think of the self in a narrative mode" has been accepted, it seems to follow quite naturally that we conceptualize "human actions...as enacted narratives."[9] "Because we

---

5. Michael Eskin, introduction to "The Double 'Turn' to Ethics and Literature?" special issue, *Poetics Today* 25.4 (2004): 557–72, here 557.
6. Alasdair MacIntyre, *After Virtue: A Study in Moral Theory* (Notre Dame, IN: University of Notre Dame Press, 1981), 2. I quote from the second edition, published in 1984.
7. MacIntyre, *After Virtue*, 205.
8. Ibid., 216.
9. Ibid., 206, 211. One of the frequently articulated criticisms launched against MacIntyre consists precisely in this seemingly natural contiguity of human actions and narrative acts. Paul Ricoeur writes: "MacIntyre is mainly considering stories told in the thick of everyday activity and does not attach any

all live out narratives in our lives," MacIntyre submits, "and because we understand our own lives in terms of the narratives that we live out...the form of narrative is appropriate for understanding the actions of others."[10] Hence, there are two overriding and intimately related questions permeating MacIntyre's study in moral theory. "Of what story or stories do I find myself a part?" is, according to MacIntyre, the primary question, which precedes the pivotal question, "What am I to do?"[11]

While, according to MacIntyre, narratives are what allow us to (anticipatorily) prescribe and (retrospectively) justify our actions and behaviors, he insists that "I am never able to seek for the good or exercise the virtues only *qua* individual."[12] MacIntyre adamantly refutes the modern and individualistic perspective "according to which the self is detachable from its social and historical roles and statutes."[13] Rather, "the story of my life is always embedded in the story of those communities from which I derive my identity. I am born with a past; and to try to cut myself off from that past, in the individualist mode, is to deform my present relationships. The possession of an historical identity and the possession of a social identity coincide."[14]

Needless to say, it is here that one of the more questionable aspects of MacIntyre's conception of narrative selfhood surges to the fore. For while he points out that "the fact that the self has to find its moral identity in and through its membership in communities such as those of the family, the neighborhood, the city and the tribe does not entail that the self has to accept the moral *limitations* of the particularity of those forms of community," it nevertheless appears as if MacIntyre's claim—according to which one has to find "moral identity in and through" one's sociohistorically determined "membership in communities"—has very little to offer to those who historically have been denied communal membership and consequently found, and find, themselves on the margins of society.[15] At any rate, what appears particularly pertinent in our context is MacIntyre's overt impatience with ventures "into a realm of entirely universal maxims which belong to man as such, whether in its eighteenth-century Kantian form or in the presentation of some modern

---

decisive importance, at least with respect to the ethical investigation he is conducting, to the split between literary fictions and the stories he says are enacted....For MacIntyre, the difficulties tied to the idea of a refiguration of life by fiction do not arise. However, he does not draw any benefit...from the double fact that it is in literary fiction that the connection between action and its agent is easiest to perceive and that literature proves to be an immense laboratory for thought experiments in which this connection is submitted to an endless number of imaginative variations" (Ricoeur, *Oneself as Another,* trans. Kathleen Blamey [Chicago: University of Chicago Press, 1992], 159).

10. MacIntyre, *After Virtue,* 212.
11. Ibid., 216.
12. Ibid., 220.
13. Ibid., 221.
14. Ibid.
15. Ibid. For a thoughtful critique of MacIntyre's narrative approach to ethics along those lines, see Hilde Lindemann Nelson, *Damaged Identities, Narrative Repair* (Ithaca, NY: Cornell University Press, 2001), 59–61.

analytical philosophies."[16] MacIntyre unambiguously asserts that "what I am...is in key part what I inherit."[17] In the light of this predication, according to which any moral theory requires a historically embedded "understanding of social life," it perhaps comes as no surprise that MacIntyre deems "the Aristotelian moral tradition...the best example we possess of a tradition whose adherents are...entitled to a high measure of confidence in its...moral resources."[18]

Indubitably, such theoretical alliance with the classic Aristotelian tradition of moral virtues is shared by other philosophers who address ethical concerns from a narrative perspective, one of them being Richard Rorty. In his 1989 *Contingency, Irony, and Solidarity*, Rorty argues that "fiction like that of Dickens, Olive Schreiner, or Richard Wright gives us the details about kinds of suffering being endured by people to whom we had previously not attended. Fiction like that of Choderlos de Laclos, Henry James, or Nabokov gives us the details about what sorts of cruelty we ourselves are capable of, and thereby lets us redescribe ourselves."[19] It is therefore that novels, according to Rorty, have become—"gradually but steadily" and in contradistinction to the philosophical treatise—"the principal vehicles of moral change."[20] Notably, this claim constitutes a critical dimension of Rorty's liberal utopia. "In my utopia," he expounds,

> human solidarity would be seen...as a goal to be achieved. It is to be achieved not by inquiry but by imagination, the imaginative ability to see strange people as fellow sufferers. Solidarity is not discovered by reflection but created. It is created by increasing our sensitivity to the particular details of the pain and humiliation of other, unfamiliar sorts of people. Such increased sensitivity makes it more difficult to marginalize people different from ourselves by thinking, "They do not feel it as *we* would," or "There must be always suffering, so why not let *them* suffer?"[21]

The notion of "solidarity" put forth here is expressly *not* to be "thought of as recognition of a core self, the human essence, in all human beings," but rather as "the ability to see more and more traditional differences...as unimportant when compared

---

16. MacIntyre, *After Virtue*, 221.
17. Ibid.
18. Ibid., 225, 277.
19. Richard Rorty, *Contingency, Irony, and Solidarity* (New York: Cambridge University Press, 1989), xvi. "The books which help us become less cruel," Rorty specifies, "can be roughly divided into (1) books which help us see the effects of social practices and institutions on others and (2) those which help us to see the effects of our private idiosyncrasies on others. The first sort of book is typified by books about, for example, slavery, poverty, and prejudice.... Such books help us see how social practices which we have taken for granted made us cruel. The second sort of book...is about the ways in which particular sorts of people are cruel to other particular sorts of people.... The most useful books of this sort are works of fiction which exhibit the blindness of a certain kind of person to the pain of another kind of person" (141).
20. Rorty, *Contingency, Irony, and Solidarity*, xvi.
21. Ibid.

with similarities with respect to pain and humiliation—the ability to think of people wildly different from ourselves as included in the range of 'us.'" Evidently more sensitive to the distinct status of communal insiders and outcasts than MacIntyre, Rorty concludes that the "process of coming to see other human beings as 'one of us' rather than as 'them' is a matter of detailed description of what unfamiliar people are like and of redescription of what we ourselves are like." And this dual task is precisely one that, according to Rorty, a philosophical treatise is less likely to accomplish than is "ethnography, the journalist's report, the comic book, the docudrama, and, especially, the novel." The paradigmatic shift from theory to fiction described here signifies, in the context of Rorty's "liberal utopia," no less than a "general turn against theory and toward narrative." Rorty considers such a turn as "emblematic of our having given up the attempt to hold all the sides of our life in a single vision, to describe them with a single vocabulary." It amounts to a "recognition" of what he calls the "contingency of language"—"the fact that there is no way to step outside the various vocabularies we have employed and find a metavocabulary which somehow takes account of *all possible* vocabularies, all possible ways of judging and feeling." The "historicist and nominalist" culture Rorty envisages (and which only obliquely ties him to MacIntyre) thus settles "for narratives which connect the present with the past, on the one hand, and with utopian futures, on the other."[22]

The predicament with this approach is that Rorty's account of literature remains confined to the propositional dimension of language while failing to acknowledge its less graspable figurative force.[23] In Rorty's theory, the pragmatist philosopher Richard Shusterman aptly notes, "literature seems almost reduced to a branch of practical moral philosophy."[24] Whereas Rorty holds that aesthetic and ethical aspects of literature are to be treated as "distinct, non-competitive goods,"[25] I would contend that aesthetic and ethical elements are inextricably linked—to the effect that a text's aesthetic features may profoundly determine its ethical thrust.

A final example of the Aristotelian approach to ethics discussed here—and understood, in the words of Geoffrey Galt Harpham, as "markedly worldly and social and...in this respect...consistent with the representational habits of

---

22. Ibid., 192, xvi.
23. See Christoph Demmerling, "Philosophie als literarische Kultur? Bemerkungen zum Verhältnis von Philosophie, Philosophiekritik und Literatur im Anschluss an Richard Rorty," in *Hinter den Spiegeln: Beiträge zur Philosophie Richard Rortys mit Erwiderungen von Richard Rorty,* ed. Thomas Schäfer et al. (Frankfurt a.M.: Suhrkamp, 2001), 325–52, here 350f., quoted in Günter Leypoldt, "Literatur als Angebot 'nützlicher Metaphern': Richard Rortys literarische Ethik," in *Literatur ohne Moral: Literaturwissenschaften und Ethik im Gespräch,* ed. Christof Mandry (Münster: LIT Verlag, 2003), 123–44, here 130.
24. Richard Shusterman and Günter Leypoldt, "The Pragmatist Aesthetics of Richard Shusterman: A Conversation," *ZAA: Zeitschrift für Anglistik und Amerikanistik* 48 (2000): 57–71, here 67, quoted in Leypoldt, "Literatur als Angebot," 130 n. 13.
25. Rorty, *Contingency, Irony, and Solidarity,* 147.

narrative"[26]—presented itself with Martha Nussbaum's voluminous and highly influential 1990 study, *Love's Knowledge,* which eventually will serve as distinct counterexample to the model I hope to develop. Nussbaum argues "for a conception of ethical understanding that involves emotional as well as intellectual activity" and gives considerable "priority to the perception of particular people and situations."[27] In correspondence with her expressly Aristotelian conception of ethics, she stresses the importance of "the study of the social conditions of human life," which she, like Rorty, argues, find a "most appropriate expression... in certain forms usually considered literary rather than philosophical." Consequently, Nussbaum not only urges us to "broaden our conception of moral philosophy in order to include these texts inside it," but indeed she seeks to provide some of the required methodological groundwork by articulating the relationship "within such a broader ethical inquiry, between literary and more abstractly theoretical elements." This involves an appreciation of "valuable aspects of human moral experience that are not tapped by traditional books of moral philosophy." If the project of moral philosophy implies "a pursuit of truth in all its forms," Nussbaum insists, "then moral philosophy requires... literary texts, and the experience of... attentive novel-reading, for its own completion."[28]

The emphasis on "*attentive* novel-reading" denotes a central tenet of Nussbaum's position and finds itself substantiated in the context of her reflections on the importance of "perception," understood as "the ability to discern, acutely and responsively, the salient features of one's particular situation."[29] The objective, in the words of writer Henry James, one of Nussbaum's central referential figures, is that of becoming "'finely aware and richly responsible.'"[30] Notably, the task "to make ourselves people 'on whom nothing is lost'" is,[31] she claims, furthered by novels not merely thematically, that is, by dint of ethical "terms and conceptions."[32] Nussbaum remarks: "Moral knowledge... is not simply intellectual grasp of propositions; it is not even simply intellectual grasp of particular facts; it is perception. It is seeing a complex, concrete reality in a highly lucid and richly responsive way; it is taking in

---

26. Geoffrey Galt Harpham, "Ethics and Literary Criticism," in *The Cambridge History of Literary Criticism,* ed. Christa Knellwolf and Christopher Norris (Cambridge: Cambridge University Press, 2001), 9:371–85, here 378.
27. Martha C. Nussbaum, *Love's Knowledge: Essays on Philosophy and Literature* (New York: Oxford University Press, 1990), ix.
28. Ibid., 139, ix, 143, 26. In *The Fragility of Goodness,* Nussbaum correspondingly states: "A tragedy does not display the dilemmas of its characters as pre-articulated; it shows them searching for the morally salient; and it forces us, as interpreters, to be similarly active. Interpreting a tragedy is a messier, less determinate, more mysterious matter than assessing a philosophical example" (Nussbaum, *The Fragility of Goodness: Luck and Ethics in Greek Tragedy and Philosophy* [Cambridge: Cambridge University Press, 2001], 14).
29. Nussbaum, *Fragility of Goodness,* 37.
30. Henry James, preface to *The Princess Casamassima,* quoted in Nussbaum, *Love's Knowledge,* 37, 148, and 199.
31. Henry James, *The Art of Fiction,* quoted in Nussbaum, *Love's Knowledge,* 148.
32. Nussbaum, *Love's Knowledge,* 157.

what is there, with imagination and feeling."³³ Correspondingly, the moral thrust of novels does not primarily hinge on "the learning of rules and principles." Rather, a "large part of learning takes place in the experience of the concrete. This experiential learning, in turn, requires the cultivation of perception and responsiveness: the ability to read a situation, singling out what is relevant for thought and action." Nussbaum avidly contends that novels "exemplify and offer such [experimental] learning: exemplify it in the efforts of the character..., engender it in the reader by setting up a similarly complex activity."³⁴

To be sure, Nussbaum's emphasis on the "experience of the concrete" presents itself as a salient feature within the purview of her argumentation, which is directed "against the claim of general description, and supports the novelist's finely tuned...descriptions as providing more of what is morally relevant."³⁵ Unsurprisingly, such pronounced skepticism toward formulas, rules, and principles evoked some discontent, such as that articulated by Hilary Putnam, who charged Nussbaum's model of a "morality of perception, which is also a morality of tender attention toward particulars" with being "dangerously lacking in general rule-guided toughness."³⁶ This reservation, which appears forceful especially if seen in the light of the requirements of public political life, was addressed in Nussbaum's 1995 *Poetic Justice,* where she ponders the "characteristics of the literary imagination as a public imagination" and investigates "the ability to imagine what it is like to live the life of another person who might, given the changes in circumstance, be oneself."³⁷ Echoing Rorty's interest in an "imaginative ability to see strange people as fellow sufferers," Nussbaum emphasizes:

> Novels (at least realist novels of the sort I shall consider) present persistent forms of human need...realized in specific social situations. These situations frequently... differ a good deal from the reader's own. Novels, recognizing this...construct and speak to an implicit reader who shares with the characters certain hopes, fears, and general human concerns, and who for that reason is able to form bonds of identification and sympathy with them.³⁸

---

33. Ibid., 152.
34. Ibid., 44.
35. Ibid., 165. "Situations are all highly concrete, and they do not present themselves with duty labels on them. Without the abilities of perception, duty is blind and therefore powerless," Nussbaum writes. She elaborates: "Obtuseness is a moral failing; its opposite can be cultivated. By themselves, trusted for and in themselves, the standing terms are a recipe for obtuseness" (156). In the words of Aristotle, to respond "at the right times, with reference to the right objects, toward the right people, with the right aim, and in the right way, is what is appropriate and best, and this is characteristic of excellence" (*Nicomachean Ethics,* quoted in Nussbaum, 156).
36. Nussbaum, *Love's Knowledge,* 198; and Hilary Putnam, "Taking Rules Seriously: A Response to Martha Nussbaum," *New Literary History* 15 (1983): 193–200.
37. Martha Nussbaum, *Poetic Justice: The Literary Imagination and Public Life* (Boston: Beacon Press, 1995), 3, 5. See also Nelson, *Damaged Identities, Narrative Repair,* 39.
38. Nussbaum, *Poetic Justice,* 7.

Prologue   xvii

What—parenthetically concealed—almost escapes attention here merely constitutes the beginning of a series of issues arising from Nussbaum's particular version of an ethics of literature: why does she restrict her argument to novels, and why only "*realist* novels"? Would not less "realism" entail more of a promise of liberation from society's established "refusals to imagine one another with empathy and compassion"?[39] Even if realist novels are deemed more amenable to a project of forming social "bonds of identification and sympathy" than, say, a Dada *lautgedicht*, why not plays, biographies, or histories?[40] Why, above all, not, as Henry James's Lambert Strether says, "poor dear old life?"[41] And further questions arise: What, for example, are we to make of the oddly dichotomic discourse imbuing Nussbaum's elaborations according to which "imagination and feeling" are linked to the reading of novels and, as such, contrasted with the more rationalistic thrust of philosophical "rules and principles"?[42] How viable is this distinction really, and how much does it serve Nussbaum's project, which sets out to undermine the oppositioning of literature and philosophy?[43]

While Nussbaum leaves these questions unanswered, she does offer one of the most elaborate accounts regarding the debate of how literature furthers our understanding of ethics. In so doing, she markedly exemplifies "the literary turn in contemporary, especially Anglo-American, philosophy—most pointedly articulated in Rorty's 'general turn against theory and toward narrative,'" which, as Michael Eskin notes, "can be viewed as a homologous response to the putative formalism of analytical moral theory in favor of a more Aristotelian—eudemonistic and aretaic—approach to human existence as it is played out by singular persons in specific situations, which are, so the claim goes, best illuminated in and through works of literature."[44] As indicated, moral philosophy's turn to narrative in general and literature in particular conversely corresponds to a certain turn to ethics in literary studies, which has been read as a "reaction against the [putative] formalism...of deconstruction,"[45] and as "the growing influence of such thinkers as Emmanuel Levinas—especially in the wake of the 'de Man controversy' in the late 1980s."[46] Moreover, it has been related "to broader institutional developments, such as the 'continuing power of feminist criticism and theory and the rising influence of

---

39. Ibid., xvii.
40. See Nussbaum, *Love's Knowledge*, 45.
41. *The Ambassadors*, quoted in Nussbaum, *Love's Knowledge*, 45. For a penetrating critique of Nussbaum's approach, see Charles Altieri, "Lyrical Ethics and Literary Experience," in *Mapping the Ethical Turn: A Reader in Ethics, Culture, and Literary Theory*, ed. Todd F. Davis and Kenneth Womack (Charlottesville: University Press of Viriginia, 2001), 30–58.
42. Nussbaum, *Love's Knowledge*, 152, 44.
43. For an insightful discussion of the last two questions, see Robert Eaglestone, *Ethical Criticism: Reading after Levinas* (Edinburgh: Edinburgh University Press, 1997), 35–60, here, 57f.
44. Eskin, introduction, 558.
45. James Phelan, "Sethe's Choice: *Beloved* and the Ethics of Reading," in Davis and Womack, *Mapping the Ethical Turn*, 93–109, here 107, quoted in Eskin, introduction, 558.
46. Eskin, introduction, 558.

African American, [postcolonial,] multicultural and queer criticism and theory, all of which ground themselves in sets of ethico-political commitments.'"[47] To be sure, the vicissitudes described here as literature's turn to (moral) philosophy and (moral) philosophy's turn to literature rely on a dichotomy of literature and philosophy that is as strategically helpful as it is methodologically problematic. "I do not deny that there are differences...between philosophy and literature...; I am suggesting that we do not understand these differences,"[48] Stanley Cavell once wrote. Decades after Cavell articulated his unease, and without intending to "solve" the case, I hope to explore the relation between philosophy and literature with regard to our focal theme of "ethics," to put in my two cents, if only obliquely. Having outlined three influential positions in the "literature and ethics debate" assumed by philosophers, and having left off with Nussbaum's renowned account, we thus shall now direct our attention to contributions put forth by prominent literary critics, commencing with Wayne Booth.

Literary Studies' Turn to Ethics

It appears safe to say that Martha Nussbaum would deem herself a "friend" of Booth's capacious *The Company We Keep: An Ethics of Fiction* (1988), according to whose central metaphor "a relationship with a literary work...is a kind of friendship."[49] Booth's conception of ethical criticism is, as Nussbaum points out, remarkably "broad and flexible,"[50] including "the entire range of effects on the 'character' or 'person' or 'self.' 'Moral' judgments are only a small part of it."[51] Booth's response to the question of "how art and ethics...should be joined or separated" develops along two trajectories. His first aim is "to restore the full intellectual legitimacy of our commonsense inclination to talk about stories in ethical terms, treating the characters in them and their makers as more like people than labyrinths, enigmas, or textual puzzles to be deciphered." Second, Booth aspires "to 'relocate' ethical criticism, turning it from flat judgment for or against supposedly stable works to fluid conversation about the qualities of the company we keep—and the company that we ourselves provide." Such hoped-for fluidity, Booth emphasizes, is at odds with preconceived ethical theorems: "What I mean by the ethical criticism of narrative...cannot be nicely confined in any preliminary definition; it will be shown more by what I do than by anything I say."[52] The performative

---

47. Phelan, "Sethe's Choice," 107, quoted in Eskin, introduction, 558.
48. Stanley Cavell, *Must We Mean What We Say?* (Cambridge: Cambridge University Press, 1976), xviii.
49. Nussbaum, *Love's Knowledge*, 231.
50. Ibid., 22 n. 36.
51. Wayne C. Booth, *The Company We Keep: An Ethics of Fiction* (Berkeley: University of California Press, 1988), 8.
52. Ibid., ix, x, 8.

power of "ethical criticism" called on here reverberates with the professed "reformatting" of the reader while reading invoked by Nussbaum.[53] It defies the determination of "rules either for what we aim to become or for the discrimination we must 'practice' on the 'way.' We seek to practice a practice, to follow a way of ways, and—as Heidegger stresses—we can never precisely *say* what the practice or way might be."[54] What, in a Boothian vein, we perhaps *can* say is what the practice or way might be like: "trust"-worthy,[55] worthy of our "assent,"[56] indeed "desirable."[57] States Booth: "What we seek...will not be words or propositions in isolation...but the total pattern of desires...that the author commits us to." The "ethical pluralism" surfacing here leaves it "to each reader to practice an ethics of reading that might determine just which...standards should count most, and just which of the world's narratives should now be banned or embraced."[58] Thus Booth challenges MacIntyre's position, "insisting in effect that narrative is not a unifying factor but a kind of discursive shrine to 'pluralism,'" and that, accordingly, "the ethics of narrative consist not in a gathering together of disparate elements, but rather in an expansion of human possibilities."[59]

While both Nussbaum and Booth are primarily interested in the link between ethics and literature, our second example of literary studies' turn to ethics, Tobin Siebers, in his 1988 *Ethics of Criticism,* expressly directs attention to the "interference between ethics and criticism."[60] His study explores "how a particular theory or school of literary criticism has justified in an ethical way its theoretical choices." The declared aim of this investigation is a more nuanced understanding of the "impact of theoretical choice on the relation between literature and the lives of human beings." Siebers's concern with the relations between literature and human life as well as the respective role of criticism emerges against the backdrop of a broader concern, namely the efficacy of language as an "instrument of human violence." Accordingly, he argues that "literary critics have a responsibility not only to supervise their own...practices as critics but to think about the way in which language carries on the work of human prejudice, racism, sexism, classism, and nationalism. Even the most ethically oriented critics must remain watchful in this regard." In order to elucidate the interrelatedness of ethics and criticism, Siebers provides "an overview of some case histories," including Plato, Aristotle, Kant, the Romantics, Nietzsche, Julia Kristeva, Northrop Frye, and J. Hillis Miller.[61] The intention behind this "necessarily incomplete overview" is to expose "how the critical enters the

---

53. On this correspondence, see Harpham, "Ethics and Literary Criticism," 379.
54. Booth, *Company We Keep,* 266.
55. Ibid., 32 n. 6.
56. Ibid.
57. Ibid., 269–70.
58. Ibid., 396, 489.
59. Harpham, "Ethics and Literary Criticism," 379–80.
60. Tobin Siebers, *The Ethics of Criticism* (Ithaca, NY: Cornell University Press, 1988), 18.
61. Ibid., 2, 7f., 18; see 14–43.

ethical, how the ethical enters the critical, and how each has tried through various means to rid itself of the other." "As it stands," Siebers states, "modern criticism has lost its sense of purpose. Perhaps its greatest failing has been its refusal to judge the difference between literature and life, for this activity is the definite characteristic of criticism." It is here, then, "in the space between literature and life," that Siebers situates the practice of literary criticism: "Criticism needs...to admit its role as a mediator between life and literature and to accept the ethical responsibilities of its judgments in both domains."[62]

The evident problem with Siebers's approach lies, as commentators have pointed out, in his unspecified employment of such concepts as "human," "humanity," "human life," "human activity," and so on. Already at the outset Siebers declares that "literature is a human activity, and the character of criticism must remain as resolutely human." This precariously sentimental approach abounds in such concluding sentences as "To be human is to tell stories about ourselves and other human beings. The finally human is literature."[63] Precisely because Siebers problematizes the ways in which language perpetuates classism, sexism, nationalism, racism, and so forth, we are perplexed at the ease with which he passes over differences of class, sex, nation, et cetera so as to bring a formulaic notion like "the human" to bear.[64] In the light of such missing differentiation of his categories, Siebers leaves many questions as to what an ethics of criticism could consist of or might involve. At the same time, what distinguishes his approach from those of both Nussbaum and Booth, who are primarily interested in the ethical ramifications of literature, is a distinct sensitivity to the ethical valences of the practice of literary criticism itself.

Such sensitivity to the ethical valences of criticism finds a prominent proponent in J. Hillis Miller, who rearticulates the relation between ethics and aesthetics with regard to questions of *reading*. "In what sense," his 1987 *Ethics of Reading* starts out, "can or should the act of reading be itself ethical or have an ethical import?"[65] Conventionally, reading is thought of as "primarily cognitive," as a matter of understanding, which may or may not turn out to be of some ethical use that, in turn, would be considered "extraneous to the primary act of reading." By contrast, Miller argues that "there is a necessary ethical moment in that act of reading *as such*, a moment neither cognitive, nor political, nor social, nor interpersonal, but properly and independently ethical." This proposition is undergirded in the course of a

---

62. Ibid., 18, 41f.
63. Ibid., 12, 239f.
64. See James Phelan, review of *The Ethics of Criticism*, by Tobin Siebers, *Modern Philology* 87.4 (1990): 435–38, here 437. No less of a concern, Phelan points out, is Siebers's employment of ethically charged categories such as "equality," "justice," and "violence." Does not Siebers's book, Phelan asks, "with its championing of equality and its condemnation of violence through appeals to an undefined, undifferentiated 'humanity,' simply serve the dominant liberal...ideology and thereby preserve a status quo in which equality is a joke and violence a commonplace?" (437).
65. J. Hillis Miller, *The Ethics of Reading* (New York: Columbia University Press, 1987), 1.

Prologue xxi

two-stage argumentation. First, Miller submits that the ethics of reading ensues *not* from the fact that "stories contain the thematic dramatization of ethical situations, choices, and judgments" but rather from a certain condition according to which "ethics itself has a peculiar relation to that form of language we call narrative."[66] "If there is to be such a thing as an ethical moment in the act of reading," Miller elaborates,

> it must be *sui generis,* something individual and particular, itself a source of political or cognitive acts, not subordinated to them. The flow of power must not be all in one direction. There must be an influx of performative power from the linguistic transaction involved in the act of reading into the realms of knowledge, politics, and history. Literature must be in some way a cause and not merely an effect.[67]

Put differently, literature is not merely a reflection *of* history; it also, and perhaps primarily, responds *to* history by generating its own speaking power and by mobilizing its own ethical force. Hence, Miller suggests that "the ethical moment in reading...enters into the social, institutional, political realms." Indeed, "the rhetorical study of literature has crucial practical implications for our moral, social, and political lives."[68]

This first stage of Miller's argument is followed by a more intricate and also more enigmatic second stage, and we shall focus on it in more detail, as it will prove valuable in situating my own understanding of the relation between ethics and narration. In order to solidify his initial claim that "there is a necessary ethical moment in that act of reading *as such,*" Miller elaborates on a well-known paradox discussed in Kant's *Foundations of the Metaphysics of Morals:*

> Respect for the law, says Kant, is like fear in that we recognize the law as *necessary,* unavoidable. In this the law is like, say, some natural catastrophe that we fear. The law is something we are subject to whether we like it or not. We accept the law, *necessarily,* without consulting that most basic of motives, self-love. Respect for the law, on the other hand, is also analogous to inclination in that we impose the law *freely* on ourselves. We really want to obey the law.... Since the law is a law for ourselves, it is something we impose *freely* on ourselves as reasonable beings.... "I *freely* impose the moral law on myself, though at the same time I respect its absolute *necessity.* I *freely* impose the moral law on myself, as a law for myself, out of respect for the law, and in respecting the law I respect myself as a *free* rational self able to have respect for the law and able to act ethically on the basis of the law."[69]

---

66. Ibid., 1, italics mine; 3.
67. Ibid., 5, italics mine.
68. Ibid., 4, 40.
69. Ibid., 21f., italics mine.

Miller now stages a dialogue between this paradoxical Kantian notion of ethics and the act of reading, arriving at the following exposition on what an ethics of reading could amount to: "By 'the ethics of reading,'" he notes, "I mean that aspect of the act of reading in which there is a response to the text that is both necessitated, in the sense that it is a response to an irresistible demand, and *free*, in the sense that *I must take responsibility* for my response and for the further effects, 'interpersonal,' institutional, social, political, or historical, of my act of reading."[70] The opacity of this paradoxical formulation comes at a high price to those trying to make sense of Miller's remarks. Just how are we to understand this "freedom" that *requires* ("I must") us to "take responsibility"? How can I, as reader, be held responsible for something that I don't choose to do but that instead is inflicted on me? "In order to make sense of this," writes Derek Attridge, one of Miller's most astute commentators,

> we have to have recourse to a different understanding of responsibility, and therefore a different sense of ethics, one not tied to freedom of choice. One such understanding would be Levinas's sense of the ethical demand of the other, a demand we cannot escape by saying "I didn't *choose* to come face to face with this person or this situation." For Levinas, ethics lies not in the responsibility implicit in my freely chosen acts but in the responsibility I find myself gripped by, "taken hostage" by.[71]

There indeed appears to be a productive resemblance between this Levinasian notion of "freedom" that only allows me "to acknowledge or deny the ethical force that already binds me" and the paradoxical Millerian conception of a reader who has to acknowledge the responsibility for his response even though he acts in response to an "implacable necessity." Time and again, Miller insists that "each reading is, strictly speaking, ethical, in the sense that it *has* to take place, by an *implacable necessity*, as the response to a categorical demand, and in the sense that the reader *must* take responsibility for its consequences in the personal, social, and political worlds." Correspondingly, he concludes: "The endpoint of my exploration of the ethics of reading...is the strange and difficult notion that reading is subject not to the text as its law, but to the law of which the text is subject. This law forces the reader to betray the text or deviate from it in the act of reading it, in the name of a higher demand that can yet be reached only by way of the text."[72]

---

70. Ibid., 43, italics mine.
71. Derek Attridge, "Miller's Tale," in *The J. Hillis Miller Reader*, ed. Julian Wolfreys (Stanford, CA: Stanford University Press, 2005), 78–82, here 80.
72. Miller, *Ethics of Reading,* 59, italics mine; 120. "The imperative of reading," as Simon Critchley paraphrases, "is not simply (but is it ever simple?) fidelity to the text as if it were one's law, but rather a *fidelity to the law to which the text is subject*. This law is the matter of...reading, which entails that the reader *should* betray the text that is being read in the name of the law to which that text is subject" (Critchley, *The Ethics of Deconstruction: Derrida and Levinas* [Cambridge: Blackwell, 1992], 46). Or, as Attridge extrapolates, "I, as responsible reader, am not...seeking to reveal an unchanging core of meaning, the text's 'secret' in the conventional sense of an unrecoverable interior, but rather attempting to

It goes without saying that the idiosyncrasy characterizing Miller's take on the relation between ethics and narration places him at a distance from most of the approaches discussed thus far. Martha Nussbaum epitomizes perhaps the most clearly identifiable theoretical antipode to Miller.[73] Whereas Nussbaum conceives of a reader who empathizes with literary characters' hopes, fears, worries, and concerns, and who learns "to form bonds of identification and sympathy," she wastes no time with the *materiality of the texts* under discussion, effectively reducing the fabric of literature to the role of an invisible transmitting device. Yet it is precisely here, in the crevices and chasms of textual constructs, that Miller locates the point of departure for his investigation into the ethics of reading.[74] Whereas Nussbaum remains blind to the workings of language, its rhetorical efficacy and allegorical force, Miller (with, in the words of Barbara Johnson, "rigorous unreliability")[75] appears crucially concerned with the narrative economy of the texts he discusses. To be sure, Miller's fixation with "language"—as opposed to "extralinguistic forces and facts"[76]—deeply confounded a great number of critics, including Tobin Siebers, who called Miller's project "absurd" and characterized it as "the creation of an isolated linguistic morality [which] robs ethical theory of its social context and renders ethics ineffectual."[77] It has been argued that for Miller, "ethics becomes just the name for a certain, albeit highly sophisticated, practice of reading,"[78] one that does not acknowledge the world's "'thickness,'" that "extra-linguistic basis with which we must engage."[79] Such "thickness of the world" would undoubtedly appear pivotal to Alasdair MacIntyre, who, in *After Virtue,* notes that virtue "has to be expounded in terms of...the narrative unity of a human life and of a moral tradition."[80] In turn, Miller's work appears to be more congenial to a position such as that put forth by Richard Rorty, who, in *Contingency, Irony, and Solidarity,*

---

perform, here and now, an affirmation of its singularity and alterity—a different kind of secret that cannot simply be revealed. If this performative response is to do justice to the singularity of the text...it must itself be singular and inventive—not merely an act of obedience to a law. It must...be irresponsible as well as responsible.... In exercising our freedom to tell stories about the text...we are obeying the text's injunction: be responsible in your irresponsibility, tell my secrets with as much care and respect as you can even though you know they will remain secret, let my inventiveness be validated in your inventiveness" ("Miller's Tale," 81).

73. See also Eaglestone, *Ethical Criticism,* 92–94.

74. "Where for Nussbaum," Robert Eaglestone astutely notes, "narratives enact and reflect back on ethical rules, for Miller, ethical or moral rules themselves can only exist in narrative form" (*Ethical Criticism,* 68).

75. Barbara Johnson, A *World of Difference* (Baltimore: Johns Hopkins University Press, 1987), 17, quoted in Lawrence Buell, "What We Talk about When We Talk about Ethics," in *The Return to Ethics,* ed. Marjorie Garber et al. (New York: Routledge, 2000), 1–13, here 4.

76. J. Hillis Miller, "Is There an Ethics of Reading?" in *Reading Narrative: Form, Ethics, Ideology,* ed. James Phelan (Columbus: Ohio State University Press, 1989), 79–101, here 81.

77. Siebers, *Ethics of Criticism,* 39.

78. Christopher Norris, *Deconstruction and the Interests of Theory* (Norman: University of Oklahoma Press, 1989), 165; after Eaglestone, *Ethical Criticism,* 80.

79. Eaglestone, *Ethical Criticism,* 81.

80. MacIntyre, *After Virtue,* 139.

claimed "that the world does not provide us with any criterion of choice between alternative metaphors, that we can only compare languages or metaphors with one another, not with something beyond language called 'fact.'"[81]

It is against this backdrop that we might have to question the thus far established framework regarding the conjunction of ethics and aesthetics, as it relies on a rather technical juxtaposition of philosophy (MacIntyre, Rorty, Nussbaum) and literary studies (Booth, Siebers, Miller). A possibly more genuine way of reflecting on the authors treated so far (and, concomitantly, of positioning my own approach) might be to ask whether ethics is problematized within the traditional purview of thematic negotiation (as is the case in MacIntyre, Rorty, Nussbaum, Booth, and Siebers) or whether the actual mechanics of language, its narrative infrastructure and figurative repercussions, are given serious consideration (as is the case in Miller) to the point where ethics may no longer translate into more or less congealed themes and positions. "Nussbaum does not find the textuality of texts problematic," Robert Eaglestone appositely remarks; "for her a text can be a direct lesson in morals or, as Henry James would say, an experiment in life.... This is epi-reading on a grand scale: literature becomes no more than a cipher, an example for philosophy, a heuristic testing ground for ideas.... Despite Nussbaum's protests to the contrary, she dissolves literature into philosophy."[82] This is a charge that, as indicated above, could similarly be held against Rorty. While it seems that for Nussbaum "ethical positions shine through [language] like light through a perfect window,"[83] the same holds true, to different degrees, for MacIntyre, Booth, and Siebers. What distinguishes Miller from these thinkers is precisely that he is deeply immersed in the architectonics of language, as he deems ethics an inherent (rather than exterior) feature of narrative structures.

Given certain correspondences between Miller's approach and my own, we shall, without digressing, delve yet a little further into *The Ethics of Reading* and spell out some crucial parallels and especially discrepancies between Miller's understanding of the relation between ethics and narration, and my own. The first claim in Miller's two-step argumentation, we noted, is that the status of ethics in literature is not merely that of "thematic reflection" or "passive mirroring" (as exemplified by Nussbaum), and I unequivocally share Miller's assumption that there is "an ethical dimension to the act of reading" that is *not* identical with the ethical themes in the works at issue. The more inscrutable second stage of Miller's argument pertains to the questions of *where* this nonthematic, nonrepresentational dimension of ethics might be located and *how* it might be configured. It is here that my concurrence with Miller falters and that important dissimilarities surge to the surface. Miller says that he is trying to shift "from the thematic representation of

---

81. Rorty, *Contingency, Irony, and Solidarity*, 20. See Eaglestone, *Ethical Criticism*, 82.
82. Eaglestone, *Ethical Criticism*, 92.
83. Ibid., 94.

ethical issues within a work of literature to the ethical issues involved in the act of reading itself." I too try to shift from the thematic representation of ethical issues (including totalitarian politics, questions of violence and terrorism) within works to the ethical issues involved in the act of reading itself. Says Miller: "I get my tip for what to do as a result of reading *What Maisie Knew* not from *What Maisie Knew* itself, but from my access, through it, to the unformulatable law it exemplifies through narration." In our case too the act of *reading* forms the basis of an ethics— a "literary ethics," which, I shall suggest, might at its heart always be an "ethics of reading." Yet just what are we to make of the "unformulatable law" that Miller seeks access to, this law that appears to constitute the centerpiece of his theorization of the relation between ethics and narration? Miller maintains that we "*must respond* to the *linguistic imperative* which is the *true* ethics of reading. Some ethical decision and act follows as an *irresistible necessity whenever I read.*"[84] This insistence on an overpowering "linguistic imperative" and the corresponding "irresistible necessity whenever I read" appears oddly nebulous and demarcates the moment at which my own project diverges from Miller's.

Whereas Miller stresses the "*irrelevance* of the thematic assertions of even the most apparently morally concerned literature" to the question of ethics (in light of that overwhelming "unformulatable law"), my focus is directed toward an ethics of reading that is emphatically invested in a work's ethical themes while examining those themes in terms of their unique interplay with particular modes of presentation and, respectively, the oddly elusive ethical force emanating from that interplay. Such a force is not one that *categorically* comes into being "whenever I read" (as with Miller) but is obliquely tied to and contingent on the ethical issues discussed within a text. Hence, I am not merely asking *what* kind of ethically concerned statements a text brings about (Nussbaum), nor am I probing some sort of ethical energy that, irrespective of the text at issue, originates in the "act of reading *as such*" (Miller).[85] My attention lies rather with how both of these dimensions interrelate with a third dimension (one that Miller is greatly concerned with without, however, conceptually spelling it out), namely the dimension of "form." We thus shall further explore the so far underexposed dimension of "form" and its relation to the act of reading. Developing this link will likely clarify my treatment of ethics as put forth in this book.

"Textual Otherness"

Among the established analyses of the relation between form and the act of reading, Derek Attridge's work, culminating in *The Singularity of Literature* (2004), presents a particularly nuanced case. Attridge suggests that "the distinctive ethical

---

84. Miller, "Is There an Ethics of Reading?" 81; 84; 87; 98; 99, italics mine.
85. Miller, *Ethics of Reading,* 98, italics mine; 99; 1, italics mine.

xxvi   *Prologue*

force of literature inheres not in the fictional world portrayed but in the handling of language whereby that fictional world is brought into being."[86] While Attridge, like Miller (and I), apparently does not direct the attention to the "portrayal" or depiction or representation of ethical issues (as does Nussbaum), the question arises, In what way does he deem "the handling of language" conducive to the coming into being of that "distinctive ethical force of literature"? "Literary works that resist the immediacy and transparency of language," Attridge argues, "engage the reader ethically; and to do justice to such works as a reader is to respond fully to an event whereby otherness challenges habitual norms."[87] The interrelatedness of the two levels evoked here—the level of form and the level of the act of reading—lies at the center of Attridge's approach. Time and again, he accentuates the importance of the latter of these two dimensions, the act of reading. "There are grounds for arguing," writes Attridge, "that the most fundamental engagement between the literary and the ethical occurs not in the human world depicted in works of literature but in the very act of reading such works, whether or not they deal with situations and relations that could be called ethical."[88] Undoubtedly, these lines recall Miller's claim regarding the *irrelevance* of the thematic assertions of even the most apparently morally concerned literature" to the question of ethics,[89] as well his corresponding insistence on "an ethical dimension to the act of reading" itself,[90] an indebtedness Attridge readily acknowledges.[91] Asking how, then, a work of art implicates the reader ethically, Attridge elaborates:

> There is...an ethical dimension to any act of literary signification, and there is also a sense in which the formally innovative work, the one that most estranges itself from the reader, makes the most sharply challenging...ethical demand. Formal innovation (of the sort that matters in literature) is a testing of the operations of meaning, and is therefore a kind of ethical experimentation. To respond to the demand of the literary work as the demand of the other is to attend to it as a unique event whose happening is a call, a challenge, an obligation: understand how little you understand me, translate my untranslatability.[92]

---

86. Derek Attridge, "Ethical Modernism: Servants as Others in J. M. Coetzee's Early Fiction," *Poetics Today* 25.4 (2004): 653–71, here 653.
87. Ibid.
88. Ibid.
89. Miller, "Is There an Ethics of Reading?" 98, italics mine.
90. Ibid., 84.
91. See Attridge, "Ethical Modernism," 653 n. 1; Derek Attridge, *The Singularity of Literature* (New York: Routledge, 2004), 143f.
92. Attridge, *Singularity of Literature,* 130f. Attridge's call, according to which we ought to "respond to the demand of the literary work as the demand of the other" of course resonates with the philosophy of Levinas, to whom Attridge frequently (if only selectively [see 141]) refers: "Levinas writes of the relation to the other as that of hostage to captor, emphasizing the randomness with which I feel myself summoned by the other—not because I am who I am but because I happen to be in a particular place and time. But the other is also vulnerable, in need of my protection, 'destitute,' to use Levinas's word.

Attridge here associates aesthetic "estrangement" with a work's "ethical demand," "formal innovation" with "ethical experimentation." Indeed, he argues that "it is in literature's *resistance* to the demands of...moral exemplification that it most distinctively engages with the ethical, and a critical practice that aims to be responsive to the ethics of literature...needs to take account of that resistance."[93] Unlike Nussbaum, whose concern appears primarily to lie with the ethical issues discussed on the level of thematic discourse, Attridge contends that "it is less a question of something we can learn than something that happens to us and through us as we read.... The distinctiveness of the ethical in literature, and in artworks more generally, is that it occurs as an *event* in the process of reading, not a theme to be registered, a thesis to be grasped, or an imperative to be followed or ignored."[94] Given this event-like occurrence of the artwork as perceived in the act of reading, Attridge puts forth the following suggestion as to what being a responsible reader might amount to:

> What I wish to argue is that doing justice to a literary work *as* a literary work (and there are many other valid ways of responding to literature) means doing justice to its *otherness:* to whatever it is about it that challenges our preferences and preconceptions, that stretches our powers of thought and feeling, that resists the encompassing grasp of our interpretive techniques. The otherness of the work is inseparable from...what we respond to when we feel that the work we are reading...is unlike any other.[95]

It is in this vein that Attridge elaborates: "If all literary works—a category which does not, for the purpose of this argument, include all works conventionally classed as 'literature' and does not exclude works not so classed—are characterized by their otherness,...their ethical significance does not depend on the representations of otherness which they may or may not contain."[96] Their "ethical significance" rather appears to be contingent on

> a recognition (whatever its writers may have thought they were doing) that literature's distinctive power and potential ethical force resides in a testing and unsettling of deeply held assumptions of transparency, instrumentality, and direct

---

Its power lies in its weakness. Literature, for all the force which it is capable of exercising, can achieve nothing without readers—responsible readers" (131). See also Zahi Zalloua's interview with Attridge, "Derek Attridge on the Ethical Debates in Literary Studies," *SubStance* 38.3 (2009): 18–30. Regarding the precarious leap from the Levinasian encounter with another human being to the encounter with a work of art, see Attridge, *Singularity of Literature,* 17–34 and 126–28; Eaglestone, *Ethial Criticism,* 129–74; Jill Robbins, *Altered Reading: Levinas and Literature* (Chicago: University of Chicago Press, 1999).

93. Attridge, "Ethical Modernism," 654.
94. Ibid.
95. Ibid.
96. Ibid., 654f.

referentiality.... The effect is one that I would want to describe as textual otherness, or *textualterity:* a verbal artifact that estranges as it entices...that speaks while it says that it must remain silent—and in so doing stages the ethical as an event.[97]

Attridge's elegant prose might be found to enact the "otherness" it discusses; "otherness" at times seems "engaged, staged, distanced, embraced...in the rupturing of narrative discourse, in the lasting uncertainties of reference."[98] And yet, just what are we to make of this incessantly employed term "otherness" that, more often than not, appears to assume the status of a concept and as such to contradict all that it presumably seeks to evoke. To be sure, Attridge spares no effort in relativizing and justifying his use of the expression. Accentuating, for instance, the constitutive force of the act of reading in relation to a work's "formal" specificity, he remarks: "Otherness, as I have stressed, is a strictly relative term—otherness is always otherness to an existing subjectivity or state of affairs."[99] *"Only in relating to me* is the other other, and its otherness is registered in the adjustments I have to make in order to acknowledge it."[100] These, like many similar sentences, evince a continuous (and perhaps deliberate) reifying spin characterizing Attridge's use of the term "otherness" that gives it gravity while appearing to be at odds with what the other, in its defiance of epistemic appropriation and instrumentalization, is meant to invoke.

While this essentially terminological issue is one that Attridge himself problematizes at length and indeed turns into an effective basis for further theorization,[101] the difference between Attridge's focus and my own lies elsewhere, in the significance attributed to the level of thematic discussion. As indicated, Attridge asks a question Miller already asked (and one I myself will ask in each of the chapters of this book), namely, Does the "ethical force" of certain works "lie in something other than the moral and political critique they ostensibly offer?"[102] His response (much like my own) revolves around the interrelation of "formal" idiosyncrasy and readerly engagement, as it is here that the distinct ethical force of literature (its "textual otherness, or textualterity")[103] is brought into being. Notably, Attridge calls this very distinction into question insofar as that which he describes as "the otherness of the literary work" is "experienced as an *event* by the reader, not as some quality"— which is why he speaks of "the event that used to be called 'form.'"[104] Yet as we found to be the case with Miller, so in Attridge the genuine "ethical significance" of literature appears programmatically dissociated from the "representation" of

---

97. Ibid., 669.
98. Ibid., 670.
99. Attridge, *Singularity of Literature,* 43.
100. Ibid., 30.
101. See Attridge, *Singularity of Literature,* 17–34; Attridge, "Innovation, Literature, Ethics: Relating to the Other," *PMLA* 114.1 (1999): 20–31.
102. Attridge, "Ethical Modernism," 657.
103. Ibid., 669.
104. Ibid., 655, italics mine; 670.

ethically charged matters.[105] And it is, once again, this structural disregard for or operational differentiation of a work's thematic discussion that distinguishes my approach from Attridge's. To be sure, Attridge concedes that a work expressly concerned with ethical issues may in fact "raise an interesting question":

> How does the staging of otherness with the fictional world relate to the work's own otherness, as experienced by the reader? Are the ethical demands played out within the work's imagined universe given peculiar intensity when the work itself makes demands as an other? And conversely, is the otherness of the literary work...more powerfully felt as an ethical force when it is in the service of a represented encounter with alterity?[106]

While literary works' ethically concerned themes or theses might add an "interesting" dimension to their "ethical significance," such "ethical significance does *not*" (to quote an already-quoted sentence) "*depend* on the representations of otherness which they may or may not contain."[107] Ethically concerned themes, according to Attridge, might well affect the question of a work's ethical import, but they remain (as with Miller) inessential, peripheral, extraneous, to what he describes as a "work's *own* otherness" as experienced by the reader.[108] In contrast, my focus is directed toward an ethics of reading integrally (rather than merely extraneously) invested in a work's ethical themes; consequently, each of my readings revolves around particular poetic enactments and the explicitly thematized ethical models *to which they respond*. My attention lies with the interdependence of ethically charged propositions and their performative enactment, morally motivated constatives and their idiosyncratic presentational manifestation as perceived in the act of reading. In each chapter, I tackle the singularly negotiated nexus of variously configured ethical "messages" vis-à-vis the particular mediatic moves by which they find themselves challenged and thwarted—an ethics of the singular that I shall now try to delineate.

Prolegomena to a "Literary Ethics"

An ethics of the singular as emerging from the singular interrelatedness of ethically concerned statements and their specific poetic enactments is always and primarily a "literary ethics." It is a literary ethics not because it is concerned with works of "literature," an attribute that, in the context of this book, would apply only to Kafka

---

105. Ibid., 654.
106. Ibid., 655.
107. Ibid., 654f., italics mine.
108. Ibid., 655, italics mine.

xxx   Prologue

and Müller.[109] What characterizes a literary ethics, rather, pertains to certain literary, filmic, or, more generally, poetic qualities, qualities that figure in "aesthetically mediated artifacts" and as such come into view only in the context of an analysis or reading that insistently focuses on the poetic moments of a text.[110] Such poetic moments of course abound in works of art such as Kafka's "In the Penal Colony," Müller's *Germania Death in Berlin,* or the film *Germany in Autumn;* yet they also surface in self-consciously "writerly" works such as those by Benjamin and Arendt scrutinized in this study. Hence, and in the light of such literary qualities, a "literary ethics" is always inherently related to the act of reading and perhaps, indeed, is to be thought of as an "ethics of reading." What, then, connects the various readings performed in this book, what ties them together and delineates their common features, what, in other words, constitutes the consistency of a model of "literary ethics," is always related to the (broadly conceived) "literary" qualities of a work in conjunction with my readerly encounter with and attentiveness to them.

These two moments—the moment of textual materiality as well as the moment of readerly response—demarcate the two poles between which a literary ethics comes into being. Everything I say in this book has to do with the way in which the details of the texts, their particular modes of performance, the question of *how* they are structured, determine their ethical "position" (for lack of a better word). The ethics generated by writers like Benjamin (whose thinking is profoundly embedded in the way in which he writes) or Arendt are, I contend, at cross-purposes to a list of fixed ideas and at odds with recognizable positions that might be allied with any school of philosophical thought on the matter. Concomitantly, what I say about ethics in Benjamin or Arendt, of course, also results from my very own readerly engagement with these thinkers' works.[111] Indeed, there is a long tradition in the second half of the twentieth century of authors (including Jacques Derrida, Judith Butler, Barbara Johnson, Carol Jacobs, and others) taking up various ethical, political, and social issues, often by way of literature and film. What unites these authors is that they all work through at times highly ambiguous texts to come to their arguments. They all *read* texts in order to "arrive" at what they have to say. Or, conversely, while one might aspire to develop a catalog of insights and positions that come out of their readings, what *does* come out of their readings, in the end, is precisely that one has to *read.*

---

109. On the intricate question of what constitutes "the literary," see Attridge, *Singularity of Literature,* 86f.

110. I am grateful to an anonymous reviewer for the expression "aesthetically mediated artifacts."

111. My reading, like any act of reading, results, to a greater or lesser degree, from a paradoxical situation, in which I seek to be "faithful" to the text by embracing it in its particularity and specificity, while hoping to remain "faithful" to myself, to my own creativity and my concrete situation as reader at this particular time and place in history. For a careful discussion of this paradox, see Attridge, *Singularity of Literature,* 89–92.

If the propensity among Neo-Aristotelian critics such as Wayne Booth, Martha Nussbaum, Alasdair MacIntyre, and Richard Rorty was to reduce literary works to moral philosophy,[112] then a "literary ethics," as understood here, directs attention to that figurative dimension that typically finds itself thwarted, kindly dismissed, or simply annulled in philosophical analyses. A literary ethics describes, within the purview of the steadfast ductus of conceptional ethics, a syncope, a moment of disruption, that challenges the meter of ethical discourses and the directives and doctrines ensuing from them.[113] As such, a literary ethics springs from specific, poetically precipitated, textual interstices and seizes its force from the fact that it posits no general and predictable but singular and unpredictable, indeed, unprecedented moments of interference—a seditious perturbance to established ethical systems of thought. A literary ethics presents, beyond any preconceived notion of ethics, the actuality of a relentlessly defiant ethical thrust, of ethical effects that, strictly speaking, elide any sort of epistemic appropriation, remain strange, strangely foreign, obstinately reluctant to be subsumed under given concepts and conceptions precisely because they cannot, in their singularity, quite be conceived *like* anything else,[114] effects that, audaciously and aporetically, no doubt, lay claim to their inconceivability.

---

112. See also Zalloua, "Derek Attridge on the Ethical Debates," 22.
113. The individual readings performed in Carol Jacob's *Skirting the Ethical* (Stanford, CA: Stanford University Press, 2008) would be exemplary in this respect.
114. To briefly spell out the etymological relation between the words employed—*concept, conceive,* and *conception:* (1) The noun *concept* derives from Latin *conceptum,* "(a thing) conceived," the past participle of Latin *concipere,* "to take effectively, take to oneself, take in and hold." (2) The verb *conceive* can be traced back to the Old French word *conceveir,* which, again, derives from Latin *concipere.* (3) Finally, the word *conception* denotes "the action of conceiving," from Old French *concepcion* and, respectively, Latin *conceptionem,* which, once again, derives from Latin *concipere (OED).* In short, *concept, conceive,* and *conception* can all be traced back to the Latin verb *concipere.* These etymological interrelations merely elucidate what has already emerged in the context of our argumentation, namely that that which defies being subsumed under any *concept* or *conception* is, strictly speaking, in-*conceivable*—such as the ethical effects at issue in this book.

Inconceivable Effects

Introduction

It goes without saying that ethics cannot be put into words....(Ethics and aesthetics are one.)
—Ludwig Wittgenstein, *Tractatus Logico-Philosophicus*

Writing and Complicity

A monograph that encompasses such different genres as political theory (Arendt), fiction (Kafka), cultural criticism (Benjamin), film (*Germany in Autumn*), and drama (Müller) raises questions: Why *these* thinkers, writers, and filmmakers? What could a configuration of Arendt, Kafka, Benjamin, German film, and Heiner Müller possibly show that cannot be shown within the confines of existing disciplines? What is the advantage of aligning political theory, fiction, cultural criticism, film, and drama? How can one account for the peculiar constellation of different genres and media, different modes of presentation? To answer these questions, it might serve us well to digress for a moment and start by simply asking what it is that is actually discussed. What are the issues that link these (theoretical, literary, cinematic) works to one another?

Thematically, the following chapters seek to relate these works through certain political, juridical, and, above all, ethical questions. Yet oddly enough, if we

2   *Inconceivable Effects*

continue to ask what connects the readings performed in this book, an ever-recurring peculiar paradox strikes the reader's eye: each of the literary, theoretical, and cinematic works under discussion seems to be dealing with some sort of ethical concern that, even as it is posited, appears to be revoked or canceled out rhetorically. For instance, Arendt, in her monumental historiography *Origins of Totalitarianism,* clearly condemns the particular logic of totalitarian domination while retaining its dubious use of metaphorical language and its ominous ways of relating to facts in her own writing. Similarly, Benjamin, in "Toward a Critique of Violence," criticizes the coercive nature of law even while enacting its duplicity in the context of his own text. The filmmakers of *Germany in Autumn* decidedly denounce the escalating violence and the concomitant dehumanizing rhetoric between the German state and the terrorist Baader-Meinhof group even as their own ethical stand regarding the struggle between state and terrorists remains disconcertingly vague. Franz Kafka's story "In the Penal Colony" revolves around the description of a morally appalling torture and execution apparatus—an impression shared by the traveler, who articulates his resolute opposition to the machine and with whom we might feel inclined to identify; however, the indifferent, detached tone suffusing the story, in addition to the traveler's ultimate disavowal of any personal responsibility, suggests some sort of collusion with the regime. And, finally, in his drama *Germania Death in Berlin* Heiner Müller outlines the convoluted German history of violence, which indubitably is meant to evoke our condemnation; but at the same time Müller also appears amenable to some sort of complicity with the described violence and, in fact, explicitly calls for such complicity in his autobiography: "You must be complicit with the violence, with the atrocity, so that you can describe it."[1] "Art holds and requires a bloody root. Complicity with the horror, with the terror, is part of the description."[2]

Of Matter and Manner

Does this mean that these works are simply unethical? Or may it be that they still generate something of an ethical momentum, though perhaps of a different kind? What if the question of ethics—in less conceivable ways—emanates from particular modes of presentation and poetic configuration? What if it is intimately tied to the singularity of each work and the specificity of each genre? What if what the constellation of Arendt, Kafka, Benjamin, New German Cinema, and Müller testifies to is precisely an understanding according to which these texts, while concerned with certain ethical questions, cannot be treated as immaterial channels of

---

1. Heiner Müller and Alexander Kluge, *Ich schulde der Welt einen Toten: Gespräche / Alexander Kluge–Heiner Müller* (Hamburg: Rotbuch, 1995), 60.
2. Heiner Müller, *Krieg ohne Schlacht: Leben in zwei Diktaturen: Eine Autobiographie,* in *Werke,* vol. 9 (Frankfurt a.M.: Suhrkamp, 2005), 227.

communication due to fundamental structural idiosyncrasies? Could it be that a "medium," rather than being a vehicle for ethical theorems, generates a certain ethical force of its own by the mere means of its mediality or its aesthetic efficacy?[3] Could it be that the question of structural difference emerges not simply as a question of manner but as one of semantic and concretely ethical relevance, that these texts' styles are fundamentally constitutive to the question of ethics, albeit in a covert way? Why might it matter how works of political theory, cultural criticism, literature, and film render their subject matter manifest, and what could be implied by taking their materiality into account?

Inconceivable Effects

If, for example, one were to describe Hannah Arendt's work *The Origins of Totalitarianism* in terms of materiality or, more concretely, genre,[4] one would likely classify it as a form of historiographical writing. Yet *Origins* (which I first read in conjunction with the recently published *Denktagebuch [Thought Journal]* [2002] and later put into dialogue with such essays as "Truth and Politics" and "Lying in Politics") is distinctly different from most historiography and likely to strike readers for its particular style. Arendt herself, in fact, speaks of her "rather unusual approach...to the whole field of...historical sciences" and elaborates on the methodological dilemma of having to reconstruct something—totalitarianism—which, rather than conserving, she felt engaged to destroy.[5] "The problem originally confronting me," Arendt writes, "was simple and baffling at the same time: all historiography is necessarily salvation and frequently justification."[6] Such vindicatory impulse, she suggests, is inherent in any putatively "objective" chronology and can hardly be overcome by dint of "the interference of value-judgments," which makes the historiographical account appear sentimental, moralistic, or biased. Yet does the absence of value judgments make her historiographical account of totalitarian domination complicit or unethical? Arendt's response to the quandary of having to reconstruct something that she felt engaged to destroy is distinctly different from the dominant positivistic paradigm in the social sciences of her day. Rather than basing her argumentation exclusively on "questionnaires, interviews, statistics, or

---

3. "Mediality" is understood here as the force engendered by a "medium." While my use of the term "medium" will assume a somewhat idiosyncratic meaning in what is to follow, the *OED*'s definition alludes to a tension not unrelated to the issues taken up by this study: "Classical Latin *medium* middle, centre, midst, intermediate course, intermediary, in post-classical Latin also means...instrument, or channel;...esp. a means or channel of communication or expression."

4. "Genre," according to the *OED*, denotes a "particular style or category of works of art; esp. a type of literary work characterized by a particular form, style, or purpose."

5. Hannah Arendt, "A Reply," *Review of Politics* 15 (1953): 76–84, here 79.

6. Ibid., 77.

the scientific evaluation of these data,"[7] Arendt feels that an all-too-heavy reliance on the explanatory power of such quantitative material eventually means the prolonging of the logic of Nazism or, more generally, the "biopolitical" logic of totalitarian politics.[8] At issue, concretely, is the insufficiency of a certain law of genre, namely the historiographical dictum of *sine ira et studio* (of presenting historical materials without indignation or partisanship) in the light of the particular thematic challenge presented by the Holocaust. "To describe the concentration camps *sine ira*," Arendt notes, "is not to be 'objective,' but to condone them; and such condoning cannot be changed by a condemnation which the author may feel duty bound to add but which remains unrelated to the description itself."[9] Since all that happened took place among human beings, and since human beings are by definition ethical beings, who, in contradistinction to animals, assume an understanding of justice,[10] the question of ethics is *intrinsic* rather than one applied to the phenomenon of the camps. There cannot be an apt description of the camps that does not apprehend them as an occurrence in the human world, and as such the phenomenon requires an ethically charged approach rather than settled fervor.

Arendt's response to this methodological and ethical challenge is that of a poetic style, which she frequently described as "storytelling," a form of transfiguration that distinguishes her own historiography from the positivistic approach she disparages. Rather than succumbing to a logic of numbers, a logic that, in talking about the politics of totalitarian extermination, entails a distinct moment of complicity, Arendt's way out of the dilemma lies in the creation of an-*other* language, an-*other* logic—a logic that, by means of its *specific* poetic configuration, establishes a certain incommensurability with and resistance to the dynamics of totalitarian systemization. She generates an edifice of images and imaginings that, in a precariously ambiguous way, contaminate and obliterate totalitarian politics within the context of its presentation. What comes into being is an ethical force never rendered manifest, though incessantly emanating from the poetic infrastructure of her text.

The question of mediality in general and of genre in particular assumes a similarly pivotal role in Walter Benjamin's "Toward a Critique of Violence." Benjamin presents his "Critique" as a philosophical treatise or tractate, a genre that he stages in a most peculiar way. At the center of Benjamin's *explicit discussion* is the

---

7. Hannah Arendt, "Understanding and Politics," in *Essays in Understanding, 1930–1954: Formation, Exile, and Totalitarianism* (New York: Schocken Books, 1994), 323 n. 1.

8. The term "biopolitics" is, of course, not to be found in the works of Arendt; it was coined by Michel Foucault and, more recently, developed and popularized by Italian philosopher Giorgio Agamben in *Homo Sacer: Sovereign Power and Bare Life,* trans. Daniel Heller-Roazen (Stanford, CA: Stanford University Press), esp. 119–88.

9. Arendt, "Reply," 79.

10. "It is the peculiarity of man, in comparison with other animals, that he alone possesses a perception of good and evil, of the just and the unjust" (Aristotle, *Politics,* trans. Ernest Barker [New York: Oxford University Press, 1998], 10f.). Cf. chapters 1, 3, and 6 of this book.

irreconcilability of human law with divine justice,[11] and law's possessive claim to justice, a claim always doomed to fail because of justice's ultimate unintelligibility. At the center of Benjamin's *performance* is an inconspicuous correspondence between, on the one hand, the coercive means-end relationship he talks *about* in the context of his expository remarks on (the means of) law and (the end of) justice, and, on the other hand, the means-end relationship he as speech-actor is caught up with in the context of his argumentation. Eventually, Benjamin will *figuratively* undercut the coercive legal order against which his "Critique" is ostensibly directed; he does not depart from certain premises or positings (*Setzungen*), narrative "means" (followed by certain forms of argumentation), so as to enforce certain narrative "ends" (certain insights into the nature of justice). He does not enact the dynamic he describes as law's positing (*setzende*) means toward the legal enforcement of just ends. Rather, Benjamin—and this is where the peculiar form of his treatise comes into play—produces narrative "means" without (purified from) identifiable narrative "ends." He rhetorically de-poses (*ent-setzt*) his argumentation, thereby undermining the philosophical treatise as the "end-oriented," "purposive literary genre in prose" that it is by definition,[12] all to the effect of free, singular ends, a strangely inconceivable ethical thrust, *beyond* the conventional enforcement of ends—an ethics, in Benjamin's words, "of a different kind."[13]

My discussion of Benjamin's treatise in many ways constitutes the center of this book: what emerges, beyond Benjamin's explicit discussion on the ethics "of a different kind" (beyond his argumentative treatment of the so-called "politics of pure means,"[14] in which means are purified from ends) is a *poetics of pure means*—a poetics in which narrative "means" are purified from narrative "ends," in which narrative means thus do "not function as a means at all, but rather *in some other way.*"[15] This poetics of pure means fundamentally relies on a refusal to operate by means

---

11. Benjamin speaks of "the stubborn prevailing habit of conceiving...just ends as ends of a possible law—that is, not only as generally valid [allgemeingültig] [which follows analytically from the nature of justice] but also as capable of generalizations [verallgemeinerungsfähig], which...contradicts the nature of justice. For ends that in one situation are just, universally acceptable [allgemein anzuerkennen] and valid [allgemeingültig] are so in no other situation, no matter how similar the situations may be in other respects" (Walter Benjamin, "Zur Kritik der Gewalt" ["Toward a Critique of Violence"], in *Gesammelte Schriften,* ed. Rolf Tiedemann and Hermann Schweppenhäuser [Frankfurt a.M.: Suhrkamp, 1977], 2.1:179–203, here 196). The irreconcilability of law and justice—resulting from law's generalizability and justice's radical singularity—finds an illustration in Anatole France's satirical remark when he notes: "Poor and rich are equally forbidden to spend the night under bridges" (after Benjamin, 198). Just because the law treats poor and rich alike doesn't mean it is just. It is ignorant of the fact that the poor, in their specific situation, may have good reasons to sleep under bridges, reasons that the rich simply don't have (and probably wouldn't dream of).

12. "Traktat, m. [lat. Tractatus = Behandlung], literar. Zweckform in Prosa" (Günther Schweikle and Irmgard Schweikle, eds., *Metzler Literaturlexikon: Begriffe und Definitionen* [Stuttgart: Metzler, 1990], 471).

13. Benjamin, "Toward a Critique of Violence," 196.
14. Ibid., 193.
15. Ibid., 196.

of coercion, a refusal to enforce conclusive ends; it is a poetics that subscribes to no-thing other than itself and as such never enforces but perhaps (or that is the question) allows for the ethical momentum that so incessantly seems to surge to the surface in the works under discussion. Yet just how are we to imagine this poetics of pure means in which medium and message no longer relate to each other in the conventional sense of a means-end relationship, but rather "in some other way"? What if we were to think of the relatedness between means and ends as a somehow dissociated relatedness, in which ends were purified of means and means purified of ends, and what if ethics had to do precisely with such purity? What if a text were to generate a force by the pure means of its mediality, an ethical force neither clearly identifiable nor definitely absent but strangely present as an inconceivable effect?

Benjamin, in his "Critique," unremittingly invokes such an-other ethics of a nonenforceable, noncoercive kind, which, provisionally, he also describes as an ethics of "higher orders."[16] He insinuates that this ethics lies *beyond* any established and socially integrated set of morals, *beyond* politico-moral discourses of "victors and vanquished," yet he does so without ever conceptually spelling it out, for that, he says, "would lead too far."[17] What would lead too far is an ethics beyond human recognition and human instrumentalization, one that will never "be recognizable as such with certainty, unless it be in *incomparable effects*."[18] Such incomparable or, more precisely, *inconceivable* effects are at the enigmatic epicenter of Benjamin's treatise and of this book; their epistemic incommensurability describes the abyss from which each of the theoretical, literary, and cinematic works under discussion seizes its ethical momentum, specifically negotiated each time. It goes without saying that such inconceivable effects of a different ethics are, strictly speaking, not simply of a higher or other order but radically out of order. They defy their deduction from *pre*rogatives and *pre*establishments and are fundamentally nondeducible, nonderivable—that is, fundamentally particular or singular.[19]

---

16. Ibid., 193.
17. Ibid.
18. Ibid., 203.
19. Benjamin, in a perhaps curious turn, does relate this ethics of the singular—both in "Critique" as well as in a posthumous fragment entitled "Notes on a Project on the Category of Justice"—to the notion of *Verantwortung*, "responsibility." The Middle High German verb *verantwürten* initially denoted "to respond in front of a court, to respond to a question" (*vor Gericht antworten, eine Frage beantworten*); it implied the imperative to respond to a *particular* question raised in the context of a trial, a juridical procedure subordinating itself to the higher order of justice. Only later did *verantworten* assume its contemporary connotation of "to stand up *for* something, to *represent* something" (*für etwas einstehen, etwas vertreten*) and, if used reflexively, "to justify oneself" (*sich rechtfertigen*) (Duden's *Das Herkunftswörterbuch: Etymologie der deutschen Sprache* [Mannheim: Dudenverlag, 1992], 777). When Benjamin speaks of *Verantwortung*, "responsibility," he employs the word, I would submit, in its original sense—"response-ability"—in the sense of an ability to respond to a particular moment, a specific situation, and to do justice to this situation by taking its uniqueness into account. For a careful discussion of Benjamin's understanding of responsibility, see Judith Butler, "Critique, Coercion, and Sacred Life in Benjamin's 'Critique of Violence,'" in *Political Theologies: Public Religions in a Post-Secular World*, ed. Hent de Vries and Lawrence E. Sullivan (New York: Fordham University Press, 2006), 201–19.

Benjamin's ethics of the singular, then, is inextricably linked to his particular poetics. In a certain way, the rhetorical intricacy of "Critique" originates in his decision to present his thoughts in the form of a philosophical treatise, a genre typically characterized by its conclusive treatment of a problem. Yet given the epistemic limits he faces—namely the conceptual unattainability of justice—and given, thus, the double bind of the law of genre and the specific economy of his subject, Benjamin attempts to explore the question of justice by the (pure) means of its poetic enactment. He addresses the methodical problem of the nonpresentability of justice via a transmutation of his treatise into a theatrical enactment, a theatrical negotiation of justice fundamentally at odds with any conceptual explication or philosophical systemization. Benjamin, in other words, undercuts the treatise's formal delimitations and dwells on its mediality—more a happening than a doing, more an event than an act. What emerges again and again in Benjamin as in the other works is a singularly negotiated relation between poetics and ethics, modes of presentation (*Darstellung*) and modes of morality (*Sittlichkeit*), a relation that Benjamin enacts by turning the thematically problematized politics of pure means into a rhetorically staged poetics of pure means—all to the effect of that somewhat different ethics.

Benjamin's essay is next put into dialogue with Sophocles' *Antigone,* in which the conflict between human law and divine justice (Creon's *nomoi* and Antigone's *dikē*) is similarly negotiated. It is this conflict between law and justice, the unrecognizability of justice, that ultimately emerges as an epistemic problem and as such relates Benjamin's treatise to the subsequent chapter on the film *Germany in Autumn* (1977–78), one of the most controversial omnibus projects of the luminaries of the New German Cinema. *Germany in Autumn* (directed by Rainer Werner Fassbinder, Alexander Kluge, Werner Herzog, and Volker Schlöndorff, among others) was shot in immediate response to the events of what was later called the "German Autumn": namely the kidnapping and murder of industrialist Hanns-Martin Schleyer by the terrorist Baader-Meinhof group, and the political crisis it triggered in the autumn of 1977. What is the relationship between mourning and the dynamics of societal inclusion and exclusion—between the public act of grieving for certain members of the socius, their stylization as "martyr" and paradigmatic "human," and the denial of public grieving as a means of excluding others, allegedly subhuman beings (*Untermenschen*)?

Within the context of this question, the chapter probes the cinematic enactment of the confrontation between the political violence of the German state and the political violence of the Baader-Meinhof group—partly in light of the "play within a play" structure of the film that takes place as a proposed television production of Sophocles' *Antigone.* But then, what kind of judgmental dynamics does *Germany in Autumn* bring about? What is the ethical stand brought to bear *beyond* the reenactment of ostensible friend-foe dichotomies of the state terror from above and the Baader-Meinhof group's terror from below? While it seems that the terrorists, in the name of natural law, and the state, in the name of positive law (paralleling the confrontation between Antigone and Creon), seek to arrogate to themselves the role of the proprietor of justice—negotiated with respect to "the human"—the filmmakers do not walk into that trap. Indeed, if one closely examines the cinematic texture and, concretely, its positions or positings (*Setzungen*) regarding the state and the terrorists, it appears that such statements are frequently left in suspense or de-posed (*ent-setzt*), much in the sense of the Benjaminian deposing (*Entsetzung*). That is to say, *Germany in Autumn*'s cinematic montage, rather than evoking simplistic identifications with preestablished political sides, produces a space of poetic ambiguities and blurred transitions, thereby unsettling identifiable political positions and undermining each political side's possessive claim to justice. What instead ceaselessly surges to the surface is an ethical momentum distinct yet not definable—perhaps deeply moral yet clearly beyond any socially established system of morals. The filmmakers' ethical intervention, rather than succumbing to the discursive dynamics of state violence and terrorist violence, comes into being as a result of the abysmal architectonics so characteristic of the film, one that portrays neither the state nor the terrorists as antagonistic political forces but focuses on individuals instead, single human beings who, *qua* humans, defy conceptual appropriation.

If *Germany in Autumn* confronts us with the question of the film's ethical stance, a question raised explicitly by the filmmakers themselves,[20] then the answer here, as in previous chapters, revolves around the relation between ethics and poetics—that is, the film's particular way of cinematically enacting an ethical concern. In terms of genre, *Germany in Autumn* clearly draws on the tradition of the *Autorenkino*, often translated as "cinema of *auteurs*," a genre that regards "the director as a film's creator" and identifies a film as an expression of that director's artistic vision.[21] As in the other works discussed here, this conception of a genre is unsettled in the light of specific thematic challenges, foremost among them the claim to justice raised by the terrorists and the German state alike. It is a challenge that seems to have prompted the filmmakers not to address the complexities raised by the struggle between the

---

20. Alf Brustellin, Rainer Werner Fassbinder, Alexander Kluge, Volker Schlöndorff, Bernhard Sinkel, "*Germany in Autumn:* What Is the Film's Bias?" in *West German Filmmakers on Film: Visions and Voices,* ed. and trans. Eric Rentschler (New York: Holmes & Meier, 1988), 133 ("Was ist die Parteilichkeit des Films?" in *Deutschland im Herbst: Terrorismus im Film,* ed. Petra Kraus et al. [Munich: Schriftenreihe Münchner Filmzentrum, 1997], 81).

21. Alexander Kluge, one of the filmmakers of *Germany in Autumn* and a distinguished proponent of the *Autorenfilm,* "developed the idea of the director as *Autor* by contrasting the new German film with what he termed a *Zutatenfilm* (recipe film). The 'recipe film' was a typical industry product, made up of ingredients such as stars, ideas, directors, technicians and scriptwriters which the producer simply went out and purchased according to requirements." By contrast, the *auteur* directors "exercised a far greater degree of authorial control than industrial production methods normally permitted." They were to "retain control over the direction and entire production process" and were provided with total financial and artistic control, all of which was to enable the development of a distinctly personal style (Julia Knight, "New German Cinema," http://www.routledge.com/textbooks/9780415409285/resources/newgermancinema.pdf).

German state and the terrorists on their own—as individual *auteur* filmmakers—but collectively—as a group of eleven—and in the form of a film-collage. It appears to be precisely the *ethical* inadequacy of conventional auteur theory (which always seems to imply some sort of partisanship of the *auteur*) that *Germany in Autumn* eludes by means of its unconventional treatment of genre, its suspension of the laws of genre. Accordingly, the undermining of aesthetic prescriptions resonates with a certain undermining of moral prescriptions: the aesthetic specificity of each contribution's mode of presentation appears to correspond to the particularity of the human beings portrayed in the film, irrespective of political allegiances and moral discourses.

Not surprisingly, such eclectic montage is incompatible with the idea of promoting a moral stand translatable into conventional political action. *Germany in Autumn* presents a collage that crosses through fictional and documentary modes alike by including interviews, archival footage from the Third Reich, fictional reenactments, and so forth. Contrary to the conventional practice of continuity editing, the film emphasizes temporal and spatial ruptures as much as it stresses its own stylistic heterogeneity. While the diverse segments are formed into a broad narrative, the film lacks stylistic as well as ethical consistency. As little as the individual characters' claim to justice, in its contextual specificity, can be subsumed under any preexisting *moral* law, so little can the film's poetic enactment be subsumed under a preexisting *aesthetic* law. Once again, laws of genre find themselves undercut to the effect of an ethics inherently tied to mediality; once again, the particularity of an ethical concern seems not merely to be reflected but indeed to be *generated* by an idiosyncratic poetic approach.

What surfaces over and over is an ethical momentum that each of these works seems to reject on the level of explicit discussion, all the while invoking it on the level of performance as that strangely elusive—poetically induced—other ethics.[22] Hannah Arendt's literary acts of *trans*-figuration relentlessly aspire toward a *beyond*—beyond the discursive boundaries of historiographical reconstruction, *beyond* the invincible logic of totalitarian politics, and toward a seemingly supersensuous sphere that statistical data, as much as conceptual language, appears unable to contain. Benjamin's peculiar mode of presentation (the constant propositions asserted only to be rhetorically eroded) brings about or stages, *beyond* any "critique" of violence, the very pure means, the very ethics "of a different kind" he talks about. And the film *Germany in Autumn* raises the question of whether

---

22. Also according to Hegel, tragedies *reflect* as much as *generate* "moral understanding and comprehension"; they function as "eternal *models* of the moral *concept*" (die ewigen *Muster* des sittlichen *Begriffs*) (Georg Wilhelm Friedrich Hegel, *Vorlesungen über die Philosophie der Religion*, in *Werke,* ed. Eva Moldenhauer and Karl Markus Michel [Frankfurt a.M.: Suhrkamp, 1969], 17:132, italics and translation mine); see also Klaus-Dieter Eichler, "Über den Umgang mit Erzählungen bei Platon und Aristoteles," in *Narrative Ethik: Das Gute und das Böse erzählen,* ed. Karen Joisten (Berlin: Akademie Verlag, 2007), 117–34, 134.

the filmmakers' ethical stance is ultimately brought to bear *beyond* the discussed discourses of political violence, whether the film's cinematic economy may precisely be one seeking to *trans*-gress the gnomic sphere of conflicting political concepts and conceptions.

Of course, Arendt does, after all, write historiography, but she effectively rejects the conventional historiographical convention of *sine ira et studio*. Of course, Benjamin does write a treatise, yet he eludes the conclusiveness of this end-oriented, purposive genre. Of course, *Germany in Autumn* is deeply rooted in the tradition of the cinema of *auteurs,* yet it resists the genre's characteristic authorial bias. And of course, as we shall see, Heiner Müller's *Germania Death in Berlin* is indebted to the tradition of bourgeois drama, yet Müller unremittingly destabilizes the genre's dialectical efficacy rhetorically. In each of these cases it seems—and that is the point here—that the specific implementation of poetic space provides not simply a mere correlative but the very conditions for that ethics of a different kind to come into being.

It is in this vein that the question of genre emerges as crucial in *Germania Death in Berlin,* insofar as Müller tackles the involuted German history of violence, spanning from the mythical time of the Nibelungs over Tacitus's *Germania* all the way to the division of twentieth-century postwar Germany. At the same time, however, Müller curiously cancels out or deposes (*entsetzt*) these morally charged historical trajectories poetically. What at the outset appears as clearly discernible discourses of victims and perpetrators, established oppositions of friends and foes—often discussed with regard to the paradigmatic "human" and its others—soon succumbs to chaos, turmoil, and a persistent conflation of political oppositions, of betrayers and betrayed, guilt and innocence. And as political discourses begin to falter, the basis for moral judgments evaporates. This, however (and it is here that the question of genre comes in), essentially concurs with Müller's dramaturgy: if bourgeois drama was characteristic with respect to variants of intersubjective confrontation, Müller's subject is deprived of the enemy. Instead of the presentation of dialectically or oppositionally evolving action along the lines of political or moral discourses, the front lines are now rhetorically rendered diffuse and eviscerated. In accordance with this absence of specifiable duels and identifiable antagonisms, in accordance with the erratic nature of "the enemy," the "theatrical" thrusts the "dramatic" aside; that is, the performative belies the constative, belies whatever discernible dramatic progress there may be. Needless to say, such performative displacement implies fundamental ethical correlatives: for as the determination of and the fight against an adversary is thwarted, politically accountable positions collapse into massacre, unstrategic brutality, and internecine struggles.

If one were to describe the link between ethics and poetics in Müller's *Germania,* then it seems as if the poetic efficacy of *Germania* is the very means that first employs and then suspends the genre-specific parameters of bourgeois drama as prescribed by its tradition of dramatic conflict and conflictional depth. This poetic means—a morally uncommitted, pure means, to be sure—aims at an exploration of the concrete complexities characterizing the situation of the two Cheruscan brothers (Flavus and Arminius) in Tacitus's *Germania* or the Nazi and his Communist brother in their respectively failed careers in the East German and the National Socialist regime or the Socialist Young Bricklayer and his ambivalent understanding of socialism. Rather than demonstrating loyalty to any conceivable moral position, Müller aspires, through intensive scrutiny of the cultural text of violence, to do justice to his characters in their specific situations and to address their individual suffering. He achieves a writerly stance ascribed less to, in Müller's own words, "established and socially integrated morals" than to a strangely elusive ethics of the singular.[23]

In line with, though distinctly different from, Heiner Müller, the nexus between ethics and poetics, between modes of morality and modes of presentation, proves to be pivotal in Franz Kafka's "In the Penal Colony." On the surface, we are, as in Müller, dealing with an unsparing description of extreme violence—that is, the meticulous depiction of an atrocious torture and execution machine in the presence of a prisoner who is about to be executed. It is unmistakable that Kafka's is a horrific, ghastly, and morally repulsive story. This surely is a perspective suggested by the story itself, through the skeptical traveler with whom, at least initially, we are encouraged to identify. Yet what unsettles our indignation and precipitates a gnawing feeling of discontent is the poetic composition, the style of the text. It is not only the unperturbed officer—the execution machine's operator—whose explanations appear ominously ordinary and obsessed with detail as he elaborates, for example, on the execution apparatus's harrow, which inscribes the sentence on the condemned prisoner's skin in the course of twelve hours. It is the traveler as well, who, though initially expressing opposition to the procedure ("I am an opponent of this procedure"), eventually revokes his unequivocal moral stance in the name of an allegedly appropriate impartiality. Time and again, Kafka's narrative appears remarkable in its plain, matter-of-fact, direct, straightforward, that is, its "prosaic," language, which seems to make the horrific situation apparent in the first place. Frequently, what turns out to be "self-evident" within the logic of the penal system is expressed as self-evident, natural, and ordinary in Kafka's prose.[24] Hence, it does not come as a surprise that the traveler, who at first protested against the execution's cruelty and announced his opposition, now shows reservations about any form of protest and recalls how "ticklish" it is "to intervene...in other people's affairs." The traveler's reticence, his tacit complicity, appears distressing precisely because, from his perspective, "the injustice of the procedure and the inhumanity of the execution were undeniable."[25]

---

23. Müller, *Krieg ohne Schlacht,* 246.
24. Franz Kafka, "In der Strafkolonie," in *Ein Landarzt und andere Drucke zu Lebzeiten* (Frankfurt a.M.: Fischer TB Verlag, 1994), 161–95, here 185.
25. Ibid., 175.

Regarding the relation between ethics and poetics, Kafka's detached rhetoric emerges as an indispensable basis for the ferocious violence to be rendered readable.[26] As in Müller, the unvarnished presentation of violence appears to be the very groundwork for the possibility of its investigation. Kafka's style, his narrative "means," as it were, inhibits the blinding gesture of moral speech and thus allows for an analysis that does not present the reader with foregone conclusions, predetermined narrative "ends," but instead induces his or her own particular insights. It is here, against the background of "ethics," that the issue of materiality once again takes center stage. Once again, genre emerges with all its weight, its narrative ramifications and semantic repercussions, its bearing on how the ethical is rendered manifest. If one were to classify Kafka's "In the Penal Colony" in terms of genre theory, one would be dealing with a *story,* more specifically, a piece of *prose* fiction. Our characterization of Kafka's writing as plain, direct, matter-of-fact, and straightforward already captures the "prosaic" in Kafka and its corresponding inhibition of moral gesture.[27] The plainness of the "prosaic" seems to be furthered by the genre-specific indeterminacy of the "story" (*Erzählung*), whose definition reads as a series of negations:

> Its laws of form are often circumscribed... negatively: the story is shorter, less related to the real world, less rich in characters and less complex in plot and substance than the novel; not as concise and suggestive as the sketch and anecdote; in contrast to the novella less sharply molded, less entangled and developed, not as strictly centered around one or two main events and surprising moments; less

---

26. Allegorically, the reading of Kafka's story presents itself in a peculiar light if contrasted with the scenes of reading discussed in the story itself. As the prisoner reads the inscriptions engraved on his body, and as the traveler tries to decipher the scriptures of law presented to him by the officer, we, as readers of Kafka's story, are engaged in deciphering his scripture. And just as we struggle to decipher Kafka's writing, the traveler takes pains with the deciphering of the scriptures of law held in front of him. What makes the act of reading so hard for the traveler is, of course, the aesthetic ornamentation of the scriptures of law (the aesthetic suspension or deposing [*Entsetzung*] of the juridical positings). "It's very ingenious, but I can't make it out," he complains (Kafka, "In der Strafkolonie," 172). And of course, it is the very same aesthetic ornamentation (the same deposing [*Entsetzung*]) that makes it so hard for the prisoner to decipher the inscriptions carved onto his body. "Reason comes to the most dull-witted" only at the sixth hour of torture, only at the sixth hour of torturous reading, a process that then proceeds for another six hours till the prisoner's death (173). As much as this allegory of reading suggests itself, it must fundamentally fail in the face of a certain discrepancy, a discrepancy that makes all the difference in Kafka's story. For while the juridical scriptures presented by the officer fall under the *general* dictum "Guilt is never to be doubted," irrespective of a particular delict, Kafka's narrative does not follow such a general axiom, such interpretative prejudgment (168). Whereas, in other words, in the penal colony every sentence yields to a pre-scribed juris-diction, a preestablished ethical framework that categorically excludes an ethics of an-*other* order, Kafka's writing presents itself as more obstinate. It is thus that we, Kafka's readers, are in a fundamentally different position from that of the reading characters in Kafka's story: while the deciphering of Kafka's story may appear torturous, it does not surrender to any preconceived metanarrative; its interpretative ends remain untethered.

27. The *OED* defines "prose," among other definitions, as "straightforward, straight, direct, ... plain, simple, or matter-of-fact."

pointed and less consistently composed toward the end than the short story; not relating to areas of the unreal and miraculous as fairy tale and legend.[28]

It is such indeterminateness or rhetorical withdrawal, such genre-specific deposing (*Entsetzung*) that brings about Kafka's narrative "ethics." The literary genre of the story (*Erzählung*) is in its formal guidelines as indeterminate as Kafka's "In the Penal Colony" is in its moral prescriptions. While the charged content of the story threatens to be absorbed by moral outrage (or rather to occasion such outrage in readers), Kafka forestalls this danger by bringing his morally uncommitted quest to bear and by problematizing and negotiating without concluding and without delivering judgments. Thus Kafka's writing appears to invoke an ethics that purely communicates itself—narrative means that insist neither on foreseeable ends nor on conceivable effects. The stylistic efficacy of the "Penal Colony" precipitates the deposing (*Entsetzung*) or undoing of conventional ethics,[29] a dynamic that provides the basis for intense analysis practiced to the point of "extra-ordinary" concretion,[30] a dynamic lending itself, once again, to an ethics of the concrete, the singular.

Toward a Poetics of Pure Means

What, we finally and once again shall ask, does an encounter of such different thinkers as Arendt, Kafka, Benjamin, the directors of *Germany in Autumn,* and Müller show? What can be taken from a constellation of modes as varied as political theory, fiction, cultural criticism, film, and drama? Does this conjunction offer any insight that could not be gained in the context of, say, a monograph on film, literature, or political philosophy? Clearly, each of the works discussed here tackles a particular ethical concern within the confines of a "medium." Yet, if with Aristotle's *Poetics* a tradition began that "systematically and prescriptively equated medium with means,"[31] then "medium" (as specified in this book) no longer functions as a means or instrument toward a thematic end. Strictly speaking, medium does not "function" at all and follows no purpose or goal other than its own mediatic force—that ethical force that forges itself in relation to explicitly discussed conceptions of ethics and displaces them. It is a force that is less the *result* of assertions, statements, or

---

28. *Metzler Literaturlexikon*, 138.
29. Newspaper critic Hans Beilhack called Kafka a "lecher of horror" (*Lüstling des Entsetzens*) who does not avoid "even the repulsive and disgusting." Beilhack was reacting to a reading in Munich in November 1916, when Kafka presented his story in the context of a literary lecture series before a small audience. Reportedly, several members of the audience swooned in consequence of hearing the described atrocities (see Peter-André Alt, *Franz Kafka: Der ewige Sohn; Eine Biographie* [Munich: Beck, 2005], 477).
30. Kafka, "In der Strafkolonie," 189.
31. Samuel Weber, *Theatricality as Medium* (New York: Fordham University Press, 2004), 101; Aristotle, *Poetics,* trans. Gerald Else (Ann Arbor: University of Michigan Press, 1970).

propositions than, as I have tried to outline, the *effect* of particular poetic configurations (that is, the effect of the particularly employed economy of a medium).

If this study, then, embarks on an exploration of the cinematic infrastructure of the film *Germany in Autumn,* whose stylistic heterogeneity seems to reverberate with the ungraspability of "the human," or if it seeks to fathom Benjamin's so unfathomable text "Toward a Critique of Violence," which appears to enact the unattainability of justice, or if, to name yet a third example, it probes into Arendt's historiography of totalitarian politics and that pervasive moment of narrative friction that appears to set itself against the cogent logicality of her object of research, totalitarian politics, if thus the study again and again investigates how each (theoretical, literary, cinematic) text's ethical force is brought about in ways distinctly different from all the others, the potential criticism still remains that I simply juxtapose different materials rather than integrate them, that I don't articulate conceptual links but content myself with adjacencies and contiguities. In a way, this is a fair complaint. It is true that the links between genres and media here are links of proximity rather than integration, of contact rather than synthesis. The reason for this, as I have tried to show, lies in the very nature of that other ethics, an ethics that defies conceptual integration of any sort.

While we earlier used the formula of a "poetics of pure means" to describe the rhetorical efficacy of the works under discussion, it goes without saying at this point that such a "poetics of pure means" might similarly describe what is at issue in my own performance, my own commentary, my own approach. This is an approach that attempts relentless readjustment so as to find "pure" ways of addressing a certain work, "pure" meaning modes of addressing a text's specificity, of "doing justice" to its idiosyncrasy. It is an approach, a poetics in constant need of decontaminating itself from preconceived methodological agendas that already anticipate their conclusions, their "insights," their narrative "ends," from the very beginning, a poetics that seeks to circumvent the temptation of reducing works of the most diverse materiality—under the pretense of thematic similarities—to "immaterial phantoms of meaning."[32]

Hence, my discussions of Walter Benjamin and Hannah Arendt probe their philosophical depths and intricacies; yet I also try to be attentive to the rhetorical registers of these theoretical texts. Chiastically reversed, the literary texts by Franz Kafka and Heiner Müller, and the cinematic presentation of *Germany in Autumn,* are read not only with an eye to their literary and cinematic traits; my readings systematically seek to unfold their philosophical and theoretical implications as well.

Rather than treating these works as if they were operating on the same level of simple content, the essays gathered here aim to address the specificity of each genre and the singularity of each text. At the same time, this study examines how the

---

32. Duncan Campbell, "Reading Phonography, Inscribing Interdisciplinarity," in *Critical Studies: Cultural Studies, Interdisciplinarity, and Translation* (Amsterdam: Rodopi, 2002), 131–45, here 132.

differences *among* media are played out *within* each work as an immanent conflict of structures. This maneuver leads to the kernel of the study, an analysis of how narratives across genres seek to capitalize meaning, and how such capitalization of meaning displays its own limits when it comes to the question of ethics. At issue is an ethics that, beyond the accumulation of moral injunctions, emanates from the fissures, chasms, and interstices of poetic enactments, an ethics that evolves as elusive effect, whose epistemic resistance this project cannot overcome but perhaps (or that would be the hope) can invoke.

1

"The Odium of Doubtfulness"

Or the Vicissitudes of Arendt's Metaphorical Thinking

All thinking [is] metaphorical.

—Hannah Arendt, *Denktagebuch*

Pondering the question of "style" in historiographical narration, Hannah Arendt notes: "The question of *style* is bound up with the *problem of understanding* which has plagued the historical sciences almost from their beginnings."[1] What is the "style" of Arendt's monumental *Origins of Totalitarianism,* the text we are primarily concerned with here? And how does its efficacy relate to the problem of *understanding* totalitarianism? In her response to political philosopher Eric Voegelin, one of the first reviewers of *Origins,* Arendt elaborates on her decision to, as it were, allocate more historiographical legitimacy to the valences of metaphorical thinking than to statistical scientificity. After conceding that she failed "to account for a rather unusual approach...to the whole field of political and historical sciences," she hypostatizes the merits of metaphorical thinking on the basis of a central

---

1. Hannah Arendt, "A Reply," *Review of Politics* 15.1 (1953): 76–84, here 79; hereafter abbreviated as R. Unless otherwise noted, all italics in this chapter are mine. For a nuanced discussion of the anachronism of Arendt's "style," see Seyla Benhabib, *The Reluctant Modernism of Hannah Arendt* (Oxford: Rowman & Littlefield, 2000), 86–95. See also Julia Kristeva, *Hannah Arendt,* trans. Ross Guberman (New York: Columbia University Press, 2001).

metaphor employed in *Origins,* that of the concentration camp as a place of "Hell" (R 79). To recapitulate the context briefly, Arendt distinguishes three types of concentration camps, each corresponding to one of the three basic Western conceptions of life after death: Hades, Purgatory, and Hell. *Hades,* Arendt explains, is represented by those "relatively mild" camps for displacing "undesirable elements of all sorts—refugees, stateless persons, the asocial and the unemployed." After those so-called displaced-persons camps, she lists the Soviet Union's labor camps, metaphorized as *Purgatory,* "where neglect is combined with chaotic forced labor." *Hell* "in the most literal sense," is embodied by those camps perfected by the Nazis "in which the whole of life was thoroughly and systematically organized with a view to the greatest possible torment" (*O* 445, *E* 918f.).[2]

Arendt frequently turns to the Nazi extermination camps, the site of Hell, as it is here that both the nature of human beings, on the threshold between life and death, and the nature of totalitarian regimes can be studied.[3] Arendt also dwells on the metaphor of Hell in explaining her rather idiosyncratic style vis-à-vis possible approaches in line with the positivistic paradigm. "Hell" is a biblical metaphor with a distinct moral connotation. Arendt explains that she parted quite consciously with the tradition of *sine ira et studio* (without indignation or partisanship), for describing a phenomenon like the extermination camps without indignation would mean to deprive them of an inherent dimension. Rather than suggest detached scholarly rigor, it would imply the dismissal of an integral element of these camps. The Nazis' extermination camps existed "in the midst of human society." "To describe the concentration camps *sine ira,*" Arendt writes, "is not to be 'objective,' but to condone them; and such condoning cannot be changed by a condemnation which the author may feel duty bound to add but which remains unrelated to the description itself" (R 79). Since all that happened took place among human beings, and since human beings are by definition ethical beings, who, in contradistinction to animals, assume an understanding of justice, the question of ethics is *intrinsic* rather than one applied to the phenomenon of the camps. There cannot be an apt description of the camps that does not apprehend them as an occurrence in the human world, and as such the phenomenon requires an inherently ethically charged approach rather than settled fervor.

---

2. See Hannah Arendt, *Elemente und Ursprünge totaler Herrschaft: Antisemitismus, Imperialismus, Totalitarismus* (Munich: Piper, 1986); and Arendt, *The Origins of Totalitarianism* (New York: Harcourt, 1968); hereafter abbreviated as *E* and *O,* respectively. Hannah Arendt wrote and published *The Origins of Totalitarianism* first in English in 1951; it appeared in German four years later. The German edition, however, is not a translation *sensu stricto* but is revised, rhetorically sharpened, and often elaborated. All citations are therefore based on the German edition. Whenever possible, I have consulted the English edition for translations; all other translations are my own.

3. Arendt's trifurcated model of Hades, Purgatory, and Hell, of course, does not take the difference between concentration and death camps within Germany itself into account—a distinction that she, however, repeatedly problematizes in interviews. See also Wolfgang Sofsky, *The Order of Terror: The Concentration Camp,* trans. William Templer (Princeton, NJ: Princeton University Press, 1996).

What one therefore faces is not merely a methodological problem but a political and philosophical one.[4] "The problem originally confronting me," Arendt writes, "was simple and baffling at the same time: all historiography is necessarily salvation and frequently justification" (R 77). Such vindicatory impulse, she suggests, is inherent in any putatively "objective" chronology and can hardly be overcome through "the interference of value-judgments," which makes the historiographical account appear sentimental, moralistic, or biased. She deems the "extraordinarily poor" scholarly literature on the history of anti-Semitism a case in point: it exemplifies the attempt "to write in a destructive way," yet "to write history for purposes of destruction is somehow a contradiction in terms" (R 77). This quandary of writing historically about totalitarianism, which one may feel engaged to destroy rather than conserve, is the fundamental challenge Arendt faces. Her metaphorical language is an attempt at a response to this challenge, a response insofar as metaphors such as "Hell" precisely do not merely reconstruct Nazism within its own judgmental efficacy, give meaning to events, and construct historical continuity, thereby ultimately condoning it. Arendt tells the history of totalitarianism in another language, another logic, a logic incompatible with that of Nazism. Rather than basing her argument exclusively on "questionnaires,...statistics, or the scientific evaluation of these data," she feels that an all-too-heavy reliance on the explanatory power of such quantitative material eventually means prolonging the logic of Nazism or, more generally, the biopolitical logic of totalitarian politics.[5] Instead of succumbing to the language and logic of numbers, a logic that, in regard to the politics of totalitarian extermination, entails a distinct moment of *complicity,* Arendt's way out of the methodological dilemma lies in creating an-*other* language, an-*other* logic, a logic allowing for an ethical *stance* (*Haltung*). As we shall see, it is not solely the thematic dimension but, beyond that, the specific performative configuration of Arendt's metaphorical language and her language in general that establishes a certain incommensurability with the dynamics of totalitarian systemization.

Between Past and Future

There is a Hasidic tale that reads as follows:

> When the Baal Shem had a difficult task before him, he would go to a certain place in the woods, light a fire and meditate in prayer—and what he had set out to perform

---

4. "Questions of method, on the one side, and of general philosophical implications on the other...of course belong together" (R 76f.).

5. Hannah Arendt, "Understanding and Politics," in *Essays in Understanding, 1930–1954: Formation, Exile, and Totalitarianism* (New York: Schocken Books, 1994), 307–27, here 323 n. 1. In "On the Nature of Totalitarianism," Arendt writes: "With the introduction of completely alien and frequently nonsensical categories of evaluation into the social sciences, they have reached an all-time low. Scientific accuracy does not permit any understanding which goes beyond the narrow limits of sheer factuality, and it has paid a heavy price for this arrogance, since the wild superstitions of the twentieth century, clothed in humbug scientism, began to supplement its deficiencies" (in *Essays in Understanding,* 328–60, here 339).

was done. When a generation later the "Maggid" of Meseritz was faced with the same task he would go to the same place in the woods and say: We can no longer light the fire, but we can still speak the prayers—and what he wanted done became reality. Again a generation later Rabbi Moshe Leib of Sassov had to perform this task. And he too went into the woods and said: We can no longer light a fire, nor do we know the secret meditations belonging to the prayer, but we do know the place in the woods to which it all belongs—and that must be sufficient; and sufficient it was. But when another generation had passed and Rabbi Israel of Rishin was called upon to perform the task, he sat down on his golden chair in his castle and said: We cannot light the fire, we cannot speak the prayers, we do not know the place, but we can tell the story of how it was done. And, the story-teller adds, the story which he told had the same effect as the actions of the other three.[6]

This little tale leads us into the center of Hannah Arendt's thought and her doings as a historian and political theorist. Hannah Arendt's art is that of storytelling, and since she knew what Rabbi Israel of Rishin knew, namely that storytelling has "the same effect as...actions," since she in fact knew that storytelling is nothing but action, and that action, respectively, can only be conceptualized as such through narrative, we may ask, from a slightly different angle now, How can one tell a story, the story of totalitarianism, without reconstructing it, without reconfiguring it as a continuum of past, present, and future, without, after all, justifying it? Hannah Arendt's response to this dilemma was one much indebted to Walter Benjamin, whose "Theses on the Philosophy of History" she had edited for the English Schocken edition, and whose understanding of history and history telling as fragmentary permeated her own oeuvre:

> I have clearly joined the ranks of those who for some time now have been attempting to dismantle metaphysics, and philosophy with all its categories, as we have known them from their beginning in Greece until today. Such dismantling is possible only on the assumption that the *thread of tradition* is broken and we shall not be able to renew it. Historically speaking, what actually has broken down is the Roman trinity that for thousands of years united religion, authority, and tradition. The loss of this trinity does not destroy the past.... What has been lost is the continuity of the past as it seemed to be handed down from generation to generation.... What you then are left with is still the past, but a *fragmented* past, which has lost its certainty of evaluation.[7]

That "the thread of tradition is broken," that it is *irrevocably* torn is a diagnosis Arendt appropriates from Benjamin: "Walter Benjamin knew that the break in tradition and the loss of authority...were irreparable," she writes. Arendt's

---

6. Gershom Scholem, *Major Trends in Jewish Mysticism* (New York: Schocken Books, 1995), 349f.; see also Annabel Herzog, "Illuminating Inheritance," *Philosophy and Social Criticism* 26.5 (2000): 1–27, 1–2.

7. Hannah Arendt, *The Life of the Mind* (New York: Harcourt, 1978), 1:212, first italics mine.

formula for this break of tradition is that of the "gap between past and future" within which we live.[8] Benjamin accounted for the postulated rupture in tradition with a fragmentary form of narration, and there is no doubt that this style had considerable impact on Arendt's own writing. Rather than constructing history as a continuous sequence of victories as would be found in most official historiography, Arendt's style is susceptible to the impasses and often traumatic ruptures of historical narrative, its event-like structure, its inconclusive logic.[9] "The continuum of history is that of the oppressors." "The history of the oppressed is a discontinuum,"[10] Walter Benjamin writes. That only a fragmentary style of historiography could tell and resuscitate the stories of the victims, and that this kind of resuscitation constitutes a form of narrative justice, a retroactive justice to those deprived of their voices, is an understanding Arendt owes to Benjamin.

Yet what does it mean to narrate history fragmentarily? Benjamin understood that the "break in tradition and the loss of authority" were irreversible, and he determined that "*he had to discover new ways of dealing with the past*" (*M* 193). Arendt credits Benjamin with mastery in the art of citation, and brilliance when he discovered "that the transmissibility of the past had been replaced by its citability" (*M* 193). It goes without saying that whereas Benjamin initially had planned for a montage of citations with respect to *Origin of the German Mourning Play* as well as *The Arcades Project,* Arendt never entertained such ambitions. At the same time, Arendt's storytelling is remarkable for its rich implementation of metaphors, analogies, proverbs, anecdotes, and literary citations—a style we shall explore in what is to come, a style, to be sure, often discredited in Arendt's role as a political thinker.[11]

---

8. Hannah Arendt, "Walter Benjamin," in *Men in Dark Times* (New York: Harcourt, 1968), 153–206, here 193; hereafter abbreviated as *M*. See also Arendt, *Menschen in dunklen Zeiten* (Munich: Piper, 1989), 185–242; Arendt, *Between Past and Future: Eight Exercises in Political Thought* (New York: Penguin Books, 1968), 3, 11.

9. On this nexus between Arendt's and Benjamin's respective understanding of storytelling, see Benhabib, *The Reluctant Modernism of Hannah Arendt,* 91–95.

10. Walter Benjamin, "Paralipomènes et variantes des *Thèses 'Sur le concept de l'histoire,'*" in *Écrits français,* ed. Jean-Maurice Monnoyer (Paris: Gallimard, 1991), 352, quoted in Shoshana Felman, *The Juridical Unconscious: Trials and Traumas in the Twentieth Century* (Cambridge, MA: Harvard University Press, 2002), 31.

11. Isaiah Berlin derided Arendt's work, revealing a certain chauvinistic bias: "I do not greatly respect the lady's [*sic*] ideas, I admit.... She produces no arguments, no evidence of serious philosophical or historical thought. It is all a stream of metaphysical free association. She moves from one sentence to another, without logical connection, without either rational or imaginative links between them" (Berlin, *Conversations with Isaiah Berlin,* ed. Ramin Jahanbegloo [London: Peter Halban, 1992], 82). On Arendt's art of storytelling in general and its historiographical implications in particular, see Kai Evers, "The Holes of Oblivion: Arendt and Benjamin on Storytelling in the Age of Totalitarian Destruction," *Telos* 132 (2005): 109–20; Maurizio Passerin d'Entrèves, *The Political Philosophy of Hannah Arendt* (London: Routledge, 1994), 3–9 and 28–34; Agnes Heller, "Hannah Arendt on Tradition and New Beginnings," in *Hannah Arendt in Jerusalem,* ed. Steven Aschheim (Berkeley: University of California Press, 2001), 19–32; Barbara Hahn, "Wie aber schreibt Hannah Arendt?" *Text und Kritik* 166/167 (2005): 102–13; Barbara Hahn, "Hannah Arendt: Wege ins politische Denken," in *Frauen in den Kulturwissenschaften: Von Lou Andreas-Salomé bis Hannah Arendt,* ed. Barbara Hahn (Munich: C. H. Beck, 1994), 262–77; Sebastian Hefti, "Zwischen Welt Sprache: Denkbilder und Hannah Arendts Schreibwerkstatt," *Text und Kritik* 166/167 (2005): 114–24. On the significance of poetic thought for Arendt's political theory, cf. Susannah Yough-ah Gottlieb, "'Seit jener Zeit.' Hannah Arendt und ihre Literaturkritik," *Text und*

Metaphorical Thinking

"What is so hard to understand about Benjamin," writes Arendt, "is that without being a poet he *thought poetically* and therefore was bound to regard the metaphor as the greatest gift of language" (*M* 166). Arendt was no poet, yet there is no question that she thought poetically and in particular, metaphorically.[12] In *Origins* she speaks of "bugs," "grasshoppers" and "lice," "mosquitoes" and "flies," "soap" and "pimples," an "iron band," "fences," "cornfields," and "chess," a "desert," a "heart," "poison," an "onion," "dogs," and so on. Arendt ponders the question of metaphorical thinking, including her own metaphorical thinking, in the *Denktagebuch* (Thought Journal), published in 2002.[13] The beginning of Arendt's notations for the *Denktagebuch* in 1950 coincides with the last working stage of *Origins*. While *Origins* is a book saturated with metaphorical language, the scattered remarks in the *Denktagebuch* expound a theory of metaphor. What is the relation between Hannah Arendt's thinking about metaphor in the *Denktagebuch*, on the one hand, and the metaphorical thinking about totalitarian politics in *Origins*, on the other?

Arendt repeatedly develops her thoughts on metaphorical thinking from a position of *defense*. For instance, in an entry titled "On the difficulties I have with my English readers," she stands up for Walter Benjamin's—and en route for her own—metaphorical thinking against "the linguistic 'philosophers'" of her day, who "*analyse* everyday speech" but do "not *clarify*" it: "For instance: I said that Benjamin thinks poetically, i.e., in metaphors. Thus far everything okay. But I then raise the question of what is a metaphor... and what does a metaphor achieve.... These considerations, according to our English friend, have nothing to do with a profile of Benjamin" (*DT* 771; English in the original).

Arendt's discontent with Anglo-linguistic philosophy is reflected in her repudiation of what she characterizes as "thesaurus philosophy," an understanding of

---

Kritik 166/167 (2005): 138–49; Marie Luise Knott, "Hannah Arendt liest Franz Kafka 1944," *Text und Kritik* 166/167 (2005): 150–61; Thomas Wild, *Nach dem Geschichtsbruch: Deutsche Schriftsteller und Hannah Arendt* (Berlin: Matthes & Seitz, 2009); Thomas Wild, "Kreative Konstellationen: Hannah Arendt und die deutsche Literatur der Gegenwart; Ein Überblick und eine Wirkungsanalyse am Beispiel Rolf Hochmuths," *Text und Kritik* 166/167 (2005): 162–73. For an almost comprehensive anthology of the essays and reviews Arendt wrote about literary texts, see Hannah Arendt, *Reflections on Literature and Culture*, ed. Susannah Young-ah Gottlieb (Stanford, CA: Stanford University Press, 2007).

12. To be sure, notwithstanding her studies with Martin Heidegger and Karl Jaspers, Arendt was not a philosopher. In fact, she herself raised this claim vehemently. "In my opinion I have said good-bye to philosophy once and for all.... There is a kind of enmity against all politics in most philosophers, with very few exceptions.... I want no part in this enmity,... I want to look at politics, so to speak, with eyes unclouded by philosophy" (Arendt, "'What Remains? The Language Remains': A Conversation with Günter Gaus," in *Essays in Understanding*, 2). While the failure of philosophy in the face of the horrors of the twentieth century triggered Arendt's unequivocal refusal to identify with philosophical thinking, her fascination with the power of metaphorical thinking seems to be yet another moment for this defiance of systematic and systematizing thinking.

13. Hannah Arendt, *Denktagebuch*, 2 vols. (Munich: Piper, 2002); hereafter abbreviated as *DT*. All translations are my own unless otherwise noted.

language as she finds it in *Roget's International Thesaurus,* where entries are listed conceptually, not defined but ordered and catalogued with respect to the "greatest possible 'variety of associations.'"[14] The impasse, in Arendt's view, is that, according to this conception of language, themes and topics are guided by certain "ideas" and, consequently, hierarchically arranged. Underlying this organizing principle is the puzzling "notion that words 'express' ideas which I supposedly have prior to having the words." In contradistinction to this perspective, Arendt deems languages the very basis of ideas: "It is more than doubtful that we would have any 'ideas' without language" (*DT* 771). Given this backdrop, Arendt, time and again, vindicates her methodology in the face of her American critics: "*Times Literary Supplement* reviewer complains of my 'ideology'; what he means is my thinking that transcends mere description. Or: similes and metaphors" (*DT* 771; English in the original). Out of a certain frustration with the school of analytical philosophy she concludes: "What this adds up to is that the whole notion of thinking a matter *through* is alien to English 'philosophy'" (*DT* 771).

"The metaphor," Arendt maintains, "is what links thought and writing. What is called a metaphor in fiction is, in philosophy, called a concept. Thought creates its 'concepts' from the visible to designate the invisible" (*DT* 728).[15] The metaphor's role here is that of a "transference" in the sense of the Greek *metapherein* (to transfer), the transference of an abstract, imageless thought from a supersensuous, inconceivable sphere to a sensuous, more conceivable one. "The metaphor's role: linking (as-if) the visible with the invisible" (*DT* 728). Notably, the metaphor is not to be situated in either the sphere of the sensuous or the sphere of the supersensuous. Its indispensable role in (philosophical) thought results precisely from its power to relate the two. "Language, by lending itself to metaphorical usage, enables us to think, that is, to have traffic with non-sensory matters, because it permits a carrying-over...of our sense experiences. There are not two worlds because metaphor unites them," Arendt writes in *Thinking,* the first volume of *The Life of the Mind.*[16] In *Origins,* then, the supersensuous corresponds to the "modern lie" of totalitarianism, a lie so big, a totality so total, that the possibility of argumentative critique appears to have evaporated.[17] At this point, only the linguistic transference of the perfect ideology of totalitarianism into a language perceivable in its immediacy seems to allow for "understanding."

---

14. Preface to *Roget's International Thesaurus,* 3rd ed. (New York: Crowell, 1962), viii, quoted in Arendt, *DT* 770.
15. "Was Denken und Dichten verbindet, ist die Metapher. In der Philosophie nennt man Begriff, was in der Dichtung Metapher heisst. Das Denken schöpft aus dem Sichtbaren seine 'Begriffe', um das Unsichtbare zu bezeichnen."
16. Arendt, *Life of the Mind,* 1:110.
17. Hannah Arendt, "Truth and Politics," in *Between Past and Future,* 227–64, here 253; hereafter abbreviated as TP.

"The Odium of Doubtfulness"

The linguistic "transference" of the metaphor leads Arendt to Immanuel Kant: "Ad metaphor:... They always have to guide us, *'where the understanding lacks the guiding threads of indubitable proofs'* [*wo dem Verstande der Faden der untrüglichen Beweise mangelt*] (*Universal Natural History and Theory of Heaven*)" (*DT* 674).[18] The Kantian *überall*... *"wo dem Verstande der Faden der untrüglichen Beweise mangelt,"* to be sure, concerns not only the sphere of "Universal Natural History and Theory of Heaven" but also, as Arendt remarks in another entry in her journal, expressly "human affairs" (*menschlichen Angelegenheiten*) (*DT* 767).[19] Incidences of the horrific, *wo dem Verstande der Faden der untrüglichen Beweise mangelt*, then, culminate in the third part of Arendt's book on totalitarianism.

> *Common sense* [*Der gesunde Menschenverstand*] reacted to the horrors of Buchenwald and Auschwitz with the plausible argument: "What crime must these people have committed that such things were done to them!"; or, in Germany and Austria, in the midst of starvation, overpopulation, and general hatred: "Too bad that they've stopped gassing the Jews"; and everywhere with the skeptical shrug that greets ineffectual propaganda. (*O* 446, *E* 919f.)

Frequently Arendt will instigate the metaphorical transference of the supersensuous into the sensuous, the invisible into the visible. Repeatedly, she will launch a translation of the unimaginable *(Unvorstellbare)*, unbelievable (*Unglaubliche*), implausible (*Unglaubwürdige*), inconceivable (*Unfassbare*), into the purportedly more graspable language of the sensuous.[20]

---

18. "Ad Metapher:... Sie müssten uns überall leiten, 'wo dem Verstande der Faden der untrüglichen Beweise mangelt' (*Allgemeine Naturgeschichte und Theorie des Himmels*)"; here translated by Ian C. Johnston http://www.mala.bc.ca/~johnstoi/kant/kant2e.htm (accessed February 13, 2007). "The metaphor provides the 'abstract,' imageless thought with an intuition drawn from the world of appearances whose function is to...undo, as it were, the withdrawal from the world of appearances that is the precondition of mental activities" (Arendt, *Life of the Mind*, 1:103).

19. "Das Unsichtbare: die 'Bilder' der Einbildungskraft, die in die Kontemplation und die Identifizierung von Wahrheit und Anschauung führen, und die 'Begriffe', welche die Sprache vorgibt. Die letzten sind immer aus dem Bereich der menschlichen Angelegenheiten gewonnen, die ersteren beziehen sich auf 'Gegebenes', Natur, Universum etc." For a more comprehensive discussion of Arendt's theory of metaphor, see Sigrid Weigel, "Dichtung als Voraussetzung der Philosophie: Hannah Arendts Denktagebuch," *Text und Kritik* 166/167 (2005): 125–37, here 133; cf. Weigel, "Hannah Arendts Passagenwerk: Das *Denktagebuch* als deutschsprachiges Palimpsest zum Werk der amerikanischen Philosophin," *Weimarer Beiträge* 50.1 (2004): 117–21.

20. The question of metaphor is, needless to say, also discussed in Arendt's long essay on Benjamin, where she rather unadventurously describes the metaphor as a correspondence "which is sensually perceived in its immediacy and requires no interpretation.... Since Homer the metaphor has borne that element of the poetic which conveys cognition; its use establishes the *correspondences* between physically most remote things" (*M* 166, Arendt's italics). The metaphor describes, according to Arendt (and, as we shall see, also within the topography of Arendt's own speech act), the paradox of a fiction that makes "reality" more graspable and "directly...concrete" not in spite of but because of its poetic mediation (165). It makes conceivable that which otherwise would remain trans-parent, *durch-schaubar* (see-through)

How exactly are we to understand this process of a linguistic transference as put forth in *Origins*? What defies understanding (*das dem Verstand sich Widersetzende*) finds an example in the species of the "human animal" (*O* 455, *E* 934). The "preparation" of this species can be divided into three stages: the *first* essential step is "to kill the juridical person in man.... This was done by putting certain categories of people *outside* the protection of the law" (*O* 447, *E* 922). Arendt speaks here of those people who became "as outlawed in their own country as the stateless" (*O* 451, *E* 928). Yet what does "stateless" or the "killing of the juridical person in man" mean; how are we to *imagine (vor-stellen)* it? Arendt translates it into the language of an image: those deprived of the "so-called Rights of Man" are turned in like a dog without a name: for of course "a dog with a name has a better chance to survive than a stray dog who is just a dog in general" (*O* 287, *E* 562).[21] Perhaps because dogs are deemed man's best friend, the stray dog must pose as a case in point here. While the *second* stage in the "mass production" of living corpses is the murder of the moral person in man, the *third* step refers to the killing of man's individuality, the uniqueness shaping a human being (*O* 453, *E* 931).[22] For this third stage Arendt, perhaps unsurprisingly, again employs the image of a dog, though this time it is Pavlov's dog, whose fame in the history of behavioral biology rested on the transmutation of its unconditioned reflexes for the sake of conditioned reflexes—which, according to Arendt, meant the killing of precisely that which defines life, namely spontaneity. In the language of images we are thus facing the juxtaposition of one dog and another dog, yet "just a dog in general," the disenfranchised person, still seems to be in a better position than a perverted dog, the undead, the dehumanized human being in the camps. Pavlov's dog describes the paradox of an inanimate living being, a "living corpse," and since this state of no longer being human appears

---

and as such *unanschaulich* (not concrete), not perceivable, that is, not susceptible to reason, *Vernunft*, which etymologically derives from the verb *vernehmen* (to perceive, to hear).

21. For Arendt's famous analysis of the perplexities of human rights and their historically fateful connection to the declining nation-states, see part 2, chap. 9 of *Origins*, "The Decline of the Nation-State and the End of the Rights of Man." As early as 1843, Karl Marx grappled with the complex question of human rights in his scandal-provoking essay "The Jewish Question," eventually disputing the Jewish or any people's alleged rights to particular rights (Marx, "The Jewish Question," in *The Marx-Engels Reader*, ed. Robert Tucker [New York: Norton, 1978], 26–52).

22. Arendt's zoological terminology for those deprived of their individuality is manifold: it ranges from "bugs," "grasshoppers," "lice," "mosquitoes," and "flies" to "dogs" and "cattle." What all these metaphors share is the reference to an anonymous population of biopolitically administered human material: "Not...men and women, children and adults, boys and girls"—that is, not representatives of mankind, but beings "brought down to the lowest common denominator of organic life itself, plunged into the darkest and deepest abyss of primal equality, like cattle, like matter, like things that had neither body nor soul, not even a physiognomy upon which death could stamp its seal" (Arendt, "The Image of Hell," in *Essays in Understanding*, 197–205, here 198). Arendt's zoological metaphors describe the *deindividualized* status of the individual in totalitarian ideology, the status of "the abstract nakedness of being human" (*O* 299, *E* 619). See also Frederick Dolan, "The Paradoxical Liberty of Bio-Power: Hannah Arendt and Michel Foucault on Modern Politics," *Philosophy & Social Criticism* 31.3 (2005): 369–80; Dana Villa, "Totalitarianism, Modernity, and the Tradition," in *Hannah Arendt in Jerusalem*, ed. Steven Aschheim (Berkeley: University of California Press, 2001), 124–48; Margaret Canovan, "Arendt's Theory of Totalitarianism: A Reassessment," in *The Cambridge Companion to Hannah Arendt*, ed. Dana Villa (Cambridge: Cambridge University Press, 2000), 24–43.

inconceivable to Arendt even *after* its metaphorical transference, she translates it yet again into another image, the metaphor of the marionette:

> For to destroy individuality is to destroy spontaneity, man's power to begin something new out of his own resources, something that cannot be explained on the basis of reactions to environment and events. Nothing then remains but *ghastly marionettes with human faces, which all behave like the dog in Pavlov's experiments,* which all react with perfect reliability even when going to their own death, and which do nothing but react. This is the real triumph of the system. (*O* 455, *E* 614)

When the dehumanized human being, the figure of the undead, is translated into the image of marionettes *behaving like* Pavlovian dogs, what then is taking place rhetorically is a double displacement. To recall Kant's formula: metaphors "must always guide us in such cases where the *understanding* lacks the guiding threads of *indubitable proofs* [wo *dem Verstande* der Faden *der untrüglichen Beweise* mangelt]." Arendt writes about the Nazi concentration camps: "Despite *overwhelming proofs* [Trotz *überwältigender Beweise*], the odium of doubtfulness [das Odium der Unglaubwürdigkeit], with which the reports from concentration camps were initially met, always remains attached to each person who reports on them" (*E* 908). The paradox Arendt faces is thus the following: despite all evidence the phenomena of the camps appear to defy understanding, appear insusceptible to the faculty of reason (*Verstand*): "What common sense [der gesunde Menschenverstand] and 'normal people' refuse to believe is that everything is possible. We attempt to understand elements in present or recollected experience that simply surpass our powers of understanding" (*O* 441).[23] Reason cannot accept certain realities despite their being "proven" beyond doubt. It deems "reality"—and we shall use these terms here only provisionally—a "fiction," yet since in totalitarian ideologies "reality" and "fiction" can no longer be discerned, "reason," as it were, forsakes humanity, and the only response provoked is a "skeptical shrug": "The films which the Allies circulated in Germany and elsewhere after the war showed clearly that this atmosphere of insanity and unreality is not dispelled by pure reportage. To the unprejudiced observer these pictures are just about as convincing as snapshots of mysterious substances taken at spiritualist séances" (*O* 446, *E* 920).

These films made about the "mass manufacture of corpses" appear like a "propaganda *trick*" meant to deceive the spectator (*O* 446, *E* 920). Despite all evidence, "'*understanding lacks the guiding threads of indubitable proofs.*'" How are we to understand this paradox?

---

23. "Was der gesunde Menschenverstand, was 'normale Menschen' nicht glauben, ist, daß alles möglich ist. Die größte Schwierigkeit, die einem angemessenen Verstehen des totalitären Phänomens entgegensteht, ist diese *Stimme des Unglaubens,* die in jedem von uns sitzt und uns mit den Argumenten des gesunden Menschenverstandes schlecht zuredet" (*E* 911f.).

The "Discovery" of the Lie

Arendt considers the "discovery" of the lie one of the Nazis' greatest "achievements," in that the immensity of their crimes guaranteed that the murderers, who "proclaim their innocence with all manner of *lies,*" will be more readily believed than the victims, whose "truths" offend any sane listener's common sense:

> Hitler circulated millions of copies of his book in which he stated that to be successful, a lie must be enormous, i.e., when you are not content to lie about individual factual data within a factual context that is left intact, whereby the intact facts already uncover the lie, but instead *cast such a web of lies around the entire factuality that all the individual constituent facts replace the real by a fictional world, coherent in itself.* (*O* 439, *E* 909f.)

Arendt speaks here of an "entire factuality," a "real" world substituted for a "fictional" world—an analysis that in the later essay "Truth and Politics" (1967) leads her to classify totalitarianism as a "modern lie": "The modern political lies are so big that they require a complete rearrangement of the whole factual texture—the making of another reality, as it were, into which they fit without seam, crack or fissure" (*TP* 253). The modern lie thus epitomizes the paradox of a lie so enormous that, in a narrow sense, it no longer can be called a "lie." For what distinguishes the "lie" from an "error" or a "mistake" is of course its *intentionality,* the deliberateness of the falsification. In the case of self-deception this intentionality is no longer given. At the same time Arendt's nominal classification of the modern lie does, as we shall see, harbor some explanatory potential for the phenomenon of collective mendacity.[24] To be sure, the concept of the modern lie, the notion of self-deception, is more than just an accompaniment to ideology. Arendt speaks about the question of ideology at length, attributing to it the analytic force of a modern, all-encompassing lie.[25] While her motivation for this interpretive symbiosis will gradually emerge, for now we shall follow her on the argumentative path of ideology.

---

24. Benjamin calls this feature of societal mendacity "objektive Verlogenheit" (objective mendacity) and deems it a phenomenon that "dominates world-historically in our time." In "Remarks on 'Objective Mendacity'" (written about 1921) he explains: "Warum 'objektive' Verlogenheit? 1) Sie herrscht objektiv weltgeschichtlich in dieser Zeit. Alles was nicht ganz groß ist, ist in unser Zeit *unecht.* 2) Es ist nicht die subjektiv, vom Einzelnen klar verantwortete Lüge. Sondern dieser ist 'bona fide'." (Why "objective" mendacity? [1] It dominates objectively, world-historically in these times. Everything not great is considered unreal in our time. [2] It is not the subjective lie for which the individual would have to take responsibility. Rather, he is "bona fide.") Benjamin, *Gesammelte Schriften,* ed. Rolf Tiedemann and Hermann Schweppenhäuser (Frankfurt a.M.: Suhrkamp, 1977), 6:60. For a discussion of the question of objective mendacity, see Peter Fenves, "Testing Right," *Cardozo Law Review* 13 (1991/92): 1099–1113.

25. In the situation of an all-encompassing state of lying, the teller of factual truths, "in the unlikely event that he survives," now is in the position the liar was in before; and it is thus that "even in Hitler's Germany and Stalin's Russia," Arendt writes, "it was more dangerous to talk about concentration and extermination camps, whose existence was no secret, than to hold and to utter 'heretical' views on anti-Semitism, racism, and Communism" (TP 251, 236).

What distinguishes totalitarian ideology from authoritarianism, tyranny, despotism, and the like is its disjunction from reality. If we try to fathom the word "ideo-logy," we are generally dealing with the *logos* of an *idea*. The pseudoscientific character of all ideologies, Arendt says, is based on the presupposition that an idea or a body of ideas—such as "Jews are inferior"—can be the subject matter of a science, as animals are considered the subject matter of zoology (see *O* 468, *E* 962). What we must ask time and again is, What is the linguistic reality or referentiality of totalitarian domination vis-à-vis the linguistic reality or referentiality of Arendt's presentation of totalitarian domination?[26]

Ideological thinking, Arendt says, is a form of political thinking and can be described by three elements:

1. Ideologies raise a claim to *total explanation*. Thus totalitarian historiography appropriates past, present, and future according to its pseudoscientific idea.[27]
2. Ideological thinking becomes *independent of experience;* it becomes emancipated from "the reality that we perceive with our five senses" and insists on a "truer" reality, of which we become aware only through a "sixth sense," acquired through ideological indoctrination.
3. Ideological thinking follows a *coercively logical procedure* that starts from an axiomatic premise and deduces everything else from it; that is, "it proceeds with a consistence that exists nowhere in the realm of reality" (*O* 470f., *E* 965).

How can Arendt expound totalitarian thinking without reconstructing it? The totalitarian-ideological element of the *emancipation from reality and experience* (2) directly corresponds to the thematic of the totalitarian lie and finds an illustration in Arendt's metaphor of the onion. First in *Origins* (1951) and then in the essay

---

26. "What we call ideology," Paul de Man writes, "is precisely the confusion of *linguistic* with natural reality, of *reference* with phenomenalism" (De Man, "The Resistance to Theory," in *The Resistance to Theory* [Minneapolis: University of Minnesota Press, 1986], 11).

27. Arendt illustrates the pseudoscientificity of ideologies through the analogy between the pseudoscientific technique of totalitarian propaganda and the pseudoscientific technique of advertisement. She analogizes totalitarian propaganda with "the advertisement columns of every newspaper...by which a manufacturer proves with facts and figures and the help of a 'research' department that his is the 'best soap in the world.' It is...true that there is a certain element of violence in the *imaginative* exaggerations of publicity men, that behind the assertion that girls who do not use this particular brand of soap may go through life with pimples and without a husband, lies the wild dream of monopoly, the dream that one day the manufacturer of the 'only soap that prevents pimples' may have the power to deprive of husbands all girls who do not use his soap" (*O* 345, *E* 733f.). What matters with respect to Arendt's speech act is that the discussed complexities of advertisement for dreaming girls with pimples and without husbands epitomize an analytical discourse *about* National Socialist propaganda without succumbing to its language or logic. The analogy constitutes a segment in Arendt's historiography of totalitarian politics, but it also remains strangely immune due to its idiosyncratic semiotic referentiality.

"What Is Authority?" (1961),[28] Arendt compares the organization of the total system with the structure of an onion (cf. *O* 366f., *E* 856; *O* 413, *E* 717f.; *O* 430, *E* 891, and A 98–100). While authoritarian governments structure their power like a pyramid, tyrannies destroy the intervening layers between top and bottom, so that the top remains suspended over a mass of completely equal individuals. By contrast, the totalitarian onion, in whose center the *Führer* is located, is specific in that all the political movement's extraordinarily manifold parts are related in such a way that each represents the façade in one direction and the center in the other; each plays the role of a normal outside world for the more extreme layer below and the role of radical extremism for the next layer toward the outside. As a result, the movement provides for each layer the fiction of a normal world. The representatives of each layer of the totalitarian onion come to believe that their convictions differ only in degree from those of other people, and they are unlikely ever to *realize* the abyss that separates their own world from what surrounds it. "The onion structure makes the system organizationally shock-proof against the *factuality of the real world*," Arendt writes (A 99f.). What is "the factuality of the real world"?

In "Truth and Politics," written in response to the controversy caused by the publication of *Eichmann in Jerusalem,* Arendt speaks of two notions of truth. Following Gottfried Wilhelm Leibniz, she distinguishes "rational truth," describing a *necessary* context ("two times two is four"), from "factual truth," denoting a *contingent* context (in the sense of George Clemenceau: no one can or will ever say that on August 4, 1914, Belgium invaded Germany) (see TP 239). Leaving the complexities involved here in suspense, it appears that the totalitarian onion makes the system organizationally shockproof against reality within the purview of a contingent discourse, the discourse of "raw facts."[29] That is, the reality initially considered "true" by those who live in the onion, in the reality of the totalitarian fiction—a reality based on racial-biological axioms, for instance—will eventually succumb to the imperviousness of the totalitarian system against experienced "facts," as the representatives in each of the onion's layers will be infiltrated by the ideological fiction disseminated by the sovereign and his propaganda apparatus from the onion's center. How are we to *imagine* this detachment from "reality"?

The ideological principle of the emancipation from experienced realities and the creation of an ideologically "truer" reality does not involve the abandonment of our five senses. Rather, it implies supplementation with a sixth sense, taught by

---

28. Hannah Arendt, "What Is Authority?" in *Between Past and Future*, 91–141; hereafter abbreviated as A. See also Jean-François Lyotard, "Survivant," in *Lectures d'enfance* (Paris: Galilée, 1991), 78.
29. Lyotard convincingly puts forth a psychoanalytic reading of the Arendtian notion of reality: "Le totalitarisme est ainsi un vast organisme 'pare-excitation,' comme disait Freud. ... Le réel est à comprendre comme *le fait* du désir et non comme *un fait* établi dans le domaine de référence d'un discours cognitif" ("Survivant," 78; Totalitarianism is...a vast system of "para-excitation," as Freud would say.... The real is to be understood as *the fact* of desire and not as *a fact* established in the referential sphere of a cognitive discourse).

the educational institutions, a sense injecting "secret meaning" into every political event and public act (*O* 471, *E* 965). The mendacity of the Stalinist dictum that the Moscow subway is the only one in the world, for instance, does not automatically mean that the existence of a subway in Paris is not perceived per se (*O* 350, *E* 742f.). Yet it does mean, and it is here that the sixth sense is required, that the "factual truth" can be reprogrammed according to the totalitarian logic that Stalin will "prove" the correctness of the assertion that there is a subway in Moscow and only there by simply destroying all the others. This "method of infallible prediction," alluding to the *third* element of ideological thinking, namely the principle of absolute logicality, signifies the assimilation of reality to the totalitarian lie or, in Arendt's words, "supreme contempt for all facts and all reality" (*O* 385, *E* 965). It entails, more generally, an equation of power and truth; it presupposes the conviction that "fact depends entirely on the power of man who can fabricate it" (*O* 350, *E* 806). Distinctions such as those "between truth and falsehood, between reality and fiction," collapse at this point. Facts are not given but wanted, and only as such, as a grammatical future anterior, given: only Moscow has a subway, for the Paris subway *will have been destroyed*. And a slogan like "Jews are inferior" is hence a totalitarian-ideological truth, a truth in which an eidetic maxim of action is already inscribed: "Jews must be exterminated."

Metaphor and Truth

An ideology's reality is in a certain sense always identical with the referentiality of its images. The lie that the Moscow subway is the only one in the world exemplifies the falsification of a truth, the truth of an image, for which the ambiguity of language allows: "Nothing reveals the peculiar *ambiguity of language*—in which alone we can establish and say the truth, through which alone we can actively remove truth from the world and which, in its necessary polished smoothness, is always in the way of finding the truth—more distinctly than the metaphor" (*DT* 46).[30] We have truth only in the ambiguity of language. Yet what does this mean? The contention articulated in this journal entry, titled "The Metaphor and the Truth," according to which the ambiguity ("Viel*deut*igkeit"), interpretability (*Deut*barkeit), that is, the meaning (Be*deut*ung) of language—"in which alone we can establish the truth"—seizes its intelligibility from metaphors, returns in more concise form: "All thinking [is] metaphorical" (*DT* 728). What emerges from this sentence, one of the most epigrammatic in the *Denktagebuch,* is the understanding that metaphorical thinking and philosophical thinking do not merely relate to each other

---

30. "In nichts offenbart sich die eigentümliche Vieldeutigkeit der Sprache—in der allein wir Wahrheit haben und sagen können, durch die allein wir aktiv Wahrheit aus der Welt schaffen können und die in ihrer notwendigen Abgeschliffenheit uns immer im Weg ist, die Wahrheit zu finden—deutlicher als in der Metapher."

like the two sides of a medal, as the transference of a thought from the supersensuous sphere into the sensuous, more conceivable sphere. Rather, the entry makes the much more profound claim—a claim Arendt insinuates without ever fully spelling it out—that all thinking is figurative and that reality is always the reality of images.[31] This means that truth *as such* remains always unreachable; it is always only the result of a mediation with the result of an *image,* the image of a "truth" or, as in the context of totalitarian politics, the image of an enormous falsehood, a "lie." The images of truths and the images of lies all of a sudden no longer appear remote from one another. "Truth" alone remains out of reach; Arendt illustrates this understanding by calling on the Enlightenment thinker Gotthold Ephraim Lessing:

> Lessing's magnificent "Sage jeder, was ihm die Wahrheit dünkt, und die Wahrheit selbst sei Gott empfohlen" ("Let each man say what he deems truth, and let truth itself be commended unto God") would have plainly signified, Man is not capable of truth, all his truths, alas, are δόξαι, mere opinions, whereas for Lessing it meant, on the contrary, Let us thank God that we don't know *the* truth. (TP 233f., Arendt's italics)[32]

The way from here to Kant's *Critique of Pure Reason,* in which reason is led to discern its own limitations, is not far.

---

31. That metaphors are not reserved for the realm of poetic thinking but that indeed all thinking is metaphorical was suggested by Nietzsche—not by chance—in a piece "on *truth* and *lie*": "The 'thing in itself' (which is precisely what the pure truth, apart from any of its consequences, would be) is likewise something quite incomprehensible to the creator of language.... To begin with, a nerve stimulus is transferred into an image: first metaphor. The image, in turn, is imitated in a sound: second metaphor.... We believe that we know something about the things themselves when we speak of trees, colors, snow, and flowers; and yet we possess nothing but metaphors for things—metaphors which correspond in no way to the original entities." These thoughts on the relationship between metaphor, truth, and lie led Nietzsche, like Arendt, to the assumption of a conceptual exchangeability of fiction and reality: "What then is truth? A movable host of metaphors, metonymies, and anthropomorphisms: in short, a sum of human relations which have been poetically and rhetorically intensified, transferred, and embellished, and which, after long usage, seem to a people to be fixed, canonical, and binding. Truths are illusions which we have forgotten are illusions; they are metaphors that have become worn out and have been drained of sensuous force" (Nietzsche, "On Truth and Lie in an Extra-Moral Sense," in *Epistemology: The Classic Readings,* ed. David Cooper, trans. Daniel Breazeale [Oxford: Blackwell, 1999], 180–95, translation modified).

Paul de Man, in turn, pushes Nietzsche's identification of truth as metaphor yet further by speaking of Nietzsche's "lie that the metaphor was in the first place. It is a naïve belief in the proper meaning of the metaphor without awareness of the problematic nature of its factual, referential foundation" (De Man, *Allegories of Reading, Figural Language in Rousseau, Nietzsche, Rilke, and Proust* [New Haven, CT: Yale University Press, 1982], 110f.). Eventually, "a text like *On Truth and Lie,* although it presents itself legitimately as a demystification of literary rhetoric remains entirely literary, rhetorical, and *deceptive* itself" (113). Similarly, we will need to explore the truthfulness or deceptiveness of the writing of Hannah Arendt, whose reliability as a writer on totalitarian politics and modern lying will prove more ambiguous than she wants us to believe.

32. On Arendt's reception of Lessing, see Sara Eigen, "Hannah Arendt's 'Lessing Rede' and the 'Truths' of History," *Lessing Yearbook* 32 (2000): 309–24.

The Question of Law and the Law of Metaphor

What, according to Arendt, is the law *in* totalitarian politics, what is the law *of* totalitarian politics, and what, eventually, is the law of Arendt's speech act in this very context? "Far from wielding its power in the interest of one man," Arendt writes, totalitarian rule "is quite prepared to sacrifice everybody's vital immediate interests to the execution of what it assumes to be *the law of History or the law of Nature*. Its defiance of positive laws claims to be a higher form of legitimacy which, since it is inspired by the sources themselves, can do away with petty legality" (O 461f., E 947). Not only does totalitarian rule not appear arbitrary, but it purports to establish the rule of justice ("the law of History or the law of Nature") on earth, thus constituting a higher form of legitimacy than that of positive law.[33] Indeed, positive law can never bring about justice in any concrete, singular case; it is always doomed to fail in the face of the irreconcilability of law and justice. By contrast, totalitarian lawfulness, enacting the "laws of Nature," does not even attempt to translate them into normative categories of "right" and "wrong" for individual citizens but relates them directly to humanity, eventually seeking to produce a *human species embodying the law*.[34]

The jurisprudential matrix clearly lies at the bottom of Hannah Arendt's theorization of totalitarian politics, yet beyond her statements, what, we may ask, is she really doing? Beyond the juridical dynamics, what kind of *rhetorical* dynamics does she attach to formulas such as the "fences of laws" and the "iron band of terror"?

> Die Tyrannis begnügt sich mit der Gesetzlosigkeit; der totale Terror setzt an die Stelle der *Zäune des Gesetzes* und der gesetzmässig etablierten und geregelten *Kanäle menschlicher Kommunikation* ein *eisernes Band,* das alle so eng aneinanderschließt, dass nicht nur der *Raum der Freiheit,* wie er in verfassungsmässigen Staaten zwischen den Bürgern existiert, sondern auch die *Wüste der Nachbarlosigkeit* und des gegenseitigen Mißtrauens, die der Tyrannis eigentümlich ist, verschwindet, und es ist, als *seien alle zusammengeschmolzen in ein einziges Wesen von gigantischen Ausmassen*. (E 957f.)[35]

Arendt says that totalitarian terror "eliminate[s]...the capacity of man to act" (O 467, E 961). Yet isn't her language precisely that—a demonstration of her

---

33. Cf. also Hannah Arendt, "Franz Kafka: A Revaluation, on the Occasion of the Twentieth Anniversary of His Death," *Partisan Review* XI/4 (1944): 412–22.
34. Hannah Arendt, "On the Nature of Totalitarianism," in *Essays in Understanding,* 340.
35. "Total terror is so easily mistaken for a symptom of tyrannical government because totalitarian government in its initial stages must behave like a tyranny and raze the boundaries of man-made law. But total terror leaves no arbitrary lawlessness behind it.... It substitutes for *the boundaries and channels of communication* between individual men a *band of iron* which holds them so tightly together that it is as though their plurality had disappeared into *One Man of gigantic dimensions*. To abolish the *fences of laws* between men—as tyranny does—means to take away man's liberties and destroy freedom as a living political reality; for the space between men as it is *hedged in by laws,* is the living space of freedom. Total terror uses this old instrument of tyranny but destroys at the same time also the lawless, *fenceless wilderness* of fear and suspicion which tyranny leaves behind. This *desert*...is no longer a living space of freedom" (O 465).

capacity to act? The long sentence quoted here seems at least as remarkable with respect to what it performs as to its content. Arendt repeatedly infringes on the rules of good rhetorical style by relating different metaphors *to one another*, evoking a stylistic dissonance correlating to a certain dis-logic. The chorale of "fences of laws" and "channels of communication," "iron band," "desert of fear," and the "One Man of gigantic dimensions" precipitates an enormous stylistic as well as political amplitude—but certainly no homogeneity or systematization, and least of all a "reconstruction" of the history of totalitarian systems. Fear, Arendt says, is the characteristic feeling within totalitarian regimes: "[Furcht] bleibt...die alles durchdringende Stimmung, die das *Herz* jedes einzelnen *verwüstet*, so wie Mißtrauen...die Beziehung aller Menschen einander *vergiftet*" (*E* 961).[36] What the calculated unpredictability of Arendt's counterenactment, what the multiplication of images, appears to invoke is precisely the epistemic control of the totalitarian phenomenon. This happens not by employing metaphors as analytic tools; what comes to the fore, rather, is the pleonastic figurative logic of Arendt's presentation *itself*: the metaphors appear to be manifesting an end *in themselves*. "Desert," "heart," and "poison" are central constituents in the political theory of Hannah Arendt.

To be sure, it would be problematic to attribute a subversive force to the narrative implementation of metaphors per se. Totalitarian systems have frequently invoked disease imagery to constitute and characterize an enemy. "As was said in speeches about 'the Jewish problem' throughout the 1930s, to treat cancer, one must cut out much of the healthy tissue around it."[37] Arendt herself alludes to the limits of metaphorical thinking when it comes to making the inconceivable conceivable. "The danger," she notes in *Thinking*, the first volume of *The Life of the Mind*, "lies in the overwhelming evidence the metaphor provides by appealing to the unquestioned evidence of sense experience."[38] Hans Blumenberg, in his *Paradigmen zu einer Metaphorologie*, traced very common figures of speech through the history of Western thought and thereby, "almost incidentally," Arendt writes,

> discovered to what an extent typically modern pseudo-sciences owe their plausibility to the lacking evidence of data. His prime example is the consciousness theory of psychoanalysis, where consciousness is seen as the peak of an iceberg, a mere indication on the floating mass of unconsciousness beneath it. Not only has that theory never been demonstrated but it is undemonstrable in its own terms: the moment a fragment of unconsciousness reaches the peak of the iceberg it has become conscious and lost all the properties of its alleged origin. (*Life of the Mind*, 1:113)[39]

---

36. "[Fear] remains... the all-pervasive feeling that lays *waste* to the *heart* of every individual, just as mistrust... *poisons* the relationship of all human beings with each other."
37. Susan Sontag, *Illness as Metaphor* (New York: Farrar, Straus and Giroux, 1978), 64f.
38. Arendt, *Life of the Mind*, 1:113.
39. See Hans Blumenberg, *Paradigmen zu einer Metaphorologie* (Frankfurt a.M.: Suhrkamp, 1998).

The evidence of the iceberg metaphor is so overwhelming that any need for demonstration appears superfluous. Leaving aside a discussion of Arendt's problematic distinction between "science" and "pseudoscience," the gist of her argument—which, of course, holds equally for the thought systems of great philosophers and metaphysicians—is the following: whereas empirical sciences are based on "real" experiences and need to account for exceptions to the rule, in the systematic order of mental constructs, the consistency of metaphorical thought seems to epitomize an end in itself. Metaphors may well allow for an *imagination* of the unknowable. But the epistemic appropriation of the unknowable always stops halfway, and the "ineffable" can never be fully handed over to us.

Despite the danger of metaphorical thought, Arendt's storytelling, one may say, appears to generate a curious double movement: on the one hand, the hyperbolic mobilization of metaphorical language, allegedly "explaining" the dynamics of totalitarianism, reads as an ongoing attempt to "destroy" totalitarianism; on the other hand, the very manifestation of her own narrative freedom, fraught with stylistic moments of the spontaneous, appears to enact the very individuality of which the living dead in the camps, reduced to Pavlovian dogs, were deprived. Arendt defies the deprivation of her voice by actualizing and dramatizing her role as a speech actor, implacably insisting on her living presence.

In this context one is, beyond the discourse of metaphors and analogies, likely to stumble across the many proverbs and the pronounced discourse of idioms and colloquial expressions in *Origins*. Arendt does not show scruples in orchestrating a round dance of sayings like "From planing come shavings," "He who says A must also say B," "Two times two is four," "You can't make an omelette without breaking eggs," and so forth in the inconclusive last chapter of her book on totalitarianism. What manifests itself here is a reality, the reality of "proverbs and idioms of everyday language" (*M* 168). Yet toward what end? The "art of taking proverbial and idiomatic speech literally," Arendt writes, "enabled Benjamin—as it did Franz Kafka, in whom figures of speech are often clearly discernible as a source of inspiration...to write a prose of...singularly enchanting and enchanted closeness to reality [verzauberte Realitätsnähe]" (*M* 168). This "enchanted closeness to reality" seems to be a poetic effect invoked by metaphors as much as by idiomatic and proverbial speech. Philosophical-conceptual sobriety, that is, an alleged *plain* closeness to the "reality" of totalitarianism, appears to be less amenable to understanding than *verzauberte Realitätsnähe*.

He Who Says A Must Also Say B

Arendt illustrates the third characteristic element of totalitarian thinking—the coercive force of logicality—not only through metaphors and analogies but also through the idiomatic saying "He who says A must also say B": "Here too, it has been shown that the vernacular was, in its own way, excellently prepared for this new kind of politics. Just like Stalin, Hitler had always had a special preference for buttressing his arguments with an 'He who says A must also say B' logicality" (*O* 472, *E* 968). "He who says A must also say B" means, according to the Duden dictionary, "He who begins something must go on with it (and if necessary also accept unpleasant consequences [und auch unangenehme Folgen auf sich nehmen])."[40] What suggests itself as rather naive in Duden's encyclopedic world—in that he who says A must "take unpleasant consequences upon *himself*"—denotes a diabolic euphemism standing for the murderous logicality of ideological reasoning. "Deductive thought's inherent coercive force, which ideologies turn into such excellent preparatory means for the coercive force of terror regimes, is extremely well expressed in 'He who says A must also say B,' because *here it is evidently identical with our fear* of embroiling ourselves in contradictions and, through such contradictions, losing ourselves" (*O* 473, *E* 968f.).

Whence does this "fear of contradicting ourselves" spring? The force of "He who says A must also say B" lies in assuming that contradictions make everything meaningless, that meaning and consistency are the same. The coercive force of total logicality ensures—on the basis of an axiomatic premise A—a stringent consistency that one will never find in reality. "The only counter-principle against this force and against the fear of contradicting ourselves," Arendt writes,

> lies in human spontaneity, our capacity to begin. Freedom as an inner capacity of man is identical with the capacity to begin.... Over the beginning, no logic, no cogent deduction can have any power, because its chain presupposes, in the form of a premise, the beginning. No necessary argumentation ever has any power over the beginning, because it is never derivable from some logical chain of reasoning, indeed, has to be assumed in all deductive thought, to bring about the inevitable. For that reason, the logic of "He who says A, must also say B" is based on the uncompromising exclusion of all experience and thought which, in itself, somehow starts to experience and imagine the new. (*O* 473, *E* 969f.)

The logical force of ideological reasoning is to forestall the chance that someone begins to think, think anew, that is, that someone says A rather than following the cogent deduction of parroting B and C and so on until the end of "the murderous alphabet" (*O* 472). To be sure, he who says A *can* by all means decide to say B, and this, as long as it does not succumb to an outer compulsion, may very well signal one's freedom to act. The point is, whatever may guarantee meaning, consistency does not guarantee it. Not raising a claim to consistency, though perhaps one to meaning, we now shall take the chance of saying A and then B, A-rendt and then B-recht.

---

40. See Duden, *Redewendungen: Wörterbuch der deutschen Idiomatik* (Mannheim: Bibliographisches Institut/Brockhaus, 2002), 11:25.

In his play *He Who Says Yes / He Who Says No,* Brecht sets a counterexample to the "murderous alphabet" of ideological reasoning: he sets an example with respect to the play's plot, but also, allegorically, with respect to his own writing process: *He Who Says Yes* was written in 1930, and *He Who Says Yes / He Who Says No* was written in 1931—yet not in the form of a consecutive succession. Rather, Brecht—in response to critical feedback from the pupils of the Karl Marx Elementary School in Berlin Neukölln with whom the script had been discussed—rewrote the play. *He Who Says Yes / He Who Says No,* as a result of the revision of *He Who Says Yes,* thus became included in the fourth issue of the (at that time still unpublished) 1931 edition of *Versuche.* Brecht knew: "He who says A need not necessarily say B. He may realize that A was wrong."[41] The 1930 version was "not right,"[42] and for that reason Brecht prepared a revised version of *He Who Says Yes,* now titled *He Who Says Yes / He Who Says No*—and he let only the later version pass.

A boy starts with his teacher and other students on a journey through the mountains to get medicine for his mother. Custom ordains that he who falls ill should not ask the expedition to turn back on his account; instead, he ought to agree to be hurled into the valley.[43] In *He Who Says Yes* during the climbing, the boy falls ill and thus gets killed:

> The friends took the jar / And, sighing for the sad ways of the world / And its bitter law / Hurled the boy down / Foot to foot they stood together / And blindly hurled him down / None guiltier than his neighbor / And flung clods of earth / And flat stones / After him.[44]

In *He Who Says No* the boy does not consent to the old custom:

> "The answer I gave was wrong, but your question was even more wrong. He who says A need not necessarily say B. He may realise that A was wrong.... As for the old Great Custom, I see no rhyme or reason in it. What I need is a new Great Custom to be introduced at once, to wit, the Custom of rethinking every new situation."[45]

---

41. Bertolt Brecht, *He Who Says Yes / He Who Says No,* in *The Measures Taken and Other Lehrstücke,* trans. Wolfgang Sauerländer (New York: Arcade, 2001), 78. See also Brecht, *Der Jasager und der Neinsager: Vorlagen, Fassungen, Materialien,* ed. Peter Szondi (Frankfurt a.M.: Suhrkamp, 1966).

42. "I think that bit about custom is not right," ten-year-old B. Korsch said in a discussion between Brecht and the pupils. In response to the general feedback, Brecht modified the drama and added *He Who Says No* with a deviating ending, a "new Custom." For the protocol of this discussion, see *Der Jasager und der Neinsager,* 59–63. For a detailed comparative analysis of both versions of the play, see Peter Szondi's commentary in Brecht, *Der Jasager und der Neinsager,* 103–12.

43. See also Barbara Hahn, *Hannah Arendt: Leidenschaften, Menschen und Bücher* (Berlin: Berlin Verlag, 2005), 27.

44. Brecht, *He Who Says Yes / He Who Says No,* 69.

45. Ibid., 78f.

The teacher raises concerns that shame and disgrace will be heaped on the boy if he turns back. But the students do not allow shame or disgrace to deter them from "doing the reasonable thing," and so they carry the boy back to the village, thereby introducing a new custom:

> The friends took the friend / And initiated a new Custom / And a new law / And brought the boy back. / *Side by side they walked together* [*Seit an Seit gingen sie zusammengedrängt*] / Towards calumny / Towards ridicule, with their eyes open / None more cowardly than his neighbour.[46]

While the old "Great Custom" corresponds to the cogent logicality of ideological reasoning, the "Custom of rethinking every new situation" epitomizes Arendt's philosophy of the beginning.[47] The "new law" allows for a new beginning, and it guarantees the liberation from the throttling nooses of the old Great Custom. To be sure, those students walking "side by side" follow their own newly developed ethical views, they are *zusammengedrängt* not in the sense of an outer compulsion, not squeezed together toward one amorphous body, but in the sense of a political community. The impetus for community formation does not resemble the compulsion of total terror in which individuals are pressed together until the space *between* them is destroyed and everyone has lost contact with everyone else. It does not refer to what Arendt describes as the "iron band" of terror, which squeezes people together until they are a homogeneous mass in the sense of the Hobbesian Leviathan, deprived of the ability for political *inter*-action, embodying "only one single human being" (*O* 474, *E* 975). The "new law" correlates with what Arendt calls "the fences of laws," laws that simultaneously protect human freedom and guarantee the continuance of a society, a pluralistic society in the sense of the Latin *inter-esse*.

Loneliness and Solitude

The outer compulsion of terror destroys the space, the freedom and thus the relationships *between* human beings, eventually precipitating the paradoxical condition of the isolation of those squeezed together. "The destruction of plurality

---

46. Ibid., 79.
47. For a careful analysis of Arendt's broader reading of Brecht, see Hahn, *Hannah Arendt,* here esp. 26–33; see also Thomas Schestag, *Die unbewältigte Sprache: Hannah Arendts Theorie der Dichtung* (Weil am Rhein: Engeler, 2006). On Arendt's philosophy of the beginning, see, among others, Doren Wohlleben, "Narrative (-) Initiative. Das 'Rätsel des Anfangs' als ethisches und poetologisches Konzept in Hannah Arendts *Denktagebuch* und ihrer Vorlesung *Über das Böse,*" in *Narration und Ethik,* ed. Claudia Öhlschläger (Munich: Wilhelm Fink, 2009), 53–63; Ludger Lütkehaus, *Natalität: Philosophie der Geburt* (Kusterdingen: Die Graue Edition, 2006); Margarete Durst, "Birth and Natality in Hannah Arendt," *Analecta Husserliana* 79 (2004): 777–97; Alison Martin, "Natality and the Philosophy of Two," *Selected Studies in Phenomenology and Existential Philosophy* 28 (2002): 134–41; Fernando Bárcena, "Hannah Arendt: Una poética de la natalidad," *Revista de Filosofía* 26 (2002): 107–23.

leaves every individual with the feeling *of being left totally on their own*." Loneliness is the politically instrumentalized feeling of totalitarian government, a feeling, to be sure, not to be confused with the state of the *flâneur* as Benjamin found it in Charles Baudelaire. The loneliness Arendt talks about is one in which human beings, individuals themselves, are deserted by themselves. "It is not good that man should be alone" Luther says; a lonely man "always deduces one thing from the other and thinks everything to the worst."[48] Luther, "whose experiences in the phenomena of solitude and loneliness probably were second to no one's," understood that the coerciveness of logical deduction can befall with all its mighty power only the one who is lonely. The experience of loneliness is inextricably linked with the compulsory process of deduction, a "curious connection" discovered by totalitarian regimes and used toward their own ends. "In loneliness, the only things that appear to remain indubitably certain are the elementary laws of the compellingly evident, the tautology of the sentence: 'He who says A, must also say B' or 'two times two is four'" (*O* 477f., *E* 976–78).[49]

The feeling of loneliness is, according to Arendt, the main feature of "that crisis...in which all of us everywhere live today [jener Krise..., in der wir heute alle und überall leben]" (*E* 971). It is in this vein that she had initially planned the title *The Burden of Our Times* for what we know as *The Origins of Totalitarianism*. This is why she brings into being so copious an edifice of images contaminating and obliterating totalitarian politics within the context of its presentation. It is thus that this performative work of destruction appears most excessive over the last pages, commenting on the "conditions under which we exist today," conditions still "threatened by [the] devastating sand storms" of totalitarian politics (*O* 478, *E* 978). Arendt's discourse here indeed seems possible only after a rather abrupt caesura, a double paragraph, and a new beginning, a beginning resulting less from the argumentative context than from her personal situation as a writer, less a thematic caesura than an overly motivated manifestation of her own capacity to act, to begin, to say A (see *O* 474, *E* 971).

Arendt's entire art of interpretation and citation oddly appears to set itself against the systematology of her research object, a politics not historicizable from a temporal distance but, once again, epitomizing a feature of "the crisis of our

---

48. Martin Luther, *Erbauliche Schriften,* after Arendt, *O* 477, *E* 976.

49. The force of total terror on the one side, which presses individuals together and "supports them in a world which has become a wilderness for them," and the coercion of deductive reasoning on the other, "which prepares each individual in his lonely isolation against all others," correspond to each other and depend on each other to sustain the movement's dynamic. Just as terror, "even in its pre-total, merely tyrannical form, ruins all relationships" between human beings, so the coercive logicality of "ideological thinking ruins all relationships with reality" (*O* 473f., *E* 970). At this point, the lying world of consistency, as conjured up by totalitarian movements, "*is more adequate to the needs of the human mind than reality itself,* in which, through sheer imagination, uprooted masses can feel at home and are spared the never-ending shocks which real life and real experiences deal to human beings and their expectations" (*O* 353, *E* 748f.).

time" (*O* 478, *E* 978). She comments on her art of interpretation and citation in a most remarkable entry of her *Denktagebuch* in November 1969: "Interpreting, citing—but only to have witnesses and friends [Das Interpretieren, das Zitieren— doch nur, um Zeugen zu haben, auch Freunde]" (*DT* 756). Saint Augustine, Benjamin, Brecht, Montesquieu, Hobbes, Kant, Kafka, Isak Dinesen, Heidegger, Luther, Luxemburg—"witnesses and friends."[50] Arendt, the Jew in exile, during the writing of *Origins* spatially and temporally distant from the world she had to leave, writing in a language foreign to her. Everyone who writes a book works in solitude. This does not necessarily imply that she or he is lonely. Arendt distinguished between solitude and loneliness.[51] While he who is lonely is deprived of the company of his equals and even deserted by himself, the one in solitude is "by himself." The solitary person still is in dialogue with himself; he does not lose contact with the world of his fellow people "because they are represented in the self" with whom he leads the internal dialogue (*O* 476, *E* 976f.). But Arendt also speaks of the "danger" of solitude turning into loneliness. In one of the perhaps most autobiographical sentences at the very end of *Origins,* Arendt describes loneliness as a feeling that comes into being "when, for whatever historical-political reasons, this shared lived world falls apart and the interwoven, interlinked people are suddenly thrown back upon themselves" (*E* 977). This sentence is, curiously enough, only in the German edition, only uttered in Arendt's mother tongue. Like so many, Arendt is also thrown back upon herself—a moment to which

---

50. The 2006 volume containing the correspondence between Benjamin and Arendt provides ample evidence of their friendship during their exile in France, a friendship that on Arendt's, but also on Benjamin's, part seemed to lack no passion: "My knights' steeds whinny with impatient anticipation to knap with your knights' steeds [Meine Springer wiehern bereits vor Ungeduld, sich mit den Ihren herumzubeißen]" (Detlev Schöttker and Erdmut Wizisla, eds., *Arendt und Benjamin: Texte, Briefe, Dokumente* [Frankfurt a.M.: Suhrkamp, 2006], 129); cf. also the Hannah Arendt Papers at the Library of Congress, http://memory.loc.gov/cgi-bin/query/P?mharendt (accessed February 13, 2007); Detlev Schöttker and Erdmut Wizisla, "Hannah Arendt und Walter Benjamin: Stationen einer Vermittlung," *Text und Kritik* 166/167 (2005): 42–57.

By contrast, Brecht, Benjamin's friend, was a witness, but certainly no friend of Arendt; numerous critical remarks throughout her oeuvre and especially the long essay on Brecht testify to Arendt's disapproval of the poet's political involvement in the Socialist project in the GDR (Arendt, "Bertolt Brecht: 1898–1956," in *M* 207–49).

51. "All thinking, strictly speaking, is done in solitude and is a dialogue between me and myself; but this dialogue of the two-in-one does not lose contact with the world of my fellow-men because they are represented in the self with whom I lead the dialogue of thought. The problem of solitude is that this two-in-one needs the others in order to become one again: one unchangeable individual whose identity can never be mistaken for that of any other. For the confirmation of my identity I depend entirely upon other people; and it is the great saving grace of companionship for solitary men that it makes them 'whole' again, saves them from the dialogue of thought in which one remains always equivocal, restores the identity which makes them speak with the single voice of one unexchangeable person." By contrast, "what makes loneliness so unbearable is the loss of one's own self which can be realized in solitude, but confirmed in its identity only by the trusting and trustworthy company of my equals. In this situation, man loses trust in himself as the partner of this thought and that elementary confidence in the world which is necessary to make experiences at all. Self and world, capacity for thought and experience are lost at the same time" (*O* 476, *E* 977). On the concept of dialogical thinking, see also Arendt, *Life of the Mind,* esp. the first volume, *Thinking.*

numerous entries in the *Denktagebuch* testify, no less than the moving essay "We Refugees." Given this background, we may have to see the performance of *Origins* with its sometimes overabundant implementation of other voices, other dialogical partners, also as a search for witnesses and friends, the struggle of one forced into exile with her unforeseen personal circumstances.

2

WHY DOES HANNAH ARENDT LIE?

Or the Vicissitudes of Imagination

> And therefore Mountaigny saith prettily, when he inquired the reason, why the word of the lie should be such a disgrace, and such an odious charge? Saith he, "If it be well weighed, to say that a man lieth, is as much to say as, that he is brave towards God, and a coward towards men." For a lie faces God, and shrinks from man.
>
> —Francis Bacon, "Of Truth"

When explaining what she was doing, Hannah Arendt typically provided the term "storytelling."[1] The storyteller, Arendt writes in the essay "Truth and Politics," confronts the seeming arbitrariness of the facts presented, constructing certain configurations of "brutally elementary data" that eventually transcend the "meaning" of the chaos of sheer events; the task is to "tell...a story."[2] The writer and the historian share this task of bestowing meaning—the art of interpretation: "The transformation of the given raw material of sheer happenings which the historian, like the fiction writer (a good novel is by no means a simple concoction or a figment of

---

1. Hannah Arendt, *Men in Dark Times* (New York: Harcourt, 1968), 22; Arendt, *Between Past and Future: Eight Exercises in Political Thought* (New York: Penguin Books, 1968), 14f.
2. Hannah Arendt, "Truth and Politics," in *Between Past and Future,* 227–64, here 239, 262; hereafter TP.

pure fantasy), must effect is closely akin to the poet's transfiguration of moods or movements of the heart" (TP 262).

The act of transfiguration is what distinguishes Arendt's historiography from the positivistic approach she disparages. Shackled by the curious double bind of seeking to interpret events to bestow meaning while upholding the imperative of telling the truth, Arendt as well as fiction writers faces the same accusation: "Fiction authors are always accused, [she writes,] of lying. And that is quite justified. We expect truth only from them (and not from philosophers, from whom we expect conceptual thought). Faced with such a demand, so terribly difficult to fulfill—how should one not lie?"[3]

How should Hannah Arendt not lie?

The Art of Lying

Facing the task of writing a history of totalitarian politics, including its tendency to rearrange the whole factual texture, that is, including the modern lie, Arendt mobilizes the traditional "art of lying" (TP 253). Both the traditional and the totalitarian/modern lie invoke a rearrangement of "factual data" that always appear or, until the arrival of the modern lie, appeared indestructible. The idiosyncrasy of the totalitarian lie is twofold. Its first difference from a traditional lie is the modern lie's all-encompassing scope. The traditional lie concerned "only particulars," by tearing "a hole in the fabric of factuality" rather than changing the whole context. By contrast, "the modern political lies are so big that they require a complete rearrangement of the whole factual texture—the making of another reality, as it were, into which they fit without seam, crack or fissure" (TP 253). Yet the mere falsification of factual truths alone does not constitute a lie; the falsification must be *intentional*. The second difference between a modern and traditional lie is that the traditional lie was "directed at the enemy and was meant to deceive only him" (TP 253).[4] The liar knew the difference between truth and falsehood and was aware of his own lying. What distinguishes the modern totalitarian lie from the traditional lie is the position of the liar: whereas the traditional lie was a *transitive* speech act and was directed away from the agent, the modern lie is primarily *reflexive* and ultimately an act of self-deception.

"The mere telling of facts leads to no action whatever: it even leads under normal circumstances toward the acceptance of things as they are," Arendt writes (TP 251). The sentence echoes Arendt's contention discussed earlier, namely that in *Origins* she faced the dilemma of reconstructing what she wishes to

---

3. Hannah Arendt, *Denktagebuch*, 2 vols. (Munich: Piper, 2002), 469; hereafter *DT*. All translations are my own unless otherwise noted.
4. "Statesmen and diplomats," Arendt writes, knew they were lying. "They were not likely to fall victim to their own falsehoods; they could deceive others without deceiving themselves" (TP 253).

destroy—totalitarianism—thereby facing the risk of condoning it. Her response to this dilemma was the employment of literary citations, proverbs, analogies, and above all, metaphorical language. Metaphorical language lends itself to a form of image making incommensurable with the self-coercive force of logical deduction fundamental to totalitarian politics. As we shall see, Arendt avails herself of the lie in a similar context in that lying, rather than embodying the "acceptance of things as they are," epitomizes a form of *performative action*. What is the performativity of the lie?[5]

Lying is action, and the liar's advantage stems from a position in the midst of it: "He says what is not so because he wants things to be different from what they are—that is, he wants to change the world." Arendt persistently associates the "art of lying" with action: the liar "is an actor by nature," she writes (TP 250). The implications are significant: "The deliberate denial of factual truth—the ability to lie—and the capacity to change facts—the ability to act—are interconnected; they owe their existence to the same source: *imagination.*"[6] The art of lying is a form of image making. The image, unlike "an old-fashioned portrait, is not supposed to flatter reality," but to offer a "full-fledged substitute" for it (TP 252). Yet, is the lie simply that? Does it not first and foremost describe a *capacity,* namely the capacity to produce images of alternative realities? Does it not, above all, denote the *ability* to imagine the world the way we would (or would not) like to change it?[7] The power, the political force of the lie, does not lie in the status quo of either this reality or that reality, but in the possibility of "an-other" reality, a potentiality for the transgression of the boundaries of "truth." It is thus that "our *ability* to lie—but not necessarily our ability to tell the truth—belongs among the few obvious, demonstrable data that confirm human freedom" (TP 250). It is thus that Arendt speaks of an "undeniable affinity of lying with action, with politics" (TP 258). It is therefore, finally, that "truthfulness has never been counted among the political virtues, because it has little indeed to contribute to that change of the world and of circumstances which is among the most legitimate political activities" (TP 251).[8]

---

5. For a critical reading of Arendt's conception of lying, see Jacques Derrida, "History of the Lie," in *Futures: Of Jacques Derrida* (Stanford, CA: Stanford University Press, 2001), 65–98. On the broader question of truth and politics in Arendt, see also John Nelson, "Politics and Truth: Arendt's Problematic," *American Journal of Political Science* 22.2 (1978): 270–301; Patrick Riley, "Hannah Arendt on Kant, Truth and Politics," in *Essays on Kant's Political Philosophy,* ed. Howard Williams (Cardiff: University of Wales Press, 1992), 305–25; Dana Villa, *Arendt and Heidegger: The Fate of the Political* (Princeton, NJ: Princeton University Press, 1996), 94–97; Theresa Man Ling Lee, *Politics and Truth: Political Theory and the Postmodern Challenge* (New York: State University of New York Press, 1997), 115–203.

6. Hannah Arendt, "Lying in Politics: Reflections on the Pentagon Papers," in *Crises of the Republic* (New York: Hartcourt, 1972), 5; hereafter abbreviated as LP. Unless otherwise noted, all italics in this chapter are mine.

7. A characteristic of human action, Arendt says, "is that it always begins something new, yet this does not mean that it is ever permitted to start *ab ovo,* to create *ex nihilo.* In order to make room for one's own action something that was there before must be removed or destroyed, and things as they were before are changed" (LP 5).

8. Whereas Arendt's notion of lying is inscribed by a distinct historical signature, Immanuel Kant, a rigorous theoretician of the lie, develops a much more formalistic concept of mendacity in "On a

Obviously, lying in the realm of politics can have devastating consequences, which Arendt underscores: "What is at stake here is [the] common and *factual reality itself,* and this is indeed a political problem of the first order" (TP 237). Lying is always defined by some sort of "denial of *factual truth*" (LP 5). Yet leaving it at that would mean missing the ambiguous nature of the "lie" and the pernicious nature of "truth."[9] For what should "factual truth" or "factuality" be? As noted in chapter 1, in "Truth and Politics," Arendt discerns two different notions of truth: rational truth and factual truth (TP 239, 249). Lying, Arendt says, is defined by the deliberate falsification of factual truths rather than the falsification of rational truths, the latter being located in the domain of ignorance, opinion, error, and so on (TP 232–37). Clearly, this distinction is fraught with difficulties and complexities: Is not the ascertaining of facts an act of interpretation? What does "storytelling" signify if not *doing* something with the raw data of factuality? What does it mean to narrate events if not to put them into a certain order, to tell them from a certain perspective, to choose them according to certain selection criteria? If there is reason to question what distinguishes factual and rational truths, the exclusive contiguity between "lying" and the falsification of "factual" rather than "rational" truth must be called into question.

Perhaps we can, if only to begin with, describe the problematic of lying by differentiating two dimensions: a "constative" or epistemological register (i.e., lying as a form of "untruth") and, more intricate and also more exciting, a "performative" or ethical register (i.e., the various motivations, intentions, maneuvers of deception, strategies of manipulation, and anticipated effects that are at the heart of every lie). Let us then embark on an excursion and explore the ethical efficacy of two Arendtian "lies," which, similar to phantasms, errors, mistakes, opinions, and so on, represent only one particular manifestation of the many detours of logic.

Supposed *Right [Recht]* to Lie Because of Philanthropic Concerns," in *Grounding for the Metaphysics of Morals,* trans. James Ellington (Indianapolis: Hackett, 1993), 63–67 (Kant, "Über ein vermeintes Recht aus Menschenliebe zu lügen," in *Gesammelte Schriften* [Berlin: Königliche Akademie der Wissenschaften, 1900], 8:423–30). For a compendium on the multifaceted phenomenon of lying, cf. Sissela Bok, *Lying: Moral Choice in Public and Private Life* (New York: Pantheon Books, 1978). Harry Frankfurt examines the related issue of "bullshitting" in *On Bullshit* (Princeton, NJ: Princeton University Press, 2005).

9. In particular, the fourth and fifth sections of Arendt's "Truth and Politics" read in parts like a manifesto for lying. The ambiguous nature that Arendt attributes to the lie retains, apart from its perversion in totalitarian politics, a certain nobility—as it also, albeit much less ambiguously, emerges in Benjamin's essay "Toward a Critique of Violence." Benjamin introduces the lie as an example of "pure means," as the lie is essentially nonviolent. He describes the prohibition of deception (*Betrug*) correspondingly as a *Verfallsprozess* (process of decline), testifying to the decreasing power of the order of right. According to Benjamin, the prohibition of fraud presents a penetration of the violent juridical sphere into the nonviolent sphere of language, which until then had not been contaminated by jurisdiction. Although Arendt tacitly dismisses her friend's treatise on violence in her own study *On Violence,* Benjamin's passages on the question of lying seem to have inspired Arendt; see, for example, TP 228f.: "Lies, since they are often used as *substitutes for more violent means,* are apt to be considered relatively harmless tools in the arsenal of political action."

Pavlov's Dog

A central moment in Arendt's anthropological philosophy (or her philosophical anthropology) is the concentration camp as the site where the nature of totalitarianism as well as the essential nature of human beings is made manifest. The objective of this "ghastly experiment," Arendt writes, is that "of eliminating, under scientifically controlled conditions, spontaneity itself as an expression of human behaviour and of transforming the human personality into a mere thing, which under different conditions will always act the same" (O 438, E 908).[10] When a human being is deprived of juridical and moral personality and ultimately loses all individuality, what remains is the figure of the undead or the living dead, a being reduced to the degree of corporeal presence—the *Muselmann* in camp jargon.

Arendt mobilizes the analogy of Pavlov's dog within her larger discourse on the figure of the undead. The point of Ivan Petrovich Pavlov's experiment was that a previously irrelevant stimulus (a bell) assumed significance as a result of the association with a conditional stimulus (food) and thus precipitated a conditioned response (salivation). This phenomenon, referred to as classical conditioning, is tantamount to the elimination of spontaneity and the substitution for conditioned behavior as seen in the camps, according to Arendt. "*Under normal circumstances* [*Unter normalen Umständen*] this can never be accomplished, because spontaneity can never be entirely eliminated.... It is only in the concentration camps that such an experiment is at all possible, and therefore they are...*the guiding social ideal* [*das richtungsgebende Gesellschaftsideal*] of total domination in general" (O 438, E 908). On the one hand, she attributes a normative power to the concentration camps by referring to them as "the *guiding principle* [*das richtungsgebende Gesellschaftsideal*] of total domination." Yet, at the same time, she claims that "under *normal* circumstances [the total conditioning of human behavior] can never be accomplished, because spontaneity can never be entirely eliminated."[11] Georg Jellinek subsumes the

---

10. See Hannah Arendt, *Elemente und Ursprünge totaler Herrschaft. Antisemitismus, Imperialismus, Totalitarismus* (Munich: Piper, 1986); and Arendt, *The Origins of Totalitarianism* (New York: Harcourt, 1968); hereafter *E* and *O*, respectively.

11. Carl Schmitt probes more fully into the intricate nature of this problem. "In mythical language, the earth became known as the mother of law. This signifies a threefold root of law and justice. First, the fertile earth contains within herself, within the womb of her fecundity, an inner measure, because human toil and trouble, human planting and cultivation of the fruitful earth is rewarded justly by her with growth and harvest. Every farmer knows the inner measure of this justice. Second, soil that is cleared and worked by human hands manifests firm lines, whereby definite divisions become apparent. Through the demarcation of fields, pastures, and forests, these lines are engraved and embedded. Through crop rotation and fallowing, they are even planted and nurtured. In these lines, the standards and rules of human cultivation of the earth become discernible. Third and last, the solid ground of the earth is delineated by fences, enclosures, boundaries, walls, houses, and other constructs. Then, obviously, families, clans, tribes, estates, forms of ownership and human proximity, also forms of power and domination, become visible. In this way, the earth is bound to law in three ways. She contains law within herself, as a reward of labor; she manifests law upon herself, as fixed boundaries; and she sustains law above herself, as a public sign of order. Law is bound to the earth and related to the earth" (Schmitt,

problem under the pithy formula of the "normative power of the factual,"[12] and Jürgen Habermas explores it in *Between Facts and Norms*.[13] Clearly Arendt is aware of the problem yet elides it—lest she might have to bury all hope with respect to the ineradicability of human spontaneity. The systematic perversion of human life, the elimination of man's freedom to act, remains an abstractum. Arendt indeed conjures up a certain projection, hope, and imagination when she states that the elimination of human spontaneity is utterly impossible under "normal circumstances." Fully aware of this maneuver of deception, she writes: "*Actually [In Wahrheit]* the experience of the concentration camps *does show* that human beings can be transformed into specimens of the human animal" (*O* 455, *E* 934). In *Origins,* such moments of deception recur quite frequently. Arendt intentionally allows for flagrant inconsistencies, paradoxes, or tensions in her speech act and generates certain wish fulfillments and imaginations that—"actually" (*in Wahrheit*)—contradict her own analysis. It is also in this vein that, as part of her exploration of the totalitarian phenomenon, Arendt implements the biblical tale of Lazarus.

Lazarus

About the "mass production of corpses" Arendt writes: "The end result in any case is inanimate men, i.e., men who can no longer be psychologically understood, whose return to the psychologically or otherwise intelligibly human world closely resembles the resurrection of Lazarus" (*O* 441, *E* 912f.). She is concerned here with the "terrible abyss that separates the world of the living from that of the living dead." She is, more concretely, concerned with the question of testimony—how camp inmates can supply a series of remembered occurrences that seem incredible to both inmates and audience. This impossibility of authentic testimony, the impossibility of survivors identifying with the experiences they recount, leads Arendt to conclude: "The reduction of a man to a bundle of reactions separates him as radically as mental disease from everything within him that is personality or character. When, like Lazarus, he rises from the dead, he finds his personality or character

---

The Nomos of the Earth in the International Law of the "Jus Publicum Europaeum," trans. G. L. Ulmen [New York: Telos, 2003], 42). Cf. also Christian J. Emden, "Carl Schmitt, Hannah Arendt, and the Limits of Liberalism," *Telos* 142 (Spring 2008): 110–34; William Scheuerman, "Revolutions and Constitutions: Hannah Arendt's Challenge to Carl Schmitt," *Canadian Journal of Law and Jurisprudence* 10.1 (1997): 141–61; Andreas Kalyvas, "From the Act to the Decision: Hannah Arendt and the Question of Decisionism," *Political Theory* 32.3 (2004): 320–46.

12. *Allgemeine Staatslehre* (Bad Homburg: Gentner, 1966), 337f.

13. See Jürgen Habermas, *Between Facts and Norms: Contributions to a Discourse Theory of Law and Democracy,* trans. William Rehg (Cambridge, MA: MIT Press), 2001. Habermas writes: "Informal public opinion-formation generates 'influence'; influence is transformed into 'communicative power' through the channels of political elections; and communicative power is again transformed into 'administrative power' through legislation. This influence, carried forward by communicative power, gives law its legitimacy, and thereby provides the political power of the state its binding force" (Habermas, "Three Normative Models of Democracy," *Constellations* 1.1 [1994]: 8).

unchanged, just as he had left it" (*O* 441, *E* 913). Arendt, of course, alludes here to the subject of the miracle recounted in the Gospel of John (11:41–44), in which Jesus performs Lazarus's resurrection. But what significance could the Lazarus tale have as an *analogy* ("closely resembles" [*auf das genaueste gleicht*]) in the context of Arendt's argument?

> On his arrival, Jesus found that Lazarus had already been in the tomb for four days. Bethany was less than two miles from Jersualem, and many Jews had come to Martha and Mary to comfort them in the loss of their brother. When Martha heard that Jesus was coming, she went out to him, but Mary stayed at home. "Lord," Martha said to Jesus, "if you had been here, my brother would not have died. But I know that even now God will give you whatever you ask." Jesus said to her, "Your brother will rise again." Martha answered, "I know he will rise again in the resurrection at the last day." Jesus said to her, "I am the resurrection and the life. He who believes in me will live, even though he dies; and whoever lives and believes in me will never die. Do you believe this?" "Yes, Lord," she told him, "I believe that you are the Christ, the Son of God, who was to come into the world." (John 11:17–27)

It is significant that Martha acknowledges Jesus, who had already gained miraculous fame by healing a man born blind (John 9:1–25), as the Messiah.

> Jesus,...deeply moved, came to the tomb. It was a cave with a stone laid across the entrance. "Take away the stone," he said. "But, Lord," said Martha, the sister of the dead man, "by this time there is a bad odor, for he has been there four days." Then Jesus said, "Did I not tell you that if you believed, you would see the glory of God?" So they took away the stone. Then Jesus looked up and said, "Father, I thank you that you have heard me. I knew that you always hear me, but I said this for the benefit of the people standing here, that they may believe that you sent me." When he had said this, Jesus called in a loud voice, "Lazarus, come out!" The dead man came out, his hands and feet wrapped with strips of linen, and a cloth around his face. Jesus said to them, "Take off the grave clothes and let him go." (John 11:32–44)[14]

The miraculous raising of Lazarus from the dead leads many Jews to accept Jesus as the promised redeemer, the *christos,* as the word for "messiah" in the Greek New Testament is translated. Whereas the Lazarus tale does elucidate the dissociation of the corporeal and "personality" or "character," Arendt's decision to compare Lazarus to the survivor, who, although once "[reduced] to a bundle of reactions," finds his personality unchanged, irritates (*O* 441, *E* 913). The central point of the biblical account, of course, is not Lazarus's revival from the dead but Jesus's appearance as the *christos,* the redeemer. The analogy of Lazarus is bewildering because

---

14. *The Holy Bible, Containing the Old Testament and the New Testament* (Colorado Springs: International Bible Society, 1983).

a messiah did not redeem any of the six million victims of the Holocaust. Arendt's analogy is profoundly disconcerting in that it insinuates a sacrificial subtext into the genocide, one, to be sure, asserted by the word "Holocaust" itself, which—being a compound of the ancient Greek *holos* (whole) and *kaustos* or *kautos* (burnt)—refers to a sacrifice "wholly consumed by fire." In contradistinction to this nominal constitution of the massive killing as a sacrifice for the gods, the Hebrew "Shoah" ("pillar of fire," a reference to Exodus) dispenses with the sacrificial connotation.

Why, then, does the analogy of Lazarus appear, which seems disconnected from Arendt's subject? The miraculous resurrection of Lazarus became the foundation of a community of Christian faith, which defined itself on the basis of collective experiences such as the witnessing of miracles. By contrast, the "resuscitation" of the undead in the concentration camps, or, with respect to the analogy, the miracle of their resurrection, was not followed by the founding of a community. Arendt's envisioned "political community or party in a narrower sense" (O 441, E 913), an initiative hoped for and *imagined* by Arendt stemming from the experiences of Holocaust survivors, did not occur. It seems, therefore, that Arendt deceptively evokes this imagined realm, one actually motivated by a hope of whose hopelessness she knows:

> The attempts to build up a European elite with a program of intra-European understanding based on the common European experience of the concentration camps have foundered in much the same manner as the attempt following the first World War to draw political conclusions from the international experience of the front generation. In both cases it turned out that the experiences themselves can communicate no more than nihilistic banalities. (O 441f., E 913)

On the one hand, Arendt asserts the impossibility of such a political community or party. At the same time Arendt, performatively, seems to refuse to bury her hopes for such a community; she reinstates her political vision—and this is the implicit ethical dynamic behind the inclusion of this analogy—through the tale of resurrection (and community foundation), a lie inspired by a wish, a lie as wish fulfillment, a wish fulfillment in the sense of a political hope for the future. Yet, is not this precisely the political potential of the lie?

"They Could Always Have Been Otherwise"

Hannah Arendt cannot undo what history has done. The point of the lie, however, which takes the form of comparing the survivors to Lazarus, resides in its inherent *possibility* to imagine "an-*other*" reality. Arendt writes a book not for the past but about the past for the future. The domain of all action, all speech action, including lying, lies in the future. "Not the past—and all factual truth, of course, concerns the past—or the present, insofar as it is the outcome of the past, but *the future is open to action*" (TP 258). The future is open to speech action, narrative action, and even historiography, as paradoxical as it may appear. According to Arendt, historians typically reject this state of affairs: "*If it is the well-nigh irresistible temptation of the professional historian to fall into the trap of necessity and implicitly deny freedom of action,* it is the almost equally irresistible temptation of the professional politician to overestimate the possibility of this freedom and implicitly condone the lying denial, or distortion of facts" (TP 250f.). It is Arendt's vacillation between these two poles of history writing and political intervention that produces the ambiguities in her performance: Arendt does not condone the "distortion of facts" (is not all narrative a "distortion of facts"?), yet she also does not condone the denial of the potentiality of facts, their inherent possibility for action:

> Newness is the realm of the historian, who—unlike the natural scientist, who is concerned with ever-recurring happenings—deals with events which always occur only once. This newness can be manipulated if the historian insists on causality and pretends to be able to explain events by a chain of causes which eventually led up to them.... *Whoever in the historical sciences honestly believes in causality actually denies the subject matter of his own science*.... He denies by the same token the very existence of events which, always suddenly and unpredictably, change the whole physiognomy of a given era.[15]

"Belief in causality," Arendt writes, is the historian's way of denying human freedom, that is, "the human capacity for making a new beginning."[16] In contradistinction to the accumulation of data for the sake of a causal, allegedly "truthful" reconstruction, Arendt considers her own historiography a quest for meaning that will never produce unequivocal results.[17] Arendt knows "reality is different from,

---

15. Hannah Arendt, "Understanding and Politics," in *Essays in Understanding, 1930–1954: Formation, Exile, and Totalitarianism* (New York: Schocken Books, 1994), 307–27, here 318f. n. 13. "Causality... is an altogether alien and falsifying category in the historical sciences. Not only does the actual meaning of every event always transcend any number of past 'causes' which we may assign to it... but this past itself comes into being only with the event itself. Only when something irrevocable has happened can we even try to trace its history backward. The event illuminates its own past; it can never be deduced from it. Whenever an event occurs that is great enough to illuminate its own past, history comes into being" (318f.). Benjamin heavily influenced the conception of history that emerges from these and other passages. Arendt describes this conception of historiography as "*Ereignis- und Elementen-Theorie*" (theory of events and elements) (*DT* 105). It is a theory that seizes meaning from the constellations of separated and juxtaposed fragments, thereby corresponding to the realities of the "elements of totalitarian domination" to which *Origins*' German title speaks—elements that "suddenly crystallize into fixed and definite forms." The moment of sudden crystallization rules out the potentialities of any occurrence and concretizes an event, and it is only "the light of the event itself which permits us to distinguish its own concrete elements from an infinite number of abstract possibilities" (Arendt, "Understanding and Politics," 325 n. 12). "An event belongs to the past, marks an end, insofar as elements... are gathered together in its sudden crystallization;... an event belongs to the future, marks a beginning, insofar as this crystallization itself can never be deduced from its own elements, but is caused invariably by some factor which lies in the realm of human freedom" (326 n. 16).
16. Arendt, "Understanding and Politics," 325 n. 13.
17. Cf. Arendt, "Understanding and Politics," 307.

and more than, the totality of facts" (TP 261). At the same time, she does not relinquish her rigid differentiation between factual truth and rational truth, and it is this resistance, this blindness to her own insights, that makes an understanding of Arendt's historiography so difficult. On the one hand, she insists: "Even if we admit that every generation has the right to write its own history, we admit no more than that it has the right to rearrange the facts in accordance with its own perspective; we don't admit the right to touch the factual matter itself" (TP 238f.). On the other hand, Arendt leaves no doubt that for the teller of history, there is no real alternative to engagement with the factual matter itself. All storytelling is composed of any number of factual truths; each narrative, no matter whether "truth" or "lie," seeks meaning (sometimes "false" meaning); each attempt to understand (or to mislead someone or oneself) is some sort of construction or interpretation of "facts." Does not such interpretation always rely on certain principles of selection that allow the telling of a story in one fashion rather than another? Yet, these principles themselves are surely not factual data, as Arendt concedes (see TP 238). Moreover, is not the question of what the facts of a given event or a series of events are, the question of testimony, fraught with complexities? Arendt's *Denktagebuch* states: "Kierkegaard said that the world kills the truth—Socrates, Jesus—, a dangerous claim because then, of course, every liar can appeal to it. *This leads us to the heart of the problem. How can we decide what truth is?*" (DT 618). Arendt leaves her question unanswered, not because she believes that there is no truth, I think, but because there is no answer. Instead, she provides an ethical imperative: "We are free to change the world and to start something new in it" (LP 5).[18] The price for this freedom to act—which includes narrative action and also lying—is that the outcome could have been different. "Facts have no conclusive reason whatever for being what they are; they could always have been otherwise, and this... contingency is literally unlimited" (TP 242). Whereas most historiography provides the impression of a conclusiveness of events—a sequence of factual data in such and such a way—any sequence could have occurred differently and only retrospectively appears predetermined. The reason for this is that, in Arendt's words, "reality...kill[s], by definition, all other potentialities...inherent in any given situation" (TP 243).

To fall into the historian's "trap of necessity" of denying "freedom of action" would mean to grant Nazism the logical consistency it claims; it would espouse

---

18. This freedom to act is, according to Arendt, the manifestation of the freedom entailed in each new birth; it is the unprecedentedness of the event of "natality." See esp. Hannah Arendt, *The Human Condition* (Chicago: University of Chicago Press, 1998), 175–247. On Arendt's interwoven concepts of "natality," "action," and their common denominator, namely "freedom," cf. Ronald Beiner, "Action, Natality, and Citizenship: Hannah Arendt's Concept of Freedom," in *Conceptions of Liberty in Political Philosophy*, ed. Zbigniew Pelczynski and John Gray (London: Athlone Press, 1984), 349–75; George Kateb, "Political Action: Its Nature and Advantages," in *The Cambridge Companion to Hannah Arendt*, ed. Dana Villa (Cambridge: Cambridge University Press, 2000), 130–50; Patricia Bowen-Moore, *Hannah Arendt's Philosophy of Natality* (London: Macmillan, 1989), esp. 42–68.

its innate claim to a higher form of legitimacy that, inspired by the law of Nature itself, can do away with positive conceptions of legality. The ideological mind-set that inhibits the potentiality of saying A and therefore settles on B serves no purpose other than to "divert the mind and blunt the judgment for the multitude of other...*possibilities*" (LP 12). By contrast, Arendt's entire act of writing appears to undermine the compulsion of totalitarian logicality. It dares to imagine, to imagine the possibility of the noneradicability of human spontaneity, and the founding of political parties or groups based on the experience of the Holocaust.

Two Keys

Imagining that the impeccable logic of totalitarian reasoning can be "cracked," that its rational immunity can be undercut, is the third lie discussed here, which is based on the metaphors of two keys. It is an image that evokes the problematic contiguity of method and the problem of understanding. In a review of *The Black Book: The Nazi Crime against the Jewish People,* Arendt writes: "*The Black Book* fails because its authors, submerged in a chaos of detail, were unable to understand or make clear the nature of the facts confronting them."[19] In other words, the authors failed to cull any explanatory substance from the vast amounts of data; they exhibited a certain inability to understand. It is this context in which Arendt's own conceptual approach to the question of understanding must be situated. In an interview, she states: "What is important for me is to understand. For me, writing is a matter of seeking this understanding, part of the process of understanding."[20] For Arendt, understanding is procedural in nature; a thought process: "Understanding, as distinguished from having correct information and scientific knowledge, is a complicated process which never produces unequivocal results. It is an unending activity."[21] Every page in *Origins* is ultimately part of this larger project of understanding. The intricacy of understanding and the subsequent travails of dispelling the systematology of totalitarian politics are rooted in their logical consistency:

> Whereas the totalitarian regimes are thus resolutely and cynically emptying the world of all structures of meaning [alle Sinnzusammenhänge] with which we normally operate and within which we normally act, they impose upon it at the same time a kind of supersense which the ideologies actually always meant when *they pretended to have found the key to history or the solution to the riddles of the universe.* Over and above the

---

19. Hannah Arendt, "The Image of Hell," in *Essays in Understanding,* 179–205, here 197f.
20. Hannah Arendt, "'What Remains? The Language Remains': A Conversation with Günter Gaus," in *Essays in Understanding,* 1–23, here 3. On the vexed relationship between truth, facts, storytelling, and understanding in Arendt, see Lisa Disch, "More Truth Than Fact: Storytelling as Critical Understanding in the Writings of Hannah Arendt," *Political Theory* 21.4 (1993): 665–94; Christina Thürmer-Rohr, "Verstehen und Schreiben—unheimliche Heimat," *Text und Kritik* 166/167 (2005): 92–101.
21. Arendt, "Understanding and Politics," 307f.

senselessness of totalitarian society is enthroned the ridiculous supersense of its ideological superstition. (*O* 457, *E* 939)

If totalitarian societies' claim of total consistency can be taken literally, they become the "nuclei of logical systems" in which everything necessarily follows once the first premise is axiomatically accepted. This claim "to have found the *key* to history" is also reflected in the juridical self-conception of the National Socialist state: the word "law" denotes the law of the movement of Nature. This law of movement is a Darwinian law of inclusion and exclusion—the exclusion of everything "unfit to live" (*O* 465, *E* 951). "In this sense the word 'law' was already used by ideologies, i.e., by those nineteenth-century *Weltanschauungen* which, based on a premise, claimed to hold in their hand *the key to all that had ever occurred*" (*E* 950). In the face of this juridical and generally ideological self-image of totalitarian systems, Arendt, committed to normative paradigms of constitutional state politics, now seeks to prove the deficiency of totalitarian logic. Yet it is precisely the foundation for such a critique that appears to have evaporated, for "all structures of meaning [alle Sinnzusammenhänge] with which we normally operate and within which we normally act" are eradicated. It is in this vein that she writes: "For those engaged in the quest for meaning and understanding, what is frightening in the rise of totalitarianism is not that it is something new, but that it has brought to light the ruin of our categories of thought and standards of judgment."[22] She also writes: "The paradox of the modern situation seems to be that our need to transcend both preliminary understanding and the strictly scientific approach springs from the fact that we have lost our tools of understanding. Our quest for meaning is at the same time prompted and frustrated by our inability to originate meaning."[23] Arendt offers further variations of this sentence that describe the same peculiar dilemma: the totalitarian system claims to "have found the *key* to history or the solution to the riddles of the universe." Thus, all philosophical arguments that Arendt adduces against this claim appear to be in vain, as far as her constative elaborations are concerned: "In this sense, the difficulty of understanding totalitarian politics and the institutions of total power is...that they are 'logically' too uncompromising in drawing the conclusions inherent in their ideologies" (*E* 938). This awareness notwithstanding, Arendt claims—and this is where she "lies"—to possess a "key to understanding" herself. In chapter 10 of *Origins,* Arendt discusses the temporary alliance between the mob and the elite as *the* central dynamic in totalitarian movements, deeming it the "essential key" to the understanding of totalitarianism (*O* 326, *E* 703):

The disturbing alliance between the mob and the elite, and the curious coincidence of their aspirations, had their origin in the fact that these strata had been the first

---
22. Ibid., 318.
23. Ibid., 313.

to be eliminated from the structure of the nation-state and the framework of class society.... For the ruthless machines of domination and extermination, the masses of co-ordinated philistines provided much better material and were capable of even greater crimes than so-called professional criminals, provided only that these crimes were well organized and assumed the appearance of routine jobs. (*O* 337, *E* 720f.)[24]

The alliance between the mob and the elite epitomizes, according to Arendt, a formula elucidating the crucial dynamics of totalitarian government; it presents "*an essential key* to the understanding of totalitarian movements...[regarding] their connection with the mob" (*O* 326, *E* 703). Arendt qualifies this pronouncement by pointing out that "one can only use this key [Dieses Schlüssels kann man sich nur dann bedienen] if one bears in mind that neither the elite nor the mob play an actual role in the totalitarian apparatus of domination.... They are essential only for the understanding of the general historical situation" (*E* 703). She writes somewhat vaguely, and it reads as if the discovery of the key must immediately be vindicated and put in perspective. Yet, in her subsequent discussion, Arendt does not revoke the idea that "this key...can be used" (*E* 703). What becomes apparent here is another moment of deception. Arendt imagines that a solid basis exists from which to attack the "not really refutable" (*schwer zurückweisbar*) systematic nature of totalitarian domination—this insurmountable total logic that "make[s] too much sense" and "is too consistent" (*O* 457, *E* 938). Arendt, who knows better, invokes the pretense that the modus operandi of Fascist government—despite its "sensible and logical" qualities within its own framework—could, in the course of more than a thousand pages, be proven somehow inadequate, dubbed tenuous, and attacked via democratic constitutional politics:

> The quest for the *nature* of totalitarianism is no longer a historical (and certainly not a sociological or psychological) undertaking; it is, strictly speaking, a question for political science, which, if it understands itself, is *the true guardian of the keys which open the doors to the problems and uncertainties* of the philosophy of history.[25]

Arendt's wish for understanding is thus directly metaphorized: the key of totalitarianism "to...the solution to the riddles of the universe" is immediately juxtaposed with Arendt's own imaginative key "which opens the doors to...the philosophy of history," including that of totalitarian domination—key versus key. The capacity of this imagination is Arendt's actual performative intervention:

---

24. The attraction of totalitarian movements for the elite results "not simply from Stalin's and Hitler's mastery in the art of lying but rather from their ability to organize the masses in such a way that their lies could turn into reality" (*E* 714). The big lie of the regime and the "masses' desire for a fictitious world" complement one another and only as such allow for the alliance between the mob and the elite (*E* 714–18).

25. Arendt, "Understanding and Politics," 326 n. 17, italics in original.

"Imagination alone enables us to see things in their proper perspective.... This kind of imagination... actually is understanding."[26]

Why Does Hannah Arendt Lie?

"To understand something which has ruined our categories of thought and our standards of judgment," Arendt resorts to imagination.[27] Only imagination can restore those standards of judgment, the "structures of meaning" (*Sinnzusammenhänge*) that totalitarianism has destroyed, for imagination or, more generally, image making enables us to "see things in their proper perspective"; imagination enables us to understand, and "the result of understanding is *meaning,* which we originate... insofar as we try to reconcile ourselves to what we do and what we suffer."[28] Arendt's lies, the images she projects, allow for meaning that totalitarian politics seemed to have obliterated once and for all.

In relentlessly distancing her storytelling from any sort of "falsification" or "distortion" of factual matter, Arendt succumbs to a kind of positivism that fundamentally contradicts her entire mission of a different historiography—a contradiction at the heart of her unconventionality. Correspondingly, she insists on the force of the traditional lie, a force that appears dubious when confronted with the modern lie (TP 231–39). It is not beyond imagination that she herself deemed this insistence her biggest lie. "Reality," Arendt writes, "is different from, and more than, the totality of facts and events, which, anyhow, is unascertainable. Who says what is—λέγει τὰ ἐόντα—always tells a story, and in this story the particular facts lose their contingency and acquire some humanly comprehensible meaning" (TP 261f.). Arendt turns to Isak Dinesen's dictum that "all sorrows can be borne if you put them into a story or tell a story about them" (TP 262). She moves from Dinesen to Hegel: "To the extent that the teller of factual truth is also a storyteller, he brings about that 'reconciliation with reality' which Hegel, the philosopher of history *par excellence,* understood as the ultimate goal of all philosophical thought, and which, indeed, has been the secret motor of all historiography" (TP 262). The motor of all historiography is reconciliation with what we suffer. Is not Arendt's art of lying precisely that? Are not the imaginations of a political community based on the experience of the Holocaust, the imagination of human spontaneity being ineffaceable, the imagination of the possibility of a political critique of totalitarian politics moments in the quest of a human being for understanding in a world that appears to have foreclosed precisely such possibility?

As paradoxical as it may sound, does not that which has been described as Arendt's "lies" eventually testify to her *integrity?* Does not her discourse, with all its

---
26. Ibid., 323.
27. Ibid., 318.
28. Ibid., 309.

tensions, contradictions, ruptures, impasses, images, and imaginations, testify to a certain truthfulness in that she presents things as they appear in her perspective, the perspective of a thinker trying to reassemble the "commonly inhabited world that has broken apart"? The intellectual efficacy of so-called objectivity finds its complement in "the disinterested pursuit of truth"—in the German translation, *dieser Haltung, der es nur um die Wahrheit zu tun ist* (TP 262f.).

Of course, any process of seeking the "truth"—that is, any process of understanding—must be based on some form of representative thinking; it must consider different viewpoints. Writes Arendt: "I form an opinion by considering a given issue from different viewpoints, by making present to my mind the standpoints of those who are absent; that is, I represent them" (TP 241). Yet understanding is not tantamount to "objectivity," at least not if objectivity involves "counting noses and joining a majority." "To understand" denotes the capacity for what Kant calls an "enlarged mentality," which enables individuals to judge.[29] "To understand" always also means "to judge."

* * *

Lying, the possibility of imagining, is a strange enterprise. But, as Arendt says, "understanding is a strange enterprise," too.[30] Imagination is "part of the dialogue of understanding for whose purposes mere knowledge erects artificial barriers."[31] Imagination, according to Wordsworth, "is but another name for...clearest insight, amplitude of mind, / And Reason in her most exalted mood."[32] Raising then the question posed at the outset—Why does Hannah Arendt lie?—the answer would probably be, because she wants to understand and judge the history of totalitarianism rather than reconstruct it; she wants to make it politically understandable and judgeable; she embarks on a political intervention, knowing that this intervention cannot undo history, but perhaps—and this is the power of imagination—can change the future. Hannah Arendt lies because she wants to "change the world" (TP 250).

"Current moral prejudice," Arendt writes, "tends to be rather harsh in respect to...lying, whereas the often highly developed art of self-deception is usually regarded with great tolerance and permissiveness" (TP 255). She shares neither the permissiveness toward self-deception nor the "prejudice" against the traditional lie. Arendt finds support here in Dostoevsky's *Brothers Karamazov*. In the famous scene in the monastery, the father, a chronic liar, asks the Staretz: "And what must I do to gain salvation?" The Staretz replies: "Above all, never lie to yourself!" (after

---

29. Immanuel Kant, *Critique of Judgment*, after TP 241.
30. Arendt, "Understanding and Politics," 322.
31. Ibid., 323.
32. William Wordsworth, *The Prelude*, book 14, lines 190–92, after Arendt, "Understanding and Politics," 323.

TP 254f.) As long as the one who lies remains aware of the distinction between truth and falsehood, the individual and the world deceived are, in the words of the Staretz, not beyond salvation. In the words of Arendt, who so often tells us about the world while commenting on her own writing: "He lied, but he is not a liar" (TP 255). She lied, but she is not a liar. Not a confession, but a concession, perhaps.

* * *

Melancholy masks the end of "Truth and Politics," this curious analysis of lying as action, political action. Arendt contends that the political sphere, "its greatness notwithstanding," is limited by "those things which men cannot change at will" (TP 263f.). It is the art of *imagination,* the ability to conjure up images of hopes and dreams, that allows us to get our bearings in the world.[33] "Conceptually, we may call truth what we cannot change; metaphorically, it is the ground on which we stand and the sky that stretches above us" (TP 264).

---

33. Arendt, "Understanding and Politics," 323.

3

"A Peculiar Apparatus"

Kafka's Thanatopoetics

> Kafka's technique could best be compared to the construction of models. Just as a man who wants to build a house or evaluate its stability would draw up a blueprint of the building, Kafka practically devises the blueprints of the existing world..., which sometimes in a page, or even in a single phrase, expose the naked structure of events.
>
> —Hannah Arendt, "Franz Kafka, Appreciated Anew"

Inclusive Exclusion

"It's a remarkable [eigentümlicher] piece of apparatus," reads the first prophetic sentence of Kafka's 1914 story "In the Penal Colony" (161, 140).[1] It is the officer who speaks this first sentence to the explorer, and in a way, Willa and Edwin Muir's mistranslation in the Schocken edition is "remarkable" in itself in that,

---

1. Chapter epigraph: Hannah Arendt, "Franz Kafka, Appreciated Anew," trans. Martin Klebes, in *Reflections on Literature and Culture*, ed. Susannah Young-ah Gottlieb (Stanford, CA: Stanford University Press, 2007), 94–109, here 104f.; "Franz Kafka: A Revaluation," in *Essays in Understanding, 1930–1954: Formation, Exile, and Totalitarianism* (New York: Schocken Books, 1994), 69–80, here 76f. Quotations from Kafka's "In the Penal Colony" are followed by two sets of page numbers. The first set refers to Franz Kafka, *Ein Landarzt und andere Drucke zu Lebzeiten* (Frankfurt a.M.: Fischer TB Verlag, 1994), 161–95; the second set refers to Franz Kafka, *The Completed Stories*, ed. Nahum N. Glatzer (New York: Schocken Books, 1988), 140–67.

though wrong, they got it just right. For *ein eigentümlicher Apparat* is, of course, not a "remarkable" but rather a "peculiar" or "singular" or "specific" or "idiosyncratic" apparatus. Yet in the eyes of the officer, the apparatus is indeed not peculiar but simply remarkable—there is nothing wrong or alarming about it. He considers the apparatus an impressive work (*Werk,* 163, 141), extraordinary, notable, outstanding, astonishing: it allows for no hesitation but solely for awe. Conversely, in the eyes of the explorer and presumably in ours (also because we shall take Kafka, at least for now, at his word), the apparatus is likely to appear peculiar or idiosyncratic. Yet what conjures up the idiosyncrasy of the apparatus? The word "apparatus" is a significant one in Kafka's story; it appears no less than twelve times within the first three paragraphs, a frequency that one may find remarkable or peculiar in itself. To be sure, the apparatus is, on a basic level, an execution machine. Yet this execution machine not only tortures and executes; it also informs the prisoner of his sentence (see 166, 143f.); and since the word "apparatus," in its most general sense, simply denotes a construct that operates according to an established set of functional rules, one perhaps could say that the apparatus constitutes the juridical institution of the penal colony.

This juridical apparatus or construct appears remarkable in its emphasis on technological details. Kafka employs an entire discourse of technological vocabulary: "Harrow," "Designer," "electric battery," "disturbances," "needles," "acid fluid," a "ladder," a creaking "wheel," "screw," "spanner," "machinery," "cogwheels," "mechanical instruments," "chemist," "draughtsman," and so forth. In the light of the officer's idealization of the mechanical parts of the juridical apparatus (see 170, 149), the emphasis on the technological seems to be at odds with the higher cause of justice—that dimension to which every juridical apparatus characteristically aspires, a dimension generally considered to be the *sine qua non* of jurisdiction. By contrast, the officer's obsession with the apparatus's innate beauty—his meticulous maintenance of the machine—seems to follow a logic of its own and serve some immanent law yet to be explored.

On the "Bed" of the apparatus lies another construct, an *"anatomical* apparatus," an expression the Duden dictionary defines as "a system of organs and parts of the body serving the same purpose."[2] This anatomical construct is the condemned man, his body, "naked, of course" (164, 142f.). The naked prisoner is strapped to the Bed of the execution machine at his hands, feet, and neck (see 164, 143). While the description of the juridical apparatus is striking for its emphasis on technical and mechanical elements, the description of the human "construct" is striking for its strong emphasis on physiological and anatomical elements (e.g., blood, saliva, vomit, skin, etc.). "For millennia, man remained what he was for Aristotle," Michel Foucault writes, "a living animal with the additional capacity for a political

---

2. Duden's *Das große Wörterbuch der deutschen Sprache,* 10 vols. (Mannheim: Dudenverlag, 1999), here 1:271.

existence."³ According to Aristotle, human beings are distinct from animals in their potentiality for an understanding of justice (*dikē*),⁴ but the condemned man in Kafka's story has largely been deprived of precisely this ethical dimension, this sense of justice. "In any case, the condemned man looked so like a submissive dog that one might have thought he could be left to run free on the surrounding hills and would only need to be whistled for when the execution was due to begin" (161, 140). The prisoner seems to have no sense of justice, no understanding of the injustice brought against him; instinctually driven, he would run to his execution if whistled for.

We are thus presented with two different apparatuses: a juridical one and an anatomical one.⁵ Both appear suspect with regard to their seeming absence of justice. Both constructs, that of law and that of life, are adjacent to one another; the condemned man lies naked on the Bed of the execution machine. Yet not only are law and life bound closely to one another (*an-einander*); they are indeed *interlocked* (*in-einander*):

> "Here at the head of the Bed, where the man, as I said, first lays down his face, is this little gag of felt, which can be easily regulated to go straight into his mouth. It is meant to keep him from screaming and biting his tongue. Of course the man is forced to take the felt into his mouth, otherwise his neck would be broken by the strap." (164f., 143)

In this description, the juridical and the corporeal seem to be intertwined. In addition, the three parts of the apparatus—"Bed," "Designer," and "Harrow"— have "acquired a kind of *popular* nickname [volkstümliche Bezeichnungen]" (163, 141f.). The apparatus is given "popular" (*volkstümliche*) names and, as such, at least nominally, relates to the people (i.e., the population, the *Volk,* the *Volkskörper,* the political body constituted by the people). Analogously "the shape of the Harrow," the part of the apparatus that inscribes the sentence on the man's skin, "corresponds to the human form" (169, 146). The Harrow indeed shows human behavior when, for example, the officer's body does not drop from the long needles: "The Harrow tried to move back to its old position, but as if it had itself noticed that it had not yet got rid of its burden, it stuck after all where it was, over the pit" (193, 165f.). The juridical and the corporeal, law and life, appear closely interrelated in the penal colony.

---

3. Michel Foucault, *The History of Sexuality: An Introduction* (New York: Vintage Books, 1978), 1:143.
4. See esp. book 1 of Aristotle's *Politics,* trans. Ernest Barker (New York: Oxford University Press, 1998).
5. For a Freudian interpretation of the "apparatus," cf. William Dodd, "Kafka and Freud: A Note on 'In der Strafkolonie,'" *Monatshefte* 70 (1978): 129–39.

In fact, the resemblance between law and life amounts to the *terminological permutation* between the juridical and the human "construct":

> "Be careful with him! [Behandle ihn sorgfältig!]," cried the officer again. He ran around the apparatus, himself caught the condemned man under the shoulders, and with the soldier's help got him up on his feet, which kept slithering from under him [Er umlief den Apparat, faßte selbst den Verurteilten unter den Achseln und stellte ihn, der öfters mit den Füßen ausglitt, mit Hilfe des Soldaten auf]. (171, 148)

The traveler "was even leaning right across the Harrow, without taking any notice of it [ohne sich um sie zu kümmern]," thus following an activity, *sich kümmern,* that humanizes the Harrow. Similarly, the officer's exclamation "Behandle ihn sorgfältig!" employs a vocable, *sorgfältig,* not typically used in reference to human beings, but to machinery, perhaps an animal, or, indeed, a baby, an infant, which in German, unlike in English, is explicitly neuter, a *thing*. It is in this vein that Kafka invokes the image of the officer catching the prisoner under the shoulders, "und stellte ihn...mit Hilfe des Soldaten auf," like a marionette, it seems, whose inanimate "feet...kept slithering from under him." The interrelatedness of law and life is thus translated into a converse rhetoric, humanizing the machine and dehumanizing the prisoner.

In *Politics,* Aristotle asserts that in addition to his potentiality for an understanding of justice (*dikē*), man is also a being capable of language (*logos*).[6] Indeed the condemned man (and perhaps also the soldier)[7] seems to distinguish himself from the officer in that he does not speak the officer's language—the language of the colonizer, the imperialist, the language of the one in power. From the perspective of the officer, the prisoner probably does not speak any language at all: "The officer was speaking French, and certainly neither the soldier nor the prisoner understood a word of French" (164, 142).

If man has language (*logos*) he has reason (*logos*); he who is without language is without reason. Language is reason, and the condemned man, consequently, is deprived of reason as much as of language: "The condemned man...was a stupid-looking, wide-mouthed creature with bewildered hair and face [ein

---

6. "Nature, according to our theory," Aristotle writes, "makes nothing in vain; and man alone of the animals is furnished with the faculty of language. The mere making of sounds serves to indicate pleasure and pain, and is thus a faculty that belongs to animals in general: their nature enables them to attain the point at which they have perceptions of pleasure and pain, and can signify those perceptions to one another. But language serves to declare what is advantageous and what is the reverse, and it is the peculiarity of man, in comparison with other animals, that he alone possesses a perception of good and evil, of the just and the unjust" (*Politics* 1253a7, trans. Barker).

7. The resemblance between the soldier and the prisoner is enacted by the soldier's gestures, seemingly in imitation of the appearance of the prisoner: "He had wound the prisoner's chain around both his wrists"; in fact, the soldier's posture prefigures the prisoner's fate: he "propped himself on his rifle, let his head hang" (163f., 142).

stumpfsinninger, breitmäuliger Mensch mit verwahrlosten Haar und Gesicht]" (161, 140). The characterization of the condemned man conjures up the innumerable illustrations pervading the cultural archaeology of nineteenth-century Western Europe: pictures of mentally ill people, photographed in the context of new academic disciplines such as psychology and psychiatry. These images—often presenting the mentally ill with tousled hair and with salivating, paralyzed, grinning faces—were etched on the collective memory of a century. It is this very image encountering us in Kafka's prisoner—a man eating the "rice pap" (from which he "can take as much as his tongue can lap"; 173, 150) as he awaits being strapped to the execution machine's Bed. In his narcotic passivity, and without the slightest understanding that his execution is imminent, the condemned man, "with a kind of drowsy persistence...directed his gaze wherever the officer pointed a finger, and at the interruption of the explorer's question he, too, as well as the officer, looked around" (164, 142). The condemned man lacks both language/reason and an understanding of justice, though he does perhaps have a potentiality for both; yet from our perspective he is solely presented as a nonhuman. In the colonial-imperialist context of the story, and in stark contrast with the officer and the traveler, he simply seems to be a "wild man"—that pervasive signifier in nineteenth-century Western European literature and philosophy, recurring in countless footnotes in the works of Kant, Hegel, and others—typically allocated to the same classificatory rubric as the still-to-become-human "child" (and extended by the "woman" to a triad). It is therefore unsurprising that the condemned man, this "insane" being, this "animal," behaves in an utterly infantile and naive manner and has nothing in mind other than horsing around with the soldier:

> When [the condemned man] put on the shirt and the trousers both he and the soldiers could not help guffawing, for the garments were of course slit up behind. Perhaps the condemned man felt it incumbent on him to amuse the soldier; he turned around and around in his slashed garments before the soldier, who squatted on the ground beating his knees with mirth. (188, 162)

The condemned man is a silly "figure," a child, a wild man, a madman, and so forth, and he is as truly naked as the officer only appears to be when he undresses,[8] drops off his uniform, that cultural signifier that ostentatiously marks him as a political being, a member of civilization, a human being (cf. 189, 162).

---

8. In his essay "Toward a Critique of Violence," Walter Benjamin distinguishes "mere life" (*bloßes Leben*) from "the living" (*das Lebendige*). Whereas "mere life" corresponds to the natural existence of a human being, "the living" partakes in a supernatural, sacred order (Benjamin, "Zur Kritik der Gewalt," in *Gesammelte Schriften,* ed. Rolf Tiedemann and Hermann Schweppenhäuser [Frankfurt a.M.: Suhrkamp, 1977], 2.1:179–203, here 200). If one were to describe Kafka's "condemned man" in Benjaminian terms, one would probably characterize him as "mere" rather than "sacred" life.

I have already indicated that the execution procedure, which strikes us first as peculiar and then as very cruel and appalling, does not seem to the officer to be peculiar at all. He finds the work of the old Commandant remarkable, places his services at the disposal of its preservation, and identifies his life entirely with the juridical procedure. It is a procedure that strikes the explorer as problematic but appears to the officer to be quite normal, even beautiful:

> Many questions were troubling the explorer, but at the sight of the prisoner he asked only: "Does he know his sentence?" "No," said the officer, eager to go on with his exposition, but the explorer interrupted him: "He doesn't know the sentence that has been passed on him?" "No," said the officer again, pausing a moment as if to let the explorer elaborate his question, and then said: "There would be *no point* [*nutzlos*] in telling him. He'll learn it on his body."... "But surely he knows that he has been sentenced?" "Nor that either," said the officer, smiling at the explorer as if expecting him to make further surprising remarks. "No," said the explorer, wiping his forehead, "then he can't know either whether his defense was effective?" "He has had no chance of putting up a defense," said the officer, turning his eyes away as if speaking to himself and so sparing the explorer the shame of hearing *self-evident matters* explained. (144f., 167)

What appears entirely inconceivable to the explorer is "self-evident" (*selbstverständlich*) to the officer; he is "eager to go on with his exposition" to spare the explorer the "shame" of hearing these self-evident matters. The basis for this discrepancy in the evaluation of the juridical procedure seems to be two diametrically opposed understandings of the meaning of law. The explorer, in accordance with most modern democratic legal constitutions, maintains an understanding of law as a tool, in the broadest sense, to protect human beings from one another. In contrast, the officer seems to assume an inextricability of law and life. In such a system there is no outside-of-politics and no outside-the-law. From the perspective of the officer—one where law and life are inextricably linked or are, figuratively, perhaps even identical—there is indeed no point in informing the prisoner of his sentence ahead of time. The individual being is registered by the system as a corpus, and the legal inscription *on his body* is therefore a quite logical form of communication. Likewise, there would be little sense in giving him an opportunity to put up a defense, for if the body is law and law is the body, to defend oneself means to defend oneself against oneself, against one's own body, and that, indeed, appears absurd.

If we follow the logic of the officer, it would ultimately appear quite inappropriate to call the execution procedure "atrocious" or "barbarous," and so on. Such taxonomy is meaningful if an *external* moral perspective, an a-nomic viewpoint, one *outside the law,* is available. In a system such as that of the penal colony, however, it can only be deemed extraneous. Notions of the "cruel," "inhuman," "unethical," and so forth do not apply; all classificatory attributes, in one way or another, are subsumed under the binary of the "politically sensible" and the "politically nonsensible." Thus the officer fails to comprehend the gist of the traveler's questions and so offers no qualifying remarks that might shed a critical light on the procedure. Thus his general *lack of understanding (Unverständnis)*; what is *selbstverständlich* (self-evident) is, according to the Duden dictionary, "without question," meaning "understanding itself out of itself," *sich aus sich selbst verstehend*.[9] Thus, after all, the officer's unperturbed mannerism, his uncanny smile "at the explorer as if expecting him to make further surprising remarks."[10]

The juridical procedure around the prisoner in Kafka's "Penal Colony" is pursued without a hearing, without a defense, and without a proclamation of the sentence prior to the execution. Given that this appears "self-evident" within a systemic logic in which law and life are identical, it only follows that the officer finally executes himself when he becomes aware that the life of the old system appears to have come to an end. The disintegration of the "logic" of justice in the penal colony, the disintegration of the old juridical system, the disintegration of the execution machine (see 192, 164) can coincide only with the disintegration of life, the officer's life, life constituting the old system. Even the explorer, whose chagrin the officer's sedate manner had provoked at the outset (167, 144f.), now yields or at least understands the logic and the consistency of the officer's action:

> Now [the officer] stood naked there. The explorer bit his lips and said nothing. He knew very well what was going to happen, but he had no right to obstruct the officer in anything. If the judicial procedure which the officer cherished were really so near its end...then the officer was doing the right thing; in his place the explorer would not have acted otherwise. (189, 163)

---

9. Duden's *Herkunftswörterbuch* (Mannheim: Dudenverlag, 2001), 760.

10. The rhetoric of the "self-evident" *obliquely* relates to what Hannah Arendt described with her formula of the "banality of evil" in her book on the trial of Adolf Eichmann (Arendt, *Eichmann in Jerusalem: A Report on the Banality of Evil* [New York: Penguin Books, 1994]). The "banality of evil" does not describe the unimaginable suffering of millions of Jews murdered in the "technically efficient" gas chambers and crematoriums of Nazi concentration camps. Nor does Arendt's formula describe the banality of an execution apparatus that can be comprehended only as the project of an insane person or a sadist. The banality of evil describes the very plain factual situation that the Holocaust was not illegal, that laws were not breached, that the entire genocide was not a criminal act in the legal sense because no juridical apparatus, no legal language, no juris-*diction* was available to classify it as "illegal," as juridically "unjust"; it follows from a judicial perspective, then, that the Holocaust was entirely "banal." At the same time, the colonial dimension of Kafka's story and the historical context of Arendt's formula of the "banality of evil," namely twentieth-century totalitarianism, are, of course, fundamentally different. And yet, perhaps the most ingenious insight of Arendt's monumental *The Origins of Totalitarianism* (New York: Harcourt, 1968) is precisely the conceptual link that she establishes in part 2 of the book: the link between colonialism and twentieth-century totalitarianism. Here Arendt argues that Germany's "failure" as a colonial empire largely motivated the imperialism and unprecedented racism of Nazi Germany in the middle of the twentieth century. While, on the one hand, it would be problematic simply to impose a conceptual framework for totalitarian politics on Kafka's colonial narrative, it seems, on the other, impossible to dismiss the repercussions that the story evokes.

The explorer understands the officer, and perhaps he even tacitly admires him. In any case, the officer does not really have any other choice, there is no *tertium datur* to living within the system and dying within the system; in the face of the "great change" (*grossen Umschwung*, 190, 163) it simply is the continuation of a political logic of which he is a political segment—thus the officer's determination and the total lack of irritation, anxiety, or panic, when discarding his clothes (see 189, 162). There also is, consequently, no need to strap the officer to the machine: "Everything was ready, only the straps hung down at the side, yet they were obviously unnecessary, the officer did not need to be fastened down" (190, 164).

If, for the moment, we ask why the officer holds a superior rank in the penal colony, he readily provides an answer: "This is how the matter stands. I have been appointed judge in this penal colony. Despite my youth. For I was the former Commandant's assistant in all penal matters and know more about the apparatus than anyone" (168, 145). The officer makes no secret of the dictatorial nature of his appointment: "Other courts...consist of several opinions and have higher courts to scrutinize them [Andere Gerichte...sind vielköpfig und haben auch noch höhere Gerichte über sich]. That is not the case here" (168, 145). While in democratic societies, power, following the *trias politica* proposed by Montesquieu, is divided *horizontally* (i.e., into executive, legislative, and judiciary branches), the penal colony's officer combines all power in his persona. Beyond that, all *vertical* allocation of power finds its end in the officer. He rules as an autocrat, epitomizing the vertex of the hierarchical pyramid; all power is *con*-centrated within his political presence.

In response to the exigencies of political crisis, the logic directing the officer's actions is a situational one: "'The new [Commandant] has already shown some inclination to interfere with my judgments, but so far I have succeeded in fending him off and will go on succeeding'" (168, 144, translation modified). According to this logic, the situation almost dictates the law (*Recht*) of situational jurisdiction, and in cases of sudden threats ("'The new [Commandant] has already shown some inclination to interfere with my judgments [hat...schon Lust gezeigt, in mein Gericht sich einzumischen]'"), "*extra*-ordinary measures" (169, 146) appear not only legitimate but imperative to further ensure order and stability that facilitate the effectiveness of jurisdiction.[11] During his encounter with the officer, the explorer comes

---

11. The juridical dynamic described here somewhat corresponds to the notion of "situational law" that Carl Schmitt popularized in the early twentieth century. "For a legal order to make sense, a normal situation must be guaranteed. [Die Ordnung muss hergestellt sein, damit die Rechtsordnung einen Sinn hat.]...All law is 'situational law' [Situationsrecht]," Schmitt writes in chapter 1 of his *Political Theology* (Schmitt, *Political Theology: Four Chapters on the Concept of Sovereignty*, trans. George Schwab [Cambridge, MA: MIT Press, 1985], 13; Schmitt, *Politische Theologie: Vier Kapitel zur Lehre der Souveränität* [Berlin: Duncker & Humblot, 2004], 19). Correspondingly, Schmitt's conception of the "state of exception" (*Ausnahmezustand*) is not one of "calculability" and "certainty," but rather one characterized by such concepts as "*state of danger*" (*Gefährdung*), "*case of necessity*" (*Notlage*), and so forth (Schmitt, "Staat, Bewegung, Volk," in *Die Dreigliederung der politischen Einheit* [Hamburg: Hanseatische

to understand how exceptional the political situation in the penal colony is and why the military infrastructure is necessary: "After all, he had to remind himself that this was in any case a penal colony *where extraordinary measures were needed and that military discipline must be enforced to the last*" (169, 146).

Given this background the question of the adequacy, the legitimacy, of the sentence of death penalty seems misplaced. Yet we may ponder its structure, its *synthetic constituency*. At the outset, the "evidence" precipitating the execution reads as straightforward:

> "A captain reported to me this morning that this man, who had been assigned to him as a servant and sleeps before his door, had been asleep on duty. It is his duty, you see, to get up every time the hour strikes and salute the captain's door. Not an exacting duty, and very necessary, since he has to be a sentry as well as a servant, and must be alert in both functions [denn er soll sowohl zur Bewachung als auch zur Bedienung frisch bleiben]. Last night the captain wanted to see if the man was doing his duty. He opened the door as the clock struck two and there was his man curled up asleep. He took his riding whip and lashed him across the face. Instead of getting up and begging pardon, the man caught hold of his master's legs, shook him, and cried: 'Throw that whip away or I'll eat you alive.'—That's the evidence." (168, 146)

I am interested here in the managerial principles, the juridical rationale, pursued by the officer. What is the officer's position that allows him to arrogate to himself a decision beyond any constitutional constraint? What are the legal grounds on which he adjudicates upon the prisoner's life? Moreover, I am interested in the normality of the exception, the simplicity of the atrocious, partly reflected in Kafka's rhetorical style[12]—a style demonstrated here in a succession of main clauses characteristic in their low stylistic temperature of affect:

1. The captain came to me an hour ago,
2. I wrote down his statement
3. And appended the sentence to it.
4. Then I had the man put in chains.
5. That was all quite simple. (168, 146)

Verlagsanstalt, 1934], esp. 43f.; and Schmitt, *Politische Theologie*, 19f.). To be sure, the officer—and this only hints at the *limits* of a dialogue between Schmitt and Kafka—is *not* a "sovereign" in the Schmittian sense. He is incessantly subservient to the old Commandant and ultimately remains within the circle of jurisdiction; thus his political incorporation eventually induces his own execution and defies such terminological attribution.

12. "The ethical possibility [ethische Möglichkeit] of literature lies in its moral indifference," Joseph Vogl beautifully writes (Vogl, *Ort der Gewalt: Kafkas literarische Ethik* [Munich: Wilhelm Fink Verlag, 1990], 3). The key word here is *Möglichkeit*, "possibility" or "potentiality"; for it is the deadening power of moralistic speech that makes the mere *possibility* of sober analysis and scrutiny (and, eventually, the *ability* to *respond* to a problem, that is, *respons-ability*) impossible.

According to the logic of the officer, everything is "quite simple." His authority as a judge (an extension of the absolute authority of the old Commandant) is not bound by any law. It is exclusively his decision that matters, tethered to whatever he considers necessary to sustain order. All of the characteristic legal procedures that precipitate deferral, allow presentation and analysis of evidence, or accommodate consideration of varied possibilities (e.g., the inquest, the calling of the accused, the interrogation, cross-examination, etc.) are suspended in the "extra-ordinary" (169, 146) political climate in the penal colony. Correspondingly and subjunctively, they are also suspended in Kafka's rhetoric:

"If I had first called the man before me and interrogated him, things would have got into a confused tangle. He would have told lies, and had I exposed these lies he would have backed them up with more lies, and so on and so forth. As it is, I've got him and I won't let him go.—Is that quite clear now? [Jetzt aber halte ich ihn und lasse ihn nicht mehr.—Ist nun alles erklärt?]." (168, 146)

In fact, hardly anything is "clear" if we actually delve into the peculiar inter-relations of crime, judgment, and punishment. If we recapitulate the "evidence" as presented by the officer, then it seems that the servant's sleeping and the resulting failure to salute is already punished through the received lashes—with Kafkaesque poignancy—"across the face." This "punishment" put forth by the captain clearly seems to be the captain's "right," or at least it finds no extra mention in the officer's exposition. The actual delict calling the death penalty down upon the servant lies in his juvenile vengeance: "Instead of getting up and begging pardon, the man caught hold of his master's legs, shook him, and cried: 'Throw that whip away or I'll eat you alive [Wirf die Peitsche weg, oder ich fresse dich].'" And it is only in response to the servant's retort that the captain makes a report (*Anzeige erstattet*) to the officer, who then, simultaneously acting as judge and prosecutor, writes down the "statement" (*Angaben*) "and append[s] the sentence to it right away [und anschließend gleich das Urteil]" (168, 146, translation modified).

What is the basis of this sentence? The officer offers a blunt answer to this question: "My guiding principle is this: Guilt is never to be doubted" (168, 145). The actual delict precisely does *not* lie in the breaching of this or that law, the breaking of this or that rule. The guilt (in the legal sense) lies in the Guilt (in the literal sense); that is, it lies not in "being guilty of having committed a crime," but rather in the sense of the Latin *in culpa esse*—as an a priori to-be-indebted-to, in this case, to the "state" (see 175, 151).[13] The condemned man by definition is always indebted to the state, yet this locks him in a relationship with the state where he must remain a culprit who can never acquit his debt himself. It is a guilt he can be released from

---

13. See Giorgio Agamben, *Homo Sacer: Sovereign Power and Bare Life* (Stanford, CA: Stanford University Press, 1998), 26f.

only in the moment of the execution, when his "illegal" claim (the claim to "individuality") simply evaporates. By executing him, the state in essence takes back a life that never was anyone's but the state's, a life with no legal claim to individuality. By executing the condemned man, the state reinserts the body of the prisoner into the political body of the *Volk* (cf. 163, 141f.; 194, 167). Since the state lent life without ever relinquishing control over it, by executing the prisoner it simply takes it back; and it is only then that, via transcendental reinsertion, the condemned man is relieved of his guilt.

It appears essential that the actual crime lies not in the infringement of a specific law but rather in the servant's "presumptuousness" of considering his body personal property rather than a possession of the state; the servant's "hubris" in decapsulating his body out of the state infrastructure—indeed, to posit his body *against* the political system—is a crime that calls for capital punishment. This crime of *separating* and *opposing* law and life amounts to an acute threat ("The man *caught hold of his master's legs*, shook him, and cried: 'Throw that whip away *or I'll eat you alive*'") and flips the established social order by menacing the state *existentially*. It is a danger emanating not primarily from the individual per se but rather in principle: the arrogation to *think* and to *act* as if the political individual had a right to a nonpolitical existence, a right to a personal body.[14]

The paradox we are facing here is the following. On the one hand, the offender seems largely deprived of an ethical understanding or a sense of justice that would qualify him as "human" (see 168, 146). The condemned man is characterized as naked (without cultural makeup), animalistic, insane, wild, and so forth; his is a body that, on top of everything else, is destroyed by a "Harrow" (*Egge*). The German word *Egge* etymologically denotes an agricultural implement used to break up clods, that is, biomaterial, and in the context of Kafka's "Penal Colony," human biomaterial. The word choice is certainly no arbitrary one: "'Yes, the Harrow,' said the officer, 'a good name for it [der Name passt]'" (164, 142).[15]

At the same time, however, an ethical dimension *does* seem immanent to the prisoner's body, immanent as potentiality, whose actualization is triggered in the very process of the execution, to then *take place:* "Now justice takes place [geschieht]" (178, 154). The body of the condemned man is, paradoxically, absorbed into the

---

14. In line with Carl Schmitt's theory of sovereignty, one perhaps could say that the crime of the servant lies in his disregard of the fact that "any decision about whether something is *unpolitical* is always a *political* decision" (Schmitt, *Political Theology,* 2, Schmitt's italics). At the same time, this Schmittian notion of "the political" as totality is undermined in Kafka's story: the old regime is in its demise, and the new Commandant's reformatory endeavors are not yet fully implemented. As a result, the executions now suffer poor attendance, much to the officer's regret ("In the old days...no high official dared to absent himself"; 178, 153f.).

15. It is not by chance that the officer later throws a "clod of earth" after the soldier, this threshold figure between human being and wild man, who by the end of the story will epitomize together with the freed prisoner another version of Kafka's "helpers" (*Gehilfen*), continuously "wrestling, half in jest" (190, 163).

socius through his execution; at the moment of the execution, the *human* quality of punishability is alleged and allows for the juridical-political treatment—the exclusion via juristically launched execution. In addition to the potentiality for justice (*dikē*), the nonhuman (in keeping with the Aristotelian double determination of human beings) also actualizes reason (*logos*) during his execution. While the officer's explications before the execution suggest that "the condemned man watched it too, but uncomprehendingly [aber ohne Verständnis]" (174, 150), during the execution, reason indeed does seem to come into being: "But how quiet he grows at just about the sixth hour! Reason comes to the most dull-witted [Verstand geht dem Blödesten auf]. It begins around the eyes" (173, 150, translation modified).[16] During the execution the presumably nonhuman entity seems to activate a potentiality for being human (through the receiving of reason, *logos,* and justice, *dikē*). In short, because the prisoner is excluded qua human being, he is included into human society.

It is this *double bind,* the deprivation of human beings to the degree of biomaterial vis-à-vis the maintaining of a person's juridical liability, that is at the center of Kafka's story. It is a paradox that also characterizes the peripheries of democratic societies in their treatment of prisoners, terrorist detainees,[17] and others, individuals who are excluded by states, excluded qua human beings, a dehumanization and desubjectization not by chance often accompanied by the deprivation of the personal name and the allocation of numeric designations.

The Power of Representation

A closer look at various linguistic discourses soon reveals how much *religious* overtones permeate the predominant *juridical* register in Kafka's narrative. In addition to the mysterious twelve-hour cycle dividing the execution procedure and inviting a number of biblical readings (cf. 178, 154),[18] an array of religious references and insinuations are apparent, ranging from the "old" (judicial/religious) law versus the "new" (judicial/religious) law to notions of "guilt," "redemption" (193), and the "scripture." In addition, the commander stands in as the "Creator" of the apparatus, while the officer serves as a kind of disciple—one who ultimately sacrifices

---

16. Richard Jayne deals with the "truth-constituting function of punishment through the infliction of pain and torture" in Kafka in the light of Friedrich Nietzsche's pertinent remarks in *On the Genealogy of Morals* and Michel Foucault's *Discipline and Punish* (Jayne, "Kafka's 'In der Strafkolonie' and the Aporias of Textual Interpretation," *Deutsche Vierteljahrsschrift für Literaturwissenschaft und Geistesgeschichte* 66.1 [1992]: 94–128, here esp. 94–101). The "body's material potential for pain, wounding, breakage, and amputation" is at the center of Malynne Sternstein's "Laughter, Gesture, and Flesh: Kafka's 'In the Penal Colony'," *Modernism/Modernity* 8.2 (2001): 315–23, here 320). Danielle Allen examines the typically underarticulated dimension of the acoustics of pain in "Sounding Silence," *Modernism/Modernity* 8.2 (2001): 325–34.

17. Cf. Judith Butler, "Indefinite Detention," in *Precarious Life* (London: Verso, 2004), 50–100, for a discussion of questions of desubjectivization and dehumanization at Guantanamo Bay.

18. Cf., for instance, Jean-François Lyotard, "Prescription," in *Lectures d'enfance* (Paris: Galilée, 1991), 59.

himself. Finally, the commander's "followers" are presented with the almost eschatological epitaph "Have faith and wait!"—possibly encapsulating hope for the commander's later rising (*Auferstehung*), and so forth (see 195, 167). The analogy between the juridical and the religious certainly does not occur coincidentally, and while, depending on one's orthodoxy as a reader and one's orthodoxy as a believer, different avenues for interpretation may or may not appear tantalizing, what remains, no doubt, is the suggested analogy between the *juridical* and the *religious*. It is an analogy Carl Schmitt, author of two books with the title *Political Theology*, found so apparent that in his analysis of the concept of sovereignty he writes:

> All significant concepts of the modern theory of the state are secularized theological concepts not only because of their historical development—in which they were transferred from theology to the theory of the state, whereby, for example, the omnipotent God became the omnipotent lawgiver—but also of their systematic structure.[19]

For an understanding of the relation between the *juridical* and the *religious* in Kafka's story, it appears vital to emphasize a third category—namely the *theatrical*. Notably, the actual execution in the colony is presented as a theatrical spectacle in "a deep hollow surrounded on all sides by naked crags" (161, 140):

> "How different an execution was in the old days! A whole day before the ceremony the valley was packed with people; they all came only to look on; early in the morning the Commandant appeared with his ladies; fanfares roused the whole camp; I reported that everything was in readiness; the assembled company—no high official dared to absent himself—arranged itself around the machine; this pile of cane chairs is a miserable survival from that epoch. The machine was freshly cleaned and glittering; I got new spare parts for almost every execution. Before hundreds of spectators—all of them standing on tiptoe as far as the heights there—the condemned man was laid under the Harrow by the Commandant himself. What is left today for a common soldier to do was then my task, the task of the presiding judge, and was an honor for me. And then the execution began! Many did not care to watch it but lay with closed eyes in the sand; they all knew: Now Justice takes place [Jetzt geschieht Gerechtigkeit]." (178, 153f., translation modified)

This *theatrum iustitiae* almost reads like a blueprint for Benjamin's contention that "virtue can be *demanded*, justice," however, "can ultimately only *be*,"[20] an insight that places "justice" outside the reach of human beings, outside the law. The officer, of course, knows of this interplay between virtue and justice: "Up till now

---

19. Schmitt, *Political Theology*, 36.
20. Walter Benjamin, "Notizen zu einer Arbeit über die Kategorie der Gerechtigkeit," *Frankfurter Adorno Blätter* 4 (1992): 41, my translation.

a few things still had to be set by hand, but from this moment it works all by itself" (162, 141). Yet what is really at the heart of this passage? How are we to understand the exposition by an officer who "know[s] more about the apparatus than anyone" and from whom we should hope to learn a lot (168, 145)?

The description of the amphitheatrical hollow in which the execution is to take place and the electrified atmosphere in the crowd underscores the blatant interplay between the *theatrical* and the *juridical*.[21] And as this theater of justice becomes a theater of cruelty, the symbiosis conjures ramifications significant in our context. It goes without saying that the juridical in its institutional manifestation typically generates a specific theatrical economy of actors, audience, costumes, dialogical forms (like cross-examination), monological forms (like opening statements), and so on; evidently the kinetics (i.e., the paralinguistic signifying dynamics) are ritualized and follow a protocol of standing and sitting, entering and leaving the courtroom, and so forth. There is, in short, an established dramatic modus operandi creating a sphere of its own, a sphere within, yet distinct from, the world outside.

Yet why is the juridical so intricately linked with the theatrical, and why does its legitimation appear so contingent on the theatrical? For a better understanding of the relation between the *juridical* and the *theatrical* in Kafka's story, we may—in line with the established analogy between the juridical and the religious—additionally consider the connection between the *religious* and the *theatrical*. What may appear confusing at this point amounts to a rather simple triangular relationship between the juridical and the religious and their point of convergence—namely the theatrical, or, more specifically, the power of (theatrical) *representation*. The relationship could be illustrated as shown in figure 1.

Clearly, the central role of theatrical elements in church resembles that in jurisdiction (and probably exceeds it with respect to its stylized proxemics: the implementation of songs, liturgical props, candlelight, incense, and so forth). What matters is that theatrical elements are constitutive to religious services and legal

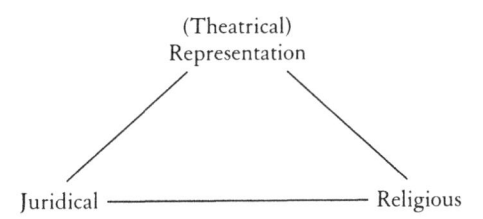

Figure 1.

---

21. For a detailed discussion of the "theatrical logic of the law" in Kafka, cf. Klaus Mladek, "Radical Play: Gesture, Performance, and the Theatrical Logic of the Law in Kafka," *Germanic Review* 78.3 (2003): 223–49.

proceedings alike; both the institution of law and that of the church employ a highly codified semiotic system of *representation,* not to be understood as a technical tool of deception, but rather as an ontological category, a category of being, of (Christ/justice) being present in being absent.[22] As represented in Kafka's "Penal Colony," the power of the law lies in the creation of a nexus between what is present (law) and what is absent yet there as an "occurrence" (justice). It is a strength situated less in presentation than in re-presentation, the re-presentation of justice[23]—justice that defies presentation but can nevertheless be apprehended as *being* ... absent. It can be apprehended because of the persuasive force of representation, bridging the epistemic gap between the present and the absent—a force that makes it ultimately unnecessary to *see* what is represented. "No discordant noise spoiled the working of the machine. Many did not care to watch it but lay with closed eyes in the sand; they all knew: Now Justice takes place [Jetzt geschieht Gerechtigkeit]" (178, 154, translation modified). In most courtroom dramas, the presence of an audience seems vital, not for passive spectatorship, but for semantic force and verifying power; and we can assume that the old Commandant in Kafka's "Penal Colony" had good reasons for having the execution carried out "before hundreds of spectators." "A whole day before the ceremony the valley was packed with people; they all came only to look on" (177f., 153). The Commandant "with his ladies," the children and the crowd—"all of them standing on tiptoe"—appear as an essential part of the juridical proceeding. "What is left today for a common soldier to do was then my task, the task of the presiding judge, and was an *honor* for me" (178, 154). The *legitimation* of the juridical apparatus in the colony appears contingent on its *public presence* as well as its *glorification,* since it is precisely the juridical *institutionalization* that seems to substantiate law's claim to justice.

An exceptional moment of such glorification can be witnessed in the officer's exposition of the guiding plans drawn by the old Commandant:

"I am still using the guiding plans drawn by the former Commandant. Here they are"—he extracted some sheets from the leather wallet—"but *I'm sorry I can't let you handle them, they are my most precious possessions.* Just take a seat and I'll hold them

---

22. In his 1923 essay, "Roman Catholicism and Political Form," published the year after his first *Political Theology* (1922), Carl Schmitt observes that the church "represents the *civitas humanas.* It presents [stellt ... dar] in every moment the historical connection to the incarnation and crucifixion of Christ. It represents the Person of Christ Himself: God become man in historical reality. Therein lies its superiority over an age of economic thinking" (trans. G. L. Ulmen [Westport, CT: Greenwood Press, 1996], 19, Schmitt's italics). While economic thinking, Schmitt contends, relies on a network of norms that stand for something else, the Catholic Church, by means of its "power of representation," develops a "specifically formal superiority," anchored in "concrete existence, full of life," and thus does not *stand for* but *is* Christ (19, 8, translation modified).

23. Justice defies presentation as much as God; "justice can ultimately only be, as a condition of the world, or as the condition of God," Benjamin writes in a posthumous fragment ("Notizen zu einer Arbeit über die Kategorie der Gerechtigkeit," 41, my translation).

in front of you like this [ich zeige sie Ihnen aus dieser Entfernung], then you'll be able to *see* everything quite well." He spread out [er zeigte] the first sheet of paper. The explorer would have liked to say something appreciative, but all he could *see* was *a labyrinth of lines crossing and recrossing each other,* which covered the paper so thickly that it was difficult to discern the blank spaces between them [daß man nur mit Mühe...erkannte]. "Read it," said the officer. "I can't," said the explorer. "Yet it's clear enough," said the officer. "It's very ingenious," said the explorer evasively, "but I can't make it out." "Yes," said the officer with a laugh, putting the paper away again, "it's no calligraphy for school children." (171f., 148)

The passage stages an oscillation between the act of *showing* and the act of (attempted) *seeing*. The officer exalts the sheets, praising them as his "most precious" possession, and this preciousness clearly enhances their representative valence, yet he does not allow the explorer to take a closer look, because the explorer perhaps would scrutinize them as the "researcher" (*Forscher,* 158, 184, translation modified) he is. The explorer compliments the sheets as "ingenious," yet they remain enigmatic and indiscernible. Holding the drawings before the explorer with due ostentatious ambiguity, the officer does not forget to say: "Yes,... it needs to be studied closely. I'm quite sure that in the end you would understand it too." Though promising meaning, he immediately, subjunctively, defers the possibility of recognition. He does not say "will" (*werden*) but "would" (*würden*) and adds "in the end" (*gewiss*) to keep the discouraged seeking for what cannot be "found."

This power of representation provides the entire basis for the officer's hopes, claims, expectations, and hallucinations, according to which the traveler will finally come to a positive opinion of the execution procedure:

"*Just watch it!*" He ran up the ladder, turned a wheel, called down: "*Look out,* keep to one side!" and everything started working. If the wheel had not creaked, it would have been marvelous. The officer, as if surprised by the noise of the wheel, shook his fist at it, then spread out his arms in excuse to the explorer, and climbed down rapidly to peer at the working of the machine from below. Something perceptible to no one save himself was still not in order; he clambered up again, did something with both hands in the interior of the Designer, then slid down one of the rods, instead of using the ladder, so as to get down quicker, and with the full force of his lungs, to make himself heard at all in the noise, yelled in the explorer's ear: "Can you follow it?" (170, 149)

Once again the officer relies on an abundance of theatrical stimuli, thereby attempting an implementation of the juridical as a means of re-presenting what defies recognition. Yet what can be achieved through the effect of this odd mélange of clownery, slapstick, "excusing" gestures reminiscent of early twentieth-century silent film, and so forth? Those residues of juridical "representation" appear to succumb to grotesqueness. The officer does and does not admit it to himself: the phrase "The officer, *as if* surprised by the noise of the wheel" suggests that unconsciously he probably suspects the penal colony's demise, for he cannot ignore the "creaking" wheel, the fading power of representation, the diminishing legitimation of the juridical apparatus. Yet he cannot avow such a decline either, not to himself and not to the explorer. And whatever the presentiments, he fortifies his insistence in addressing the explorer: "Just *watch* it! [Sehen Sie doch!]...Can you follow it? [Begreifen Sie den Vorgang?]." The officer insinuates a transition from the *sensory* to the *cognitive level*—a transition encumbered precisely by the apparatus's lack of representative strength; what the performance does *not* achieve is precisely a fusion, an ontological shaping, an *identity* of jurisdiction.

We said that the status of the theatrical, of theatrical representation, lies in making the absent present by *staging* its absence. Law acts in the name of justice, yet justice defies its instrumentalization—thus the irreconcilability of law and justice, and thus the need for a power to bridge the hiatus between representation (juridical performance) and represented ("justice"); and since the notion of "justice" in the penal colony is particularly perverted, its proprietor—the old Commandant—wisely put a particular emphasis on the enactment of the execution.

Yet in contrast to the crowds of spectators once witnessing the spectacle of the execution and the "occurrence" of justice, the explorer refuses his complicity. Why so? Why does the representative power of the juridical procedure, once banning the crowd, now fail before the eyes of the explorer? That the juridical procedure seems to have forfeited its *credibility* (*Glaubwürdigkeit*), its *authenticity,* certainly has a number of causes. First of all, the old Commandant, being the apparatus's creator, who, by means of his power of decision, previously ensured the apparatus's claim to "justice," is dead. Further, the apparatus's institutional integrity seems undermined by the new Commandant's antagonistic reformatory endeavors. The people, at least outwardly, have lost faith in the old system, thereby robbing the penal proceeding of one of its most central configuratory constituents: its public participation (see 177, 153). Finally, the machine has begun to show significant signs of wear: its straps are broken, and its canes are worn. The officer laments the disgusting felt gag "which more than a hundred men have...slobbered and gnawed in their dying moments" (176, 152). The "acid fluid" used in the machine has been prohibited, and without it "the machine can no longer wring from anyone a sigh louder than the felt gag can stifle" (178, 154). In short, its deteriorating state deprives the apparatus of its power to represent and consequently its legitimating foundation, also in the eyes of the explorer. Moreover, the explorer describes himself as a "stranger" (*Fremder*)—that is, someone unfamiliar with the apparatus's ethical idiosyncrasy. Yet what precisely is it that the explorer condemns, what is the apparatus's *force,* and what is the nature of its law enforcement? What is the kernel of its "peculiarity" that its "inadequate" act of representation fails to concretize?

The Force of Law

While law's power of representation is directed at the nonpresent, its force (*Geltung*) and its enforceability rely on its access to the body. The force of law constitutes a moment of violence, leaving law and justice irreconcilable; it is the very violence that requires the law's legitimation via representation in the first place. Law "needs" the body,[24] for only on naked flesh can it inscribe itself. Correspondingly, in systems like the one in Kafka's penal colony, the body gives validity to the law by allowing the law to punish the body. "I do not approve of your procedure," the explorer says; he even offers an "explanation"—without ultimately "explaining" anything (185, 159, translation modified), perhaps because he knows that the juridical procedure is as immune to his critique as it is immune to the remarks of the new Commandant's "ladies": "'In our country we have a different criminal procedure,' or 'In our country the prisoner is interrogated before he is sentenced,'... or 'We haven't used torture since the Middle Ages'" (180, 155f., translation modified). "All these statements," the officer says, "are as true as they seem natural to you, harmless remarks that pass no judgment on my methods." They are "statements" attesting to a hypothetical "core" of the procedure—statements trying to challenge the inadequate means employed by the old law to ensure its force (*Geltung*). The "ladies'" progressivism, however, does not allow them to grasp the officer's ideas, because from his perspective the legitimacy of law cannot be deduced from a rationalistic assessment of its "recognized" "brutality"; rather, it must be deduced from its phenomenological effect exclusively. The question is one rooted in its representativeness, its power of persuasion: "'So you did not find the procedure *convincing* [Das Verfahren hat Sie also nicht *überzeugt*],' he said to himself and smiled" (186, 160).

Once more we shall ask: What is the logic of the old system? How, concretely, does its law acquire *force* (*Geltung*), the force of law?

> "As soon as the man is strapped down, the Bed is set in motion. It quivers in minute, very rapid vibrations, both from side to side and up and down. You will have seen similar apparatuses in hospitals [Heilanstalten]; but in our Bed the movements are all precisely calculated; you see, they have to correspond very exactly to the movements of the Harrow. And the Harrow is the instrument for the actual execution of the sentence [Dieser Egge aber ist die eigentliche Ausführung des Urteils überlassen]." (165f., 144)

What does it mean that "der Egge ist die... Ausführung des Urteils überlassen"? In the first place it means, as the translation indicates, that the Harrow carries out the execution by inflicting injuries on the condemned man's body. Yet the German idiom

---

24. For a discussion of "law's desire to have a body," see also Agamben, *Homo Sacer,* 124. On the portrayal of the law in Kafka with regard to the complexities and shortcomings of Agamben's reading of Kafka, see Susanne Lüdemann, "'Geltung ohne Bedeutung': Zur Architektonik des Gesetzes bei Franz Kafka und Giorgio Agamben," *Zeitschrift für deutsche Philologie* 124.4 (2005): 499–519.

jemandem etwas überlassen conveys a certain ambiguity because it can also mean "to leave something up to someone"; in this sense, the execution of the sentence is left to the discretion of the Harrow. Not only does the Harrow carry out the judgment, but given that human qualities appear to be attributed to it, it may in fact have a certain agency in this process of execution (i.e., "The carrying out of the execution is left up to the Harrow"). The Harrow appropriates a certain autonomous quality by being put in position to decide how exactly the sentence is to be carried out.

Yet doesn't this contradict the officer's assertion that the inscriptions are prescribed by the old Commandant's sketches? And, after all, isn't "guilt...never to be doubted"? "We should not be deceived by all the Constitutions framed throughout the world..., the Codes written and revised, a whole continual and clamorous legislative activity: these were the forms that made an essentially normalizing power acceptable," Foucault writes in *The History of Sexuality*.[25] The Harrow's partial autonomy to decide on the prisoner's fate is juxtaposed with total predetermination—a predetermination that, at the moment of inscription, manifests itself by turning life into a political matrix. "Dieser Egge aber ist die eigentliche Ausführung des Urteils überlassen" means, after all, no more than that whatever the political inscription of life, whatever its "specificity" is or may turn out to be, never will it transgress the referential framework of the extraordinary state in which everyone's guilt is a priori.[26] Every inscription is preceded by a prescription—a prescription not only in the primary *temporal* sense of the word, but also in its *normative,* normalizing sense. The inscription makes a promise that evaporates with the Harrow's first prick, a promise of an individualized inscription, a promise that succumbs, however, to the vehemence of the preestablished sentence of the politicization of life, tantamount to the individual's death.[27]

The Birth of the Nation, or the "Wisdom" of the Commandant

The condemned man's execution figuratively stages the birth of a human being (see 173, 150); his inclusion into human society via inscription reenacts the process

---

25. Foucault, *History of Sexuality*, 1:144.

26. That the traveler does not lend himself to the officer's propaganda, that the officer's rhetoric leaves no *im-pression* (*Ein-druck*) sympathetic to the old system, results precisely from his already-being-inscribed—seemingly by a more democratic texture—and his not-being-naked-anymore: "The officer kept watching the explorer sideways, as if seeking to read from his face the impression [Ein-druck] made on him by the execution, which had been at least cursorily [oberflächlich] explained to him" (174, 151).

27. Stanley Corngold, in his nuanced chapter on "In the Penal Colony" in *The Necessity of Form* (Ithaca, NY: Cornell University Press, 1988, 228–49), discusses the motif of "inscription" as a reflection on the "rigors of writing." Beate Müller reads the story as a problematization of "censorship": "In the process of his execution, the offender is supposed to decipher the inscription the machine administers to his body.... Taking the narrated world of the island colony as a frame of reference, the figures embody the narrative functions of author, fictional character and reader, engaged in creation and reception. But ultimately, the literary text acts as censor: It does not yield to the reader's knocking on the gate" ("Die grausame Schrift: Zur Ästhetik der Zensur in Kafkas 'Strafkolonie,'" *Neophilologus* 84 [2000]: 107–25, here 107).

of the politicization of a child. The prisoner lies on the Bed under the Harrow where he is born into the political realm—an experience of birth, the experience of a "naked" being, someone not yet inscribed. The juridical apparatus inscribes the naked flesh of the delinquent, because it considers it as much a threat as every child is considered a threat—a threat in the sense of what Jean-François Lyotard calls "l'innocence criminelle du corps."[28] The naked body of the child is dangerous because of its existence outside of the law; the child epitomizes a blank space, an interruption within the communicative texture of the state. In the perspective of the state, the naked flesh feigns innocence and pretends to an innocuous, apolitical existence that officially does not exist and must not exist, a state of existence only the state can adjudicate upon by virtue of its "sovereignty"[29]—in itself again an act of politicization. The state deems the event of birth, which, as Heidegger says, "throws" us into the world, disconcerting precisely for what Arendt (in the context of twentieth-century totalitarian politics) calls "natality": "The beginning of a being that itself has the ability to begin: it is the beginning of a beginning, the beginning of beginning itself."[30] The event of birth, an event of novelty and unprecedented potentiality for the new, challenges the system of the old Commandant. In fact, it potentially threatens to subvert the thanatopolitical regime in Kafka's "Penal Colony." The strength of the old regime then lies in its capacity to obliterate the "infinitely improbable" promised by each birth, and to transform the naked body into a political body, a body of the nation. (Notably, the word *nation* is an etymological derivative of the word *nascere,* "to be born.") Thanks to the "wisdom" of the old Commandant, the children can watch the execution procedure from nearby, witnessing the prisoner's inscription that enacts their own inscription:

"It was impossible to grant all the requests to be allowed to watch it from nearby. The Commandant in his wisdom ordained that the children should have the preference; I, of course, because of my office had the privilege of always being at hand; often enough I would be squatting there with a small child in either arm." (178, 154)

The Commandant is a "wise" man, for he knows that the political upbringing of the children and adolescents amounts to a new generation of biomaterial, the essential resource and existential guaranty of his government. The wisdom of the Commandant lies, in the words of Foucault, in the implementation of the power

---

28. Lyotard, "Prescription," 44.
29. For an analysis of Kafka's story in its relation to the peculiar efficacy of "sovereignty," see Andreas Gailus, "Lessons of the Cryptograph: Revelation and the Mechanical in Kafka's 'In the Penal Colony,'" *Modernism/Modernity* 8.2 (2001): 295–302.
30. Hannah Arendt, *The Origins of Totalitarianism* (Cleveland: Meridian, 1958), 166, after Werner Hamacher, "The Rights to Have Rights (Four-and-a-Half-Remarks)," *South Atlantic Quarterly* 103.2/3 (Spring/Summer 2004): 356.

76   *Inconceivable Effects*

"to 'make' live and 'let' die."³¹ It is the power allowing for the growth of an entire population—a population soon to be inscribed, politicized, and judiciously registered. It is the power of inserting the human being, from the moment of birth, into the body of the nation. And it is not by chance, then, that the question of nationality and citizenship plays an important role in Kafka's story:

> The explorer thought to himself: It's always a ticklish matter to intervene decisively in other people's affairs. He was neither a citizen [Bürger] of the penal colony nor a citizen [Bürger] of the state to which it belonged. Were he to denounce this execution or actually try to stop it, they could say to him: You are a foreigner [Fremder], mind your own business.... Yet here he found himself strongly tempted. The injustice of the procedure and the inhumanity of the execution were undeniable. No one could suppose that he had any selfish interest in the matter, for the condemned man was a complete stranger [war ihm fremd], not a fellow countryman or even at all sympathetic to him [kein Landsmann und ein zum Mitleid gar nicht auffordernder Mensch]. (175, 151f.)

Evidently this passage touches on questions regarding the notion of citizenship. The officer is a "citizen [Bürger] of the state to which [the colony] belonged," a state which he refers to as his "home" (*Heimat*, 162, 141).³² Also the explorer is identifiable as a citizen, for "the condemned man was a complete stranger [war ihm fremd], not a fellow countryman [kein Landsmann]"; the explorer is a citizen in an Occidental country (*Abendlandes*, 181). Yet what juridical status has the condemned man? He does not appear to be a citizen, he seems deprived of any civil rights, he has no right to rights and is juridically naked.³³ The question of human rights (that is, rights that technically precede the rights of state citizens) is one addressed in Kafka's story:

---

31. Michel Foucault, *Society Must Be Defended: Lectures at the Collège de France* (New York: Picador, 2003), 241.

32. Claudia Albert and Andreas Disselnkötter explore the colonial dimension of Kafka's story in terms of its invocation of cross-cultural practices (Albert and Disselnkötter, "'Inmitten der Strafkolonie steht keine Schreibmaschine': Eine Re-Lektüre von Kafkas Erzählung," *Internationales Archiv für Sozialgeschichte der deutschen Literatur* 27.2 [2002]: 168–84). Danilyn Rutherford tackles the question of colonialism from an anthropologically informed perspective and focuses on "the alterity of power" and the space for subversion it may open (Rutherford, "The Foreignness of Power: Alterity and Subversion in Kafka's 'In the Penal Colony' and Beyond," *Modernism/Modernity* 8.2 [2001]: 303–13, here 312).

33. With respect to the prisoner's exclusion from human society, it seems interesting that even the explorer "was...not...at all sympathetic [Mitleid] to him" (175, 151f.). "Commiseration," *Mitleid*, is not an emotion that can be shared between human beings and animals; commiseration is possible only if the one who is commiserated with (*der Bemitleidete*) himself can feel commiseration (*Leid mit-empfinden*)—a quality the prisoner lacks, whose characterization better fits that of an animal than of a human being, and who consequently "does not call commiseration upon himself" (ein...zum Mitleid gar nicht auffordernder Mensch). A "human being not calling commiseration upon himself" is a nonhuman, whose human insufficiency lies in the absence of an ethical potentiality, the potentiality for an understanding of justice.

"'A famous Western investigator [Ein großer Forscher des Abendlandes], sent out to study criminal procedure *in all the countries of the world,* has just said that our old tradition of administering justice is *inhumane* [*unmenschliches*].'... You may want to interpose that you never said any such thing, that you never called my methods *inhumane* [*unmenschlich*], on the contrary your profound experience leads you to believe they are *most humane and most in consonance with human dignity* [*das menschlichste und menschenwürdigste*]." (181)

Presumably the existence of human rights, rights that are prior to the rights of citizens of nation-states—"in all...countries of the world"—would save the prisoner. His privation will be inflicted on European Jewry barely three decades after Kafka writes this story. The prisoner is no citizen, and as such, without a pre-right to citizen rights, he epitomizes the extreme of political existence in the penal colony. The officer also is politically encoded, yet his status differs in degree. If one wanted to schematize the political sectors in Kafka's story, the echelons could be represented as shown in figure 2 (moving from the inside to the outside).

The extreme of the penal colony's political system is situated "*in* the penal colony" (1) (and the preposition in the story's title makes all the difference here): the juridical logic appears to be a situational one, where "extra-ordinary measures" ensure order (169, 146). The penal colony itself (2) presents a military regime, in which a "great change" is about to come into being for the sake of another, still military ("the new Commandant") yet more moderate, order. Moreover, citizen

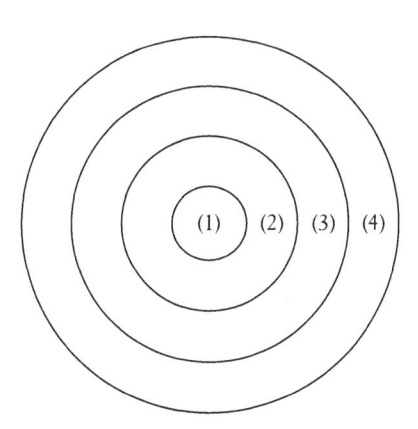

(1) "*in* the penal colony"—condemned man
(2) "citizen of the penal colony"—officer
(3) "citizen of the state to which it belonged"—officer's "home" (*Heimat*)
(4) "Occident"—"stranger"/"foreigner" (*Fremder*)—explorer

Figure 2.

rights exist. We learn little about the state to which the penal colony belongs (3), except perhaps its spoken language—French. The explorer, coming from the outside (4), "from far away" (*aus der Fremde*), is "neither a citizen [Bürger] of the penal colony nor a citizen [Bürger] of the state to which it belonged." In addition, he, in contrast to the officer, does not wear a uniform, and he appears to come from a "modern" time: "I am an opponent of this procedure" (*Ich bin ein Gegner dieses Verfahrens,* 185, 159, translation modified). If we limit the geopolitical radius to that of the penal colony[34]—whose one extreme is that of the peculiar extraordinary state within, and whose other extreme is a state with civil rights, rights of citizens (*Bürgerrechte*)—what can be said about the topographical gradation of the different sectors? What is the relation between the extremes, between inside and outside, and between outside and inside? In a diary entry of October 8, 1911, Kafka writes:

> Would like to know Yiddish literature, which is obviously characterized by an uninterrupted tradition of national struggle that determines every work. A tradition, therefore, that pervades no other literature, not even that of the most oppressed people. It may be that other peoples in times of war make a success out of a pugnacious national literature, and that other works, standing at a greater remove, acquire from the enthusiasm of the audience a national character too.[35]

What manifests itself in this entry appears to be an understanding according to which the marginal may at times precipitate a more forceful dynamic than does the center of a system. It is an insight Joseph K., the protagonist of Kafka's novel *The Trial,* appears to heed in orchestrating his trial from the suburbs of the city and from law offices in remote attics—that is, the horizontal and the vertical extremes. It is an epistemological insight that equally pertains to Kafka's "Penal Colony"—an insight according to which history presents itself from the perspective of its extremes rather than from political middle ground. The secluded space "*in* the penal colony," the prisoner exposed in it—all this is not merely exception, but exception determining as well as characterizing the rule. We know more about "the state to which it belonged" than Kafka explicitly states. We know in particular what happens to those deprived of the rights of citizens (of the colony as much as of the state to which it belongs), those excluded from the socius. And we know of the unremitting reproduction of this condition, of children being inscribed with a political status in the act of seeing: "Often enough I would be squatting there with a small child in either arm. How we all absorbed the look of transfiguration on the face of

---

34. For documentation of the geopolitical-historical context of Kafka's story, cf. Walter Müller-Seidel, *Die Deportation des Menschen: Kafkas Erzählung "In der Strafkolonie" im europäischen Kontext* (Stuttgart: Metzler Verlag, 1986).
35. Franz Kafka, *The Diaries of Franz Kafka, 1910–1913,* ed. Max Brod, trans. Joseph Kresh (New York: Schocken Books, 1965), 87.

the sufferer, how we bathed our cheeks in the radiance of that justice, achieved at last and fading so quickly!" (178, 154).

Postscript: "Have faith and wait!"

After the officer's execution the explorer glances at the face of the corpse:

> It was as it had been in life; no sign was visible of the promised redemption; what the others had found in the machine the officer had not found; the lips were firmly pressed together, the eyes were open, with the same expression as in life, the look calm and convinced, through the forehead went the point of the great iron spike. (193, 166)

The officer finds no redemption; his eyes remain open, like those of a living person; the legal system embodied by the officer continues to maintain its force. This latent power, its perennial force (*Geltung*), is one Kafka rhetorically enacts with three asterisks—no closure but a rupture, no end but deferral, a suspension.

The persistent power characterizing the peculiar situation in the penal colony—that state within which the law withdraws all the while maintaining its presence, an omnipresence precisely due to its withdrawal—finds an enactment in the eerie atmosphere of the "teahouse," where the old Commandant, the physical body of the deceased ruler, lies buried:[36]

> As the explorer, with the soldier and the condemned man behind him, reached the first houses of the colony, the soldier pointed to one of them and said: "There is the teahouse." In the ground floor of the house was a deep, low, cavernous space, its walls and ceiling blackened with smoke. It was open to the road all along its length. Although this teahouse was very little different from the other houses of the colony, which were all very dilapidated, even up to the Commandant's palatial headquarters, it made on the explorer the impression of a historic tradition of some kind, and he felt the power of past days. (193f., 166)

The explorer *feels* the power of past days, a power that is past yet still sensible and as such present. Together with the old Commandant, the law retreats while relentlessly sustaining its force: the "people" (*Volk,* 194, 167, translation modified) sit around the grave, the *Volk* whose etymology can be traced back to the Germanic word *fulka,* "das Kriegsvolk" (the war-waging people). The correspondence between the old Commandant and the political body of the people (*Volkskörper*) does not seem interrupted as a result of the old Commandant's death:

---

[36]. Cf. also Ernst Kantorowicz, *The King's Two Bodies: A Study in Mediaeval Political Theology* (Princeton, NJ: Princeton University Press, 1997).

"Where is the grave?" asked the explorer.... They pushed one of the tables aside, and under it there was really a gravestone. It was a simple stone, low enough to be covered by a table. There was an inscription on it in very small letters.... "Here rests the old Commandant. His adherents, who now must be nameless, have dug this grave and set up this stone. There is a prophecy that after a certain number of years [nach einer bestimmten Anzahl von Jahren] the Commandant will rise again [auferstehen] and lead his adherents from this house to recover the colony. Have faith and wait! [Glaubet und wartet!]." (194, 166f.)

The officer's demise, at least at first glance, does not seem to make a difference at all; the soldier does not even consider it a message worth being reported: the socius generates its force no longer from concrete incidences of conviction and execution, but from its inherent void, a void drawing "dock laborers," "poor, humble creatures," the population, into its ban, leaving them in a deactivated state of drinking "tea." To be sure, these secluded, destitute men are "adherents," *Anhänger,* "onhangers," hanging on to the old order, segregated within the Commandant's ban,[37] condemned to remain in a static state of believing and waiting (*Glauben und Warten*).

It is impossible to say how long the old Commandant's adherents will wait, how long they will still remain subordinate to his omnipresent power. The latent power of the old Commandant, the faith in his resurrection (*auferstehen*) "after a determined number of years" is very indeterminate, for the *act* thus far having constituted the *potency* of the colony (namely the execution of prisoners) will, due to the officer's death, not take place anymore. The particular political situation in the penal colony gained its entire power from the act of execution, an act now abolished, perhaps bequeathing the prophecy of the "recovery of the colony" (*Wiedereroberung der Kolonie*) to obliteration and foreclosing the actualization of all potency. The execution of prisoners was, one may say, the old system's last hope—in spite of the difficult conditions, the constant shortages of material, the lack of public participation, and so forth. Without the executions, we may have to read the epitaph "Have faith and wait!" (Glaubet und wartet!) somewhat differently: as believing (*Glauben*) and waiting not only for the actualization of the prophecy (i.e., the resurrection [*Auferstehung*] of the old Commandant), but also for the fading of their own belief (*Glauben*), the belief in their own waiting (*Warten*).

* * *

Yet perhaps the adherents latently know and always knew of this fate and thus have been reading the "Glaubet und wartet!" in this sense for a long time already: as waiting for the end of their own belief, an *act,* once again, reinvigorating the potency—an act of believing, once again constituting the socius anew.

---

37. Cf. also Jean-Luc Nancy, *L'impérative catégorique* (Paris: Flammarion, 1983); Nancy, "Abandoned Being," in *The Birth to Presence,* trans. Brian Holmes (Stanford, CA: Stanford University Press, 1993).

4

A Strike of Rhetoric

Benjamin's Paradox of Justice

> Nothing is understood about this man until it has been perceived that of necessity and without exception, everything—language and fact—falls for him within the sphere of justice.... For him, too, justice and language remain founded in each other.
>
> —Walter Benjamin, "Karl Kraus"

Before beginning, a few prefatory remarks appear necessary to maintain at least the hope for what Benjamin would have condemned: communication. Call it an act of violence, an act of communicative violence, if you will. But is not all language, that is, "impure" language, all language after the Fall, as Benjamin would say, violent? And does he himself not battle and ultimately fail in the face of language: fail either by instrumentalizing it as a tool for communication, or fail in failing to communicate, fail as a communicator, so to speak?

Given this aporetic situation that guarantees failure no matter what, we shall—violently—assure ourselves of some fundamental assumptions recurring in what is to come. In his 1921 essay "Toward a Critique of Violence" Benjamin is concerned with law, law's denial of its inherent violence (*Gewalt*). He is concerned, more concretely, with the nature of juridical force (*Gewalt*) and what he calls its law-positing and law-preserving character. All law is characteristic in that it violently establishes boundaries, divides, discriminates between "legal" and "illegal," so as to then coercively—if not violently—maintain these divisive moments of lawmaking. That is to say, law assumes its authority very much as a result of an ever-present latent threat, the threat of physical violence, directed against the people, the citizens. Why is this so remarkable? Because law is supposed to attain justice. Yet given law's coercive or latently violent nature, justice and law appear to be irreconcilable—exactly contrary to the way in which democracy, democratic jurisprudence, usually understands itself.

At first, it seems as if there will probably never be an alternative to the particular nature of legal violence. But then, in the last third of his essay, Benjamin actually offers an alternative, an-*other*, form of violence: divine violence. While he links positive law with mythic violence, which posits and preserves itself, posits and insists on this initial moment of instituting, institutionalization, divine violence is different in that it also posits itself but then immediately withdraws; it posits and does not insist, does not adhere to any ends, does not institutionalize itself; it posits and withdraws. This divine or—if enacted in the human sphere—"pure" violence is a nonviolent violence, a violence that posits itself without insisting on its moment of foundation.

My interest in Benjamin's essay begins precisely at the point where questions arise that he does not posit explicitly, questions, however, that his essay indeed raises, questions like, If law is characteristic in positing and preserving itself violently, and if one were to translate Benjamin's narrative act into the language of speech-act theory, is not any text, including his critique of violence, similarly characterized by constant moments of constative language, moments positing and preserving narrative violence? And if this is so, if a speech act is characteristic for its continuous violent moments of narrative positing and preserving, is there perhaps an alternative to this, an alternative like that of divine violence to mythic violence, an alternative violence that does not posit and preserve but one somehow in line with pure means, pure in that its means adhere to no ends but rather posit and immediately withdraw? Is not this, after all, where the peculiar narrative form of Benjamin's essay, the series of flagrant contradictions, comes into play? The essay is remarkable in that Benjamin constantly sets up binaries such as those between positing and preserving violence, natural and positive law, means and ends, mythic and divine violence, Niobe and Korah, and so forth. Benjamin posits these and other dichotomies, yet soon after their setting up they get drawn into contradictions, paradoxes, and tensions and ultimately collapse. He posits but then does not appear to insist on this once-instituted moment of narrative violence, performs no institutionalization; what is insisted on is narrative means without narrative ends, a speech act that does not adhere to its ends, a speech act of pure means, very much in line with what in the long 1916 essay on language Benjamin calls pure language, which in the critique of violence he also discusses as a form of pure means. Finally, if the divine or pure violence Benjamin talks about constitutes a form of justice, a contention invoked throughout the essay, does the narrative spectacle staged in "Toward a Critique of Violence" bring about or stage something we are inclined to call narrative justice?

* * *

Given these prolegomena, two questions will motivate the remaining discussion: What does Benjamin do? And what does he say?

> The task of a critique of violence can be circumscribed as that of expounding its relation to law and justice. For a cause, however effective, becomes violent, in the precise sense of the word, only when it enters into moral relations [sittliche Verhältnisse]. The sphere of these relations is defined by the concepts of law and justice. ("Toward a Critique of Violence," 179)[1]

It is from these sentences that "Toward a Critique of Violence" departs. Generally, they address the relationship between violence, on the one hand, and law and justice, on the other. Yet since, "in the precise sense of the word," a cause "becomes violent" only when it enters into moral relations (that is, the sphere defined by the concepts of law and justice), the juxtaposition of violence, on the one hand, and law and justice, on the other, is not really what is at issue here. Violence, rather, is something to be sought and scrutinized *within* the sphere of moral relations, "defined by the concepts of law and justice." What matters, hence, is the relation between law and justice. Finally, "the task of the critique of violence" also entails the "presentation" (*Darstellung*, 179) of this relation, raising the question of the critique's presentability or unpresentability.[2]

Immediately following his initial elliptical sentences, Benjamin introduces a couple of categories, which are difficult to grasp in their entirety here (cf. 179).[3] Notably, Benjamin, as if commenting on his observations, adds a sentence that could almost be read as a warning: "These observations provide a critique of violence with premises that are *more complex and more intricate than they may perhaps appear*" (179). If we want to apprehend what is "more complex and more intricate," we may need to pay attention to Benjamin's utterances, to what is *happening* in his narrative act. The questions, again and again, will be the following: What is the story Benjamin tells? Is it the entire story? Or is there perhaps another component, another story of narrative action rather than simple truths—one that, though

---

1. In general, in this chapter and the next, quotations from Benjamin refer to Walter Benjamin, *Gesammelte Schriften,* ed. Rolf Tiedemann and Hermann Schweppenhäuser, vol. 2.1 (Frankfurt a.M.: Suhrkamp, 1977). As a rule, all translations are my own. Whenever possible, I have consulted the translations in Walter Benjamin, *Selected Writings,* ed. Michael W. Jennings, 4 vols. (Cambridge, MA: Harvard University Press, Belknap Press, 1996–2003). Unless otherwise noted, all italics are mine.

2. "Die Aufgabe einer Kritik der Gewalt läßt sich als die *Darstellung* ihres Verhältnisses zu Recht und Gerechtigkeit umschreiben."

3. 1. "With regard to [law], it is clear that the most elementary relationship within any legal system is that of ends to means."
   2. "Violence can first be sought only in the realm of means, not in the realm of ends." (179)

inseparably linked, may question and at times even belie Benjamin's explicit statements? What are the rhetorical dynamics within which "Toward a Critique of Violence" operates? What is the economy of Benjamin's performative speech act?

The relation between law and justice lies at the center of "Critique." As discussed earlier, law is the means to the end of "justice," and because of its discriminating character, it is always violent. The decisive question, then, is this: Can we think of justice only as a result of violence, or are there perhaps means different from the violent means of law, means that are "pure," and as such much more related to the idea of justice? "To decide this question [zu ihrer Entscheidung] a more exact criterion is needed, which would discriminate [Unterscheidung] within the sphere of means themselves, without regard for the ends they serve" (179). This strategic mode of discrimination (*Unterscheidung*) and decision (*Entscheidung*) seems predetermined by the method of "Critique," in German "Kritik," from the Greek κρίνειν *(krinein),* meaning "to separate, decide." Toward the end of the essay, Benjamin, in fact, speaks of his "critical, discriminating, and decisive" (*kritische, scheidende und entscheidende*) approach (202). As we shall see, there is a curious tension between Benjamin's assertion that law is violent in respect to its discriminating character, and his own rhetorical moves in "Critique"—moves of discrimination, separation, differentiation, moves to establish frontiers, divide, in short, a dynamic of exclusion and inclusion, as the ubiquitous use of the word *Ausschaltung* ("exclusion"; e.g., 180, 181, 196) suggests. An understanding of Benjamin's notoriously difficult essay requires an understanding of these rhetorical moves. Thus, in line with Benjamin's "critical" (i.e., discriminating and decisive) approach, we shall ask: What is it that shifts (*schaltet*)? What is the out-side, what the in-side, of the excluded? What is the relation between the inside and the outside? And perhaps most interestingly, *Quo iudice?* That is, who is to decide, and who is to judge?

Part One: A Dogma of Violence (within the Circle)

Antigone

The fundamental question, in Benjamin's words, is "whether violence, as a principle, could be a moral means...to just ends" (179). Can one call the judicial *enforcement* of human rights, for instance, moral? This is one of the most precarious issues the essay raises, for both the early twentieth century and today. It is a question to which Benjamin's answer would without a doubt be no. But are human rights not just? What is a just law? Is it an aporia? Is it what in colloquial language one would call "a myth"? "Is there anyone," Jacques Lacan asks, "who doesn't evoke *Antigone* whenever there is a question of a law that causes conflict in us even though it is acknowledged by the community to be a just law?"[4] What can *Antigone,* in anticipation of Benjamin, tell us about the paradoxical notion of just laws?

---

4. Jacques Lacan, *The Ethics of Psychoanalysis,* trans. Dennis Porter (New York: Norton, 1992), 243.

Antigone defies the decree of her uncle, King Creon, by burying the corpse of her brother Polyneices.[5]

ANTIGONE: Will you take up that corpse along with me?
ISMENE: To bury him you mean, when it's forbidden?
ANTIGONE: My brother, and yours...
I never shall be found to be his traitor. (Sophocles, *Antigone* 44–46; 98–99)[6]

Antigone invokes the rights of blood lineage (*genos*) and, citing the gods of Hades, acts in allegiance to her brother Polyneices by enacting his burial rites. This insistence on family kinship stands in contrast to Creon's laws (*nomoi*), which, on the one hand, guarantee the city's greatness, yet, on the other, require civic obedience and alliance. Creon (who by name is a "ruler") presents his edict as essential to the manifestation of security in the state. In his view Polyneices is a traitor who attacked the city of Thebes and thus forfeited the honors of a ceremonial burial.

> Remember this:
>> Our country is our safety.
>> Only while she voyages true on course
>> Can we establish friendships, truer than blood itself. Such are my laws [nomoisi].
>> They make our city great. (184–91)

Creon and Antigone follow antagonistic notions of law, an antagonism that initially seems to present a conflict between natural and positive law.[7] The natural law Antigone cites with reference to the nether gods is frequently associated with justice (*dikē*) and stated in contradistinction to the positive law of the state (*nomos*) enforced by Creon. As we will see, the paradox of just laws is one ultimately rooted in

---

5. Antigone's name etymologically denotes the offspring who opposes her ancestors. Judith Butler points out a certain ambiguity in the etymology of Antigone's name, which is "construed as 'anti-generation' (*gonē* [generation])." Butler herself refers to Stathis Gourgouris's perceptive comments on "'the rich polyvalence of Antigone's name.... The preposition *anti* means both 'in opposition to' and 'in compensation of'; *gonē* belongs in a line of derivatives of *genos* (kin, lineage, descent) and means simultaneously offspring, generation, womb, seed, birth. On the basis of this etymological polyphony (the battle for meaning at the nucleus of the name itself), we can argue that Antigone embodies both an opposition of kinship to the polis (in compensation for its defeat by the *demos* reforms), as well as an opposition *to* kinship, expressed by her attachment to a sibling by means of a disruptive desire, *philia* beyond kinship" (Butler, *Antigone's Claim: Kinship between Life and Death* [New York: Columbia University Press, 2000], 22 n. 24).
6. Passages of *Antigone* in the text are from Elizabeth Wyckoff's translation in *Sophocles I: Oedipus the King, Oedipus at Colonus, Antigone*, in *The Complete Greek Tragedies*, ed. David Grene and Richmond Lattimore, vol. 3 (New York: Modern Library, 1960). The line numbers in the text refer to the edition by R. C. Jebb (Cambridge: Cambridge University Press, 1966).
7. *Natural law*, the *OED* reads, encompasses "the principles of morality, held to be discernible by reason as belonging to human nature or implicit in the nature of rational thought and action; such principles are the basis for man-made laws." *Positive law*, by contrast, connotes "a body of laws artificially instituted or imposed by an authority, often as contrasted with natural law rooted in the requirements of justice."

the *irreconcilability* of law (*nomos*) and justice (*dikē*), rather than in the conflict between natural law and positive law on which the paradox is only inflicted. We shall return to the relation between law and justice and, for the sake of cross-elucidation, occasionally probe into the correspondences between Benjamin's and Sophocles' texts. What will emerge in both texts, beyond the juridical antithesis of natural laws and positive laws, is a subterranean discourse revolving around the *epistemic* status of justice.

The Dogma: Violence as a Means to "Just Ends"

The diametrical relationship between positive law and natural law plays a crucial role in Benjamin's critique: "If natural law can judge all existing law only in criticizing its ends, so positive law can judge all evolving law only in criticizing its means. If justice is the criterion of ends, legality is that of means" ("Critique," 180). This antithetical relation notwithstanding, both natural and positive law meet in what Benjamin calls their common "basic dogma":

> Just ends can be attained by justified means, justified means used for just ends. Natural law attempts, by the justness of the ends, to "justify" the means, positive law to "guarantee" the justness of the ends through the justification of the means. (180)

If we were to translate this dogma into a language of temporality, one could perhaps say, with justice as the common point of reference, that natural law operates *retrospectively* ("justify") and positive law *anticipatorily* ("guarantee"). Benjamin considers this antinomy

> insoluble if the common dogmatic assumption were false, if justified means on the one hand and just ends on the other were in irreconcilable conflict. No insight into this problem [and it is the pursuit of such insight, after all, that motivates "Toward a Critique of Violence"] could be gained, however, *until the circular argument had been broken* [*bevor der Zirkel verlassen*], and mutually independent criteria both of just ends and of justified means were established. (181)

This circle of the two juridical-philosophical schools (as we shall become aware of with an increasing sense of urgency) is the circle from within which Benjamin operates and shifts (*schaltet*): "The realm of ends, and therefore also the question of a criterion of justness, are *excluded* [*schaltet...aus*] for the time being from this study" (181). What is the efficacy of this and the many subsequent instances of "exclusion"? If we consider only for a moment the larger topography of Benjamin's essay, the numerous exclusions in his narrative suggest themselves as the very incidences of law-positing violence (*setzende Gewalt*) he talks *about* critically. Benjamin's critique of violence, as in a double movement, tells the story of his own speech act: it is not only a critical account *about* violence, but also a tale about itself—a tale *of* narrative violence indeed.

The "Hypothetical Basis"

Benjamin institutes a series of preliminary strategic distinctions. First, the realm of ends is excluded from the study in favor of the realm of means that constitute violence. Next, principles of natural law are excluded, for natural law is blind to the contingency of means and would lead to "bottomless casuistry" (181). As a result of these two distinctions, a first cornerstone is set (*gesetzt*): the positive theory of law is considered acceptable as a "hypothetical basis" at the outset of the study, since it fundamentally distinguishes between kinds of violence "independently of cases of their application" (181). This discriminating rhetorical dynamic continues when Benjamin distinguishes such "kinds of violence," namely sanctioned and unsanctioned violence. "Although the following considerations proceed from this distinction [between sanctioned and unsanctioned violence]," Benjamin writes:

> It cannot, of course, mean that given forms of violence are classified in terms of whether they are sanctioned or not. For in a critique of violence, a criterion for [violence] in positive law can concern not its *uses* [*Anwendung*] but only its *evaluation* [*Beurteilung*]. The question that concerns us is, What light is thrown on the nature of violence by the fact that such a criterion or distinction can be applied to it at all? In other words, what is the meaning of this distinction? (181)

While the explicitly raised "question that concerns us" (as readers of Benjamin's statements) may appear rather straightforward, the question that concerns us (as readers of Benjamin's speech act) is, I suggest, much more tenuous, for how could Benjamin himself render a critical judgment (*Beurteilung*) without wielding narrative power—that is, without using (*Anwendung*) narrative violence? If, as Benjamin goes on, a standpoint *outside* positive legal philosophy and *outside* natural law must be found (since only from this external standpoint will light be shed on this sphere in which distinctions can be made; see 181f.), then this may well be read as an imperative for his own speech act—the imperative, namely, to find a narrative standpoint *outside* all narrative positings and *outside* all narrative violence. "For this critique," Benjamin writes, "a standpoint outside [den Standpunkt außerhalb] positive legal philosophy but also outside natural law must be found. The extent to which it can be furnished only by a philosophico-historical view of law will emerge [wird sich herausstellen]" (181f.). What will emerge (*sich heraus-stellen*) is a sphere of pure means, an inaugurated "beyond"—beyond sanctioned and unsanctioned, legitimate and illegitimate, legal and illegal means.

"The Only Secure Foundation": Law-Positing Violence

Benjamin calls "the only secure foundation" of his critique the dynamic of "law-positing violence" (*rechtsetzende Gewalt*), which can found and modify legal conditions (185). He names martial law as an example for this law-positing violence and points out the contradiction according to which "legal subjects sanction violence whose ends remain for the sanctioners natural ends" (185). This contradiction, double standard, or hypocrisy legally sanctioning one's predatory violence, one's taking possession of another person's goods, property, or life, makes a peace ceremony absolutely necessary. According to Benjamin, the word "'peace,' in the sense in which it is the correlative to the word 'war,'" denotes an a priori, necessary sanctioning; "this sanction consists precisely in recognizing the new conditions as the new 'law,' quite regardless of whether they need de facto any guarantee of their continuation" (186). Benjamin's terminological characterization of the word "peace" here as "correlative to the word 'war'" is particularly interesting, for, as he notes only parenthetically, "there is also an entirely different [ganz andere] meaning..., the one used by Kant in talking of 'Eternal Peace'" (185). Benjamin characterizes this different meaning of peace as "unmetaphorical," as it is not signifier in a chain of "peace" and "war," and thus not part of a series of substitutions of one political order by another. Kant's "Eternal Peace," as Benjamin interprets it, *stands outside the circle of all positing violence*—an "entirely different" sphere still to be explored.

The Police, or a Ghost in the "Critique of Violence"

In addition to this first dynamic of law-positing violence, Benjamin observes a second dynamic—the more "conservative" "law-preserving violence" (*erhaltende Gewalt*)[8]—thereby instituting a duality whose parts will prove indistinguishable.[9] The indistinguishability of law-positing and law-preserving violence is embodied

---

8. Jacques Derrida, "Force of Law: 'The Mystical Foundation of Authority,'" *Cardozo Law Review* 11 (1990): 919–1045, here 1001. Derrida delivered his reading of Benjamin's "Toward a Critique of Violence" as a keynote address at "Deconstruction and the Possibility of Justice," a symposium held at the Benjamin N. Cardozo School of Law in October 1989. The proceedings of that conference were published in volume 11 of the *Cardozo Law Review*. Benjamin's "Critique" was the subject of a subsequent symposium in October 1990; the proceedings of that second conference were published in volume 13 of the *Cardozo Law Review*. Two anthologies (and a number of challenging analyses of Benjamin's "Critique") grew out of these conferences: Drucialla Cornell et al., eds., *Deconstruction and the Possibility of Justice* (New York: Routledge, 1992); Anselm Haverkamp, ed., *Gewalt und Gerechtigkeit: Derrida–Benjamin* (Frankfurt a.M.: Suhrkamp, 1994). For a careful critique of Derrida's "Force of Law: 'The Mystical Foundation of Authority,'" cf. Burkhardt Lindner, "Derrida, Benjamin, Holocaust: Zur politischen Problematik der 'Kritik der Gewalt,'" *Zeitschrift für kritische Theorie* 5 (1997): 65–100.

9. Benjamin refers to a certain auto-destructive nature of the law toward the end of his essay when he says that "all law-preserving violence, in its duration, indirectly weakens the law-positing violence it represents, by suppressing hostile counterviolence" (202).

most idiosyncratically by the police. And as we shall see, the specificity of the police as a threshold phenomenon is not only asserted, but also rhetorically enacted.

According to Benjamin, the police's "right of disposition" (*Verfügungsrecht*) and "right of decree" (*Verordnungsrecht*) allude to a mixture of legislative and executive power, which he describes as a blurring of law-positing and law-preserving violence:

> If [law-positing violence] is required to prove its worth in victory, [law-preserving violence] is subject to the restriction that it may not set itself new ends. Police violence is *emancipated* from both conditions. It is law-positing, because its characteristic function is not the promulgation of laws but the assertion of legal claims for any decree, and law-preserving, because it is at the disposal of these ends. (189)

The police both assert decrees and promulgate the law, being liberated from the confines of both law-positing and law-preserving violence. The police are neither one nor the other, but they are both singularly in a movement of passing, and are, as such, the epitome of an emancipatory momentum Benjamin also calls "ignominious" (189).[10] While the law is put in place a priori by lawmakers as a "metaphysical category" (189), which then, however, is determined by temporal and spatial moments in which a subject either complies with the law or transgresses the law, the police are "in no way essential" (*nichts Wesenhaftes*). The police present themselves without any specifiable juridical existence; their juridical presence is that of an absence, their body is a no-body.[11]

Benjamin's emphatic discussion of the police, in turn, is remarkable itself in that the police's hybrid nature is reenacted within his narrative. A discourse of ghosts and specters pervades the essay: Benjamin characterizes the police as "spectral mixture," speaks of their "formless" (*gestaltlos*) and "emancipated" power, their "nowhere-tangible, all-pervasive, ghostly presence," their *Geist* ("spirit"/"ghost"), and so forth (189f.). He, in short, mobilizes a linguistic arsenal of ominous attributes contaminating the juridicality that characterizes "Critique" at the outset. The conflation of law-positing and law-preserving violence characterizing the police

---

10. Contrary to common intuition, Benjamin suggests, it is not the case that the ends of police violence are related to those of general law, a law decided on by representatives of the people, in which case the police would act as an executive power on behalf of the people's political consensus. Rather, the law is enforced by the police at the point at which the state "can no longer guarantee through the legal system the empirical ends that it desires at any price to attain" (189). The police really mark the point of a gray zone, within which they enjoy full discretion, protected by the state, even when their actions go beyond or against the interests of the citizenry.

11. And "it cannot finally be denied," Benjamin writes, "that in absolute monarchy, where they represent the power of a ruler in which legislative and executive supremacy are united, their spirit is less devastating than in democracies" (189f.). The "spirit"/"ghost" (*Geist*) of the police is uncanny in democratic systems where a separation of powers provides precisely the anonymous space in which the police cannot be held responsible either as an executive or a legislative power, a situation that induces "the greatest conceivable degeneration of violence" (190).

finds, in the context of Benjamin's description, a ghostly mirror-image in the incessant intersection of two registers: namely that of mere analytical description and that of ambiguously charged (dis)qualifications.[12] Benjamin emancipates the treatise from the constraints of propositional language; he elides systematic conceptualizations, thus depriving his narrative of accountability. We will see how a rhetoric of Jewish versus Greek, divine versus mythic, pure versus impure violence, just life versus mere life, and so on initially appears to structure but eventually haunts Benjamin's text in a way that one may find rather disturbing. This is so particularly if one thinks of his later admiration for Carl Schmitt (which I cannot pursue in detail here),[13] that famous jurist who soon would enjoy a reputation as the "crown jurist" of the Third Reich. At the same time though, the charged language in the essay, as troubling as it may appear, can (as I hope to show) be evaluated solely with regard to the specific economy of Benjamin's text. And as such it appears entirely incommensurable with the decisionism of a Carl Schmitt.[14] While Schmitt's systematic politics, including those of the state of exception (*Ausnahmezustand*),[15] remain within the circle of traditional violence, Benjamin seeks to transgress this sphere, including its oppositional extremes.

---

12. Correspondingly, Benjamin characterizes the legal order (*Recht*) as "ambiguous" (*zwei-deutig*) (190) and "demonically-ambiguous" (198). On Benjamin's concept of the demonic, cf. Giorgio Agamben's essay "Walter Benjamin and the Demonic: Happiness and Historical Redemption," in Giorgio Agamben, *Potentialities: Collected Essays in Philosophy*, trans. Daniel Heller-Roazen (Stanford, CA: Stanford University Press, 1999), 138–59. For a discussion of Benjamin's conception of *Recht* (legal order), see Axel Honneth, "Zur Kritik der Gewalt," in *Benjamin-Handbuch: Leben-Werk-Wirkung*, ed. Burkhardt Lindner (Stuttgart: Metzler, 2006), 193–210, here 197–99.
13. See Benjamin's letter to Carl Schmitt from December 1930 (Benjamin, *Gesammelte Schriften*, 1.3:887).
14. On the relation between Benjamin's and Schmitt's thinking, cf. also Giorgio Agamben, *State of Exception*, trans. Kevin Attell (Chicago: University of Chicago Press, 2005), 52–59; Christian J. Emden, *Walter Benjamins Archäologie der Moderne: Kulturwissenschaft um 1930* (Munich: Fink, 2006), 35f.; Horst Bredekamp, "From Walter Benjamin to Carl Schmitt via Thomas Hobbes," *Critical Inquiry* 25 (Winter 1999): 247–66; Jan-Werner Müller, "Myth, Law, and Order: Schmitt and Benjamin Read Reflections on Violence," *History of European Ideas* 29 (2003): 459–73; Samuel Weber, "Taking Exception to Decision: Walter Benjamin and Carl Schmitt," *Diacritics* 22.3 (1992): 5–18; Susanne Heil, *Gefährliche Beziehungen: Walter Benjamin und Carl Schmitt* (Stuttgart: Metzler, 1996); Günter Figal, "Vom Sinn der Geschichte: Zur Erörterung der politischen Theologie bei Carl Schmitt und Walter Benjamin," in *Dialektischer Negativismus*, ed. Emil Angehrn et al. (Frankfurt a.M.: Suhrkamp, 1992), 252–69; Robert Sinnerbrink, "Violence, Deconstruction, and Sovereignty: Derrida and Agamben on Benjamin's 'Critique of Violence,'" in *Walter Benjamin and the Architecture of Modernity*, ed. Andrew Benjamin and Charles Rice (Melbourne: re.press, 2009), 77–92.
15. See Carl Schmitt, *Political Theology: Four Chapters on the Concept of Sovereignty*, trans. George Schwab (Chicago: University of Chicago Press, 2006), esp. chap. 1. For a discussion on the often-unrecognized discrepancy between Schmitt's notion of the "state of exception" (*Ausnahmezustand*) and Benjamin's distinctly altered implementation of the same term in the 1928 *Trauerspielbuch* and the 1940 "Theses on the Philosophy of History," see Sigrid Weigel, *Walter Benjamin: Die Kreatur, das Heilige, die Bilder* (Frankfurt a.M.: S. Fischer, 2008), esp. 89–92 and 108f.; Herbert Marcuse, afterword to *Zur Kritik der Gewalt und andere Aufsätze*, by Walter Benjamin (Frankfurt a.M.: Suhrkamp, 1965), here 99–101; Werner Hamacher, "Afformative, Strike," trans. Dana Hollander, *Cardozo Law Review* 13.4 (1991): 1149f. n. 34.

Part Two: A Politics of Pure Means (beyond the Circle)

Mise-en-Scène

In a famous letter to Benjamin dated September 20, 1934, Gershom Scholem describes the role of the Scripture (the Law in Kafka) as a severed correlation of "being in force" without "significance" (*Geltung ohne Bedeutung*).[16] But what if what Scholem calls "the Scripture" has lost not only its signification but also its validity? "All violence as a means is either law-positing or law-preserving. If it lays claim to neither of these predicates, *it forfeits all validity* [*so verzichtet sie damit selbst auf jede Geltung*]," Benjamin writes in "Toward a Critique of Violence" (190). In his letter to Benjamin, Scholem describes the "stage in which revelation does not signify [bedeutet], yet still affirms itself by the fact that it is in force [Geltung]," as a "zero point"; after the emptying out of all significance, the Law is still in force, for "there the Nothing appears."[17] But what is beyond the zero point, beyond the potentiality for a re-signification? What is the beyond-the-Nothing? Beyond the Nothing is the Other. For Benjamin the Other is synonymous with *purity*, and it is here that the abyss of Benjamin's politics of "pure means" opens up in its entirety.

If violence does function as a *means*, if it does function as a *means* of enforcement, it is implicated in what Benjamin considers the "problematic nature of law itself" (190). "And if the importance of these problems cannot be assessed with certainty at this stage of the investigation [Wenn auch deren (der Problematik des Rechts) Bedeutung an dieser Stelle der Untersuchung noch nicht mit Gewißheit *abzusehen* ist]," Benjamin notes in a not-so-conspicuous gesture of ambiguity,

> the legal order [das Recht] nevertheless *appears*, from what has been said, in so ambiguous a moral *light* that the question *posits itself* whether there are no other than violent means for regulating conflicting human interests. (190)
>
> so *erscheint* doch nach dem *Ausgeführten* das Recht in so zweideutiger sittlicher *Beleuchtung*, daß die Frage *sich von selbst aufdrängt*, ob es zur Regelung widerstreitender menschlicher Interessen keine anderen Mittel als gewaltsame gebe.

What appears morally ambiguous is not only the tradition of positive law, but also a certain duplicity on Benjamin's part as a writer. For what the reader/spectator of his performance is about to see (*abzusehen*) appears (*erscheint*) from what has been said (*dem Ausgeführten*) and also staged (*dem Aufgeführten*) in not merely an "ambiguous,"[18] but specifically a *zwei-deutig*,[19] moral light (*Beleuchtung*). If the

---

16. Hermann Schweppenhäuser, ed., *Benjamin über Kafka: Texte, Briefzeugnisse, Aufzeichnungen* (Frankfurt a.M.: Suhrkamp, 1981), 82, my translation.
17. Ibid.
18. From Latin *ambiguus*, meaning "shifting, changeable, doubtful."
19. Literally, "of dual interpretability."

92   *Inconceivable Effects*

question "whether there are no other than violent means" for regulating conflicting human interests "posits itself" (*sich von selbst aufdrängt*) rather unpretentiously at this point, it soon will undergo a metamorphosis and arise as a ubiquitous *Aufgabe* (task, surrender, etc.) regarding "the question of a pure immediate violence," a nonviolent violence (199). At the same time, the question of the violent or nonviolent nature of Benjamin's performance will become increasingly urgent and ultimately suggest itself as a criterion on which the credibility of Benjamin's critique of violence hinges.

Contamination

Pursuing the question, then, "whether there are no other than violent means for regulating conflicting human interests" (190), Benjamin first juxtaposes the violent "compromise" between contractual partners with the pure, nonviolent "agreement" as found in the "relationships among private persons" (191). While relations between contractual partners are peacefully intended, but, because of their legal nature, inherently violent, "relationships among private persons" are considered nonviolent: "Nonviolent agreement is possible wherever the culture of the heart allows the use of pure means of agreement [den Menschen reine Mittel der Übereinkunft an die Hand gegeben hat]" (191). Agreement (*Übereinkunft, Einigung*) relies on "courtesy, sympathy, peaceableness, [and] trust" as its subjective preconditions. While compromise "is motivated not internally but from outside, by the opposing effort," and while it is always imbued with a "compulsive character" (191), agreement, in contrast, consists solely of itself.[20]

---

20. Benjamin's discussion of nonviolent means is in miniature already foreshadowed by his word choice of nonviolent "agreement" (*Übereinkunft*) as opposed to violent "compromise" (*Kompromiss*). Grimms *Deutsches Wörterbuch* traces *Übereinkunft* to the Middle High German word *kunft* as the general noun for *komen* (to come): "Künftig ist, dessen kunft man weisz, was oder wer kommt." (About to come is the one of whose coming one knows.) *Über-ein-kunft* is thus the coming (*komen*) of two persons toward each other to the degree of Ein*igkeit* (agreement), Ein*heit* (unity), total fusion—and as such evocative of what Benjamin has in mind when speaking of "pure means" or "immediacy" (*Unmittelbar-keit*). Benjamin's semantic coding comes full circle in Ein*igung* (agreement), a word he transposes from its conventional juridical context into a sphere of pure mediacy.

Über-ein-kunft and *Einigung* stand in contrast to the violent *Kompromiss*, which derives from the Latin *compromittere*, roughly translatable as "to make a mutual promise" or "to abide by an arbiter's decision," in which case the arbiter is a judging authority exterior to the contractual partnership. The word *promittere* means "to send (something) forth" or to "fore-tell." The compromise is a representational agreement, an agreement regarding future times. It can be understood only in regard to what it stands *for*; it not merely *is*, does not just stand for *itself*, but it stands for some*thing beyond itself*; its identity is split; it connotes precisely not unity, as does *Über-ein-kunft*. There is a fissure between the *pro-* and the *mittere*, and it is in this fissure that violence originates. The ground sense of *promittere* is that of a declaration made about some future condition or event, some act to be done or not done (see the *Oxford Latin Dictionary*). And it, of course, is the *not*, the danger of the other *not* complying with the contractual agreement, the potential danger of a new law-positing violence, seething under the surface of every compromise. It is also in this context that Benjamin writes about compromise: "It confers on each party the right to resort to violence in some form against the other, should he break the agreement" (190).

The project of investigating pure means is fraught with difficulty due to their insusceptibility to conceptualization. Their "objective appearance" is in fact "determined by the law," according to which

> pure means are never those of immediate [unmittelbarer] solutions but always those of indirect [mittelbarer] solutions. They therefore never apply immediately to the resolution of conflict between human being and human being, but apply only to matters concerning objects. The sphere of pure means opens up in the realm of human conflicts relating to goods. For this reason, technique [Technik] in the broadest sense of the word is their most particular area. Its profoundest example is perhaps conversation, considered as a technique of civil agreement. (191)

To say that pure means are conceivable only as indirect (*mittelbar*) solutions implies a confession on Benjamin's part that his critique of violence will never allow us to apprehend these pure means head-on. The indirectness (*Mittelbarkeit*) of his communicative act is, at least in its objective appearance, characterized by an inevitable referentiality to external objects, in which the relationship between human being and human being, writer and reader, between Benjamin and us and you and me, is undermined.

And yet Benjamin tells us that conversation is the most profound domain of pure means; he wants to substantiate this claim on the basis of the historical condition that "there is no penalty for lying" (192). Historically there is no penalty for lying, because the sphere of language is "nonviolent to the extent that it is *wholly inaccessible to violence.*" But how can it be, we may ask, that "only late and in a peculiar process of decay *has it been penetrated* by legal violence in the penalty placed on fraud"? (192) If the penetration of legal violence into the domain of nonviolent language precipitated the decay of language as a pure means, how did the fissure that allowed for the distinction between violent and nonviolent, nonpure and pure, occur in the first place? Benjamin names the problem only to leave it suspended— "as cannot be shown in detail here" (see 199f.). How can pure language, something that by definition should be immune to any kind of otherness, friction, contamination, ultimately be "penetrated" by something alien? Benjamin's 1916 essay, "On Language as Such and on the Language of Man," presents itself as a possible avenue for exploration here. In line with the rhetoric generated in this early essay on language, we could ask, How, in a mediality of pure language, can the human word *suddenly* "communicate something (other than itself)"? It goes without saying that Benjamin's 1916 essay provides an answer consistent with its own argumentation: "The Fall marks the birth of the *human word,* in which name no longer lives intact and which has stepped out of name-language...from what we may call its own immanent magic" (153, 71). The question, though, is how satisfying an answer this reference to the Fall is with regard to the political chaos of the Weimar parliaments and the rise of Nazism. How are we *politically* to understand the legal violence of compromise, if language exists only in its very own "sphere of 'understanding'" (*Sphäre der "Verständigung"*) and is as such "wholly inaccessible to violence"? (192).

> Only late and in a peculiar process of decay has [language] been penetrated by legal violence in the penalty placed on fraud. For whereas the legal system at its origin, trusting to its victorious power, is content to defeat lawbreaking wherever it happens to appear, and deception, having itself no trace of power about it, was, on the principle *ius civile vigilantibus scriptum est,* exempt from punishment in Roman and ancient Germanic law, the law of a later period, lacking confidence in its own violence, no longer felt itself a match for that of all others.... It turns to fraud, therefore, not out of moral consideration but for fear of the violence that it might unleash in the defrauded party. Since such fear conflicts with the violent nature of law derived from its origins, such ends are inappropriate to the justified means of law. They reflect not only the decay of its own sphere but also a *diminution of pure means. For in prohibiting fraud, law restricts the use of wholly nonviolent means because they could produce reactive violence.* (192)

How can fraud—supposedly nonviolent in nature—unleash violence in the defrauded party, and consequently conjure up the state's fear? If we were simply to declare this scenario inadequate (and we cannot if we grant Benjamin authority as a *political* thinker), and if we wanted to hold on to the idea of a nonviolent sphere of human agreement (and thus Benjamin's voice regarding language as such and the language of man) as his example of pure means in the private sphere, then the pressing question would still remain: Where exactly does the threshold between pure, nonviolent language and impure, representative language lie? The urgency of the matter lies in the "*diminution* of pure means" (*Minderung* der reinen Mittel, 192), an ontological impossibility, it might seem. In prohibiting fraud, Benjamin writes, "law restricts the use [Gebrauch] of nonviolent," pure means. If pure means can be *restricted,* and if they, astonishingly, can be *used,* how then is pure language different from instrumental language, and how are nonviolent means different from violent means? With regard to this collapse of distinctions that so far have rendered Benjamin's critique of violence viable, how (if at all) are we still to think of a sphere outside-the-law and beyond violence, that is to say, of justice?

The Politics of Pure Means, or a Strike of Rhetoric

Benjamin's discussion of pure means as the medium of peaceful relations between private persons is complemented by a discussion of pure means in the political sphere. With Georges Sorel, Benjamin distinguishes two essentially different kinds of strikes: the political general strike and the proletarian general strike. The contrast, of course, concerns their antithetical relation to violence. Of the partisans of the political general strike, Benjamin, in the words of Sorel, says:

"The strengthening of state power is the basis of their conceptions; in their present organizations the politicians (namely, the moderate socialists) are already preparing the ground for a strong centralized and disciplined power that will be impervious to criticism from the opposition, and capable of imposing silence and issuing its mendacious decrees." "The political general strike demonstrates how the state will lose none of its strength, how power is transferred from the privileged to the privileged, how the mass of producers will change their masters." (193)

In contrast to the political general strike,

> the proletarian general strike sets itself the sole task of destroying state power.... "This general strike clearly announces its indifference toward material gain through conquest by declaring its intention to abolish the state." (194)

The perplexing conclusion that Benjamin draws from his comparison is presented in a curiously simple formula: "Whereas the first form of interruption of work is violent, since it causes only an external modification of labor conditions, the second, as a pure means, is nonviolent" (194). If one refuses to simply buy into Benjamin's rhetoric of persuasion, his proposition can only strike one as counterintuitive: a strike that seeks "external modification" is "violent"; a strike, however, that "sets itself the sole task of destruction" (*die eine einzige Aufgabe der Vernichtung*) is considered "nonviolent" (194). An understanding of the paradox of nonviolent destruction requires us to delve into the series of dichotomies Benjamin delineates, beginning with the one of the political general strike versus the proletarian general strike:

> Whereas the [political general strike] is violent, since it causes only an external modification of labour conditions, the second, as a pure means, is nonviolent. For it takes place not in readiness to resume working conditions, but in the determination to resume only a wholly transformed work, no longer enforced by the state, an overthrow that this kind of strike not so much occasions as carries out [vollzieht]. (194)

The proletarian general strike *carries out* an overthrow; its signification does not lie beyond this carrying out. It serves no-*thing* other than itself. There are no means serving ends; there are, conventionally speaking, no means at all, only pure means, which, as we shall see, according to Benjamin, do not serve but rather allow for the coming into being of justice.

A remark, seemingly intended to facilitate things, soon proves intricate because of an entirely new set of ramifications: "The [political general strike] is law-positing but the [proletarian general strike] *anarchistic*" (194). It would not get us very far to explain Benjamin's idiosyncratic notion of "pure means," deliberately veiled in ambiguity, with the word "anarchistic." We may well ask, however, why Benjamin chooses the word "anarchistic" (cf. also "childish anarchism," 187), a concept that connotes a teaching, a school, a normative, perhaps ethical, framework, instead of the more commonly used "anarchic" or "anarchy" (194).[21] "Anarchism" is not synonymous with "anarchy"—anarchism is the dogma of anarchy.

I would suggest that the very tension between "anarchism" and "anarchy" is highly pertinent for Benjamin's own presentation (*Darstellung*) of the politics of pure means.[22] On the surface, to be sure, Benjamin's interest in the semantics of "anarchism" is less one of opposition or rebellion (that is, a directed movement, an antimovement) than it is one of dis-order or law-lessness (dis-organization, that is, a deferral of systemization). Correspondingly, the proletarian general strike is not directed against *the* law or against *the* order; it is also not against *any* order or *any* law. Rather it is precisely against the "against." That is to say, it is not directed at all, but it is *Vollzug* (carrying-out/execution).

The proletarian general strike's *Vollzug*, however—and this is where the deliberateness of Benjamin's rhetorical staging comes to the fore—is aligned with a rhetoric that (purportedly elucidating the notion of pure means) unremittingly unsettles the semantics of his textual edifice. On the one hand, Benjamin degrades the political strike because it means "to *resume* [aufzunehmen] work after a *modification* to working conditions," yet, on the other hand, the workers of the proletarian general strike are also ready "to resume a...transformed work [eine...veränderte Arbeit...wieder aufzunehmen]" (194). Both strikes rely on some kind of modification or transformation of working conditions. In both strikes, the workers "*resume*" a transformed or modified work, and the antipodes that seemed to motivate Benjamin's narrative begin to falter. On the one hand, Benjamin speaks of the law-positing impetus that pervades every political general strike. At the same time, the *Vollzug* of the proletarian general strike—allegedly beyond the dialectics of law-positing and law-preserving violence—itself relies on a "*determination*"

---

21. *Anarchie* is the *absence* of any form of political authority. The word was borrowed in the sixteenth century from the Greek *an-archia*, from *an-archos*, "without a ruler." In contrast, the German *Anarchismus* gained political currency in the late eighteenth and early nineteenth centuries and signifies an active resistance *against* all forms of coercive control and authority. While *Anarchie* connotes an *absence*, *Anarchismus* implies a *directed* movement (Duden's *Herkunftswörterbuch* [Mannheim: Dudenverlag, 2001], 34).

Benjamin's choice of "anarchistic" in contrast to "anarchic" is particularly striking in light of its deviation from Sorel. Sorel uses the word *anarchique*, which translates to the German *anarchisch* (or the English *anarchic* or *anarchical*). Sorel does not speak of *anarchiste*, the adjective corresponding to the German *anarchistisch* (or the English *anarchistic*) (Georges Sorel, *Réflexions sur la violence* [Paris: Librairie Marcel Rivière, 1946], 238, 253, etc.). For a nuanced contextualization of Benjamin's essay, see Uwe Steiner, "The True Politician: Walter Benjamin's Concept of the Political," *New German Critique* 83 (2001): 43–88, here esp. 69–71; and Steiner, *Walter Benjamin: An Introduction to His Work and Thought*, trans. Michael Winkler (Chicago: University of Chicago Press, 2010), esp. 75–79. Cf. also Chryssoula Kambas, "Walter Benjamin liest Georges Sorel: 'Réflexions sur la violence,'" in *Aber ein Sturm weht vom Paradiese her: Texte zu Walter Benjamin*, ed. Michael Opitz and Erdmut Wizisla (Leipzig: Reclam, 1992), 250–69.

22. On Benjamin's politics of pure means, cf. also Hamacher, "Affirmative, Strike," 1133–57; Beatrice Hanssen, *Critique of Violence: Between Poststructuralism and Critical Theory* (New York: Routledge, 2000), 16–29; Peter Fenves, "'Out of the Order of Number': Benjamin and Irigaray toward the Politics of Pure Means," *Diacritics* 28 (1998): 43–58; Günter Figal, "Die Ethik Walter Benjamins als Philosophie der reinen Mittel," in *Zur Theorie der Gewalt und Gewaltlosigkeit bei Walter Benjamin* (Heidelberg: FEST, 1979), 1–24.

or "*decision*" (*Entschluß*) to resume work. It seems that the radicality of a pure carrying-out (*reiner Vollzug*) is undermined by this "*determination*" or "*decision*" "to *resume* a...transformed work."[23] The idea of "pure means" is forfeited for the perspective of a future order—a future time beyond the revolutionary ones of the proletarian general strike. Indeed, whether enforced through the state or not, any "determination" or "decision" to "resume...work" (*Arbeit...wieder aufzunehmen*), even if a "wholly transformed" (*gänzlich veränderte*) work, will by definition entail a moment of positing (*Setzung*). Thus, the purportedly nonviolent proletarian general strike and the inherently violent political strike are left less distinct than they appeared at the outset.[24]

---

23. This decision "to resume a...transformed work" in Benjamin's characterization of the proletarian general strike closely resembles his description of the political strike, which is inherently violent precisely because "it takes place in the context of a conscious readiness to resume the suspended action" (183).

24. Benjamin asserts that no objection can stand that seeks "to brand such a [proletarian] general strike as violent" (194). No objection can stand that seeks to brand "the sole task of the destruction of state power" (die eine einzige Aufgabe der Vernichtung der Staatsgewalt) as violence because, Benjamin insists, "the violence of an action can be assessed...only from the law of its means" (195). Perhaps we can develop a better understanding of "the sole task [Aufgabe] of the destruction of state power" by turning to another "task" (*Aufgabe*), the "task of diplomats" (195). "More clearly than in recent class struggles, the means of nonviolent agreement have developed in thousands of years of the history of states. Only occasionally does the task of diplomats in their transactions consist of modifying legal systems" (195). One may find it striking that the tasks of diplomats, even if only occasionally, consist of "*modifying* legal systems," for it was the "*modification* to working conditions" in the case of the extortionary political strike that exemplified impure, violent means.

If this wording allows for merely a proximity between the alleged antipodes of diplomats on the one side and political general strikers on the other, Benjamin's narrative spectacle, built on a series of binary oppositions, is about to precipitate the implosion of the text. "Fundamentally [Im wesentlichen] they [the diplomats] must, entirely on the *analogy* of agreement between private persons, resolve conflicts case by case, in the name of their states, peacefully and without contracts. A delicate task that is more robustly performed by referees, but a method of solution that in principle is above that of the referee because it is *beyond all legal systems and therefore beyond violence*" (195). Benjamin reminds us that we are dealing with an *analogy* here when he discusses "pure means in politics as *analogous* to those which govern peaceful intercourse between private persons" (193). Yet this analogy immediately begins to vacillate: for if diplomats essentially seek to "resolve conflicts...*in the name* of their states," this representative relationship distinguishes itself drastically from the "pure" "agreement" between private persons (191). It lies precisely at the core (*im wesentlichen*) of the "relationships among private persons" that "the culture of the heart allows the use of pure means of agreement [die Kultur des Herzens den Menschen reine Mittel der Übereinkunft an die Hand gegeben hat]"—thus in the context of Benjamin's elaboration on language embodying an antithesis to representative, that is to say, impure, language (191).

To complicate matters, this compromised "analogy" now is extended to a chiasm that again moves on the brink of collapse, for the analogy between "the intercourse of private persons" and the "intercourse...of diplomats" (195) is drawn not only in regard to their common *core* (*Wesen*), but also in regard to their external *appearance* (*äußere Erscheinung*). Benjamin writes: "Accordingly, like the intercourse of private persons, that of diplomats has engendered its own forms and virtues [Formen und Tugenden], which were not always a question of appearance, even though they have become so [die, weil sie äußerlich geworden, es darum nicht immer gewesen sind]" (195). While the intercourse of diplomats has engendered its own immediate (*unmittelbare*) forms and virtues, their appearance is precisely not "*like* the intercourse of private persons," whose "objective appearance [objektive Erscheinung]...is determined by the law (whose enormous scope cannot be discussed here) that says pure means are never those of direct [unmittelbarer] solutions but always those of indirect [mittelbarer] solutions" (191). In summary, the analogy between the intercourse of diplomats and private persons (that is, between "pure means in *politics*" and pure means of agreement "among *private* persons") appears unstable; in essence,

98   Inconceivable Effects

Hannah Arendt wrote about Karl Marx that "such fundamental and flagrant contradictions...rarely occur in second-rate writers; in the work of the great authors, they lead into the very center of their work."[25] Likewise, what presents itself as contradictory here in Benjamin's discussion of pure means will, I suggest, lead us into the very center of his thought. From Arendt's perspective, the contradictions she discovered in Marx actually showed not Marx's failure to think clearly, but instead his "integrity in describing phenomena as they presented themselves in his view." Similarly Benjamin's description of the general strike, "this...genuinely revolutionary conception" (194), will testify to his integrity in describing phenomena as they present themselves in his view. That the series of contradictions that we did and are about to discover were more true to the world than any consistent system could ever have been is, as I hope to show, the very center of his performance.

Toward a Performatory Justice

If, for the moment, we strictly follow the reading instructions that "Critique" offers, the task (*Aufgabe*) of the general proletarian strike appears to be (similarly to the task [*Aufgabe*] of diplomats) "a method of solution...*beyond* all legal systems and therefore *beyond* violence [eine Methode der Lösung...jenseits aller Rechtsordnung und also Gewalt]" (195). Of course, this method (means) of a solution (ends) *beyond* all legal systems metonymizes pure means, which Benjamin paradoxically seeks to invoke from his operating position on the "inside" of the circle of all historical violence; and, of course, we have reason to assume that he will never escape this circle. But are we justified in assuming that Benjamin himself believes that he will leave the circle? Does he not quite explicitly concede that such an aspiration would actually lead too far?

> To induce men to reconcile their interests peacefully without involving the legal system, there is, in the end, apart from all virtues, one effective motive that often enough puts into the most reluctant hands pure instead of violent means: it is the fear of mutual disadvantages that threaten to arise from violent confrontation, whatever the outcome might be. Such motives are clearly visible in countless cases of conflict of interests, since the *higher orders* that threaten to overwhelm equally victor and vanquished are hidden from the feelings of most, and from the intelligence of almost all. Here the seeking out of *such higher orders* and the common interests corresponding to them, which constitute the most enduring motive for a politics of pure means, *would lead too far*. (193)

---

diplomats and private persons, at the core *(im wesentlichen)* and in appearance *(objektive Erscheinung)*, lose their rhetorical specificity and distinguishing force. Perhaps it is, quite literally, the "enormous scope" *(gewaltige Tragweite)* of the peculiar law that rules *(zum walten kommt)* here and throughout *Walter* Benjamin's text. In any case, the implosion of the chiasm, an implosion not discussed but performed, seems to contribute to what one does not dare to call the "quintessence" of "Toward a Critique of Violence."

25. Hannah Arendt, *The Human Condition* (Chicago: University of Chicago Press, 1998), 104f.

What "would lead too far" is the possibility of a critique of violence (and thus the critique of a critique of violence); according to Benjamin, a proper critique lies out of reach. What appears uncanny about Benjamin's critique is that he seems to know all this from the beginning. He is, after all, *on his path* "*Toward* a Critique of Violence," on the threshold, perhaps, but without the slightest chance of ever arriving, for that "would lead too far." The "where" that "Toward a Critique of Violence" aspires to lies "*beyond* all legal systems and...*beyond* violence."[26] Benjamin is moving "toward" it, but the belief in the actualization of a critique, the belief in the success of "the seeking out of such higher orders" he appears long to have given up. In the word "Toward" (*Zur*, which is lost in the English translation) all hope of the critique lies buried. The essay's first sentence, which testifies to the impossibility (cf. *Aufgabe*) of the critique,[27] seems merely to confirm what the title already implies. The initially pronounced *presentation* (*Darstellung*) of the critique of violence cannot attain the "higher order of freedom" as long as Benjamin is caught *within* the topography of all legal violence while justice is waiting in the "beyond" (187). And yet Benjamin launches a critique of violence, perhaps (and we will return to this) because he still has hope for "incomparable effects" (203).

For the time being and in accordance with the proletarian general strike, which is not "anarchic" but "*anarchistic*" because of its inherent ethics,[28] its "deep, moral" nature (194), I would suggest for the performative act of Benjamin's critique of

---

26. The "Toward" in the title of Benjamin's "Critique" by no means should be misunderstood as a movement directed "toward" a telos. As the "Theologico-Political Fragment," written in the same year as "Critique," evinces: "Only the messiah himself puts an end to history, in the sense that it frees, completely fulfills the relationship of history to the messianic. Therefore, nothing that is truly historical can want to relate by its own volition to the messianic. Therefore the kingdom of God is not the telos of the dynamics of history, it cannot be posited as its aim; seen historically *it is not its aim but its end*" (Benjamin, *Gesammelte Schriften*, 2.1:203; here translated after Paul de Man, "'Conclusion': Walter Benjamin's 'The Task of the Translator,'" in *The Resistance to Theory* [Minneapolis: University of Minnesota Press, 1986], 93). The unmaintainability of a teleological understanding of history, especially with regard to Benjamin's discussion of the parliamentarian crisis in "Critique," is unequivocally disavowed in the "Theses on the Philosophy of History": "Social Democratic theory, and even more its practice, have been formed by a conception of progress which...made dogmatic claims. The concept of the historical progress of mankind cannot be sundered from the concept of its progression through a homogeneous, empty time. A critique of the concept of such a progression must be the basis of any criticism of the concept of progress itself" (*Gesammelte Schriften*, 2.1:701, here translated after Walter Benjamin, *Illuminations*, ed. Hannah Arendt, trans. Harry Zohn [New York: Schocken Books, 1968], 260f.).

27. "*Die Aufgabe einer Kritik der Gewalt* läßt sich als die Darstellung ihres Verhältnisses zu Recht und Gerechtigkeit umschreiben" (179).

28. Cf. also Benjamin's remarks on an "ethical anarchism" in volume 4 of *Gesammelte Schriften:* "An exposition of this standpoint is one of the tasks [Aufgaben] of my moral philosophy, and in that connection the term 'anarchism' may very well be used to describe a theory that denies a moral right not to force as such but to every human institution, community, or individuality that either claims a monopoly over it or in any way claims that right for itself from any point of view, even if only as a general principle, instead of respecting it in specific cases as a gift bestowed by a divine power, as *absolute power*." "On the other hand (invalid as 'ethical anarchism' may be as a political program), a form of action along the lines it recommends can...elevate the morality of the individual or the community to the greatest heights in situations where they are suffering because God does not appear to have commanded them to offer violent resistance" (*Gesammelte Schriften*, 6:107; *Selected Writings, 1913–1926*, 1:233).

violence—an act conveying a distinct (though not definable) ethical impetus—the terminology of a *performatory* rather than merely a *performative* speech act. In a footnote from his first lecture in *How to Do Things with Words,* John Austin says that while he used the word "performatory" in previous writings, he now employs "performative," which "is to be preferred as shorter, less ugly, more tractable, and more traditional in formation."[29] Austin equates the two, and, to be sure, the *OED* also treats "performatory" and "performative" alike without making further delineations. While both "perfomative" and "performatory" have an adjectival surface structure (*-ive/-y*), "performatory" carries a deeper layer: the *-or* following the morpheme *performat-* denotes a nominative noun agent, an act-*or,* a speech act-*or,* whose speech act, like every human act, is inevitably inherently normative. In the case of "performative" and "performatory," the suffixes make all the difference. It is the agental suffix that materializes the matrix of an ethical imperative; the *-or,* the action, generates a moral efficacy that lies at the center of Benjamin's performance.[30] In light of the efficacy of Benjamin's rhetoric analyzed so far, I would thus suggest a definite value of such terminological differentiation—a differentiation that will eventually undermine the feasibility of his task as a translator between, on the one hand, the sphere of violent means and, on the other hand, "just ends" (196).

"Performatory" is what a critique of violence cannot state; it is what, as a promise, can be generated only by "interests" that ultimately define a politics of pure means (193). "Performatory" is a gesture generating a potentiality (though never an actuality) of justice, an ethical imperative allowing for "moral relations" (179). "Performatory," finally, is the imperative of a *"responsibility"* (a word Benjamin relates to *justice* in a posthumous fragment)[31]—a responsibility that insists on and, paradoxically, puts forth in spite of all tacit constraints the critique of violence.

---

29. John Austin, *How to Do Things with Words* (Cambridge, MA: Harvard University Press, 1962), 6 n. 3.

30. In much the same vein, though more conventional, the words "authoritative" and "authoritarian" differ due to the latter's more coercive thrust. The agental suffix *-ar* (the vowel shifting is not relevant in this context) again denotes an act or action and thus conveys a normativity that "authoritative" lacks. Accordingly, the *OED*'s definitions of "authoritative" read: "1. Of authority, of the nature of authority, exercising or assuming power; imperative, dictatorial, commanding. 2. Possessing due or acknowledged authority; entitled to obedience or acceptance. 3. Proceeding from a competent authority." In contrast, the more coercive "authoritarian" is defined as either "Favourable to the principle of authority as *opposed* to that of individual freedom" or "One who supports the principle of authority."

Finally, the suggested contention according to which "performatory" carries more of a normative connotation than "performative" can be solidified by the occurrence of linguistic contaminations: in contrast to "performative," "performatory" resonates with words such as "oratory" and especially "hortatory"—both of which carry a normative connotation into "performatory" that distinguishes it from "performative."

31. Walter Benjamin, "Notizen zu einer Arbeit über die Kategorie der Gerechtigkeit," *Frankfurter Adorno Blätter* 4 (1995): 41–51, here 42. For a more elaborate discussion of the question of responsibility in Benjamin's "Critique," see Judith Butler, "Critique, Coercion, and Sacred Life in Benjamin's 'Critique of Violence,'" in *Political Theologies: Public Religions in a Post-Secular World,* ed. Hent de Vries and Lawrence E. Sullivan (New York: Fordham University Press, 2006), 201–19.

5

Pernicious Bastardizations

Benjamin's Ethics of Pure Violence

> Kraus accuses the law in its substance, not in its effect. His charge: high treason of the law against justice.... He has seen through law as have few others. If he nevertheless invokes it, he does so precisely because his own demon is drawn so powerfully by the abyss it represents.
>
> —Walter Benjamin, "Karl Kraus"

The pronounced inauguration of "the task of a... presentation" (*Aufgabe einer... Darstellung*) in "Toward a Critique of Violence" (179) positions Walter Benjamin as an author engaged in the scholarly tradition of the philosophical treatise. While "presentation," on the one hand, generates the transience of the present rather than re-presenting the pre-existing and pre-dictable, on the other hand, it carries the weight of a philosophical genre and the aura of a scholarly habitus that seems to foreclose the true possibility of *presenting,* that is, generating the new.

> Among all the forms of violence permitted by both natural and positive law, not one is free of the gravely problematic nature, already indicated, of all legal violence. Since, however, every conceivable solution to human tasks [jede Vorstellung einer irgendwie denkbaren Lösung menschlicher Aufgaben], not to speak of deliverance [Erlösung] from the confines [aus dem Bannkreis] of all the world-historical conditions of existence obtaining hitherto, remains impossible if violence is totally excluded in

principle [unter völliger und prinzipieller Ausschaltung jedweder Gewalt], the question necessarily arises as to what kinds of violence exist other than all those envisaged by legal theory. (195–96)

It is in this context that we may want to ponder the ramifications of representation's (*Vorstellung*) (196) *narrative implementation as theatrical strategy*. While Benjamin is seeking to attain presentation (*Darstellung*), *Vorstellung*—be it translated as mental representation (i.e., imagination) or theatrical representation (i.e., performance)—will always at least imply a claim, more or less openly conveyed, that what is re-presented is in fact present. The duality of *Vorstellung* and *Darstellung* appears precarious in light of Benjamin's announced task to present his critique's "relation to law and justice": "The task [Aufgabe] of a critique of violence can be circumscribed as that of expounding [Darstellung] its relation to law and justice" (179). How could justice—metonymizing singularity and alterity and heterogeneity and otherness—possibly be done justice while dealt with in a philosophical treatise, which is still more a *doing* than a *happening,* more an *act* than an *event*? The question is whether Benjamin's narrative performance exacerbates or mitigates the conflict between *act* and *event,* whether he moves "toward a critique of violence," or whether he loses sight of it. Whatever rhetorical finesse will distinguish his performance in the face of the double bind of the law of genre and the specific economy of his text, it will no doubt fail to circumvent the possibly graver impasse of the idiosyncratic non-presentability (*Nicht-Darstellbarkeit*) and non-re-presentability (*Nicht-Vorstellbarkeit*) of justice.[1]

Yet every claim of *Vorstellung* also entails a *promise,* the promise that perhaps a critique of violence qua *Vorstellung* may still allow for "deliverance" (*Erlösung*) from the dialectical dynamics of traditional violence and, as such, provide an arena for the solution of tasks, distinctively "human tasks." This epistemological bifurcation epitomizes the abyss across which Benjamin's hope for "human tasks" is built. And it precipitates corollaries of a paradoxical nature: on the one hand, Benjamin seems to situate the solution to such human tasks *outside* the human sphere by relating it to a "violence...*other* than" legal violence. This, however, is not a straightforward reference to the divine sphere, to "divine violence" (199), but leads back to the human sphere, where "divine violence" is enacted as "pure violence" (202, 203)—an a-nomic "violence...other than all those envisaged by legal theory." In the human

---

1. Even if in this text I translate *Vorstellung* as "representation," it goes without saying that *Vorstellung* can also present and *Darstellung* can also represent. The etymology of the two German words does not allow for a clear distinction. Both words connote a *moment of stability* as well as a *relation,* in which the *-stellen* is always already pre-determined by a contextual relatedness (*woher-stellen, wohin-stellen, wie-stellen, wann-stellen,* etc.). Thus Benjamin's notion of justice cannot be done justice to by either *Dar-stellung* or *Vor-stellung,* as both rely on a moment of *fixation* encapsulated in the *prefix,* a moment that freezes the *momentum* of *-stellen.* It is this moment of stability, this break or rupture, that is incommensurable with justice, for justice is pure mediacy.

sphere, divine violence finds its *"highest manifestation"* (202) as pure violence. Hence, what initially appeared to be an ineluctable discrepancy between human tasks and the divine *does* anticipate a "solution" qua "highest manifestation."

* * *

Benjamin's verbatim reiteration of the basic dogma common to natural as well as legal law may well be read as a "revolutionary" beacon (202), a beacon proclaiming the third, most dramatic and most enigmatic act of his performance: "Just ends can be attained by justified means, justified means used for just ends" (196). Does this closure of the circle reconfirm Benjamin's entanglement in the constrictive dynamics of "dispatch" and "exclusion" (*Aus-schalten;* e.g., 180, 181, 196), or does it announce a breaking out of the confines (*aus dem Bannkreis*) of all the world-historical conditions of existence, a redemption (*Erlösung,* 196) indeed?

> How would it be... if all the violence imposed by fate, using justified means, were of itself in irreconcilable conflict with just ends, and if at the same time *a different kind of violence arose* [*eine Gewalt anderer Art absehbar werden sollte*] that certainly could be either the justified or the unjustified means to those ends but was *not related* to them as means at all *but in some different way* [*irgendwie anders*]? (196)

What if this other violence made all the difference regarding the proclaimed "task of a critique of violence"? What if it offered itself as an unthought-of, perhaps unthinkable (and thus unfalsifiable) possibility of writing, an unpredicted player in the arena of narratology? "This would throw light [damit würde ein Licht fallen]," Benjamin writes,

> on the curious and at first discouraging discovery of the ultimate indistinguishability [von der letztlichen Unentscheidbarkeit] of all legal problems (which in its hopelessness [Aussichtslosigkeit] is perhaps comparable only to the possibility of conclusive decisions on "right" and "wrong" in evolving languages). For it is never reason that decides [entscheidet] on the justification of means and the justness of ends: fate-imposed violence decides [entscheidet] on the former, and God on the latter. (196)

Reason appears not to be a trustworthy point of reference for conducting a critique of violence. In spite of or perhaps because of all the descending light ("This would throw a light..."), one has to be dubious of one's faculty of sight and perception. Indeed what at the outset still came along as a *"plan"* to investigate "a different kind of violence" ("violence... other than all those envisaged [ins Auge faßt] by legal theory") is soon reduced to a mere hope for "conceivability" ("if a different kind of violence arose [absehbar werden sollte]") and appears finally to be truly "unpromising," beyond perception, view or vision (*Aussichtslosigkeit*) (196).

Manifestation, Bastardization

A long dash leads Benjamin from the realm of speculation into the discussion of that "different kind of violence" (196). Anger, an "example" of immediate violence from everyday experience, impels human beings to the most visible outbursts of a violence that is "not related as a means to a preconceived end. It is not a means but a manifestation" (196). The "objective manifestation" of divine violence is to be found in *myth,* and it is here, in the discussion of the "manifestation of the gods," that a deep rupture pervading Benjamin's "Critique" comes to the fore. For mythic violence is a "*mere* manifestation of the gods" (197), comparable to man's "stepping outside the purer language of name," making language "a *mere* sign" (153, Benjamin's italics), comparable, finally, to "the living" *(das Lebendige),* that is, ethical life, as opposed to "*mere* life" (200).

Mythic violence "in its archetypal form" (*in ihrer ur*bild*lichen Form*) is mere manifestation, "not a means to [the gods'] ends, scarcely a manifestation of their will, but primarily a manifestation of their existence" (197). There would be some benefit at this point in considering the role of the Jewish prohibition of the image—a commandment informing almost all areas of the Benjaminian oeuvre.[2] A recapitulation of Benjamin's discussion of divine violence must suffice here, and it shows that Benjamin never discusses divine violence in its own right but only via examples of *manifestation:* as proletarian general strike, as anger, as language, as myth (in the case of the Niobe story), as education (194, 196, 197, 200). However, if pure mediacy generally occurs merely as *manifestation,* then it is not actually pure. It consequently "exists" solely in "bastardized," hybrid form as both mythic and divine violence—not as pure existence, but manifested "existence," not *Sein* (being), but *Da-sein* (existence) (203, 197). The only place in the essay where we may hope for pure mediacy is a place that does not draw on examples, one that is not manifested and is therefore unintelligible.

The ~~Law~~ of Justice

What has so far appeared nebulous in Benjamin's description of pure violence and its manifestations results from Benjamin's constant directional shifts, continuous positings and re-positings with regard to the *(un)attainability* of the critique of legal violence. It is in the same context that "further illumination" again allows for a "conclusion," and it appears that the long-awaited presentation of nonviolent violence—that is, "immediate violence"—actually moves farther away with every sentence.

---

2. For an astute discussion of imagelessness in Benjamin's thought, see Winfried Menninghaus, "Walter Benjamin's Variations of Imagelessness," in *Jewish Writers, German Literature: The Uneasy Examples of Nelly Sachs and Walter Benjamin,* ed. Timothy Bahti and Marilyn Sibley Fries (Ann Arbor: University of Michigan Press, 1995), 155–73.

Instead of investing much faith in the establishing and renouncing rhetoric of "higher orders" that prove too high, plans that appear to be "unpromising," and "conclusions" that "lead too far," Benjamin offers the decisive hint (with all the reservation a subjunctive allows) that pure violence "was *not related* to [just ends] as means at all [überhaupt nicht als Mittel zu (gerechten Zwecken)...sich verhalten würde]" (196). In the next sentence, Benjamin provides an indispensable link to his 1916 essay on language: he compares (*zu vergleichen*) the discouraging discovery of the indistinguishability of all legal problems with the impossibility of evolving languages to distinguish "right" and "wrong." How does pure language compare to the immediacy of violence, and how are we to imagine the curious *relatedness of an immediacy*?

In his 1916 essay on language, Benjamin distinguishes between instrumental and pure language. While instrumental language is characterized as a mere sign that communicates some-*thing* other than itself (a means of a knowledge inappropriate to man), pure language "communicates itself *in* itself; it is in the purest sense the 'medium' of the communication" (142, Benjamin's italics). After making the comparison encouraged by Benjamin, one may conclude: since pure language has no speaker, "if this means someone who communicates *through* these languages" (142, Benjamin's italics), there is, similarly, in the case of pure mediacy, no means *through* which an end would be pursued, but only a "pure medium" *in* which "just ends" *occur* (148, 196).

If virtue is something that can be *demanded* and that can be *complied with,* then justice, ultimately, is solely a *condition* of the world, a *condition* of God. Benjamin suggests precisely this in a posthumous fragment:

> Justice does not appear to correspond to the good will of a subject, but rather it is a condition of the world; justice describes the ethical category of the existing, and virtue is the ethical category of the demanded. Virtue can be demanded; justice can ultimately only be, as a condition of the world, or as the condition of God.[3]

Pure mediacy or justice is nothing that can be "enforced" or translated into legal language. The difference between law and justice is not embedded in the nomenclature of means and ends, which Benjamin retains even when speaking about justice. The difference hinges on the notion of *power:*

> For the function of violence in lawmaking is twofold, in the sense that lawmaking pursues as its end, with violence as the means, *what* is to be established as law, but at the moment of instatement does not dismiss violence [die Gewalt nicht abdankt]; rather, at this very moment of lawmaking, it specifically establishes as law not an end

---

3. Walter Benjamin, "Notizen zu einer Arbeit über die Kategorie der Gerechtigkeit," *Frankfurter Adorno Blätter* 4 (1995): 41–51, here 41, my translation.

unalloyed by violence [einen von Gewalt freien und unabhängigen...Zweck] but one necessarily and intimately bound to it, under the title of power. Lawmaking is powermaking, assumption of power, and to that extent an immediate manifestation of violence. Justice is the principle of all divine endmaking, power the principle of all mythic lawmaking. (198, Benjamin's italics)

The means of lawmaking are not pure precisely because at the moment of instatement the lawmaking violence does not "abdicate" but rather establishes itself as power. Power is the ongoing predominance of means that do not allow for the *independence* of ends, as with pure means that by nature entertain solely relations to *free, singular* ends. If there is power, all ends remain tied to their law-positing violence, sustaining its constituting claim, its claim to power. It all hinges on the question of the *relatedness of means and ends* in conjunction with a *specific temporality*. On one occasion a means manifests itself and does so with (perhaps almighty) power, but *abdicates instantaneously;* the relation between this means and its ends remains pure, uncontaminated by any insisting claim for iteration. Another time, the initial manifestation posits itself in such a way that it claims its prevalence (i.e., the generalization of its law-positing violence); it does not allow for the singularity of the specific relation between means and ends but rather insists that from that point on all means serve the once-proclaimed end. While in the first scenario the relation between means and ends is immediately dissociated, in the second the law-positing violence insists, via *(mittels)* (increasingly weakened) law-preserving iteration, on its initial law-positing violence, its once-instituted relation, and this institutionalization is *power*.

"Pernicious" Identity

Because in the case of divine violence the singularity in the relatedness of means and ends (justice) distinguishes itself so clearly from mythic violence's claim to generalization (law), Benjamin devotes an unequivocal passage to the problem. He discovers

> the stubborn prevailing habit of conceiving those just ends as ends of a possible law—that is, not only as generally valid [allgemeingültig] (which follows analytically from the nature of justice) but also as capable of generalizations [verallgemeinerungsfähig], which, as could be shown, contradicts the nature of justice. For ends that in one situation are just, universally acceptable [allgemein anzuerkennen], and valid [allgemeingültig] are so in no other situation, no matter how similar the situations may be in other respects. (196)

The impossible conciliation of law and justice is reflected in the irreconcilability of their attributes: while just ends are generally valid (*allgemeingültig*) (Benjamin calls this an "*analytical*" characteristic of justice), the ends of legal violence are generalizable (*verallgemeinerungsfähig*). At the same time, just ends are not capable of generalization (*verallgemeinerungsfähig*), and the ends of legal violence are conversely not generally valid (*allgemeingültig*); the mediality of justice is incommensurable to the relatedness of means and ends of legal violence. Where, then, do we situate the structural difference? Justice is generally valid (*allgemeingültig*) in the sense of a multiple singularity—a singularity that constitutes itself anew each time, a singularity also that defies its deduction from any *pre*rogative, any *pre*establishment, any juris*diction*. "In God," Benjamin writes, "all virtues have the form of justice; the epithet 'omni' in omni-gracious, omniscient and others, testifies to this condition [das Beiwort all in all-gütig, allwissend u.a. deutet darauf hin]."[4] The singularity of justice is *all-* (*omni-*); the law of human law, however, is *verall-*. It is within the *ver* that the instrumental force of every law-positing violence is located,[5] a force that seeks to ensure the general validity of a specific law-positing moment for the most diverse situations and for all times, a force whose power is diametrically opposed to the ethics of the singular event. The generalizability (*Verallgemeinerungsfähigkeit*) of legitimate ends relies on an *abstraction* to which the *concretion* of justice does not succumb.[6]

The gap between law (*Recht*) and justice (*Ge-recht-igkeit*), which finds no support in the German etymology of the two words, is evoked by Latin, Greek, and Hebrew, which is why Benjamin writes: "The enormous abyss opening up between the essential composition of law and justice is signified by other languages."

ius θέμις משפט[7]
fas Δίκη צרק[8]

The differentiation Benjamin *asserts* for law and justice is severely challenged in the context of his own speech act, which reflects the very ambiguity he attributes to mythic violence. The law of Benjamin's narrative is, on one side, clearly attributed to a higher end, namely that of justice; the emerging insight, however, as to the unattainability of justice is met with ongoing iterations *asserting* its attainability and

---

4. Benjamin, "Notizen," 41, my translation.
5. It is thus that—in contradistinction to *verwaltende Gewalt* (law-preserving, "administrative" violence)—a *waltende* (sovereign) violence signs the essay (203).
6. It is in this vein that, in his long 1916 essay on language, Benjamin juxtaposes the *concrete* with the *abstract*—as the third aspect of a threefold significance of the Fall for the essential composition of language: "For good and evil, being unnameable and nameless, stand outside the language of names.... Name, however, with regard to existing language, offers only the ground in which its *concrete* elements are rooted. But the *abstract* elements of language—we may perhaps surmise—are rooted in the word of judgment." Judgment, or better "the magic of judgment" itself, Benjamin considered to have risen from the Fall in exchange for the immediacy of the name that was damaged by it" (153f.).
7. Greek: *themis;* Hebrew: *mischpat* (law [*Recht*]).
8. Greek: *dikē;* Hebrew: *zedek* (justice); Benjamin, "Notizen zu einer Arbeit," 42.

vindicating the initial claim of "Critique." The ambiguity of "Critique" consists precisely of Benjamin's awareness of the unintelligibility of justice. Yet instead of "abdicating" its critical objective, he perpetuates it, transforming it into an *end in itself,* eventually instigating "Critique" as the self-sufficient dynamic of his (narratological) *power.* "Lawmaking is powermaking," Benjamin writes, seemingly commenting on his own enactment. However, "lawmaking is powermaking, assumption of power, *and to that extent an act of immediate manifestation of violence*" (198). Is Benjamin's performance an "*act* of immediate *manifestation*" or an "act of *immediate* manifestation" (198)? It is both, of course, because what was separate at the outset now is "identical":

> Far from inaugurating a purer sphere, the mythic manifestation of immediate violence [unmittelbare Gewalt] shows itself fundamentally *identical* with all legal violence, and turns suspicion concerning the latter into certainty of the perniciousness of its historical function, the destruction of which thus becomes obligatory [deren Vernichtung damit zur Aufgabe wird]. This very task [Aufgabe] of destruction poses again, ultimately, the question of a pure immediate violence that might be able to call a halt to mythic violence. (199)

Benjamin calls the indistinguishability of the manifestation of immediate violence and legal violence "pernicious" in regard to its "historical function." It ruins all politics of pure means, compromises and bastardizes all revolution; it is a mournful compromise.[9]

On Mythic Constitutional Law, or the Contested Right to Sleep under Bridges

> Of all the masterpieces...the *Antigone* seems to me to be the most magnificent and satisfying work of this kind.
> —G. W. F. Hegel, *Aesthetics: Lectures on Fine Art*

> Like Hegel, we have been fascinated by Antigone, by this unbelievable relationship, this powerful liaison without desire, this immense impossible desire that could not live, capable only of overturning, paralyzing, or exceeding any system and history, of interrupting the life of the concept, of cutting off its breath...of supporting it from outside or underneath a crypt.
> —Jacques Derrida, *Glas*

---

9. "Mournful," Benjamin writes, is the "'overnaming' [*Überbenennung*]—the deepest linguistic reason for all melancholy and (from the point of view of the thing) for all deliberate muteness. Overnaming as the linguistic being of melancholy points to another curious relation of language: the overprecision that obtains in the tragic relationship between the languages of human speakers [die im tragischen Verhältnis zwischen den Sprachen der sprechenden Menschen waltet]" (155–56).

Mythic violence finds an outstanding example in the legend of Niobe.[10] While, Benjamin says, she may appear to be punished by Apollo and Artemis, their violence actually establishes a law rather than punishes the infringement of an already existing law. Niobe calls down fate upon herself, and the violence that arrives from the uncertain sphere of fate can only be *ambigious* (*zwei-deutig*) because of the lack of a fixed juridical framework (197). The hybrid nature of myth, its position between divine laws and the human sphere, is reflected in the ambiguity of fate, which can be challenged with "dignified courage," as in the case of Prometheus, or brought upon oneself through "arrogance," as in Niobe's case. Niobe, however—and this is the crux—*does not infringe any law* and hence is *not punished* by mythic violence. In a world where challenging of fate still corresponds to a certain hope of establishing a legal right, laws are still *unwritten,* and a law that cannot be violated does not result in punishment but "retribution":

> Laws and circumscribed frontiers remain, at least in primeval times, unwritten laws. A human being can unwittingly infringe upon them and thus incur retribution. For each intervention of law that is provoked by an offense against the unwritten and unknown law is called "retribution" (in contradistinction to "punishment"). But however unluckily it may befall its unsuspecting victim, its occurrence is, in the understanding of the law, not chance, but fate presenting itself once again in its deliberate ambiguity [das sich hier nochmals in seiner planvollen Zweideutigkeit darstellt]. (198–99)

The mythic violence that bursts upon Niobe from the uncertain sphere of fate is "not actually destructive." It stops short of claiming the life of the mother, whom it leaves "only more guilty" than before, "both as an eternally mute bearer of guilt and as a boundary stone on the frontier between men and gods" (197).[11]

An application of the "ambiguous" principle of all mythic lawmaking has immense consequences in constitutional law, which Benjamin similarly calls

---

10. Section epigraphs: Georg Wilhelm Friedrich Hegel, *Aesthetics: Lectures on Fine Art,* trans. Thomas Malcolm Knox (Oxford: Clarendon Press, 1975), 2:1218; and Jacques Derrida, *Glas,* trans. John P. Leavey and Richard Rand (Lincoln: University of Nebraska Press, 1986), 166.

11. Also in his "Storyteller" essay, Benjamin speaks of the "need [Not] created by the myth," to then continue: "Whenever good counsel was at a premium, the fairy tale had it, and where the need was greatest, its aid was nearest. This need was the need created by the myth. The fairy tale tells us of the earliest arrangements that mankind made to shake off the nightmare which the myth had placed upon its chest. In the figure of the fool it shows us how mankind 'acts dumb' toward myth; in the figure of the youngest brother it shows us how one's chances increase as the mythical primitive times are left behind; in the figure of the man who sets out to learn what fear is it shows us that the things we are afraid of can be seen through; in the figure of the wiseacre it shows us that the questions posed by the myth are simple-minded, like the riddle of the Sphinx; in the shape of the animals which come to the aid of the child in the fairy tale it shows that nature not only is subservient to the myth, but much prefers to be aligned with man. The wisest thing—so the fairy tale taught mankind in olden times, and teaches children to this day—*is to meet the forces [Gewalten] of the mythical world with cunning and with high spirits*" (Benjamin, *Gesammelte Schriften,* 2.2:457f., translated after Benjamin, *Illuminations,* ed. Hannah Arendt, trans. Harry Zohn [New York: Schocken Books], 102).

"demonically ambiguous" (198). In constitutional law the establishing of frontiers is the "primal phenomenon of all lawmaking violence":

> Where frontiers are decided, the adversary is not simply annihilated; indeed, he is accorded rights even when the victor's superiority in power is complete. And these are, in a demonically ambiguous way, "equal" rights: for both parties to the treaty, it is the same line that may not be crossed. Here appears, in a terribly primitive form, the mythic ambiguity of laws that may not be "infringed"—the same ambiguity to which Anatole France refers satirically when he says, "Poor and rich are equally forbidden to spend the night under bridges." (198)

It would be just if all people had a bed in which to sleep, but it seems that the law's concerns lie elsewhere—that is its mythic ambiguity. Mythic violence is characteristic in regard to its establishing of frontiers, and the establishing of frontiers is a matter of power. The law is inevitably contaminated with power. It is entirely inconceivable, Benjamin suggests, that at any time in history, law and power could have been separate.

> It also appears that Sorel touches not merely on a cultural-historical truth but also on a metaphysical truth when he surmises that in the beginning all right [Recht] was the prerogative ['Vor'recht] of kings or nobles—in short, of the mighty; and that, *mutatis mutandis,* it will remain so as long as it exists. (198)

That all right (*Recht*) was the prerogative (*'Vor'recht*) of the ones in power means no less than that all prerogative (*'Vor'recht*) was power. Hence, all law (*Recht*) succeeding this prerogative (*'Vor'recht*) will (whatever the ends) always be reducible to a smallest common denominator—that of power. The law (*Gesetz*) is the law (*Recht*) of the ones in power; and this, *mutatis mutandis,* will be so as long as the law exists.

It is this ambiguous interrelatedness of law, justice, and power that similarly takes center stage in Sophocles' *Antigone*. Creon's decree stands vis-à-vis Antigone's unwritten laws. Creon questions Antigone about her knowledge of the royal decree that prohibits the burial of her brother Polyneices:

> CREON (to Antigone): You knew the order not to do this thing?
> ANTIGONE: I knew, of course I knew. The word was plain.
> CREON: And still you dared to overstep these laws?
> ANTIGONE: *For me* it was not Zeus who made that order.[12]

---

12. Hölderlin's German translation of *Antigone* underscores my own reading of the contested unity of justice most appropriately, although it diverges from all standard English translations: "*Mein* Zeus berichtete mirs nicht" (*My* Zeus did not report me), Hölderlin's italics. Friedrich Hölderlin, *Sämtliche*

> Nor did that Justice who lives with the gods below
> Mark out such laws to hold among mankind.
> Nor did I think your orders were so strong
> That you, a mortal man, could over-run
> The gods' unwritten and unfailing laws.
> Not now, nor yesterday's, they always live...
> So not through fear of any man's proud spirit
> Would I be likely to neglect these laws...
> I knew that I must die; how could I not?
> Even without your warning. (Sophocles, *Antigone* 450–61)

Antigone is not the only one who legitimizes her actions by citing the gods of Hades; Creon also solidifies his disputed edicts with reference to justice, *dikē* (see line 746). And Creon is not alone in attributing the term *nomos* to his laws (e.g., lines 449, 663); Antigone in her famous speech also remarks on the unwritten *nomoi* to which she remains faithful. Why then must Antigone die? Mythic violence burst upon Niobe in response to her display of "arrogance"; is this not also the situation of Antigone? Is not her one-sided interpretation of divine law, her *hybris*, the actual crime?[13] Not only does she dismiss the necessity of orderly life in the city, but she also stands against the family, since her self-sacrificial pathos renders the continuation of her father's lineage virtually impossible.

And does not Creon also call guilt upon himself, since though he acts in good faith as a state sovereign who must guarantee security through the enforcement of political laws, he nevertheless remains blind to the gravity of Antigone's situation? Her brothers had killed each other in battle, and not until the end—not until the moment blood stains his own family, not until Haemon (whose name seems to foreshadow his fate) dies by his own hand, not until the guilt of blood sin has come full circle—does Creon understand Antigone's actions. *Hybris* seduces Creon to infringe on the unwritten laws of the chthonic gods, thereby provoking a burst of mythic violence, which, as with Niobe, is "not actually destructive"—it leaves him alive and instead annihilates his family. Benjamin refers to the hybrid nature of

---

Werke: Historisch-kritische Ausgabe, ed. D. E. Sattler, vol. 17 (Frankfurt a.M.: Stroemfeld, 1991). This distinction between one justice next to a second and perhaps a third uncertain one corresponds to my understanding of the play in respect to both Antigone's and Creon's *possessive claims to justice,* claims dismissing any notion of justice's defiance of human attempts of instrumentalization. Also Vernant discusses the chasm inflicted on justice, *dikē,* thereby distinguishing Antigone's "*Dikē* infernale, différente de celle de Créon, des hommes, des cités, différente aussi peut-être de cette autre *Dikē* qui siège dans le ciel à côté de Zeus" (Jean-Pierre Vernant and Pierre Vidal-Naquet, *Mythe et tragédie en Grèce ancienne* [Paris: Maspero, 1972]). Cf. Hans-Thies Lehmann on the significance of the concept of *dikē* for the formation of a juridical discourse for the Greeks in Lehmann, *Theater und Mythos: Die Konstitution des Subjekts im Diskurs der antiken Tragödie* (Stuttgart: Metzlersche Verlagsbuchhandlung, 1991).

13. At the same time, of course, Antigone, in contrast to Niobe, *does* infract a given law, namely Creon's decree.

myth as "the spirit of law" (*Geist des Rechts*); from the moment of its birth, it haunts the discourse of jurisdiction (199).[14]

Das 'Vor'recht der Bevorrechteten

Benjamin juxtaposes the legend of Niobe with the biblical account of the destruction of the group of Korah in Numbers to illustrate the divine violence of God. The latter strikes "privileged Levites [*Bevorrechtete, Leviten*]," that is, those powerful ones who possess the *'Vor'recht* (prerogative) of establishing frontiers. Divine violence strikes the privileged "without warning, without threat" (198), and thus it strikes in a way that is different from yet reminiscent of Benjamin's characterization of mythic violence. In both the mythic sphere as well as the divine sphere, we encounter a judgment without a fixed juridical catalog, the execution of a sentence without the pronouncing of a judgment, a violence incurred unwittingly.

If mythic violence is law-positing, divine violence is law-destroying; if mythic violence sets boundaries, the latter boundlessly destroys them; if the former brings at once guilt and retribution (*Sühne*), the latter only expiates (*entsühnend*); if mythic violence is threatening, divine violence is striking; if the former is bloody (*blutig*), the latter is lethal without spilling blood (*unblutig*) (see 199). But what can be said about this curious dichotomization of mythic and divine violence, Greek and Jewish violence under the seals of Niobe and Korah, in respect to the biblical text to which Benjamin merely alludes?

"You Levites have gone too far!"

How apt is Benjamin's reference to Korah regarding "the *lack of bloodshed* and the *expiatory* [*entsühnenden*] character" of divine violence? How appositely does it elucidate the "*boundless*" divine violence that "*strikes... without warning*" (199)? To what degree can the account of Korah shed light on the so-far enigmatic rhetorical implementation of "divine violence"? Korah, who is followed by 250 "well-known community leaders who had been appointed members of the council," is said to rebel against the leadership of Moses:

> "*You have gone too far!* The whole community is holy, every one of them, and the Lord is with them. Why then do you set yourselves above the Lord's assembly?" When Moses heard this, he fell facedown. Then he said to Korah and all his followers: "In the morning the Lord will show who belongs to him and who is holy, and he will have that person come near him.... You, Korah, and all your followers are

---

14. Already Hermann Cohen in *Ethik des reinen Willens* (*Ethics of the Pure Will*), Benjamin remarks, speaks of the "'inescapable realization' that it is 'fate's orders themselves that seem to cause and bring about this infringement, this offense'" (Cohen, quoted in "Critique," 199).

to do this: Take censers and tomorrow put fire and incense in them before the Lord. The man the Lord chooses will be the one who is holy. *You Levites have gone too far!*" (Num. 16:2–3)[15]

While there is no explicit mention of annihilation here, Moses does insinuate that the Lord will choose with his almighty power. Moses reiterates Korah's reproach ("You have gone too far!"), and in the succeeding lines it will be said that Moses summons Dathan and Abiram, two of Korah's followers, who in turn refuse to appear before the Lord. "Will you gouge out the eyes of these men? No, we will not come!" What we are witnessing here is a climactic back and forth, a sequence in which the very *naming of a violent act* allows—not inadvertently—for its actualization to be feared. Korah's rebellion is contemptuous ("These men have treated the Lord with contempt," Num. 16:30) and as such is from the first moment doomed to fatal consequences. I recapitulate the communication in this passage in such detail because it seems to me that divine violence does not strike as surprisingly and "*without warning*" as Benjamin suggests.

The actual execution is carried out in multiple renderings. First "the ground... split apart and the earth opened its mouth and swallowed them, with their households and all Korah's men and all their possessions. They went down alive into the grave, with everything they owned; the earth closed over them, and they perished and were gone from the community." After the first killing, Korah and his followers are killed again: "And a fire came out from the Lord and consumed the 250 men who were offering the incense" (Num. 16:35). Of the grumbling Israelite community, which accuses Moses and Aaron of the murder of the Lord's people, another "14,700 died from a plague, in addition to those who had died because of Korah" (16:49). In contrast to Benjamin's brief allusion to this passage, there is virtually no evidence that would support the attribution of "without spilling blood" to an act of divine violence.

As a matter of fact, the crux of the story seems exemplary of what Benjamin termed "mythic violence." Benjamin said that divine violence destroys "*boundlessly*" (199). But is this, in view of the story of Korah, actually the case?

> When Korah had gathered all his followers... at the entrance to the Tent of Meeting, the glory of the Lord appeared to the entire assembly. The Lord said to Moses and Aaron, "*Separate yourselves* from this assembly so I can put an end to them at once." (Num. 16:20–21)

I am additionally consulting the German translation by Luther, who translates "Separate yourselves from this assembly" as "Scheidet euch von dieser Gemeinde."

---

15. *The Holy Bible, Containing the Old Testament and the New Testament* (Colorado Springs: International Bible Society, 1983).

It is precisely the moment of dividing, *scheiden,* that Benjamin found characteristic of the mythic "act of establishing frontiers." Yet another salient moment of establishing frontiers follows in anticipation of the destructive power of a plague that God sends to the grumbling people. The Lord commands Moses and Aaron: "Get away from this assembly so I can put an end to them at once" (Num. 16:45). Instead of destroying boundlessly, God distinguishes between the life he wants to preserve and the life he hands over to the swallowing earth, to the fire and to the plague. These moments of divine border establishment are followed by yet a third famous moment:

> The next day the whole Israelite community grumbled against Moses and Aaron. "You have killed the Lord's people," they said.... Then Moses said to Aaron, "Take your censer and put incense in it, along with fire from the altar, and hurry to the assembly to make atonement for them. Wrath has come out from the Lord; the plague has started." So Aaron did as Moses said, and ran into the midst of the assembly. The plague had already started among the people, but Aaron offered the incense and made atonement for them. *He stood between the living and the dead, and the plague stopped.* But 14,700 people died from the plague, in addition to those who had died because of Korah. (16:41–49)

Again divine violence is not borderless, but quite the contrary, as Aaron, by means of his *corporeal presence,* establishes a frontier *"between the living and the dead,"* a border that stops the plague. This passage is interesting in yet another respect, namely that of Aaron's "atonement" for the people. The point of mythic violence for Benjamin was that one who unwittingly infringes on unwritten laws will incur "retribution" (*Sühne*). Yet if divine violence really *"expiates"* (*entsühnt*), as Benjamin asserts, could Aaron then, by making atonement for the people, really ward off divine violence and save the Israelites?[16]

---

16. While my reading of the Korah passages questions the distinguishability of Benjamin's two categories of divine and mythic violence, the central thematic of the biblical passage, which is that of representation, does, as a matter of fact, inform our reading of Benjamin's essay, in which the question of representation and representational language (cf. 192) is pivotal. The central question of the story—namely, "Why does a community in which each one is holy need a leader, a representative?"—is one that Benjamin does not ask. Korah and his followers raise this question at the time of their initial reproach against Moses and Aaron: "The whole community is holy, every one of them, and the Lord is with them. Why then do you set yourselves above the Lord's assembly?" (Num. 16:3) The paradox is one between the assertion of the community's holiness and the commandment that requires obedience to an even holier representative. Benjamin will problematize this contradiction, this double bind in his discussion of justice and its impossible representation through human laws. Why can the historical realization, the historicization of divine holiness, only exist, and that is, not exist, through representation? Why is the manifestation of holiness contingent on a rupture, thereby forfeiting its all-encompassing quality, its wholeness? It is this paradox that in his *Moses* Martin Buber (whom Benjamin held in limited esteem) analyzes as the impasse of Judaism, ultimately necessitating the normative framework of Jewish customs. The possibility of the divine lies buried in its manifestation, yet the aporia of divine manifestation alone seems to allow for religious rituals and practice.

It is perplexing that Benjamin should choose this biblical passage to elucidate his category of divine violence, as it leaves mythic and divine violence fraught with ambiguities and ultimately indistinguishable. Throughout "Critique" the antipodes of both violences remain unsettled, amounting to what may be called Benjamin's felicitous speech act, in which the asserted ambiguities appear reenacted in the course of performance.

The Abyss

We encountered an "identity" of the mythic manifestation of immediate violence and legal violence—reverberating with the just-discussed indistinguishability of divine and mythic violence—but we have not yet asked how legal violence actually came into being. At a late point in his essay Benjamin addresses exactly this question of the "origin" of legal violence. "The triggering of legal violence," he writes, "stems (as cannot be shown in detail here) from the guilt of *merely natural life*" (199–200). What "cannot be shown in detail here" is at least hinted at in the beginning of "Critique." The triggering of legal violence, with all due ambiguity,

---

Yet there are further complexities underlying Korah's accusation. For it is not only Moses who speaks *in the name* of the Lord, but also Korah and his 250 followers, who *represent* their—holy—communities. Moreover, there is a certain hypocrisy underlying Korah's accusation, since Korah does not reject the legitimacy of Moses' priesthood with respect to its representational dynamic but rather suggests himself as the righteous spokesman of the Lord. The theme of representation is even furthered when Korah and his 250 followers are told to appear equipped with censers, "and *present* it before the Lord" (Num. 16:17). After the annihilation of Korah and his followers, God instructs Moses: "Tell Eleazar son of Aaron, the priest, to take the censers out of the smoldering remains and scatter the coals some distance away, for the censers are holy—the censers of the men who sinned at the cost of their lives. Hammer the censers into sheets to overlay the altar, for they were *presented* before the Lord and have become holy. Let them be a *sign* to the Israelites" (Num. 16:36–38). Once the bodies of Dathan, Abiram, and the other leaders have vanished, their censers, as if delivered from their previous *representational* relationship, assume a new meaning, the meaning of a warning "sign to the Israelites." They are "to remind the Israelites that no one except a descendant of Aaron should come to burn incense before the Lord, or he would become like Korah and his followers" (16:39–40).

Finally the Lord orders Moses to get twelve staffs from the Israelites, "one from the leader of each of their ancestral tribes." The name of each man is written on his staff. On the staff of Levi, Moses is to write Aaron's name. The staff belonging to the chosen man will sprout, and this will calm down the complaining Israelites (see Num. 17:1–4): "So Moses spoke to the Israelites, and their leaders gave him twelve staffs, one for the leader of each of their ancestral tribes, and Aaron's staff was among them. Moses placed the staffs before the Lord in the Tent of the Testimony. The next day Moses entered the Tent of the Testimony and saw that Aaron's staff, which *represented* the house of Levi, had not only sprouted but had budded, blossomed, and produced almonds. Then Moses brought out all the staffs from the Lord's presence to all the Israelites. They looked at them, and each man took his own staff. The Lord said to Moses: 'Put back Aaron's staff in front of the Testimony, to be kept *as a sign* to the rebellious. This will put an end to their grumbling against me, so that they will not die.' Moses did just as the Lord commanded him" (17:6–11).The sprouting and budding tree instigates yet another incidence of *representation*. I do not hope to engage in a detailed exegesis of this passage; the point is that Benjamin's reference to Korah impedes rather than endorses its antithetical status to the story of Niobe. The passage is so imbued with a rhetoric of establishing borders—encompassing instances of *corporeal* as well as *semiotic* representation—that it appears to comment on "mythic violence," all the while rendering Benjamin's category of "divine violence" unintelligible.

is derived from a certain understanding of violence as natural product, as "raw material" (*Rohstoff*). Benjamin discusses natural violence, violence as a product of nature, by (following Spinoza's *Tractatus Theologico-Politicus*) drawing on the natural-law theory that assumes that the individual, before the conclusion of a rational state contract, has *de jure* the right to use at will the violence that is *de facto* (i.e., *de natura*) at his disposal. The problem for Benjamin lies at the threshold, the transition, the short step from the dogma of natural history to the one of legal philosophy—and popular Darwinistic philosophy solidifies his concern. The rekindling of Darwin's biology stimulated in a "thoroughly dogmatic manner" a view that "regards violence as the only original means, besides natural selection, appropriate to all the vital ends of nature" (180). Benjamin suggests that what may be appropriate to natural ends is not necessarily legitimate, let alone just. He refuses to acknowledge bare life as sacred per se, for he knows of the (biopolitical) complicity between bare life and legal violence; it is in this vein that he attacks promoters of the doctrine of the sanctity of life, "which they either apply to all animal and even vegetable life, or limit to human life" (201). Benjamin finds the "canonization" (*Heiligsprechung*) of bare life at its extreme in Kurt Hiller, whose argument runs as follows:

> "If I do not kill, I shall never establish the world dominion of justice . . . that is the argument of the intelligent terrorist. . . . We, however, profess that higher even than the happiness and justice of existence stands existence itself." (Kurt Hiller, *Anti-Kain*, quoted in "Critique," 201)

Benjamin refutes the dogma of the sanctity of life in its Hillerian version if existence means nothing other than bare life ("*Dasein nichts als bloßes Leben bedeuten soll*," 201). However, Benjamin does find a mighty truth in Hiller's sentence by attributing a second semantic layer to the word "existence" (*Dasein*):

> It contains a mighty truth, however, if "existence" . . . means the irreducible, total condition that is "human being"; if the proposition is intended to mean that the nonexistence of man is something more terrible than the (admittedly subordinate) *not-yet-attained condition of the just human beings.* . . . A human being cannot, at any price, be said to coincide with the mere life in him, any more than it can be said to coincide with any other of his conditions and qualities, including even the uniqueness of his bodily person. However sacred man is (or however sacred that life in him which is identically present in earthly life, death, and afterlife), there is no sacredness in his condition, in his bodily life vulnerable to injury by his fellow human beings. What, then, distinguishes it essentially from the life of animals and plants? (201–2)

The life of humans is different from that of animals and plants primarily in that it is ethical. Benjamin juxtaposes "bare life" (*bloßes Leben*) with the category of "the living" (*Lebendigkeit*) (200).[17] While "bare life" entails a *promise* for justice, "the living" *is* just.[18]

Benjamin not only characterizes divine violence as expiating, striking, and without bloodshed, but also "by the absence of all lawmaking": "To this extent it is justifiable to call this violence, too, annihilating; but it is so only relatively, with regard to goods, right, life [Leben], and suchlike, never absolutely, with regard to the soul of the living [die Seele des Lebendigen]" (200). Benjamin's aligning of the divine with "the living" (as opposed to mere "bodily life vulnerable to injury") feeds the predictable accusation that the premise of the extension of divine power, taken to its logical conclusion, "confers on men even lethal power against one another." However,

> the question "May I kill?" meets its irreducible answer in the commandment "Thou shalt not kill." This commandment *precedes the deed*, just as God was *"standing before"* the deed. But just as it may not be fear of punishment that enforces obedience, the injunction becomes inapplicable, incommensurable, once the deed is accomplished. (200)

Precisely because the commandment *pre-cedes the deed*, it does not lend itself to any form of instrumentalization "within" the legal sphere. The spheres of the commandment and law are as incommensurable as the spheres of law and justice:

> Those who base a condemnation of all violent killing of one person by another on the commandment are therefore mistaken. It exists not as a criterion of judgment, but as a guideline for the actions of persons or communities who have to wrestle with it in *solitude* and, in exceptional cases, to take on themselves the *responsibility* of ignoring

---

17. The dichotomy of "bare" and "just" life is one Benjamin borrows from the Greek tradition, where the difference between human and animal life is not only demarcated by the possession of *logos* but also by the existence of an understanding of justice, *dikē*. See Marcel Detienne, *Les maîtres de vérité dans la Grèce archaique* (Paris: Maspero, 1967); Detienne, *Dionysos mis à mort* (Paris: Gallimard, 1977).

18. Benjamin's antithetical treatment of mythic and divine violence ends with this enigmatic conclusion: "Mythic violence is bloody power over bare life for its own sake; divine violence is pure power over all life for the sake of the living. The first demands sacrifice; the second accepts it" (200). Some elucidation is provided by the "Outline of the Psychophysical Problem" in volume 6 of *Gesammelte Schriften*, a series of fragments written around 1922/23 and much indebted to Husserl's phenomenology. The opposition of bare life and just "living" (*Lebendigkeit*) figures here as the antipodes of "body and corporeal substance" (*Leib und Körper*): "Man's *body* [*Leib*] and his *corporeal substance* [*Körper*] place him in universal contexts. But a different context for each: with his *body*, man belongs to mankind; with his *corporeal substance*, to God" (80). "This corporeal substance [Körper] is...a substance [Substrat] in contrast to our body, which is only a function [Funktion]. Our corporeal substance is objective in a higher sense" (79). "Objective" means: "The body...was created to fulfill the Commandments. It was fashioned at the Creation according to this purpose" (82).

Benjamin's peculiar remark, according to which mythic violence demands sacrifice, whereas divine violence accepts it, is now commented on, as it were, in a more intelligible fashion: "Bodily nature [i.e., bare life] advances toward its dissolution; that of corporeal substance [i.e., just life, the living], however, advances toward its resurrection" (80f.) (*Gesammelte Schriften*, 6:79–82; *Selected Writings, 1913–1926*, 1:394–96).

it. Thus it was understood by Judaism, which expressly rejected the condemnation of killing in self-defense. (200)

How does the Judaic rejection of the condemnation of killing in self-defense relate to justice? We should not, I think, interpret it as a *suspension of the commandment*. For what "stands before" can be considered only in its existence "outside the law" (200). In "exceptional cases" the killing of one person by another is left to one's *responsibility,* an authority *beyond all legal right,* one that cannot be deduced from a logos, a jurisdiction, and for precisely this reason is difficult and exceptionally solitary. Because "the soul of the living" stands outside the law, it cannot be threatened by even the most powerful legal violence. "For with bare life, the rule of law over the living ceases" (200; Denn mit dem bloßen Leben hört die Herrschaft des Rechtes über den Lebendigen auf).

It is precisely this condition that both Creon and Antigone dismiss, thus calling guilt upon themselves. Antigone and Creon invoke justice (*dikē*) to justify their actions (256, 208); neither recognizes that the justness of Polyneices' life is one that *pre-cedes all logification,* be it Antigone's theo*logical* or Creon's polito*logical* one. The blind prophet Teiresias prognosticates to Creon:

> Know well, the sun will not have rolled its course
> Many more days, before you come to give
> Corpse for these corpses, child of your own loins.
> For you've confused the upper and lower worlds.
> You sent a life to settle in a tomb;
> You keep up here that which belongs below
> The corpse unburied, robbed of its release.
> Not you, nor any god that rules on high
> Can claim him now
> You rob the nether gods of what is theirs.
> So the pursuing horrors lie in wait
> To track you down. The Furies sent by Hades
> And by all gods will even you with your victims. (Sophocles, *Antigone* 1065–77)

Justice does not yield to human discourse, and he who does not recognize this (as does Creon, who seeks to deprive Polyneices the status of a just life, thereby infringing on the unwritten laws of the chthonic gods) incurs "retribution" (*Sühne*). Antigone as much as Creon seeks to appropriate justice (one of the state, the other of the chthonic gods; see lines 536, 737). But justice is essentially as ungraspable as God; justice is God or at least the principle of all divine making. Benjamin says precisely that: "Justice is the principle of all divine endmaking" (198). Does this mean that any striving for justice is doomed a priori? What results from the insight into the unattainability of justice? "Unaged in time," chants the Chorus in *Antigone,* "[Zeus] you rule of Olympus' gleaming light. / Near time, far future, and the past, / One law controls them all: / Any greatness in human life brings doom" (Sophocles, *Antigone* 609–13). That greatness brings doom is essentially *tragic.* The tragic condition is one not precipitated by human *hybris* alone but rooted in the chasm, the abyss, at the bottom of judicial discourse. Prometheus's greatness ("dignified courage") is as tragic as the conflict between Antigone and Creon, a conflict not reducible to arrogance or blindness or a cursed ancestry beginning with Oedipus. The conflict *carried out* behind the shields of natural law (by Antigone) and positive law (by Creon) is *rooted* within the sphere of law; it can be traced to the *unrecognizability of justice.*

"Unless it be..."

Why, then, does Sophocles stage a play (written at a time when juridical thinking came into being) in mythic time; and, one consequently and finally may ask, what is the status of the theatrical in Benjamin's critique of violence? In *Antigone* the mythic discourse seems to suspend the juridical "discourse," thus allowing for it to be scrutinized, for an exploration of the interrelation of law and justice, dismantling and disclosing its aporetic link. Yet is this not much like what Benjamin achieves with the rhetorically staged distinction between an indistinguishable *within-the-circle* (*Bannkreis,* 195–96) (i.e., law) and a nonrecognizable *beyond-the-circle* (i.e., justice)? Nothing less than this refusal of philosophical systematization of the question of justice motivates those uncanny quotation marks around "philosophy":

> The critique of violence is the philosophy of its history—the "philosophy" of this history because only the idea of its development makes possible a critical, discriminating, and decisive approach to its temporal data. A gaze directed only at what is close at hand can at most perceive a dialectical rising and falling in the law-positing and law-preserving forms of violence.... This lasts until either new forces or those earlier suppressed triumph over the hitherto lawmaking violence and thus found a new law, destined in its turn to decay. On the breaking of this cycle maintained by mythic forms of law [Durchbrechung dieses Umlaufs im Banne der mythischen Rechtsformen], on the deposing of law [Entsetzung] with all the forces on which it depends as they depend on it, finally therefore on the abolition of state power, a new historical epoch is founded. (202)

To what degree does Benjamin's performance generate a new historicity? How convincingly can a text, caught in the dialectics of law positing and law preserving, speak of *de-posing (Entsetzung),* how wide a hiatus can there be between the constative and the performative of a text for it to still function as speech act?

But if the existence of violence outside the law, as pure immediate violence, is assured [Ist aber der Gewalt auch jenseits des Rechtes ihr Bestand als reine unmittelbare gesichert], this furnishes proof that revolutionary violence, the *highest manifestation* of pure violence by human beings, is possible, and shows by what means. (202)

The "highest manifestation" of pure violence is possible also, one may add, within a critique of violence. Yet the conditionality ("But if...") of highest manifestation in the human sphere also implies the possibility of its impossibility. Just how much Benjamin's rhetoric is informed by prognosis and prophecy is indicated by the peculiar grammatical pace of the next sentence, a sentence that inflicts some strain on the German ear: "Less possible and also less urgent for humankind, however, is to decide when pure violence has been realized in particular cases" (202–3; Nicht gleich möglich noch auch gleich dringend ist aber für Menschen die Entscheidung, wann reine Gewalt in einem bestimmten Falle wirklich war). The grammatical category of an implicit future anterior forfeits the possibility of indicative assertions about the realizability of pure violence and resembles a language we encounter once more in the essay's last sentence, where the mentioning of a "sovereign" (*waltende*) violence testifies to its existence—yet again only as manifestation. "Divine violence, which is the sign and seal [Insignium und Siegel] but never the means of a sacred execution [heiliger Vollstreckung], may be called 'sovereign' [waltende] violence" (203). "Sovereign" violence is immediate, but also this immediacy (*Unmittel-bar-keit*) is not entirely deprived of an "ethical anarchism"[19]—a directed immediacy, which, as such, contaminates all pure immediacy. "Less possible and also less urgent [Nicht gleich möglich noch auch gleich dringend] for humankind...is to decide [Entscheidung] *when pure violence has been realized in particular cases*" (202–3). For what is *scheidend und entscheidend* (discriminating, and decisive), such as the approach "Toward...Critique," implies both, a perpetual law-positing, dividing (*scheidend*) movement, and also its undividing (*Ent-scheidung*), de-posing (*Ent-setzung*), the withdrawal from the dialectical rising and falling in the law-positing and law-preserving forms of violence and therefore the circularity of means and ends. This abyss in the juridical discourse Benjamin speaks *about,* as well as the abyss in the presentation *(Darstellung)* of "Critique," could never be subject to *judgment* but only *negotiation.* As in *Antigone,* "Critique"'s narrative staging of indistinguishabilities would not merely be a form of *refusal* to explicate the unattainable—justice—but, in the form of a reenactment, the very center of performance. The impossibility of logification is performed as gestures of *abstention* ("omission," 184).[20] One may say that Benjamin hovers in a

---

19. See Benjamin's remarks on an "ethical anarchism" in *Gesammelte Schriften,* 6:107.
20. With regard to Benjamin's "Goethe's Elective Affinities," one could say that "the expressionless" (*das Ausdruckslose*) is the "standstill" in the aesthetic realm; it falls into line with Benjamin's example of the proletarian general strike, the standstill of all production ("omission of an action") in the political sphere. Both are intricately related in their moral claim, a claim that finds expression precisely in the

dual state of refusal—a refusal as to "philosophy,"[21] and a refusal in the sense of the Jewish prohibition of the image. And it is this gesture of refusal that puts us, the spectators of his spectacle, into a position of sitting-in-judgment without being able to judge, a negotiation of the undeterminable.

The not-possible *Ent-scheidung* (un-dividing/decision) suspends all certainty about the factuality of pure violence: "Once again all the eternal forms are open to pure divine violence, which myth bastardized with law" (203). "Once again" is to say "again and again"—like the "dialectical rising and falling." Myth bastardizes all the eternal forms—again and again. This means nothing less than the continuous positing *(Setzung)* and de-posing *(Ent-setzung)* of divine violence followed by still another bastardization. No doubt, also the *waltende* (sovereign) violence is compromised by the dialectical rising and falling—as a result of its combination with a *schaltende* (executive) violence. For *schalten und walten* as an idiomatic phrase,[22] of course, connotes the kind of indeterminacy, undecidability, we "at once" *(nicht gleich)* fail to unravel. "For only mythic violence, not divine, will be *recognizable* as such with certainty, unless it be in incomparable effects [es sei denn in unvergleichlichen Wirkungen]" (203). What defies recognizability forecloses presentation *(Darstellung)*, remains dependent on imagination *(Vorstellung)*, in spite of and precisely because "the coming age *is not so unimaginably remote* [jenes Neue nicht in so unvorstellbarer Fernflucht (liegt)]" (202). The critique of violence epitomizes the compromise of presentation *(Darstellung)* and representation *(Vorstellung)* on the one side, and their "beyond" on the other—a compromise between task *(Aufgabe)* and "resignation" *(Aufgabe)*, a performatory speech act that perpetuates the aporia of an event we cannot witness. "Unless it be..."(203).

---

withdrawal of all state-ment and thus all discriminating violence. "The expressionless is the critical violence which, while unable to separate semblance from essence in art, prevents them from mingling. It possesses this violence as a moral dictum" (Benjamin, *Gesammelte Schriften,* 1:181).

21. "Joy, *jouissance, to come,*" Jean-Luc Nancy writes, "have the sense of birth: the sense of the inexhaustible imminence of sense.... It is a question of the pre-venience of the flower in the fruit.... It merely invites a simple thought, withdrawn and coming forth, careful, graceful, attentive: pre-venient. It is a question of preventing philosophies, of preventing appropriate thinking" (Nancy, *The Birth to Presence,* trans. Brian Holmes et al. [Stanford, CA: Stanford University Press, 1993], 5f.).

22. For a penetrating analysis of this idiomatic phrase, see Peter Fenves, *The Messianic Reduction: Walter Benjamin and the Shape of Time* (Stanford, CA: Stanford University Press, 2011), 222f.

6

THE RETURN OF THE HUMAN

Germany in Autumn

> Murder, it is true, is a banal fact: one can kill the Other; the ethical exigency is not an ontological necessity.... It also appears in the Scriptures, to which the humanity of man is exposed inasmuch as it is engaged in the world. But to speak truly, the appearance in being of these "ethical peculiarities"—the humanity of man—is a rupture of being. It is significant, even if being resumes and recovers itself.
>
> —Emmanuel Levinas, *Ethics and Infinity*

Terrorism in postwar West Germany culminated in a series of traumatic events during seven weeks in the autumn of 1977.[1] On September 5, Hanns-Martin Schleyer, chairman of the Daimler-Benz Company and president of the Federation of German Industries (Bundesverband der Deutschen Industrie) was kidnapped by members of the Red Army Faction (RAF) in a gun battle on the streets of Cologne.[2] His four companions were shot to death. In a videotaped statement,

---

1. Chapter epigraph: Emmanuel Levinas, *Ethics and Infinity,* trans. Richard A. Cohen (Pittsburgh: Duquesne University Press, 1985), 87.
2. The RAF is also known as the Baader-Meinhof group, after Andreas Baader and Ulrike Meinhof, two of its founders and protagonists of the "first generation." For a general account of the organization, see Stefan Aust, *The Baader-Meinhof Complex* (New York: Harcourt Brace, 1989); Jillian Becker, *Hitler's Children? The Story of the Baader-Meinhof Terrorist Gang* (New York: Lippincott, 1977); more recently, Wolfgang Kraushaar, ed., *Die RAF und der linke Terrorismus,* 2 vols. (Hamburg: Hamburger Edition, 2006).

Schleyer was forced by his kidnappers to appeal to the chancellor, Helmut Schmidt, for his release in exchange for that of eleven imprisoned terrorists. In contrast to a previous prisoner exchange, the government this time refused to negotiate. On October 13, a Lufthansa plane carrying eighty-six passengers was hijacked in an attempt to force the release of the captured RAF members. After a long ordeal, including several stops around the Mediterranean, the aircraft eventually landed in Mogadishu, Somalia. On October 18, an antiterrorist elite unit was able to liberate all hostages from this hijacking. On the same day, in the maximum-security prison of Stammheim, Andreas Baader, Gudrun Ensslin, and Jan-Carl Raspe, three members of the RAF, were found dead. The circumstances of these suspected suicides, two of them committed with handguns, were so mysterious that an international commission had to investigate the matter. On October 19, Schleyer's corpse was found in the trunk of an abandoned car on the road to Mulhouse across the French border.

Two Funerals

Germany in Autumn (1977/1978),[3] perhaps the most famous omnibus project of the luminaries of the New German Cinema, including Rainer Werner Fassbinder, Alexander Kluge, Werner Herzog, Volker Schlöndorff, and Edgar Reitz, among others, was shot in immediate response to the events of what was later called the "German Autumn."[4] It is a film about two funerals: the state funeral of Hanns-Martin Schleyer, murdered by members from the RAF; and the joint funeral of Andreas Baader, Gudrun Ensslin, and Jan-Carl Raspe. The film commences as a documentary of the funeral of Schleyer,[5] which was notable for the number of well-known visitors among the congregation. Appearing first is ex-chancellor Kurt Georg Kiesinger, who had joined the Nazi Party in 1933 and worked in the German Foreign Ministry's radio propaganda department. Other political and industrial elites of West Germany follow, figures such as Flick, Quandt, Filbinger, and

---

3. *Deutschland im Herbst* (*Germany in Autumn*) (Filmverlag der Autoren, Hallelujah Film, Kairos Film, 1977/1978; US distributor: New Line Cinema), 134 min.

4. Among the critical literature on *Germany in Autumn* mention should be made of Thomas Elsaesser, "Antigone Agonistes: Urban Guerilla or Guerilla Urbanism? The Red Army Faction, *Germany in Autumn*, and Death Game," in *Giving Grounds: The Politics of Propinquity*, ed. Joan Copjec and Michael Sorkin (London: Verso, 1999), 267–302; Miriam Hansen, "Alexander Kluge's Contribution to *Germany in Autumn*," *New German Critique* 24/25 (Fall/Winter 1981/82): 35–56; Eric Rentschler, *West German Film in the Course of Time* (New York: Redgrave, 1984), esp. the epilogue, "Life with Fassbinder: The Politics of Fear and Pain," 191–202; Anton Kaes, *From Hitler to Heimat* (Cambridge, MA: Harvard University Press, 1989), 22–28; Marc Silberman, "Germany in Autumn," *Discourse* 6 (Fall 1983): 48–52.

5. For a discussion of the "documentary," "semi-documentary," and "fictional" segments in *Germany in Autumn*, see Alexander Kluge and Klaus Eder, *Ulmer Dramaturgien: Reibungsverluste* (Munich: Carl Hanser Verlag, 1980). On the intricate conception of "reality" in the work of Alexander Kluge, who coordinated the film and arranged its montage structure, together with editor Beate Mainka-Jellinghaus, see Alexander Kluge, "On Film and Public Sphere," trans. Thomas Levin and Miriam Hansen, *New German Critique* 24/25 (1981/82): 206–20.

von Brauchitsch, who are known to the German audience for having paved or accompanied the Nazis' route to power, and who also gained, rather preposterously, prominence after the war in the context of West Germany's foundation and economic rise. These very visible continuities in the history of the German elite are figuratively engraved into the face of a particular older gentleman, which is marked by scars ensuing from Mensur fencing, the traditional form of fraternity dueling in which the wounds resulting from a hit were seen a badge of honor. This man tries to avert his gaze from the camera yet remains as much a focal point of the lens as the entire assembly of the former elite gathering in the name of the Federal Republic of Germany. In the background flags of the oil company ESSO flutter—"ESSO"—four letters amid which the "SS" can hardly hide, that "SS" in which Hanns-Martin Schleyer held the rank of an officer, an *Untersturmführer*.

Notable are the many journalists with cameras and microphones. What is documented here for media distribution are condolences as part of a public act of grieving, that is, the passing of someone worth being mourned. The significance of this contiguity of mourning and public discourse, the discursive constitution of something notably grievable, becomes apparent in contrast to the funeral of Baader, Ensslin, and Raspe two days later. This funeral, shown at the end of *Germany in Autumn,* is contested with respect to both its legitimization and its legitimacy; only under difficulties and because of the dismissal of official authorities can a burial place be obtained. A friend of the Ensslin family tells Kluge of the difficulties Gudrun Ensslin's father, Pastor Ensslin, experienced in finding a grave for his daughter and for Baader and Raspe:

> Father Ensslin tried hard, despairingly hard, to find graves. In Stuttgart itself he had unbelievable problems convincing the citizens or anyone at all to bury three terrorists, in any case, people who stand outside society [Leute die außerhalb der Gesellschaft stehen], within the city walls, or within the community [innerhalb von Stadtmauern oder innerhalb einer Gemeinde]. Outside on the land, all right, but not where so-called normal people are buried.[6]

Baader, Ensslin, and Raspe stand "outside society" as "abnormal people"; "normal people," by contrast, are buried "within a community." Perhaps "normal people" are humans, fellow human beings (*Mitmenschen*) whose death causes us pain, people we recognize and with whom we therefore identify, in whose doom we partake. Acts of grieving, *symbolically* taking into society those whom the event of death has placed physically outside society, binding affect energies in the course of mourning rituals, quelling a pain and filling a vacuum left by the deceased, thus ensuring societal order and continuity for the polity, such acts of grieving seem

---

6. While all quotations of *Germany in Autumn* are based on the English subtitles, many of those translations were modified.

entirely superfluous when it comes to the deceased Baader, Ensslin, and Raspe—or this at least is public opinion. Ensslin's sister tells us: "When I came back from my vacation, the first thing I read in the paper was, 'Into the sewage,' and I knew that the people had already begun to call, 'Let them rot!'" Evidently, Raspe, Baader, and Ensslin appear less worthy of grief and, as such, perhaps less human.

The cinematic narrative emerging here could be characterized as a surface discourse largely revolving, on the one hand, around the state funeral of Hanns-Martin Schleyer and involving the participation of the highest dignitaries, and, on the other, around the funeral excluded from public discourse of Baader, Ensslin, and Raspe. In addition, we find a more subterranean discourse emerging, juxtaposing one funeral aligned with the generation of the Fascist fathers with another aligned with a younger generation of sons and daughters who morally discredit their parents for their crimes of the past and their crimes of the present.[7] What, we will have to ask, are the implications of Baader, Ensslin, and Raspe's funeral, which suggests that they are unworthy of mourning and should be deprived of any public form of recognition, in contrast to Schleyer's appearance as the grievable par excellence? "As to Eteocles,... there shall be such funeral / as we give to the noblest dead," Creon says in Sophocles' *Antigone,* as cited in the short *mise en abyme* television production later in the film. "But as to his brother, Polyneices,.../ it has been proclaimed / that none shall honor him, none shall lament over him." We will return to the question of the interrelation of mourning and the dynamics of societal inclusion and exclusion, the public act of grieving for certain members of the socius, their stylization as "martyr" and paradigmatic "human," and the denial of public grieving as a means of excluding others, allegedly subhuman beings, *Untermenschen.*[8]

Clearly, the question of humanization or dehumanization is intimately bound up with the question of *presentation,* and it is the task of *cinematic presentation* that *Germany in Autumn* pursues. In the 1978 manifesto "What Is the Film's Bias [*Parteilichkeit*]?" the eleven filmmakers collectively proclaim: "Autumn 1977 is the

---

7. "The unreformed continuation of the country's affairs in the style of the old German ruling classes," Norbert Elias writes, "was certainly one of the main reasons why many young people in the upcoming generation had the feeling that, in essence, nothing had changed and they were still living in an authoritarian state, but whether that sentiment was right or wrong, the decisive aspect was quite simply the fact that a considerable group of young people, increasing numbers of whom had not experienced the past at first hand, arrived at this conviction. This is certainly where one of the roots of their radicalization lay and hence, in extreme cases, their later terrorism" (Elias, "Gedanken über die Bundesrepublik: Herbst 1977," *Merkur* 9/10 [Sept./Oct. 1985]: 745).

8. As Volker Schlöndorff reports, the Filmverlag der Autoren had approached Rainer Werner Fassbinder and himself the day after the suicide of Baader, Ensslin, and Raspe, pondering what could be done in light of the univocity of all television channels, radio stations, and the press. There Schleyer was established as "demi-saint," as "martyr," whereas the RAF members were depicted as "subhumans" and "the scum of humanity." Thus they agreed that a more eclectic counter-public sphere needed to be constituted (interview with Volker Schlöndorff on *Deutschland im Herbst* [Kinowelt Home Entertainment, 2004], DVD, 119 min).

history of confusion. Exactly this must be held on to. Whoever knows the truth lies. Whoever does not know it seeks."⁹ In a less sweeping voice, filmmaker Bernd Sinkel, in the context of an interview with the directors, says: "We did...not attempt to present the events of autumn 1977 or parts of them, *but to show what kind of statement film can or cannot make about them.*"¹⁰ When a film like *Germany in Autumn*, embarking on an exploration of that spectral atmosphere of autumn 1977, with its anxiety, paranoia, public denunciation, and state authoritarianism, does *not* seek to present the events of the tragic fall ("nicht versucht die Ereignisse des Herbstes 1977 darzustellen"), what then can it do or state or probe? What can or cannot a film "say" *about* the events of the German Autumn ("was der Film darüber aussagen kann oder nicht") *beyond* their cinematic presentation? Those who rhetorically, cinematically, poetically eschew the dominant discourses of intelligibility and reason may be prepared for the traps of truth, whose narration is always only obtainable together with the lie. "Whoever knows the truth lies. Whoever does not know it seeks."¹¹ Yet are the filmmakers of *Germany in Autumn* merely seekers? Is not every narration, even that of a documentary, allegedly objective, always also judgment? Does this then not inevitably present us with the question of the ethical stance of the film? Would it be imaginable that another, whether friend or enemy or merely *Other*, dies, and those who tell the story give their account from a "neutral" perspective? Beyond the ambiguous rhetoric of the "humane," beyond the problematic efficacy of "humanist" endeavors, are not the question of "the human" and the act of grieving intricately linked?¹² Are not the problems of "what is a human" and what it means to present a human being one way rather than another or perhaps not at all—are not these the very questions *Germany in Autumn* raises?

Let us then begin with one of the longest scenes of the film, the twenty-six-minute Fassbinder segment immediately following the funeral of Schleyer. Here the various "conditions" (*Zustände*), political, social, juridical, psychological,

---

9. Alf Brustellin, Rainer Werner Fassbinder, Alexander Kluge, Volker Schlöndorff, Bernhard Sinkel, "Germany in Autumn: What Is the Film's Bias?" in *West German Filmmakers on Film: Visions and Voices*, ed. and trans. Eric Rentschler (New York: Holmes & Meier, 1988), 133 ("Was ist die Parteilichkeit des Films?" in *Deutschland im Herbst: Terrorismus im Film,* ed. Petra Kraus et al. [Munich: Schriftenreihe Münchner Filmzentrum, 1997], 81).

10. "'Deutschland im Herbst' oder 'Modell Deutschland,'" interview with the filmmakers, *Filmfaust* 2 (1978): 3–15, here 4. Unless otherwise noted, all italics in this chapter are mine.

11. "'Deutschland im Herbst' oder 'Modell Deutschland.'"

12. It should be noted that I by no means seek to advocate a form of "identity politics" here, as one so frequently encounters it when political analyses succumb to a rhetoric of the "humane," a rhetoric susceptible to a sentimentality that limits the very possibility of political scrutiny. It would be interesting to ask to what extent the particular mode of presentation of the human faces depicted in the film invites or resists acts of identification. The very "*being* of human being" may turn out to have "more to do with *setups* and *sets* than with *subjects* and *objects*, unified in and through self-consciousness" (Samuel Weber, *Mass Mediauras: Form, Technics, Media* [Stanford, CA: Stanford University Press, 1996], 4, Weber's italics). Cf. Samuel Weber and Laurence A. Rickels, "Theory on TV: 'After-Thoughts,'" in *Religion and Media*, ed. Hent de Vries and Samuel Weber (Stanford, CA: Stanford University Press, 2001), 94–111.

are presented in the disputes between a representative of the parental generation and a representative of the descendants' generation, a mother, Lilo Pempeit, and her son, Rainer Werner Fassbinder.

The "Evil" of Democracy

The provocative Fassbinder episode is staged in the filmmaker's poorly lit Munich apartment. It commences with the shot of an exhausted, somewhat scruffy man with exposed belly introducing himself with "It's me, Fassbinder" to the person on the phone and to us, his viewers. In a staged interview with a journalist, Fassbinder (or his narrator double) characterizes marriage as an "artificial" institution and explains that he makes films in order that, among other things, marriages, rather than surviving unquestioned, "fall apart" (in die Brüche geht)[13]—only a minute later to call his wife, Ingrid Caven, in Paris to hear news about the hijacked aircraft in Mogadishu. At the same time, Fassbinder is bossing around his gay lover, Arnim, who for evident reasons nicknames him "bully." Fassbinder, no doubt, is not only the oppressed son but also a "patriarch," so that the mother against whom he rails does not merely epitomize the oppressive parent but also the oppressed. Yet what is it that really lies at the center of this episode?

The first shot shows Fassbinder speaking on the phone, alluding to his own "hysteria," stuttering inconsistently, dismayed, frantic, beleaguered, anxious, agitated. It is into this atmosphere that interlocutory scenes with his mother, Pempeit, are embedded, the first explicitly revolving around societal "hysteria." On the basis of her experiences during the Nazi period, the mother notes that she would not advise anyone to discuss the matter of terrorism openly, in light of current political problems: "Because I don't know what someone else would do." She recounts a recent experience of speaking favorably of the writer Heinrich Böll, who had called for "safe conduct

---

13. The link between the initial problematization of the institution of marriage and the question of terrorism emerges with respect to Fassbinder's understanding of "anarchy." The *institution of marriage* and the *institution of democracy* equally require "constant movement," "constant questioning and criticism," Fassbinder says. His notion of anarchy, much indebted to the classical, idealistic anarchism in the nineteenth century, is incompatible with any form of terrorism: "I am...an extreme advocate of democracy with a concrete utopia of anarchy in mind, another minority. Actually that's something one shouldn't even mention these days, the part about anarchy. *We have learned from the media that anarchy and terrorism are synonymous.* On the one hand there is a utopia of a form of government without hierarchies, without fears, without aggressions, and on the other a concrete societal situation in which utopias are suppressed. The fact that terrorism could develop here is a sign that the utopias have been suppressed much too long" (Rainer Werner Fassbinder, "The Winter Years," in *Politics, Poetics: Documenta X, The Book*, ed. Catherine David and Jean François Chevrier [Ostfildern-Ruit: Cantz, 1997], 480, 482). Cf. the interview with Beate Mainka-Jellinghaus on the DVD recording of Fassbinder's *Die dritte Generation* (Kinowelt Home Entertainment, 2004), 105 min.; Robert Fischer, ed., *Fassbinder über Fassbinder: Die ungekürzten Interviews* (Darmstadt: Verlag der Autoren, 2004), 194, 309f., 562f.; Rainer Werner Fassbinder, *Die Anarchie der Phantasie: Gespräche und Interviews*, ed. Michael Töteberg (Frankfurt a.M.: Fischer TB Verlag, 1986), 90–93.

for Ulrike Meinhof,"[14] and consequently found himself in the cross fire of the conservative Springer Press, exposed to defamation, denounced as a "sympathizer" with the terrorists.[15] "You understand," she says, "you don't know in this *hysterical situation* at the moment what will be made out of something that you say." What suggests itself as exceptional here, both on a private level (in Pempeit's, or her narrator double's, social environment), and on a societal level (with respect to the slander of Böll), is an atmosphere reminiscent of Nazi Germany: "You see, it reminds me a lot of the Nazi times, when people simply were quiet to avoid falling into the fat [in der man einfach geschwiegen hat, um sich nicht in Teufels Küche zu bringen]." This state of exception, as she perceives it, determines both the explicit discourse of subsequent dialogues and the performatively engendered atmosphere in the apartment.

Fassbinder then speaks to Ingrid Caven on the phone about the terrorists' suicides: Ensslin hanged herself, and Baader and Raspe shot themselves, unbelievably enough, with "real guns." To Fassbinder it strains credulity that pistols could have been smuggled into the cells of the maximum-security prison, implicitly raising the suspicion of a state-condoned assassination of the terrorists, a suspicion also expressed on the banners of attendees at the funeral of Baader, Ensslin, and Raspe.[16] It is also during this phone conversation that the infamous *Kontaktsperregesetz* is mentioned, whose necessity the Social Democrat Herbert Wehner seeks to justify in a speech incorporated later in the film. To the German audience the *Kontaktsperregesetz* registers as a signal word: based on the assumption that the imprisoned terrorists continued to direct operations via communication through their lawyers, the federal minister of justice, Hans-Joachim Vogel, had directed his subordinates "to prevent any contact whatsoever between imprisoned terrorists and the outside world."[17] The order had been harshly criticized because "the constitutional

---

14. Heinrich Böll, "Will Ulrike Gnade oder freies Geleit?" *Der Spiegel,* January 10, 1972, 54–57.

15. The jurisdiction of opinion (*Gesinnungsstrafrecht*) describes, in the words of Felix Guattari, the "collective emotional context in which these opinions take shape, that is, one of the essential components in the massive foundation of any opinion that becomes law" (Guattari, "Like the Echo of a Collective Melancholy," *Semiotexte* 4.2 [1982]: 102–10). Among the many theorizations of the sociocultural dynamics of terrorism, see Noam Chomsky, *The Culture of Terrorism* (Boston: South End Press, 1988); Jean Baudrillard, "Our Theatre of Cruelty," trans. John Johnston, *Semiotexte* 4.2 (1982): 108–15; Jean-Paul Sartre, "Schreckliche Situation," interview with Alice Schwarzer, *Der Spiegel,* February 12, 1974, 166–69; Jacques Derrida, *Rogues: Two Essays on Reason,* trans. Pascale-Anne Brault and Michael Naas (Stanford, CA: Stanford University Press, 2005). The painter Gerhard Richter subjects the problematic of the mythos of the RAF to critical scrutiny in his *Atlas,* then in the famous 1988 *October 18, 1977* series, and again in his 1995 *Stammheim.*

16. This assumption, lending itself to one of the most viable legends permeating the history of the RAF, had deliberately been evoked by Baader and Raspe, who theatrically shot themselves in the neck from behind. See "Mythos RAF: Im Spannungsfeld von terroristischer Herausforderung und populistischer Bedrohungsphantasie," in Kraushaar, *Die RAF und der linke Terrorismus,* 2:1186–1210, here 1195–97; Karl-Heinz Weidenhammer, *Selbstmord oder Mord? Das Todesermittlungsverfahren: Baader/Ensslin/Raspe* (Kiel: Neuer Malik Verlag, 1988), 45f.

17. *Dokumentation zu den Ereignissen und Entscheidungen im Zusammenhang mit der Entführung von Hanns-Martin Schleyer und der Lufthansa-Maschine 'Landshut'* (Bonn: Presse- und Informationsamt der Bundesregierung, 1977), 18, after Wolfgang Kraushaar, "Der nicht erklärte Ausnahmezustand: Staatliches

principle had to take second place to a reason of state";[18] it indeed was associated with the notion of the "state of exception" (*Ausnahmezustand*), which does not appear in the German constitution but had been popularized by the legal theorist Carl Schmitt since the 1920s.[19] The extraordinary emotive status of this law mentioned by Fassbinder corresponds to a grotesque reenactment: Fassbinder sits on the floor, deplores the disproportionality of the state actions, at the same time facing the camera, naked, with spread legs, masturbating, his bare body, skin soft as an infant's, appearing heavy and massive and at the same time vulnerable.

In another telephone conversation with Caven, Fassbinder discusses the government's call for the population to help out with the investigation of Schleyer's kidnappers by reporting suspicious behavior of fellow citizens to the police via anonymous phone calls. Fassbinder asserts that this is a more general tactic to fortify state authority: "It forces people to denounce others; it actually forces them to give names! You don't really believe that...you don't really believe that something will change. It remains the same, that's exactly what they want."[20] Suddenly, Fassbinder, infuriated, shouts at the wall: "Yes, feel free to listen to my conversation." This seemingly random remark alludes to the wiretapping to which Fassbinder considers himself subject, and corresponds biographically to his infamous personal encounters with Ulrike Meinhof and Andreas Baader that indeed subjected him to wiretapping. The widespread implementation of wiretapping—also commented

---

Handeln während des sogenannten Deutschen Herbstes," in *Die RAF und der linke Terrorismus*, 1015f. For a detailed discussion of the legal complexeties of the *Kontaktsperregesetz*, see Kraushaar, "Der nicht erklärte Ausnahmezustand," 1011–25, esp. the section "Die Einführung des Kontaktsperregesetzes," 1015f.

18. Kraushaar, "Der nicht erklärte Ausnahmezustand," 1014.

19. See, among others, Ernst-Wolfgang Böckenförde (former judge at the Federal Constitutional Court in Germany), "Der verdrängte Ausnahmezustand: Zum Handeln der Staatsgewalt in außergewöhnlichen Lagen," *Neue juristische Wochenschrift* 31.38 (September 1978): 1881–89. It should be noted that the "term of a 'state of exception'...as a constitutional concept in the Basic Law [*Grundgesetz*]...does not appear; instead [there are] varying degrees of deviance from the 'standard constitution' (emergency legislation, case of tension, internal emergency, case of defense and, in addition, catastrophe and disaster)" (Ulrich K. Preuß, e-mail message to author, April 11, 2007). It is in this vein that Wolfgang Kraushaar, a political scientist working at the Hamburg Institute for Social Research, talks of "a state of exception applied but not announced" (Kraushaar, "Der nicht erklärte Ausnahmezustand," 1017). See also Wolfgang Kraushaar, "Die Schleyer-Entführung: 44 Tage ohne Opposition; Die Linke im Zirkelschluss von RAF und Staat," in *Revolte und Reflexionen: Politische Aufsätze 1976–87* (Frankfurt a.M.: Verlag Neue Kritik, 1990), 91; Carsten Polzin, "Kein Austausch! Die verfassungsrechtliche Dimension der Schleyer Entscheidung," in Kraushaar, *Die RAF und der linke Terrorismus*, 1026–47; Herfried Münkler, "Sehnsucht nach dem Ausnahmezustand," ibid., 1211–26; Uwe Wesel, "Strafverfahren, Menschenwürde und Rechtsprinzip," ibid., 1048–57.

20. This concern regarding the instrumentalization of terrorism finds a tragicomic manifestation with a joke in Fassbinder's film *The Third Generation*: "Capital hires the terrorists to force the state to protect it better. In other words: everything serves to protect the powerful; even the apparent threat is only a dramatized threat in the sense of securing the continuation of existing power relations." Fassbinder expressed the same thought in an interview, saying: "It's not terrorism that appalls me personally so much, but what the state makes out of it to equip itself with more authority and more power." See Fischer, *Fassbinder über Fassbinder*, 564.

on by Max Frisch later in the film—again epitomizes a strong emotive momentum in the cinematic production of an exceptional atmosphere.[21]

This purportedly "political" narrative is permeated by a subsequent allegedly "private" moment, presenting a transgression, a destabilization of borders: Fassbinder jumps up, runs to the bathroom, and throws up. The spectator is invited to follow Fassbinder's deteriorating condition—as both a politically troubled and physically suffering human being, a condition aligned to a discursive establishment of showing and recognizing "the human." "What are you looking at?" Fassbinder asks, having just vomited, now gazing at Arnim and gazing into the camera at us, that is, at other humans who are in a position to *recognize* or *not recognize* him as human. We will have to return to this question of what it means to present a human being one way rather than the other, what the valences of representation can be or imply. Fassbinder shouts: "I'm depressed! I don't know..." The private appears as little private here as the political remains confined to the outside world: Fassbinder's psychological deterioration (depression) and his physical deterioration (emesis) emerge both as product and as impulse of a perceived state of exception. This perceived state is concretized in the disputes between mother and son:

FASSBINDER: When the pilot was shot in Mogadishu or in Aden, you said that for everyone shot in Aden you'd like a terrorist to be shot in Stammheim.
MOTHER: Yes, publicly....
FASSBINDER: And that's democratic!
MOTHER: *No, that's not democratic. Neither was it democratic to hijack this plane and say: "Now we'll shoot each, one by one..."* If you'd been sitting there, or if I'd been there, how would you react!
FASSBINDER: An eye for an eye, a tooth for a tooth.
MOTHER: Not an eye for an eye, a tooth for a tooth, *but in such a situation you can't get by simply with democracy.*[22]

---

21. Wolfgang Kraushaar considers "implementing bugging operations" and the law on limiting contact of detainees with the outside world (*Kontaktsperregesetz*) as the two central moments that justify characterizing the period as an "applied state of exception." For the period of the German Autumn, he diagnoses "under the conditions of the Schleyer kidnapping which were removed from any public and parliamentary control, one of the largest bugging operations in the history of this still relatively young republic" (Kraushaar, "Der nicht erklärte Ausnahmezustand," 1021f.). As *Der Spiegel* noted in one of its issues of August 1987, "The breach of the constitution was so blatant that Richard Meier, then director of the Cologne Federal Office for the Protection of the Constitution, rejected telephone eavesdropping. But his minister Werner Maihofer insisted on it." ("Die Deutschen sind irrsinnig geworden," *Der Spiegel*, August 31, 1987, 111). Paragraph 34 codified "the legal concept of the justified state of emergency [Notstand]." According to Kraushaar, "*This paragraph defines the entire period,*" i.e., as relying on a supralegal state of emergency. "As...utilizing Paragraph 34 to justify the illegal bugging praxis shows, the legal concept contained within it was converted into an instrument of state action against the constitutionally guaranteed rights of the individual citizen. It was used as an all-purpose weapon for operations that could not be made compatible with the Basic Law (*Grundgesetz*). In the hands of an executive that had become uncontrollable, it served as a legal anti-tank gun" (Kraushaar, "Der nicht erklärte Ausnahmezustand," 1021f.).

22. As the motto for his film *Die dritte Generation* (The Third Generation), Fassbinder selected a comment made by Chancellor Helmut Schmidt in a *Spiegel* interview, on the freeing of the Mogadishu

Fassbinder's mother does not contemplate the suspension of the legal order "*in such a situation*" as a *permanent* solution, but solely as a temporary response to the terrorists, "who also did not act democratically." What she ponders here is explicitly not to be understood as a form of retaliation ("Not an eye for an eye, a tooth for a tooth"), but as a means of serving the protection of the passengers of the hijacked aircraft and the political order putatively threatened by the terrorists. The logic of this argument according to which the exceptionality of a societal situation justifies an exceptional juridical response (resembling Carl Schmitt's notion of "situational law")[23] is reenacted in the subsequent scene. Here, Fassbinder—whose elaborations on democracy are continuously undermined by his own performance, that is, his abusive behavior toward Arnim and Lilo Pempeit—suffers through a panic attack precipitated by the sound of police sirens on the street. He flushes cocaine and marijuana down the toilet lest he be charged by the police—who turn out to be going up the stairs to a higher floor. This scene, seemingly entirely dissociated from the kidnapping of Schleyer, gains significance precisely with regard to the ubiquitous paranoia, the seeming undermining of constitutional reason, shedding uncertainty on the constituency of the legal framework of the FRG. "If they'd have come in...!" Fassbinder says, seeking to defend his overreaction in front of Arnim. "And if one of us makes a wrong move, they shoot." The "situation" echoes Lilo Pempeit's words—*"But in such a situation you can't get by simply with democracy"* (*in einer solchen Situation, da kannst du einfach nicht ankommen mit Demokratie*)—with respect to the retrenchment of basic rights because of an *emergency situation*. Once again, we are witnessing an "intrusion" of the political into the private sphere and the transmutation of seemingly private views into political acts, that is, the interlacing of the private and the political. In this atmosphere of a state of exception, private paranoia and public paranoia have become interdependent and indistinguishable. The dispute between Fassbinder and his mother aims precisely in that direction:

MOTHER:...*in such a situation!*
FASSBINDER: You just said laws didn't interest you. But you are a democrat....
MOTHER: [The terrorists] disregard the laws, not I.
FASSBINDER: An ordinary murderer does that, too!
MOTHER: Then they're murderers, the terrorists.

---

hostages: "I can only thank the German jurists retrospectively for not adhering to constitutional procedures" ("Leistung liegt im Deutschen drin," Interview mit Bundeskanzler Helmut Schmidt, *Der Spiegel,* January 15, 1979, 42). Significantly, this comment is excerpted from a discussion in which Schmidt was asked to explain what he understood by "state of emergency."

23. Rather than succumbing to a logic of "calculability" and "certainty," *Situationsrecht* is characterized by such concepts as "state of danger" and "case of necessity." On Schmitt's conception of *Situationsrecht*, see his *Political Theology: Four Chapters on the Concept of Sovereignty,* trans. George Schwab (Cambridge, MA: MIT Press, 1985), 13f. (*Politische Theologie: Vier Kapitel zur Lehre der Souveränität* [Berlin: Duncker & Humblot, 2004], 19f.); Schmitt, "Staat, Bewegung, Volk," in *Die Dreigliederung der politischen Einheit* (Hamburg: Hanseatische Verlagsanstalt Hamburg, 1934), esp. 43f.

FASSBINDER: Of course they are. For all I care. *But there are not exceptional laws for murderers....* An ordinary murderer doesn't simply have what's called...bad reasons or none at all for his murderous deed. The bad thing about the terrorists is that *they may have reasons which you understand.*
MOTHER: *Surely, but they don't use the right means, Rainer.*
FASSBINDER: But you're not interested in laws either. You said you didn't care [das Gesetz ist dir wurscht, wenn es drauf ankommt].
MOTHER: *In this situation...*
FASSBINDER: *Is it at all acceptable that there are situations where you aren't interested in who makes the laws? And which?*

The relation between means and ends in the conflict between state and terrorists seems to lie at the crux of this exchange. The mother's statement of the deficiency of the terrorists' means (*"but they don't use the right means"*) for "reasons [one] could understand" is as comprehensible as it is incommensurable with the logic of action of the RAF, whose entire reasoning is along the lines of natural law, that is, based on the conviction that revolutionary justice will eventually justify the violent means. The interview later with Horst Mahler will revolve precisely around this assumption. Fassbinder aptly relates the terrorists' dismissal of the constitutional order of positive law to the idea of situational law—as advocated by the mother—according to which constitutional loyalty may have to suffer: "You're not interested in laws *either*. You said you didn't care [das Gesetz ist dir wurscht, wenn es drauf ankommt]." It seems that the precarious proximity is one between the state's putative suspension of law (in the sense of pre-legal or extra-legal forces) for the preservation of state order, on the one hand, and the pre-legal or extra-legal forces upon which the terrorist's actions are settled in the name of some higher natural law, on the other.[24]

What keeps erupting at the surface in almost every segment of Fassbinder's contribution to *Germany in Autumn* is the exceptionally paranoiac atmosphere: Arnim invites a stranger home, offering him a place to sleep only to have to make him leave

---

24. Social contract theorists "from Hobbes to Rousseau [have argued that] only those who cede their natural, admittedly precarious, rights can recover some of them in a *guaranteed* form. However, since contract theorists assumed that the few guaranteed rights were more than the many uncertain ones, they were able to view, overall, the establishment of the state and the transition from 'the state of nature' to 'civil society' as progress." By contrast, the terrorist, who does not accept that the state has, in the words of Max Weber, a "monopoly on the legitimate use of physical force within a given territory," appeals to a natural right prior to or beyond positive law, because s/he is no longer ready to accept the purpose of this natural law and natural force in the sense of some kind of social progress. Terrorism discredits the concrete dogma of a society's progress, even if not necessarily the belief in progress per se, which, in the case of the RAF, was only supposed to be given a new ideological connotation that was "in some way" Marxist (Herfried Münkler, "Sehnsucht nach dem Ausnahmezustand," in Kraushaar, *Die RAF und der linke Terrorismus,* 1212; Max Weber, "Politics as a Vocation," in *From Max Weber: Essays in Sociology,* ed. H. H. Gerth and C. Wright Mills [New York: Routledge, 1991], 77–128, here 78, translation modified; Weber, *Politik als Beruf* [Stuttgart: Reclam, 1992], 4).

the very next moment upon receiving Fassbinder's dictate. Fassbinder: "Where's he from?" Arnim: "Don't really know. Hamburg, I think." Fassbinder: "Throw him out." That the stranger comes from Hamburg amounts to yet another signal moment, for Hamburg's anonymous residential housing projects were known as relatively safe hideouts for terrorists from police operations. The manifestation of the tense political situation as an atmospherical state of exception in the Fassbinderian world is solidified when the exasperated Fassbinder, peering through the window after the intruder departs, breaks down both physically and mentally, sobbing and pressing his face against the floor. Immediately after, the dialogical to and fro between Fassbinder and his mother reaches its ineluctable pinnacle:

FASSBINDER: Democracy is the most human form of government, isn't that right?
MOTHER: You see, it's the least of all evils [es ist das kleinste aller Übel].
FASSBINDER: The least of all evils.
MOTHER: At the moment, it's really an evil.
FASSBINDER: Democracy? What would be better...something authoritarian?...
MOTHER: The best thing would be a kind of authoritarian ruler, who is quite good and quite kind and orderly.

What throughout has been identified as an exceptional state, substantiated by constative landmarks such as the *Kontaktsperregesetz,* wiretapping, the subordination of jurisdiction under executive authorities as a form of situational law, and a corresponding atmospherical dimension of hysterical outbreaks, panic attacks, vomiting, and crying fits, reaches its amalgamation in the projected "good," "kind," "orderly" "authoritarian ruler," the personified embodiment of a sovereign. The cinematic production of the atmosphere of a state of exception marks the emotive topography for the subsequent contributions of *Germany in Autumn*.

Faces of Friends and Foes

The incipient documentation of Schleyer's funeral resumes with the High Mass in the St. Eberhard's Church in Stuttgart. A long escort of Mercedes limousines carries those who come to collectively mourn the death of the industrialist Schleyer, some perhaps the *Untersturmführer* Schleyer, others certainly the former chairman of the Daimler-Benz Company. Gigantic flags flutter, resembling idiosyncratic shots in the films of Leni Riefenstahl,[25] though this time showing the Mercedes emblem rather than swastikas. Officials in uniform mingle in front of the church, and hundreds of men in black are seated inside, among them Chancellor Schmidt;

---

25. See also Melissa Goldsmith, "Montage, Music, and Memory: Remembering *Deutschland im Herbst,*" *Kinoeye* 2.20 (2002): 1; James Franklin, *New German Cinema: From Oberhausen to Hamburg* (Boston: Twayne Publishers, 1983), 48–53.

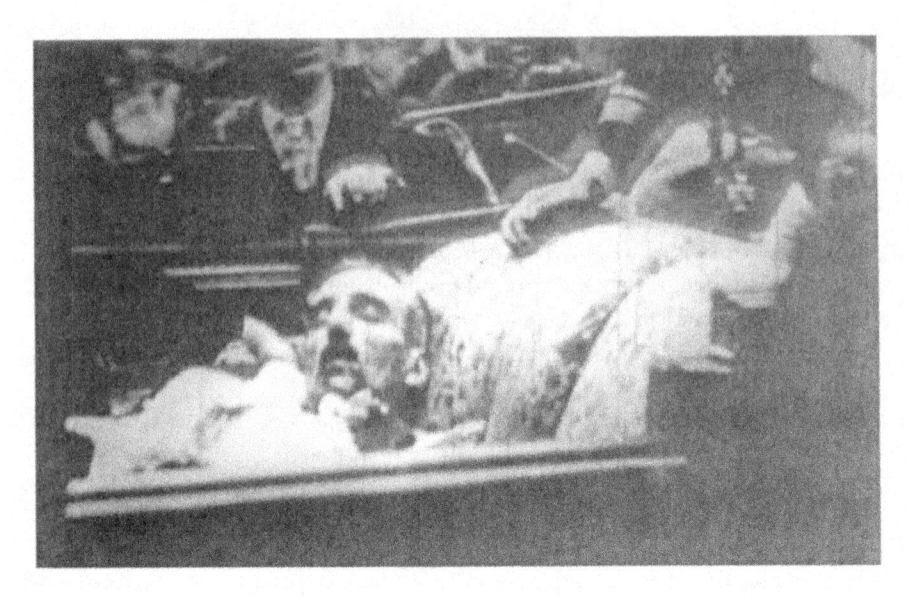

Figure 3.

Franz Josef Strauß, minister-president of Bavaria; Helmut Kohl, opposition leader; ex-chancellor Kiesinger; Walter Scheel, federal president of West Germany; and so forth. An orchestra plays Mozart's *Requiem;* priests walk to the altar. The *cinematic picture* drawn here assembles the trinity of politics, industry, and church. At issue is the question of the (re)presentation of political power and powerful people, that is, conceptually speaking, the connection between the "political" and "the human" with respect to forms of presentation. Then a sudden rupture: Alexander Karadjordjevic, the king of Serbia, on a state visit to France, being driven through the streets of Marseille in an open limousine. The crowds are cheering—and suddenly a gunman steps from the street and shoots the king, who is instantly dead (fig. 3). "The King of Serbia. A murder committed by the German Secret Services in 1938 in Marseille." The ostensible statement of this fragment of historical footage is that a high state official, a king, falls victim to the Macedonian terrorist Vlado Chernozemski, and, as such, resembles Schleyer, who also is murdered by terrorists. In addition to this explicit narrative analogy, however, the performative dimension, the question of the concrete cinematic presentation, is no less significant. For what is not being said here is that this piece of historical footage was the first assassination captured on film: the shooting coincidentally occurred right in front of the cameraman.[26] The newsreel of Alexander I's assassination, depicting the face of the dead monarch close-up, raises a number of questions concerning the politics of representation and the representability of politics, both of which lie at the

---

26. See François Broche, *Assassinat de Alexandre Ier et Louis Barthou* (Paris: Balland, 1977); Robert Seton-Watson, "King Alexander's Assassination: Its Background and Effects," *International Affairs* 14.1 (1935): 20–47.

Figure 4.

center of *Germany in Autumn:* What does it mean to be shown on film? What does it mean for one's face to be filmically or photographically captured, distributable to others and recognizable by others? What does it mean for us to look at this face of a human whose humanness depends on the recognition of the onlooker?

It is not by chance that this fragment interrupts the scene showing the High Mass and the obsequies for Schleyer, as it raises questions about the relatedness of (re)presentation, grievability, and humanness. Both events are televised, and the broadcast is picked up in the main hall of the Automobile Museum, where *"delegated employees and representatives of the plants from all over the world"* have gathered to pay a last tribute to Schleyer. The act of grieving centers, not fortuitously, on an image of this seemingly superior human, an image of Schleyer multiplied on television monitors and, in an enlarged version, posed *before the eyes* of the mourners (fig. 4). What is the dramaturgical status of this image in the context of the funeral ceremony with all its ritualistic pomp, the obsequies witnessed by an array of hundreds of workers, most of them uninvolved yet lined up like believers facing the altar? In honor of Schleyer, the workers at the factory assembly belts in the Mercedes plant in Stuttgart must—simultaneously with the memorial service in the Automobile Museum—stop their work "for three minutes of silence." "Ninety-five percent of the workers on this phase of the assembly line are foreigners," the voice-over comments while following the apathetic faces of employees, most of whom, as Volker Schlöndorff notes, probably invest little interest in the political drama around Schleyer.[27] Through this spectacular veneer Schleyer, as we see him in the

---

27. Interview with Volker Schlöndorff on *Deutschland im Herbst.*

136   *Inconceivable Effects*

Figure 5.

still photo, functions here primarily as a political signifier, as part of a discourse regulated by the state that invokes Schleyer as the martyr of German rebuilding after the war, German industry, German patriarchy. In contradistinction to Baader, Ensslin, and Raspe, Schleyer stands for the *good* dead, as a result of a meticulously programmed discourse, and as this picture of the sanctity appears on millions of TV screens in German households, it appears to establish "the human" that the viewers are to revere, absorb, and internalize.

Concerning a possible equivalent of the inflated Schleyer portrayal in the depiction of the faces of Baader, Ensslin, or Raspe, the focus shifts to the scene in which a female pianist is visited by an alleged terrorist who asks for emergency medical assistance. The image of the chairman of the Daimler-Benz Company and president of the German Federation of Industry finds its discursively regulated counterpart, perhaps unsurprisingly, in the mug shot of Raspe, as publicized in a newspaper lying on a table (fig. 5). Given the classic crime thriller atmosphere of the scene, the mug shot of Raspe appears amenable to the state's discursive constitution of the enemy as "a gruesome thing to see" (as Creon anticipates the corpse of Polyneices),[28] certainly not

---

28. In line with our analysis of depicted faces of friends and foes, one could meditate on the corporeal representation of the political antagonists. It seems that Fassbinder's massive naked body is concatenated, as it were, with Polyneices' naked corpse, which in turn relates to the dead body of Gudrun Ensslin laid out in the coffin. Moreover, Ensslin's corpse appears to correspond to the Communist freedom fighters' corpses sung about in one of Alexander Kluge's contributions. In contrast to the dead or naked children, representatives of the fathers' generation are never displayed naked or dead—that is, their lives never appear bare.

grievable and perhaps not even inhuman but subhuman or nonhuman.[29] The female pianist's gaze out of the window at the departing intruder appears to be an intrafilmic reference to Fassbinder's gaze out of the window at the suspected terrorist from Hamburg. The scene protracts the atmosphere of exception of the Fassbinder segment and as such also precedes Edgar Reitz's contribution to *Germany in Autumn,* the episode at the border checkpoint where, again, mug shots evoke a sensation of the uncanny. The scene is atmospherically permeated by the music of Schubert's *Frühlingstraum* (Dream of Spring), notable for its turbulent minor variations, slow arpeggios, abrasive contrasts of meter (6/8 and 2/4), disjunctions of tempo, dissonances, alternations between diatonic and chromatic strains, changes of tonal direction—in sum, musical devices for sustaining a continual state of suspense as to the next disjunction. The border police officer, gently holding his submachine gun, compares a poster with mug shots of "Wanted Terrorists!" to the face of a woman hoping to pass the border with her lover. In a somewhat ironic, somewhat eerie tone, he compares the woman's physiognomy with that of one of the wanted terrorists: "Come here, young lady! That's not you, by chance? The chin...and the hair.... No, you haven't got the fanatical eyes. Don't be afraid, I know it's not you. But it could well be. All right, young lady. You can go!" The petrified woman shows relief when cleared to cross the border.

The pictographic logic of exclusion, which denies humanness through dehumanizing visualizations, finds yet another variation in Wolf Biermann's diegetic recitation of his ballad "The Girl From Stuttgart," about Ulrike Meinhof:

Ich werde wohl bald ihr Foto sehen
Es wird in der Reihe mit anderen stehen
Beim Bäcker im Fenster
Und eine Hand
Mit Kugelschreiber *bewaffnet* wird dann
Auskreuzen mit einem Krakelstrich
Ihr Menschengesicht.

I'll probably be seeing her picture soon
It'll be in a row with the others
In the window of the bakery
And a hand *armed* with a pen
Will scratch out with a scrawl—
Her human face.

---

29. For a discussion of the "inhuman" and "not human," see also Slavoj Žižek, Eric L. Santner, Kenneth Reinhard, *The Neighbor: Three Inquiries in Political Theology* (Chicago: University of Chicago Press, 2005), 159f.

The face of the "enemy" Ulrike Meinhof must be effaced in order to deprive her of the politico-discursively *attributable* status "human."

A Spontaneous Decision

Hanns-Martin Schleyer functions as the paradigmatic human and, concomitantly, as a political signifier of a discourse defining itself in contradistinction to the RAF and its "sympathizers." As such, he serves as the embodiment of a *raison d'état,* whose veracity is recognized and verified by the funeral congregation and those witnessing the event on television. Yet what exactly is the reason here, what is the *raison d'état* of the FRG? Federal President Scheel notes in his oration:

> Just as those who spiritually and materially support terrorism have completely misunderstood the meaning of a democratic way of life, so have those who recognize the human dignity of the terrorists envisioned the goals of democracy [die Demokratie zu Ende gedacht].

When the conservative press stokes the public rage with phrases like "Into the sewage!" it apparently is not too concerned about "the dignity of the terrorists." According to Scheel they do not "think democracy to its end." This begs the question, however, of what it means in this context "to think democracy to its end." Federal President Scheel, in his role as the supreme representative of the people, and as such allegedly a democrat par excellence, exhorts: "We all affirm the principles of democracy, the struggle about different opinions and points of view.... We cannot improve our State without being aware of its shortcomings." Scheel knows of the significance of speaking and being heard publicly. He knows that the eruption of the "struggle about different opinions and points of view" (Kampf der Meinungen und der Argumente) is a political act par excellence, an act allowing or not allowing for the "general," the *demos,* to constitute itself as veritable subjects. In a similar vein, another speech later in the film, that of Max Frisch, presents itself as a plea for "more democracy," uttered from the position of the guest speaker at the yearly convention of the Social Democratic Party. Frisch states and performs what lies at the center of any configuration of public speech, its participatory and distributional dynamics that ultimately distinguish intelligible speech from "noise."[30] That is what Antigone, in the *mise en abyme* scene, insinuates when refuting Ismene's

---

30. In his analysis of what happens in the case of a disruption of a dominant order of the political, Jacques Rancière differentiates "speech... understood as discourse" from "noise." "Political activity... makes heard a discourse where once there was only place for noise.... This term means the open set of practices driven by the assumption of equality between any and every speaking being and by the concern to test this equality." Rancière, *Dis-agreements: Politics and Philosophy,* trans. Julie Rose (Minneapolis: University of Minnesota Press, 1999), 29, 53 (*Mésentente: Politique et Philosophie* [Paris: Galilée, 1995]).

invocation to keep the burial plan secret: "No, but cry it aloud! I will condemn you more / If you are silent than if you proclaim my deed to all."[31] It goes without saying that the question is not one of dichotomizing the political and the nonpolitical or reason and nonreason per se. Rather, the question, alluding to the very frontiers and conceptual borders of "the human," is one of making oneself heard in public discourse, being conceived of as a "reasonable" subject, recognized as an equal member of the polity, that is, being allowed to be "human."

Given the political struggle between the German state and the RAF, *Germany in Autumn*'s bias (*Parteilichkeit*), to be sure, is not that of advocating one side over the other or even engaging in heretical or apologetic speech. On a primary level, the film plainly asks, What does it mean to be a citizen of the Federal Republic of Germany in 1977? The extreme cases of Hanns-Martin Schleyer, on the one hand, and Baader, Ensslin, and Raspe, on the other, epitomize an answer to that question. While the former is invoked as a model for national self-identification,[32] the latter are a scandal; he is symbolically included into the socius, whereas they are symbolically excluded; while the one's public "grievability" typifies "the human," the disavowal of public "grievability" concerning Baader, Ensslin, and Raspe amounts to their dehumanization.

This differential allocation of humanness is similarly exemplified in a comparison of the two different funeral repasts, starting with the reception following Schleyer's funeral in the New Palace. The maître d' speaks of a buffet for an expected 1,100 guests. As if in a dress rehearsal, the waitresses and waiters walk down a grand staircase, receiving the last corrections of the maître d', who, clapping his hands, comments on posture and mimics: "Quiet, I say! My God, always the same! Hurry up! Get a move on. As usual...keep smiling, polite, quick service. Remember, it must go fast. Please, don't forget...trays held level to your chest. March, off you go." The funeral reception revolving around the figure of Schleyer, staged in an aura of sublimity, is juxtaposed with the repast of the funeral of Baader, Ensslin, and Raspe, which comes into being only because of the spontaneous decision of an innkeeper.

INNKEEPER: I *decided spontaneously* [*spontaner Entschluss*], after I found out that Mr. Ensslin had been refused for certain reasons.
INTERVIEWER: How did you find that out?
INNKEEPER: A couple who own a restaurant told me this, with a corresponding commentary, and that made me so mad that I went straight to the phone and called Mr. Ensslin and told him that *out of purely humane reasons,* I would serve food for him at the funeral repast.

---

31. While Antigone, the "terroristic woman" (as she is called in the *mise en abyme*), refuses to figure as the wild woman in the attic of the house of reason, the RAF, correspondingly stigmatized as "female" (that is, "unreasonable"), no longer seeks participation in public communicative discourse.
32. On the question of national self-recognition, see Judith Butler's nuanced remarks in *Precarious Life: The Powers of Mourning and Violence* (London: Verso, 2004), 19–49 and 128–51.

What the "spontaneous decision" of the innkeeper leaves in suspense is a logic of friends and foes inculcated both by the RAF as well as the German state. It is a decision not for the RAF or for the state or against the RAF or against the state; rather, the innkeeper's decision transgresses such logicality "out of purely humane reasons." It remains to be seen how the film's bias (*Parteilichkeit*) posits itself in relation to the two political discourses, whether it merely confines itself to citing "humane" positions, or whether it perhaps succeeds in producing something one might be tempted to call an "authentic" voice in the course of its cinematic performance.

The Transgression of Morality

Discursive thinking along the lines of a friend-foe logic, a logic of humanization and dehumanization, is of course brought to bear by the terrorists no less than by the state. Insightful in this respect is an interview with the prisoner Horst Mahler, a former lawyer and ostensibly the cofounder of the RAF, who has now served seven years of a fourteen-year sentence. The interview, which takes place in Mahler's prison cell, revolves around the question of the legitimization of the RAF's terrorist acts. "How does a person like Ulrike Meinhof," Mahler ponders,

> come to kill other people or, at least, to run the risk of doing so? A murderer [krimineller Mörder] departs from the moral value system [verlässt das moralische Wertsystem]; the revolutionary [Revolutionär] transgresses it [übersteigert es]. That is, the moral rigorousness [moralische Rigorismus] of the revolutionary, which can turn itself into arrogant presumptuousness [einem subjektiven, anmaßenden Eigendünkel], at the same time provides the basis for overcoming the scruples that a leftist has about killing someone.

Mahler's juxtaposition of the "murderer" (*krimineller Mörder*) and the "revolutionary" (*Revolutionär*) is noteworthy, given that §1 of the Basic Law (*Grundgesetz*) of the FRG—"Human dignity is inviolable"—also postulates an integral component of the "moral value system" of West German society.[33] For example, one could say: the "murderer departs from the moral value system" by dismissing the dignity of his victims. In contrast, "the revolutionary transgresses it [übersteigert es]" means that, adhering to Mahler's examples, the dignity of the Vietnamese population massacred by the American military is also to be considered inviolable because human dignity is a universal value. The revolutionary, bound to his "moral rigorousness" (*moralische Rigorismus*), thinks of the American soldier and

---

33. In its well-known Lüth judgment, the German constitutional court postulated this principle of applying the Basic Law's fundamental rights to create an objective value system for the entire legal system (see Thomas Henne and Arne Riedlinger, eds., *Das Lüth-Urteil in [rechts-]historischer Sicht: Die Grundlegung der Grundrechtsjudikatur in den 1950er Jahren* [Berlin: Berliner Wissenschaftsverlag, 2004]).

the German politician supporting him as "murderers" and, as such, as his enemies, both of whom he is ready to eliminate. Mahler, who at this point meditates from a somewhat distant perspective on the motivations of the RAF,[34] rightly notes that this "moral rigorousness" "can turn itself into arrogant presumptuousness" and at times produce entirely grotesque results. This is the case "in Mogadishu," where, according to Mahler, the RAF's "practical political action" solidifies, where indeed it almost would have caused a "massacre," the murder of "defenseless civilian women, children and elderly hostages," that is, the very scenario the terrorists were fighting in its Vietnamese version. To be sure, the "moral rigorousness" Mahler elaborates on is not at all radical but merely extreme. It deduces a set of ideas under the terms of a compulsive logicality geared toward a dead end that may still be logical, albeit void of meaning.[35] How then does the RAF's "practical political action," inspired by "moral rigorousness," define the relation between the political and the human? Mahler explains:

> [The revolutionary] sees the moral degeneracy of the capitalist system; one sees the people who deal corruptly with this system, morally judges them, condemns them, and with this moral judgment *evil has been personified* [*verkörpern sie das Böse*]. That is to say, one believes that personal guilt plays a role, and that it is *necessary for liberation and therefore also justified* [*es zur Befreiung notwendig und daher auch gerechtfertigt ist*] to destroy this evil, even if personified, that is, to kill people [dieses Böse, auch wo es sich personifiziert, zu vernichten, dass heißt also, Personen zu vernichten].[36]

Of course the argumentation, "necessary...*and therefore* also justified,"[37] is never commensurable with justice, for justice, beyond all generalizability, can be thought

---

34. It should be noted that "the ideology of West German terrorism used to legitimate the group's actions initially largely served an ethical-political argument by claiming the liberation of the suppressed and disenfranchised, the poor and suffering...in Germany and, first and foremost, in the Third World, as the group's decisive political goal. However, after these 'as affected suppressed third parties' refused to become the political addressees of terrorism, the *anthropological* argument came increasingly to the fore: liberating people, through the struggle, to liberate themselves from a subject mentality ingrained by the state" (Münkler, "Sehnsucht nach dem Ausnahmezustand," 1213).

35. What is at issue here is, in the words of Hannah Arendt, an "extremism of the utmost evil," which "has nothing to do with a genuine radicalism" and in which "free and controlled thought...appears to suffer" (Arendt, *Elemente und Ursprünge totaler Herrschaft: Antisemitismus, Imperialismus, totale Herrschaft* [Piper: Munich, 1986], 978, my translation).

36. In another interview, Mahler focuses on this point: "It was a moral duty to kill, that's what you can call it." "In some way we subjectively were at war and accordingly regarded ourselves as soldiers" (Mahler, "Terrorismus und die Bewusstseinskrisen der Linken," *Frankfurter Rundschau*, March 22, 1978, 14, after Klaus Wasmund, "The Political Socialization of West German Terrorists," in *Political Violence and Terror: Motifs and Motivations,* ed. Peter Merkl [Berkeley: University of California Press, 1986], 215f.).

37. In line with the above-described political dynamics of terrorism, one could with Max Weber differentiate between the conceptions of *Verantwortungsethik* (ethics of responsibility) and *Gesinnungsethik* (ethics of conviction). Whereas the *Verantwortungsethiker* is in a position to effectively practice politics as a "profession," the *Gesinnungsethiker* seizes his or her inspiration from "the flame of pure conviction."

of only in terms of a universalizability by succumbing to the absoluteness of given singularities.[38] What matters, for this argument, is that the described logic of the elimination of persons does not signify the murder of humans as humans but as the "embodiment of evil" (*Verkörperung des Bösen*). As such, it posits an equivalent to the state's political discourse that depicts Baader, Ensslin, and Raspe in mug shots as the epitome of dehumanized evil. This dynamics of dehumanization is illustrated even more drastically in a text by Ulrike Meinhof whose ideological thinking serves Mahler as a case in point. Meinhof outlines the "problem":

> When one... has to deal with the pigs [Bullen] the argument goes that, due to their function, they are naturally brutal and, due to their function, they have to beat people up and shoot and, due to their function, they have to engage in suppression, but of course it's just the uniform and it's only the function, and the man who's wearing it is maybe a really pleasant person to be around at home.... That's a problem and we say, *naturally, the pigs [Bullen] are pigs [Schweine], we say the guy in the uniform is a pig [Schwein], that's not a person, and that's how we have to encounter him*. That means we're not there to talk to him and it's wrong to talk at all to these people, and naturally shots may be fired. Because we don't have the problem that these are human beings.[39]

That the fight of the RAF, this extremist branch of the student protest movement germinating in the cultural revolution of the 1960s, that the "war" against

---

S/he follows the principle according to which the end justifies the means in order to attain "absolute justice on earth *by means of* force" (Weber, *Politik als Beruf,* 52f., 56, 58f., translation and italics mine).

38. While Mahler analyzes the RAF's mission as *empirically* insufficiently informed ("our consciousness wasn't in tune with the times"), he does not question its *normative* dimension, that is, its precarious logic of actions based on "natural law." The nature of natural law that Mahler invokes here, this law always referring to some higher authority beyond the human sphere, is so intimately entangled with the possibility for abuse that Kant in *The Metaphysics of Morals* almost entirely abstains from it. Yet since there is always the possibility of a "despotic government," Kant, in an importantly ambiguous move, *does* seem to allow for a *ius necessitatis (Notrecht)* when he speaks about the confrontation between moral responsibility and official prosecution: "Hence the deed of saving one's life by violence is not to be judged *inculpable (inculpabile)* but only *unpunishable (impunible),* and by a strange confusion jurists take this *subjective* impunity to be *objective* impunity (conformity with the law)" (Immanuel Kant, *The Metaphysics of Morals,* trans. Mary Gregor [Cambridge: Cambridge University Press, 1996], 28, 93–96). Hegel, who decisively rejected the right of resistance, was equally decisive on the framework of *social* conflicts: "The person who is starving has the absolute right to violate the property of another; he violates the other person's property only to a limited extent, however; the *jus necessitatis* implies that he does not violate the right of the other as a right per se. The interest is directed solely to the piece of bread; he does not treat the other as without rights" (Georg Wilhelm Friedrich Hegel, *Vorlesungen über die Philosophie der Religion,* ed. Walter Jaeschke [Felix Meiner Verlag: Hamburg, 1985], 341). Whereas Kant's conception of the *ius necessitatis* pertains to an exceptional condition, Hegel's notion is inspired by the everyday exceptionality of the poor: "The poor man feels himself to be relating to arbitrariness, to human fortuitousness, and this is what is outrageous..., that the arbitrariness puts him into this dilemma. Self-consciousness appears to be driven to this extreme where it has no rights anymore, where freedom does not exist" (Georg Wilhelm Friedrich Hegel, *Philosophie des Rechts: Die Vorlesung von 1819/20 in einer Nachschrift,* ed. Dieter Henrich [Frankfurt a.M.: Suhrkamp, 1983], 194–95).

39. Ulrike Meinhof, "Natürlich kann geschossen werden," *Der Spiegel,* June 15, 1970, 75.

the state of which Mahler speaks,[40] depleted itself in the perversion of the student movement's indignation, in the killing of uninvolved people in bloody shoot-outs, and so forth, seems, in the words of Volker Schlöndorff, to be continuing the tragic legacy of all German revolutions.[41] Yet the panning shot to Mahler's prison window by the end of the scene, the long fixation of the window appears to portend a hope, a future, or at least an uncertainty. For the grammar of revolution, according to Rosa Luxemburg's dictum, cited in the film, follows the conjugation "I was, I am, I will be."[42]

Unfaithful Officials, or the "Desert Fox" and His "Sovereign" Son

In *Germany in Autumn,* the dichotomization of two antagonistic forms of violence (the political violence of the German state under Helmut Schmidt's Social Democratic government vis-à-vis the terrorist violence of the RAF) is enacted within several semiotic systems: two funerals, two obsequies, two funeral repasts, two systems of pictographical representation, two conceptions of law (natural and positive law), and their sporadic problematization within the *mise en abyme* scene of the television production of *Antigone*. Yet what kind of political intervention does *Germany in Autumn* bring about? What is its ethos *beyond* the reenactment of these ostensible friend-foe dichotomies? Indeed, to reduce the film to a series of conflicting concepts or notions or positions or positings (*Setzungen*) clearly would elide its artistic potential and the poetic force that characterizes it as a cinematic work of art. Such a form of "reconstruction" would be tantamount to an equation of the film's cinematic economy with the discursive dynamics of state violence and terrorist violence, a gnomic sphere *Germany in Autumn* may precisely transgress.

We thus shall follow the film into the infrastructure of yet another dualism, as part of a piece of historical footage contributed by Alexander Kluge, with an eye to what the film does and what it allows for beyond the dynamics of thesis and counterthesis, violence and counterviolence. "Field Marshal Erwin Rommel, hero of Africa... father of today's Mayor of Stuttgart, Manfred Rommel": the footage displays Erwin Rommel at work, driving in a military vehicle in a desert somewhere

---

40. Cf. Andreas Musolff, "Bürgerkriegs-Szenarios und ihre Folgen: Die Terrorismusdebatte in der Bundesrepublik 1970–1993," in Kraushaar, *Die RAF und der linke Terrorismus,* 1171–84.
41. Interview with Volker Schlöndorff on *Deutschland im Herbst.*
42. See also Rosa Luxemburg, "Die Ordnung herrscht in Berlin," *Die Rote Fahne,* January 14, 1919, in *Gesammelte Werke,* vol. 4 (August 1914–Januar 1919) (East Berlin: Institut für Marxismus-Leninismus beim ZK der SED, 1974), 538. "At the beginning of *Being and Time,*" Alexander Kluge writes, "Heidegger asks extremely exactly why the 3rd person present singular has become the object of philosophy and not, for example, 'we are' ['wir sind'], 'you are' ['ihr seid'], i.e., the collective flections" (Kluge, *Die Patriotin: Texte/Bilder* [Frankfurt a.M.: Zweitausendeins], 391). In a different context, the Italian philosopher Adriana Cavarero notes: "Indeed, many revolutionary movements (which range from traditional communism to the feminism of sisterhood) seem to share a curious linguistic code *based on the intrinsic morality of pronouns*" (Cavarero, *Relating Narratives* [London: Routledge, 1997], 90f., after Judith Butler, *Giving an Account of Oneself: A Critique of Ethical Violence* [Assen: Koninklijke Van Gorcum, 2003], 25).

in North Africa. The voice-over proceeds: "[Rommel], killed with poison by the state in autumn 1944...followed by a state funeral, public mourning...his son witnesses the state funeral." The fragment shows bits of the state ceremonies, including a brief shot of Rommel's son, all accompanied by Haydn's String Quartet in C Major, Op. 76, No. 3 ("Emperor"), which provides the melody of the German national anthem. The cinematic narrative of Erwin Rommel, who gained fame under the nickname "Desert Fox," is continued later in the film, for Rommel's son, briefly shown during the obsequies, again appears in his position as the mayor of Stuttgart.

Needless to say, there are several parallels between Rommel's funeral in 1944 and Schleyer's funeral in 1977: two acts of state, two official funeral services, and the visual appearance of Erwin Rommel's son against the acoustical appearance of Schleyer's son during the funeral. In fact, the parent-child dyad could be extrapolated further with respect to Fassbinder and his mother. Regarding the question of the bias (*Parteilichkeit*) of *Germany in Autumn,* Rommel's funeral appears indicative, since what first presents itself as yet another manifestation of antagonistic forms of political violence, another binary opposition of Fascist parents and their anti-Fascist children, now begins to falter in that both political discourses are left performatively in suspense. Although the film does not remind us of this, in 1977 Erwin Rommel is not merely a father among fathers, one of Hitler's helpers, but also one of those generals let into the planned plot to kill Hitler (albeit without having been involved in the planning or execution of the attempted assassination of Hitler on July 20, 1944). Yet because of his suspected involvement in the plot, on top of having openly expressed skepticism as to the feasibility of Hitler's military objectives in North Africa, Rommel was forced into suicide in 1944. Within the cinematic topography of *Germany in Autumn,* then, the legacy of Erwin Rommel, Hitler's all-too-critical general, is asymmetrical to the political discourse of the conformist generation of Fascist fathers. Similarly, Manfred Rommel, as we learn later, does not simply pose as a servant within an established political discourse, as one would expect of the mayor of a major German city, but instead acts against the official discourse. Feeling bound to a logic outside his political alliance, as Ensslin's sister explains, Rommel had "*decided entirely sovereignly [ganz souverän beschlossen], without asking the city council,*" that Baader, Ensslin, and Raspe would be buried in Stuttgart's Dornhalden Cemetery—next to deserving people, such as the industrialist Robert Bosch, ex-federal president Theodor Heuss, and former minister president Reinhold Maier. Manfred Rommel explains his motivations for rendering the funeral possible without the officially required approval:

> MANFRED ROMMEL: About the question of the burial of the three dead terrorists, it seemed to me obvious [es erschien mir eine Selbstverständlichkeit] that it had to be decided on quickly and cleanly.

INTERVIEWER: Clean in what sense, in the sense of the administration, or in the human sense?
MANFRED ROMMEL: *Clean in the human sense.* It would have been unbearable for me to be responsible or collectively responsible that the question of the proper burial of the terrorists was discussed for weeks and months. Therefore, *I decided quickly,* so that the *decision* was binding.

To be sure, the political, ethical, and ultimately moral contexts within which one would have to situate the actions of Manfred Rommel and Erwin Rommel are disparate and too incongruous to be put into direct dialogue here. And I certainly do not mean to suggest that they are compatible or amenable to one another. The point is that *Germany in Autumn*'s concrete cinematic montage, rather than evoking simplistic identifications with preestablished political sides, produces a liminal space of poetic ambiguities, of blurred transitions, thereby unsettling and obliterating identifiable political positions. Perhaps it is such performative suspension that ultimately allows for a bias (*Parteilichkeit*) of the film on behalf of "purely human reasons," beyond antithetical ascriptions of Erwin Rommel as signifier of one political system and Manfred Rommel as signifier of another political system. Perhaps *Germany in Autumn*'s bias (*Parteilichkeit*) has to be thought of as a deposing (*Entsetzung*), that is to say, not in terms of the negation of political orders, nor in the sense of *another* politics but in the sense of eluding all political systematology.[43]

Four Humans

"Fiat justitia pereat mundus," Kant famously declares in his third *Critique*. "Let justice prevail, though all the knaves in the world perish!" "There is no doubt," writes Alexander Kluge, "that the Stammheimer proceed de facto in line with 'fiat

---

43. A similar dynamic of constative positing (*Setzung*) and performative deposing (*Entsetzung*) suffuses the stylized funeral reception revolving around Schleyer, whose sublimity is first established and then undercut, as the behind-the-scene view of the headwaiter turns the reception into a farce about servitude to the upper echelons of society. Still another example of *Germany in Autumn*'s peculiar cinematic dynamic manifests itself in the long Fassbinder episode. On the one hand, Fassbinder's statements in defense of democracy explicitly align him with the generation of anti-Fascist, antiauthoritarian, and antipatriarchal "children," who convene at the funeral of Baader, Ensslin, and Raspe at the end of the film. On the other hand, Fassbinder's own authoritarian behavior toward his mother (who hopes for an "authoritarian ruler") and his demeaning, if not abusive, treatment of Arnim (who, again, not by chance nicknames him "bully") align him with the detested parental generation assembling at the Schleyer funeral at the beginning of the film. That is to say, Fassbinder's actions performatively undermine his ostensible statements and expose them as "empty rhetoric." It is precisely this dynamic of positing and deposing that unremittingly threatens the film's oppositional narrative structure, its political dichotomies. Importantly, this dynamic eventually allows for the filmmakers' own ethical intervention, their *Parteilichkeit* to emerge—not in spite of but indeed as a result of their refusal to identify with political orders and, as we shall see, to logify what cannot be logified, namely justice.

justitia pereat mundus.' But the other side [the German state] does so too."[44] And in the *mise en abyme* television production later in the film, Creon also seeks to arrogate justice to himself through a polito*logical* claim in the name of civic order, thereby succumbing to *hybris*. Antigone, who opposes Creon's secular order, follows this dictum with respect to a the*ological* claim; she is equally prone to *hybris* given her insistence on being able to read the unwritten laws of the chthonic gods. To be sure, for the Greeks, justice, *dikē*, sunders the human from the animal in that the human's aspiration toward justice, *dikē*, allows one to enter into contractual relationships and orient social life according to certain laws, *nomoi*.[45] But justice still belongs to the gods, stands beyond all logic, beyond all human appropriation and instrumentalization. Disavowing justice's opacity, both the West German state and the RAF arrogate to themselves the role of its proprietor. As in a Sophoclean drama, a tragic fate befalls the West German state.

Toward the end of the film, Alexander Kluge reads a letter by Schleyer written during his captivity on September 9–10, 1977, and addressed to the entrepreneur Eberhard von Brauchitsch: "If they're going to refuse to give in, they should do it soon. *Even though the human in one [der Mensch], as it always was during the war, would like to survive.* It is never sweet and agreeable [süß und angenehm] to die for the fatherland." Schleyer himself speaks of two Schleyers, "the human" Schleyer and the political functionary. The political functionary is ready to die just as the SS officer Schleyer was ready to die, to sacrifice himself even though it is not pleasant to die for the fatherland, neither during the Nazi period nor in 1977. By contrast, "the human" "wants to survive," the human whose image—already shown during the funeral ceremony, multiplied and inflated—now appears once more, decontextualized this time, torn out of any discursive environment, shown as a long-take close-up (fig. 6). The Schleyer presented here is not primarily chairman of the Daimler-Benz Company and president of the German Federation of Industry, or SS officer, and perhaps not even husband of the mourning widow shown during the funeral or father of the son whom we get to know as the addressee of a letter. What comes to the fore here is the individual Schleyer,[46] elusively located somewhere in the fissures and chasms of stratified representational systems, a Schleyer who qua human defies conceptualization. Immediately after the Schleyer image two more images are

---

44. Kluge, *Die Patriotin*, 35.

45. Cf. Marcel Detienne, *Les maîtres de vérité dans la Grèce archaïque* (Paris: F. Maspero, 1967); Detienne, *Dionysos mis à mort* (Paris: Gallimard, 1977).

46. At the same time, to be sure, a picture of a human can never really capture that human but, in accordance with Levinas, always depicts its own failure to represent this human. "The face is signification, and signification without context.... The face is meaning all by itself.... In this sense one can say that the face is not 'seen.' It is what cannot become a content, which your thought would embrace; it is uncontainable, it leads you beyond" (Emmanuel Levinas, *Ethics and Infinity*, trans. Richard Cohen [Pittsburgh: Duquesne University Press: 1985], 87).

Figure 6.

depicted, one of Raspe (fig. 7) and one of Baader and Ensslin (fig. 8). In the context of the diversified relationships of the film, they are invoked without any disparagement or discursive contradistinction to the Schleyer portrayal.

Shown here are not terrorists or state enemies or political warriors. In the cinematic space of *Germany in Autumn,* Raspe, appearing so different from his mug shot, does not, however, merely figure as a "private" person either. And Baader, who caresses his girlfriend Ensslin in this legendary shot during a court hearing, does not just pose as the lover. Ensslin, in turn, does not appear merely as Baader's lover or as the daughter of Pastor Ensslin, who so frenetically tries to ensure a proper burial for his daughter, and also not solely as sister of Christiane Ensslin. After one and a half hours of discursive representation of friends and foes, state servants and state antagonists, Fascists and anti-Fascists, "subhumans" and "martyrs," and even husbands and fathers and daughters and sisters and lovers, what emerges, beyond the multitude of discourses in the crevices of an ambiguous semantic field, are four humans. Four humans: Schleyer, Baader, Ensslin, and Raspe, all of them dead now, all of them—and perhaps this is the bias (*Parteilichkeit*) of the film— treated alike with respect to their individuation.

"We have to treat the dead equally," Alexander Kluge insists in light of the irreverent media coverage during the first meeting of the contributors of *Germany in Autumn,*[47] echoing Antigone's claim for equal burials for her brothers, Eteocles and Polyneices. Antigone maintains that if all humans enter life at the moment

---

47. Interview with Volker Schlöndorff on *Deutschland im Herbst.*

148   *Inconceivable Effects*

Figure 7.

Figure 8.

of birth, it must be insisted that death—the moment of exiting life—is a question of human dignity, an absolute value and, as such, is not susceptible to Creon's secularist power.[48] Antigone's all-encompassing insistence on *philia,* bound to cycles and

---

48. See also Alexander Kluge and Oskar Negt, *Geschichte und Eigensinn* (Frankfurt a.M.: Zweitausendeins, 1981), 768. For discussions of the act of mourning with respect to the cultural codification of "the human" in Greek antiquity, see Walter Burkert, *Structure and History in Greek Mythology and*

rhythms of generations, a temporality of the *dead* and perhaps the *unborn,* disrupts Creon's linear and politico-pragmatic discourse of the living,[49] his logic of friends and foes, inclusion and exclusion, his decisionism as to the precarious nexus between the political and the human. What is at stake here, then, may be not so much a problem of conflicting political conceptions but ultimately an epistemological difficulty as to the conceptualizability of "the human." It may be this sphere *beyond,* a sphere suspending any dynamics of re-presentation, identification, decision, to which *Germany in Autumn* aspires.[50] It is precisely in the context of such a transgression of the temporality of the living that we must situate the drawing of an embryo, an *unborn,* by Leonardo da Vinci—placed right before the funeral of Baader, Ensslin, and Raspe, the *dead.* Perhaps it is this imagery invoked by Leonardo da Vinci's embryo that soon after is undergirded by yet another child, the child of the hippie mother walking down the street, accompanied by Joan Baez's "Here's to You." Perhaps, indeed, it is this pictorial conglomerate to which we might want to allot the long, seemingly arbitrary shot focused on a blond young boy watching the caskets being placed in the grave, which cuts then to a boy the camera still follows in one of the departing cars after the funeral. What is not said is that this is Gudrun Ensslin's son, who as a result of the mother's death is now an orphan (the father, Bernhard Vesper, had died in 1971). It is hard to make sense of or find truth in the child's situation along the lines of any "political" logicality.

The frailty of the human emerging here *beyond* the contours of politico-discursive violence, *beyond* the logic of whence and whither, surges to the surface once more with the very last shot of the film, a textual quotation that at the outset of the film already appeared as follows:

> When atrocity reaches a certain point, it no longer matters who initiated it; it only matters that it should stop. [An einem bestimmten Punkt der Grausamkeit angekommen, ist es schon gleich, wer sie begangen hat: sie soll nur aufhören.]
> 8. April 1945—Frau Wilde, 5 Kinder

We do not know Frau Wilde, but from the note we can infer the following: Frau Wilde, presumably a German woman, mother of five, utters this sentence on April 8, 1945, shortly before the capitulation of Germany after twelve years of Nazi domination and a war causing a loss of human life of roughly 72 million people including 47 million civilians, 61 million on the Allies' side, 11 million on the side

---

Ritual (Berkeley: University of California Press, 1979); Nicole Loraux, *The Invention of Athens: The Funeral Oration in the Classical City,* trans. Alan Sheridan (Cambridge, MA: Harvard University Press, 1986); Maurice Bloch, *Ritual, History, and Power: Selected Papers in Anthropology* (London: Athlone Press, 1989).

49. For a detailed discussion of the notion of temporality in Sophoclean drama, see Hans-Thies Lehmann, *Das politische Schreiben: Essays zu Theatertexten* (Berlin: Theater der Zeit, 2002), 32f.

50. Sophocles' language, Hölderlin writes, allows human understanding (*des Menschen Verstand*) to wander likewise "amid the unthinkable" (*unter Undenkbarem*) (Friedrich Hölderlin, "Anmerkungen zur Antigonä," in *Sämtliche Werke,* ed. Franz M. Knaupp and D. E. Sattler [Frankfurt a.M.: Stroemfeld/Roter Stern, 1988], 16:413).

of the Axis powers. "It no longer matters who initiated it" does not mean that it *does not matter* who initiated it; rather, "no longer" addresses a certain rupture of temporality, a rupture denoting the point where a human being discovers an incapacity to think toward a promised *telos,* and the incapacity to think the logic of friends and foes. This is how Frau Wilde's sentence appears a second time at the end of the film:

> When atrocity reaches a certain point, it no longer matters who initiated it; it only matters that it should stop. [An einem bestimmten Punkt der Grausamkeit angekommen, ist es schon gleich, wer sie begangen hat: sie soll nur aufhören.]

Who is speaking here, and what do we make in this second sentence of the absence of Frau Wilde's name, her role as a mother of five, her role as a German woman on April 8, 1945? Of course, we know or believe we know, or remember, that "Frau Wilde" is speaking here, that this is her sentence. Yet what is the semantic efficacy of this so-evident presence of the absence of an author, what may be implied here without being uttered? "When atrocity reaches a certain point," when "it no longer matters who initiated it," when all that matters is that the atrocities stop, it perhaps no longer matters who signs the plea. It no longer matters whether Frau Wilde signs it or, in her name, the eleven filmmakers, without her but for her and perhaps even for one another—as humans who, after all, also recognize each other and themselves, under the impression of the traumatic events of the German Autumn, beyond all discursive calculation, in a state of distress.

7

A Politics of Enmity

Müller's Germania Death in Berlin

Give / Me a gun and show me an enemy.

—Heiner Müller, *The Duel*

The Cauldron

Germania Death in Berlin (1956/1971), together with *The Battle* (1951/1974), *Life of Gundling Lessing's Sleep Dream Cry* (1977), and *Germania 3 Ghosts at the Dead Man* (1995), testifies to Heiner Müller's intense occupation with German history, particularly the history of violence. The play, which consists of thirteen miscellaneously interrelated scenes, generates a certain politics of enmity—a politics whose poetic itinerary has neither an evident beginning nor an end. We thus may well begin in the middle of the play, in a scene titled "Hommage à Stalin 1," and we shall, for the time being, "imagine" *(vorstellen)* "*Snow. Battle noise. Three Soldiers. Their bodies aren't complete anymore. Enter, in the snowstorm, a Young Soldier*":

SOLDIER 2: Comrade, where from?
YOUNG SOLDIER: The battle.
SOLDIER 3: Comrade, whereto?
YOUNG SOLDIER: Where there is no battle.

SOLDIER 1: Comrade, your hand.
Tears off his arm. The Young Soldier screams. The dead laugh and begin to gnaw at the arm.
SOLDIER 3 *offering the arm:* Aren't you hungry?
The Young Soldier hides his face with his remaining hand.
SOLDIER 1: Next time it's your turn. There is meat for all of us in this cauldron [Der Kessel hat für alle Fleisch]. (20f., 56f.)[1]

What presents itself here in concentrated form is a kind of humor that Müller relentlessly culls from the difference between the literal and the figurative meanings of words and phrases. It is in this sense that a hand ostensibly extended in a gesture of comradeship ("Comrade, your hand") results in an act of dismemberment. Similarly, the infamous Stalingrad "Cauldron" (*Kessel*)—the site of one of Hitler's bloodiest defeats and a turning point during World War II[2]—is literally employed as a "kettle" in which the Young Soldier's arm is cooked and offered to him for his own consumption. This kind of sardonic irony, especially in conjunction with the repeated stage direction *"Laughter,"* forms a comic counterpoint to the ubiquitous fear of death felt by those trapped inside the cauldron.[3] And it is from this oscillating dynamic between laughter and death, humor and fright, that a moment of the absurd emanates, not with a sense of a historical nihilism but rather with respect to a peculiar beyond, a moment of *horror* characteristic of the theater of Heiner Müller.

Within Müller's dramatic economy, the *Kessel,* with its *literal* gastronomic and its *metaphorical* military meanings, functions *metonymically* as an affective conglomerate of the tragedies of German history and beyond. To this anachronistic, world-historical battleground, Napoleon, "pale and bloated," enters the stage, and

---

1. Quotations from Heiner Müller's *Germania Death in Berlin* are followed by two sets of page numbers. The first set, unless otherwise noted, refers to Heiner Müller, *Germania, Germania Tod in Berlin, Germania 3 Gespenster am toten Mann* (Frankfurt a.M.: Suhrkamp, 2001); the second set refers to *Explosion of a Memory: Writings by Heiner Müller,* ed. and trans. Carl Weber (New York: PAJ Publications, 1989). In most cases I have modified Weber's translation, often consulting the other available English translation by Dennis Redmond, *Germania Death in Berlin,* 2002, http://www.efn.org/~dredmond/Germania. html. As a rule, with the exception of Heiner Müller's italicized stage directions, all italics are mine.

On *Germania Death in Berlin,* cf., among others, Volker Bohn, "Germania Tod in Berlin," in *Heiner Müller-Handbuch: Leben-Werk-Wirkung,* ed. Hans-Thies Lehmann and Patrick Primavesi (Stuttgart: Metzler, 2003), 207–14; Georg Wieghaus, *Heiner Müller* (Munich: C. H. Beck, 1981), 88–99; Norbert Otto Eke, "Geschichte und Gedächtnis im Drama," in *Heiner Müller-Handbuch,* 52–58. For a historical contextualization of *Germania Death in Berlin,* see Jost Hermand, "Braut, Mutter oder Hure? Heiner Müllers *Germania* und ihre Vorgeschichte," in *Mit den Toten reden: Fragen an Heiner Müller,* ed. Jost Hermand and Helen Fehervary (Cologne: Böhlau, 1999), 52–69.

2. The Stalingrad Cauldron was a trap for Hitler's Sixth Army, ultimately defeated by the Red Army in the winter of 1942–43 after 199 days and combined casualties of about 1.5 million.

3. For a penetrating analysis of Müller's poetics of laughter, see Bernhard Greiner, "'Jetzt will ich sitzen wo gelacht wird': Über das Lachen bei Heiner Müller," *Jahrbuch zur Literatur in der DDR* 5 (1986): 29–63; see also Nikolaus Müller-Schöll, "Tragik, Komik, Groteske," in *Heiner Müller-Handbuch,* 82–88.

Caesar, "his toga bloodied and torn," follows after him (21, 57). *"More and more soldiers stagger or crawl on the stage, fall down, remain on the ground"*; additionally— and perhaps not surprisingly for a play titled *Germania* and inspired by the myth of the battle in Eztel's castle—the Nibelungs (Gunther, Hagen, Volker, and Gernot) appear "clad in rusted armor" (21, 57):

> GUNTHER *crushing the dead underfoot:* Malingerers. Shirkers. Defeatists. Pack of cowards.
> VOLKER: They think that when they're rotting, they've done everything that can be demanded of them.
> HAGEN *sneering:* They think they are out of it.
> GERNOT: They'll be surprised. (21f., 57)

The dead will be surprised, for in a seemingly perennial history of calamity and violence, they are to exercise the rhythm of death and "resurrection" (*Auferstehung*, 31, 66) again and again; this is a rhythm Müller dramatically implements throughout the play, and it repeats itself sometimes "every night" (23, 58).[4] And it is here, in the implacable cycle of horror and violence, that a distinct feature of Müller's theater manifests itself. Not by chance are the Nibelungs *überlebensgroß (larger than life-sized):* they are *überlebensgroß*, of course, in the comic respect of their grotesque height as well as in the heroic respect of their Wagnerian pathos.[5] Yet to be *überlebens-groß* in this context is also and particularly significant in that *überleben* is precisely what appears so difficult in the cauldron: "I don't want to die every night," laments Gernot (23, 58). Such discontent appears incompatible with the ways of life and death in the cauldron.

> GUNTHER: Take up your swords, all of you Nibelungs.
> The Huns are coming back. IN GOD WE TRUST.
> *The Nibelungs arm themselves with corpses, or limbs of corpses,*
> *and hurl them yelling at imaginary Huns so that an irregular wall of corpses piles up.*
> See, Attila, the harvest our swords reaped.

---

4. On Müller's theater of resurrection, see Günther Heeg, "Totenreich Deutschland—Theater der Auferstehung," in *Der Text ist der Coyote: Heiner Müller Bestandsaufnahme,* ed. Brigitte Maria Mayer and Christian Schulte (Frankfurt a.M.: Suhrkamp, 2004), 35–50.

5. Müller deems the *Nibelungs* the "most German of all German material and also still a German reality. The *Nibelungs* continues to be performed in Germany" ("'Germany Still Plays the *Nibelungs*': Interview with Urs Jenny und Hellmuth Karasek," *Der Spiegel,* May 9, 1983, 196–207). For a discussion of the arguably problematic implications correlating with Müller's evaluation of the Nibelung myth, see Genia Schulz and Hans-Thies Lehmann, "Protoplasma des Gesamtkunstwerks: Heiner Müller und die Tradition der Moderne," in *Unsere Wagner: Joseph Beys, Heiner Müller, Karlheinz Stockhausen, Hans Jürgen Syberberg,* ed. Gabriele Förg (Frankfurt a.M.: Fischer, 1984), 50–84; Jonathan Kalb, *The Theater of Heiner Müller* (Cambridge: Cambridge University Press, 1998), 138–63.

The Nibelungs sit on the wall of corpses, take off their helmets, and drink beer from their skulls.
GERNOT: Always the same thing. *The others look at him outraged.* I'm not saying that I don't want to play along anymore. But what is it all about, actually? (22, 57f.)

The question of what it is all about is taken up by Hagen: *"Because we can't get out of this cauldron,* that's why we keep scuffling with the Huns" (22, 58). The fact that the enemy here is merely constituted of *"imaginary Huns"* appears extraneous; after all, it is not the killing of Huns per se but the *performative dynamics* of enmity that allows for the foundation of a political community, a community germinating from the ethnic or tribal cleansing of the "dastard" (cf. "aus dem Hinterhalt") Huns (22, 58). The political self-identification of the Nibelungs' *Volksgemeinschaft* operates via an imagined contradistinction to the Huns, and it promises to reinvigorate the polity successfully as long as the Huns can be instituted and sustained as the "enemy" in an ongoing drive for tribal purity. The goal is an ethnically "immanent" community.[6] Gernot has not yet entirely understood the rigorousness of this conception of communal politics:

GERNOT: But we only need to stop, and then there's no more cauldron.
GUNTHER: Did he say: stop.
VOLKER: He still doesn't get it.
HAGEN: He'll never learn. (23, 58)

What Gernot has not yet understood is the nature of a certain concept of the political, a concept according to which "to stop"—that is, ceasefire, armistice, peace—cannot actually ensue from withdrawal, for without "the concrete determination of the enemy"[7] not only is it impossible to wage war, but, more importantly, it would be inconceivable to institute peace.[8] Within the poetic space of *Germania* this logic is taken to heart and run through step by step. First, Gernot must be sacrificed:

The three Nibelungs, in a protracted fight, hack [GERNOT] to pieces. Then they masturbate together.
VOLKER *masturbating:* I'd like to do something else, for a change. That thing with women, for instance. I've forgotten what it's called. *The Nibelungs laugh.*

---

6. For an analysis of the societal efficacy of "immanentism," see Jean-Luc Nancy, *The Inoperative Community,* trans. Peter Connor et al. (Minneapolis: University of Minnesota Press, 1991); Nancy, *La communauté désoeuvrée* (Paris: C. Bourgois, 1986). Cf. also Slavoj Žižek, "Heiner Müller aus den Fugen," in *Der Text ist der Coyote,* ed. Brigitte Maria Mayer and Christian Schulte, 274–98.
7. Carl Schmitt, *Der Begriff des Politischen* (Berlin: Duncker & Humblot, 2002), 57. On Müller's poetics of war, cf. Günther Heeg, "Deutschland—Krieg," in *Heiner Müller-Handbuch,* 89–93.
8. See Schmitt, *Der Begriff des Politischen,* 26.

HAGEN *likewise:* I don't even know anymore what that is, a woman. I think I wouldn't even find the hole anymore. *The Nibelungs laugh.*
GUNTHER *likewise:* War is men's business. Anyway, now the money needs only to be split in three. And we'll find the hole in the cauldron, don't worry. (23, 59)

The associative leap from the necrophiliac act to the "hole in the cauldron" alludes to an exit, a potential way out of the lethal mechanisms of the politics of enmity. Yet the three remaining Nibelungs appear tied up in it, and, accordingly, the persistently erratic role of the "enemy" is passed around one by one, all the way to the end, or in the words of Hermann Göring, "to the last man."[9]

The Nibelungs laugh. VOLKER tunes his violin.
GUNTHER: Leave your violin out of this. I know your tricks. He wants to soften us with this song-and-dance routine. SLEEP LITTLE PRINCE SLEEP TIGHT. And then he hauls off and pinches the loot for himself.
HAGEN: Better, we take care of him right away.
GUNTHER: Let's go. *They arm themselves.*
VOLKER: Comrades.
They hack him to pieces.
GUNTHER: Now it's only the two of us.
HAGEN: One too many.
Hack each other into pieces. (24, 59)

The massacre taking place here on a thematic level involves an unstable role of the "enemy" and invokes far-reaching theatrological correlatives: as a result of the nonpresence of specifiable duels and identifiable antagonisms, the performative/"theatrical" dimension belies the constative/"dramatic" dimension. The theatrical efficacy of the scene seems, in other words, to thwart the determination of and the fight against an "enemy." The *enemy remains undefinable* ("But what is it all about, actually?"), only appears as "mirror-image" (Gernot vs. Hagen vs. Volker vs. Gunther),[10] or proves identical with the battleground (cauldron).[11] An instance commensurate with this interlacing of friends and enemies is epitomized by

---

9. "Rede Hermann Görings, gehalten am 30.1. 1943 im Reichsluftfahrtsministerium vor Abordnung der Wehrmacht," in *Die Nibelungen: Ein deutscher Wahn, ein deutscher Alptraum; Studien und Dokumente zur Rezeption des Nibelungenstoffs im 19. und 20. Jahrhundert,* ed. Joachim Heinzle und Anneliese Waldschmidt (Frankfurt a.M.: Suhrkamp, 1991), 180.
10. See "Ein Gespräch zwischen Wolfgang Heise und Heiner Müller," in *Brecht 88: Anregungen zum Dialog über die Vernunft am Jahrtausendende,* ed. Wolfgang Heise (Berlin: Henschelverlag Kunst und Gesellschaft, 1989), 194.
11. For a discussion of Heiner Müller's dramaturgy, see Hans-Thies Lehmann, *Das politische Schreiben: Essays zu Theatertexten* (Berlin: Theater der Zeit, 2002), 338–53, here 346; Andreas Keller, *Drama und Dramaturgie Heiner Müllers zwischen 1956 und 1988* (Frankfurt a.M.: Peter Lang, 1994), esp. 206–25; Norbert Otto Eke, *Heiner Müller: Apokalypse und Utopie* (Munich: Ferdinand Schöningh, 1989), 20–66.

"Stalin," the "hero" to whom the "Hommage" is devoted, but who also is on a par with Hitler in his role as a mass murderer ("Heil Stalin," 40, 72). This degree of discursive inconsistency eludes any framework of dramatic conflict. The evaporation of conflictual depth becomes most evident with the transformation at the end of "Hommage à Stalin 1":

> A moment of silence. The battle noise also has stopped. Then pieces of corpses crawl towards one another and form themselves, with a terrible din of metal, screams, and snatches of songs [Lärm aus Metall, Schreien...], into a monster made of scrap-metal and body-parts [zu einem Monster aus Schrott und Menschenmaterial]. (24, 59)

What is rendered indistinguishable here are the processes of human history, natural history, and technology. The symbiosis of "scrap-metal" and "body-parts," metal and flesh, embodies the politics of "foes" and "friends," within which all human beings are potential "enemies" in a society resigned to technology. The monster is, on the one hand, machine,[12] yet, on the other, still capable of articulating anxiety and fright ("screams")—and as long as the "screams" prevail, this "inhuman" being remains an ideologically instrumentalizable correlative for any humanist quest. "Humanism is the ideology of the machine," Müller hyperbolically states in his autobiography. What he alludes to is the precarious ideological ambiguity of "humanism," which is always based on principles of selection and exclusion, mechanisms of enmity, and the expulsion of enemies, thereby producing the "inhuman" that proves to be an incessant supplement of "the" human and, perhaps, as we shall see, the most genuinely and inherently "human" there is.[13]

Ghosts in Müller's *Germania*

"Hommage à Stalin 1" ends with *"The noise continues into the next scene"* (24, 59); the next scene, "Hommage à Stalin 2," transmutes this noise into *"Sirens [and b]ells ringing."* This acoustic transmutation is aligned with a thematic iteration: "PETTY-BOURGEOIS [KLEINBÜRGER] 1: Stalin is dead. / PETTY-BOURGEOIS 2: It took him long enough" (24, 60). Death matters to Müller, yet as already noted, not as a last stop, but as a dramatic impetus for the next "resurrection" (*Auferstehung*, 31, 66) and the next death. As the Nazi brother later says in *Germania*, "Don't worry, it's a slaughterhouse, brother. / If you want to see something around here

---

12. On Müller's poetics of the machine, see Thomas Weitin, "Technik-Ökonomie-Maschine," in *Heiner Müller-Handbuch*, 104–8.
13. Heiner Müller, *Jenseits der Nation: Heiner Müller im Interview mit Frank M. Raddatz* (Berlin: Rotbuch Verlag, 1991), 43; Müller, *Krieg ohne Schlacht, Leben in zwei Diktaturen, Eine Autobiographie*, in *Werke* (Frankfurt a.M.: Suhrkamp, 2005), 9:244–46.

which has a future / Better go to a factory where they make coffins" (50, 80). Correspondingly, Müller says: "One function of drama is the invocation of the dead—the dialogue with the dead must not come to an end, until they hand over that of the future which has been buried with them."[14] We will return to this notion of a potentiality buried with the dead, a potentiality yet to be actualized. Given this temporal dynamic of death and resurgence, Müller's *Germania* seems to manifest an entire discourse of ghostly figures: Napoleon, "dragging behind him a soldier of his Grand Army by the feet"; Caesar, "his face green"; the "imaginary Huns" and the "larger than life-sized" Nibelungs, transformed into the "monster made of scrap-metal and body-parts." In addition are the "Skull-Seller" (*Schädelverkäufer*) in "Hommage à Stalin 2," the vampire of Frederick the Great in "Brandenburg Concerto 1," the specters associated with the People's Uprising on June 17, 1953 (see 51, 82), and the *revenant* of "Red Rosa [Luxemburg]" appearing in "Death in Berlin 2." These ghosts, still situated in the dramatic discourse of *Germania,* yet already anachronistically hovering in a heterogeneous sphere between the centuries and between "reality" and "fiction," now find support from the specters inhabiting the play's crevices and chasms: specters as they rise amid a temporal, spatial, and stylistic chaos,[15] constituted of countless intertextual references, explicit (as with Tacitus, Virgil, Georg Heym, or Beckett) and implicit (as in the case of Kafka[16] or Brecht[17] or German Arthurian literature).[18] The uncanniness of *Germania,* of course, is largely due to the dramaturgical structure of the dyadic scenes—scenes in which the second, often

---

14. *Gesammelte Irrtümer,* vol. 2, *Interviews und Gespräche* (Frankfurt a.M.: Verlag der Autoren, 1990), 64.

15. *Germania Tod in Berlin* amounts to a conglomerate of immense stylistic heterogeneity: the styles employed include historical drama, a citation from Tacitus's *Annales,* lyrical forms such as the ode from Virgil's *Bucolica* and the sonnet by Georg Heym, the surreal "nocturne" "Night Piece," the clownish comic in "Brandenburg Concerto I," fantastic grotesque tones as in "Hommage à Stalin 1," and Socialist *Aufbauliteratur* (literature of reconstruction) with its typified, often numbered characters in "Workers' Monument" and "Death in Berlin 2." Müller's dramatic art, which increasingly will turn out to be anything but "dramatic," develops its poetic force, its velocity very much based on this eclectic exuberance, situated between manifold styles and centuries.

16. "*Tears his jacket off, shows his back, covered with old scars.* / Do you recognize their handwriting. It's / Still legible. It was a little faded," says the Communist to his brother in "The Brothers 2" (48, 78f.). Kafka's story "In the Penal Colony" reads: "The Harrow is beginning to write; when it finishes the first draft of the inscription on the man's back, the layer of cotton wool begins to roll and slowly turns the body over, to give the Harrow fresh space for writing.... It keeps on writing deeper and deeper for the whole twelve hours.... You have seen how difficult it is to decipher the script with one's eyes; but our man deciphers it with his wounds." Franz Kafka, *The Completed Stories,* ed. Nahum N. Glatzer, trans. Willa and Edwin Muir (New York: Schocken Books, 1988), 149f. (*Ein Landarzt und andere Drucke zu Lebzeiten* [Frankfurt a.M.: Fischer, 1994], 172f.).

17. Cf. the clown scene in "Brandenburg Concerto 1" with the clown scene in Brecht's *Badener Lehrstück vom Einverständnis.*

18. "Oh, don't ever ask me, Lohengrin," Petty-Bourgeois 1 says in the scene "Hommage à Stalin 2" (27, 62). The mention of Lohengrin poses yet another moment of the spectral. For this son of Parzival and knight of the Holy Grail of course requests from the maiden he frees that she must never ask his name. It is not the case that he *does not have* an identity, but that it must not be inquired about and thus must remain strangely undetermined.

concerned with the present history of the GDR, is haunted by corresponding moments in history: the November Revolution, Prussia under Frederick II, the perpetual quarrel between brothers as already found with the Cheruscan brothers Arminius and Flavus, and so forth. Within the poetic space outlined by five couplets and three single scenes, an enormous efficacy of cross-elucidation comes into being, lending itself to an array of constellations in which the performative invocation of specters peculiarly merges with the explicit narrative of ghosts. *"The Skull-Seller has gotten up, he picks up his bag and approaches, tottering a bit,"* we read in "Hommage à Stalin 1":

WHORE 1: What's he want.
YOUNG BRICKLAYER: That's Santa Claus. Missing something?
SKULL-SELLER: A beautiful couple. Allow me to offer you a little souvenir.
Pulls a human skull from the sack. WHORE 1 screams.
A memento mori for the new home. IN THE MIDST OF LIFE WE ARE / SURROUNDED BY DEATH. I dug him up myself. And boiled three times. A clean specimen....
SKULL-SELLER *sits down at team leader's table:* I work deep underground. So to speak. We're moving cemeteries, unbeknownst to the public. Reburying, as it is called in the language of the bereaved [Umbetten, wie es in der Sprache der Hinterbliebenen heißt]. I am a bereaved person [Ich bin ein Hinterbliebener], I rebury. (30f., 65f.)

Müller, no doubt, is a skull-seller himself.[19] Unremittingly he piles up corpses;[20] time after time he lets the dead rise. Frequently, like the Skull-Seller, he reburies them to or from entirely different graveyards, that is, to or from entirely different plays: for instance, in the case of "Red Rosa" (and her *Doppelgänger* "Siegfried a Jewess from Poland" in *Germania 3 Ghosts at the Dead Man*) or the Nazi and his Communist brother (and the brothers "A" and "B" in *The Battle*) or the Nibelungs (also staged in Müller's prologue to Jürgen Flimm's production of Hebbel's *The Nibelungs* as well as *Germania 3*). The Skull-Seller is "a bereaved person" (*ein Hinterbliebener*) and as such *[ein] naher Angehöriger eines Verstorbenen* ([a] close relative of a deceased person).[21] The word *Angehöriger* corresponds to the verb *angehören* and denotes, according to the etymological dictionary "Teil von etwas sein" (to be part of something).[22] An *Angehöriger* is "part" of a family, and when his/her relatives

---

19. My use of the name "Müller" refers, needless to say, to an authorial voice, not the psychological constituency of the dramatist or the "private individual" Heiner Müller.
20. In his translation of *Hamlet* in collaboration with Matthias Langhoff, Heiner Müller translates Hamlet's famous words "as this fell sergeant, Death, / Is strict in his arrest"—epigrammatic in our context—as "der Tod ist ein Beamter und / Verhaftet pünktlich" (Müller, *Shakespeare Factory* [Berlin: Rotbuch Verlag, 1989], 2:121).
21. Gerhard Köbler, *Etymologisches Rechtswörterbuch* (Tübingen: Mohr, 1995), 189.
22. Ibid., 18.

die, s/he is part of something that no longer exists in its entirety, is perhaps half or one third or one fourth, and so on of what it was before; yet the *Angehöriger* appears, with respect to his/her identity as kins(wo)man, as quasi material, or as "Whore 2" points out, a "ghost," a ghost precisely in his/her role as *Hinterbliebene* (25, 66). On a different level, Heiner Müller, skull-seller within the scope of his profession as a dramatist, is also a *Hinterbliebener* in that he literally "stands behind" (*bleibt hinter*) the *Gestalt* ("figure," 24, 60) of the Skull-Seller, concealed behind a mask, ensconced without disclosing his authorial identity. And it is precisely from this hiding place that Müller brings to bear his morally uncommitted quest: "I cannot read morally, just as little as I can write morally."[23] "We work nights. Under the influence of alcohol, because of the danger of infection. [Wir arbeiten nachts. Unter Alkohol, wegen der Infektionsgefahr]," the Skull-Seller says ambiguously (32, 66). The Skull-Seller counters the hazard of getting infected with the disinfectant alcohol. The work "under the influence of alcohol" guarantees a certain "immunity" ("I have become immunized," 32, 66). It is in a similar vein that Heiner Müller's own close examination of the conflagration of history (we will return to this question) requires immunity against infectious diseases such as "sentimentality" or "piety." Not by chance, a "Drunk" (*Betrunkener*) in "Hommage à Stalin 2," appearing strikingly inconspicuous, "reconstructs" the horrors of the Cauldron of Stalingrad, after "Hommage à Stalin 1" dealt with nothing else:

> DRUNK:...In Stalingrad
> They've cooked me tender. That was more than war.
> We would have eaten grass. But I did not
> See any grass. We didn't ask a bone
> If it came from a horse, or rather: I
> ONCE HAD A GOOD COMRADE.
> But man gets used to everything. Who's sitting here.
> I was the only N.C.O.
> Who was commander of a company.
> The Captain croaked, and the Lieutenants too.
> We got finally out of the cauldron
> All of us twenty-four, except for ten.
> I got them safely out....
> TEAM LEADER: You ought to know.
> DRUNK: Oh yes, and just today
> I've met one. He's with the government.

---

23. Müller, *Krieg ohne Schlacht*, 220f. On Müller's autobiography, cf. Jost Hermand, "Diskursive Widersprüche: Fragen an Heiner Müller's 'Autobiographie,'" in *Mit den Toten reden*, 94–112; Gerd Gemünden, "The Author as Battlefield: Heiner Müller's Autobiography *War without Battle*," in *Heiner Müller: ConTEXTS and HISTORY*, ed. Gerhard Fischer (Tübingen: Stauffenberg Verlag, 1995), 117–27.

160   Inconceivable Effects

> State-Secretary, or whatever they call it now.
> That boy has got it made: Way up he is.
> But right away he recognized me. You, Boss?
> Always the same, says I. And he: Come on
> Let's celebrate. I went along. His wife
> Spit fire when we tried to *reconstruct*
> With beer on her parquet floor our cauldron
> Of Stalingrad. He locked her in the kitchen.
> And then we *reconstructed* our cauldron.
> *And after the fourth bottle* I ask: Could you
> Still crawl on elbows, Willi, you old pig.
> And what shall I tell you, you won't believe this:
> He could, and how. That well I drilled them boys. (29, 63f.)

The drunk man's contention "We got finally out of the cauldron" is illustrated by a "*re-construction*" that amounts to no less than an actual *enactment*. And perhaps because the Drunk, like the Skull-Seller, is so well disinfected ("after the fourth bottle") and has gotten "accustomed" (*[sich] gewöhnt*) to the horrors, he feels incited to "*reconstruct*" or compulsively repeat the traumatic experiences from the cauldron once again, this time graphically:

> DRUNK *pours beer on the table:* This is the Volga. Here is Stalingrad.
> TEAM LEADER: That is my beer.
> DRUNK: Not interested, huh.
> The war isn't over. It's just starting. (29, 64)

"The war...is just starting" appears to be the motto permeating Müller's *Germania,* rendered possible by Müller's imperturbability, his *Einverständnis* with the killing, the violence, the horrors: "You must be complicit with the violence [Du mußt einverstanden sein mit der Gewalt], with the atrocity, so that you can describe it."[24] Again and again the dead must "rise" (*auferstehen*) (31, 66), and die and "rise": "One must unearth the dead, again ánd again, for only from them can one obtain the future."[25] This is Müller's understanding of the "memento mori" (30, 65). Müller writes: "SO THAT SOMETHING CAN ARRIVE SOMETHING HAS TO GO THE FIRST SHAPE OF HOPE IS THE FEAR THE FIRST APPEARANCE OF THE NEW IS HORROR [SCHRECKEN]."[26] The German word *Gespenst* derives etymologically from the Old High German *spanan*, meaning

---

24. *Ich schulde der Welt einen Toten: Gespräche / Alexander Kluge-Heiner Müller* (Hamburg: Rotbuch, 1995), 60.
25. Müller, *Jenseits der Nation,* 31.
26. Heiner Müller, "Notes on *Mauser,*" in *The Battle: Plays, Prose, Poems by Heiner Müller,* trans. Carl Weber (New York: PAJ Publications, 1989), 133.

"reizen, verlocken, überreden,"[27] and it seems as if the most spectral dimension of the cultural text of horror[28] read and written by Müller lies in the fact that he, Müller, paradoxically demonstrates a propensity to perpetuate what he aspires to scrutinize: the involuted history of violence.

The Thalidomide Wolf

The grotesque-humorous scene "The Holy Family," integral to our question of the politics of enmity, stages Hitler in the biblical role of the father and redeemer, Joseph Göbbels as Maria, and the "enormous" personified "Germania" as midwife of the childbearing Göbbels and progenitor of Hitler (see 35, 69). The action does not take place in Nazareth but in the *Führerbunker*. Alleged "traitors" infiltrate *Germania* (see 22, 58; 28, 63; 45, 76; 50, 81; 51, 81), and "Hitler" indubitably fears them to the point of paranoia. In conversation with Göbbels he explains:

[Röhm] was a *traitor*.... The little slut.... I shot the entire magazine into him.... You were holding him, do you remember. You and Herrmann. Also a *traitor*. I'm surrounded with *traitors*.... Everywhere they are lying in wait for me. There. And there. *Walks faster and faster back and forth, always whirling around suddenly.* They are behind me. They won't dare to confront me. They are keeping themselves in my back. You see. But I'll get all of them. Providence holds its guiding hand over me. (35, 68f.)

The ramifications of the imputation of treachery emerge inconspicuously:

GUARD: Upstairs, a dog ran by [the *Führerbunker*].
HITLER: You hear that, Joseph. They are disguising themselves.
They won't dare anymore to confront us openly. But I see through their tricks.
I see through everything. A dog. Laughable! Continue.
GUARD: He pissed in the grass. That's all, my Führer.
HITLER: Keep your eyes open. The enemy is everywhere.
GUARD: Yessir, my Führer. *Exit Guard*. (34, 68)

The enemy also figures as a dog in Carl Schmitt's *Theory of the Partisan,* a work that Müller, in the context of his later intensive studies of Schmitt, called a "key text" (*Schlüsseltext*) to his thinking.[29] Schmitt writes:

---

27. Duden's *Das Herkunftswörterbuch: Etymologie der deutschen Sprache* (Mannheim: Dudenverlag, 1992), 237.
28. Lehmann, *Das politische Schreiben,* 365.
29. Müller, *Krieg ohne Schlacht,* 213.

When the internal, immanent rationality and regularity of the thoroughly-organized technological world has been achieved in optimistic opinion, the partisan becomes perhaps nothing more than an irritant. Then, he disappears simply of his own accord in the smooth-running fulfillment of technical-functional forces, *just as a dog disappears on the highway*.[30]

Müller, who in another context speaks of "the rebirth of the revolutionary out of the spirit of the partisan,"[31] will question Schmitt: "The partisan in an industrialized society may be a dog on the highway. But it depends how many dogs come together on the highway."[32] In *Germania,* soon after the first appearance of the dog that Hitler believes he has unmasked as the enemy, once again a dog, in the Schmittian sense of the dog as enemy, shows up. The Guard reports meaningfully: "The dog ran by again. He pissed again" (35, 69). No doubt, dogs matter to Müller, and *Germania* is full of them (see 15, 52; 18, 54; 20, 56; 36, 69; 37, 70). Notably, the dogs in *Germania* are accompanied by numerous other animals: the *"Thalidomide wolf"* is in *"sheep's"* clothing" (39, 71); Hilse's *Krebs* creeps no less than five times over a single page (39, 84). And there are mice crawling through Müller's play, so small that they are virtually invisible as they hide behind words: "We smashed the guns against the curbstones," the "Old Man" remembers of the failed revolution of 1918–19; "we crept back into the holes we lived in [krochen zurück in unsre Mauerlöcher]," *Mauerlöcher* that, in contiguity with *krochen,* for good reason may be (mis)read as *Mauselöcher.* A few lines down the page Müller implements the image of bird and cage: "A funny bird.... He's looking for a cage.... You've got to have luck. Bird, you are in luck. There goes a cage, he's looking for a bird" (9, 47). Kafka, among whose aphorisms Müller finds this enigmatic image,[33] generally appears to inspire the Müllerian art of metaphor.[34] "Art," Müller writes, "is perhaps also an experiment in '*becoming-animal*' [*Tierwerdung*] in the sense of Deleuze's and Guattari's book about Kafka."[35] Still before Deleuze and Guattari, Walter Benjamin noted: "[Kafka] often attributes the behavior patterns which are of most interest to him to animals."[36] The question of "*becoming-animal*" (*Tierwerdung*), a question of

---

30. Carl Schmitt, *Theorie des Partisanen: Zwischenbemerkung zum Begriff des Politischen* (Berlin: Duncker & Humblot, 1975), 80 (*Theory of the Partisan: Intermediate Commentary on the Concept of the Political,* trans. G. L. Ulmen [New York: Telos Press Publishing, 2007], 77).
31. In his speech given upon the reception of the Kleist-Prize, Müller writes: "The figure of the ghost-driver [*Geisterfahrer:* also wrong-way driver] belongs to the highway" (*Jenseits der Nation,* 62).
32. Müller, *Krieg ohne Schlacht,* 273.
33. "Ein Vogel geht einen Käfig suchen." See Franz Kafka, *Beim Bau der chinesischen Mauer und andere Schriften aus dem Nachlaß* (Frankfurt a.M.: Fischer, 1994), 231.
34. *Der Bau* started as a play adapted from the novel by Erich Neutsch, and, as Müller writes, moved increasingly in the direction of the story by Kafka. "It became increasingly metaphorical, more and more of a parable" (Müller, *Krieg ohne Schlacht,* 153).
35. Müller, *Krieg ohne Schlacht,* 247.
36. Walter Benjamin, *Aufsätze, Essays, Vorträge,* in *Gesammelte Schriften,* ed. Rolf Tiedemann and Hermann Schweppenhäuser (Frankfurt a.M.: Suhrkamp, 1991), 2.3:1261f.

significance in Müller's work, must be seen in the context of his occupation with the barbarian mechanisms of selection as characteristic of humanist ideology, which declares the human being "an enemy of human kind."[37] Humanist ideology disparages the enemy as "inhuman," thereby, as already indicated, invoking something genuinely "human," which continuously exists between the representative paradigm of "the" human and its *negativum* as inevitable supplement of society. Müller is interested in the "inhuman," which obstinately is engendered in the context of societal processes of decontamination or purification. The inquiry into the "inhuman" beyond moral concerns ("at least...[the] established and socially integrated morals") lies at the center of his conception of art.[38]

Notably, the action taking place in "The Holy Family" is a very festive one. Even "the three Magi of the Occident" (the Western Allies France, Great Britain, and the United States) have come from afar, and they have brought "presents," for what is about to be born here is nothing less than West Germany (see 38, 71). Yet in the context of the actual delivery the unexpected occurs:

Long scream from Göbbels.
GERMANIA:...Gentlemen, it's time. Where's my forceps. Why don't you give me a hand.
Germania applies the forceps, pulls, MAGI 1 pulls at GERMANIA, 2 at 1, 3 at 2.
HITLER: My people!
GUARD OF HONOR: GERMANY AWAKEN! SIEG HEIL!
THREE MAGIS: HALLELUJA! HOSANNA! *A wolf howls.*
Germania and the three Magi fall on their behinds. Before them stands a *Thalidomide wolf [Contergan-Wolf]. Startled.* Oh.
GERMANIA gets up, pulls a family-size box of SUNIL from her midwife's bag and pours detergent over the wolf. White Light. The wolf stands in sheepskin.
GÖBBELS dances like a whirling dervish. GERMANIA screams.
HITLER *laughs.* (38f., 71)

The popular German detergent Sunil quickly whitewashes the Fascist wolf so that it appears as a democratic wolf. Yet it seems as if during pregnancy Joseph Göbbels took the medication Thalidomide, the ominous drug predominantly recommended to pregnant women as an antiemetic to fight morning sickness and as a sedative. As a result of the side effects associated with the drug, Göbbels gives birth to an infant with a condition called phocomelia, that is, "abnormally short limbs with toes sprouting from the hips and flipper-like arms" (dysmelia) or, in

---

37. Müller, *Krieg ohne Schlacht,* 246.
38. Ibid., 247.

other cases, missing limbs or internal organs (aplasia).[39] The Fascist malformation of the West German Thalidomide wolf is ostentatiously ignored by the three Magi: "THE THREE MAGI *assuming the position of the three monkeys:* HALLELUJAH! HOSANNA!" (35, 72). They neither smell nor see nor hear the fascism still so alive in the Federal Republic of Germany. Hitler, disappointed with Germany's future, gets at Germania's, that is, "Mama's," throat: he "tortures Germania" and finally kills her with a "cannon" (35, 69; 39, 71f.). "*Curtain with the explosion*" (39, 72).

As with Kafka, one no doubt could say for Müller that the animal metaphors relentlessly displace their "signifiers"; that is to say, Müller's animals no longer "represent" human beings but rather decide things among themselves. In this sense Müller's conception of "becoming-animal" seems largely indebted to Kafka, and yet it appears—when Müller's art is most Müllerian—that the moment of becoming-animal presents us with a *radicalization* of Kafka. Indeed, one can*not* read Müller's animals "without realizing" (*ohne überhaupt wahrzunehmen*), as Benjamin noted in Kafka, "that they don't stand for humans at all" (*daß es sich gar nicht um Menschen handelt*).[40] The West German Thalidomide wolf, malformed progeny of Nazi Germany's "racial"-ethnic selection machinery, maintains its idiosyncrasy with respect to a notion of "inhumanity" inevitably associated with *Auschwitz* (a word crucial to Müller's understanding of "humanism"). This is not to say that any "humane" society, perhaps any society at all, could ever dispense with the politics of selection and exclusion; indeed, the inhuman capacity equally determines the "progressive" potential of "the" human as it establishes, intimately linked, its perversity (as is metaphorized by the "Thalidomide wolf").[41] What distinguishes the "metaphor" of the Thalidomide wolf from Kafka's "metaphors" is that whereas Kafka's animals merely *forebode* Auschwitz, Müller's malformed Thalidomide wolf *knows* of Auschwitz. In an interview with Alexander Kluge, Müller problematized the transformation of human beings into animals, plants, and stones in the poetics of Ovid—a characteristic equally pertinent to Kafka—and said: "The motif of metamorphosis is...what makes the matter theatrical [Das Verwandlungsmotiv ist das was...die Sache theatralisch macht]."[42] Perhaps we can provisionally turn Müller's observation about Ovid upon Müller's *Germania* in that the *radicalization* and *distortion* of transformation as explored here is what makes Müller's matter theatrical.

---

39. Trent Stephens and Rock Brynner, *Dark Remedy: The Impact of Thalidomide and Its Revival as a Vital Medicine* (New York: Perseus, 2001), 61–78; David J. Bloch, *The Fundamentals of Life Sciences Law* (Washington, DC: American Health Lawyers Association, 2007), 4.

40. Benjamin, *Aufsätze, Essays, Vorträge*, 2.3:1261f.

41. Cf. Jean-François Lyotard, *L'inhumain: Causeries sur le temps* (Paris: Galilée, 1988), 10. For a discussion of "the inhuman" in Müller, see Nikolaus Müller-Schöll, *Das Theater des "konstruktiven Defaitismus": Lektüren zur Theorie eines Theaters der A-Identität bei Walter Benjamin, Bertolt Brecht und Heiner Müller* (Frankfurt a.M.: Stroemfeld Verlag, 2002), 578–82.

42. "Heiner Müller in Time Flight," http://muller-kluge.library.cornell.edu/en/video_record.php?f = 110.

Silence. Pause.

The politics of enmity finds one of its most embroiled variants in the scene "The Brothers 2." The scene takes place in a prison in the GDR—allegedly *the* prison "GDR"—among murderers, saboteurs, Nazi criminals, and a Communist. The People's Uprising of June 17, 1953, starting in East Berlin, is the backdrop for the encounter of a Communist, who in the Gestapo's torture chambers was forcefully converted into a Nazi, and his nonconformist Communist brother, who is also imprisoned by the new Communist regime:

> NAZI *steps forward:* He's my brother.
> SABOTEUR: The Red?
> GANDHI *laughs:* IN MY HOMETOWN IN MY HOMETOWN
> THAT'S WHERE WE MEET AGAIN.
> COMMUNIST: My brother the traitor. *Silence.*
> You've made quite a career.
> NAZI: So did you.
> *Pause. Noise of a crowd outside. Rhythmic beating on steam pipes*
> *in the prison that continues throughout the following scene.*
> SABOTEUR *at the window:* It won't take long now anymore.
> COMMUNIST *at window:* What's that?
> SABOTEUR: That is the people rising up. (46f., 77f.)

Two words almost get lost in this passage, two words that make all the difference: "*Silence*" and "*Pause.*" What do "*Silence*" and "*Pause*" signify here? What do they omit while perhaps expressing all the more perspicuously? When the Communist says: "My brother the traitor. You've made quite a career [Mein Bruder der Spitzel. Du hast es weit gebracht]"; when he, in other words, accuses his Nazi brother of having betrayed their common Communist cause, a betrayal, of course, equally directed against the anti-Fascist self-conception of the GDR, within which Müller writes, if such an accusation is succeeded by "*Silence,*" then this silence implies a great deal: conjectures perhaps as to the reasons that led the brother to comply with the Fascist enemy; perhaps the silence denotes a reference to the many Communists murdered by Nazis; and perhaps it alludes to the struggles among the parties of the Left during the Weimar Republic with their fatal consequences, the rise of the Nazi Party and the fratricide. Yet the ambiguity of this "*Silence,*" its precarious meaning, is brought to bear only in light of the subsequent lines and the eerie "*Pause*":

> COMMUNIST: My brother the traitor. *Silence.*
> You've made quite a career.
> NAZI: So did you.
> *Pause.*

The uncanny (and from the perspective of GDR censors actually outrageous) does *not* preside in the Nazi's accusation against his Communist brother ("So did you")—an allusion to both of their failed careers in the service of opposite and opposing ideologies that lead both to an encounter in the same prison cell. The audacity in those few lines lies in the fact that Müller, in his putative role as the author, refuses to intervene by virtue of his authorial authority—refuses to intercede as an omniscient narrator, withholding comment in order to suggest that the Nazi's insinuated comparison of his career with that of his brother in the GDR is ridiculous if not absurd. Instead Müller performatively corroborates the Nazi's constative parallelization by leaving the Nazi's infamous assertion uncontradicted. He offers only an abysmal *"Pause"*—a *"Pause"* accompanying the Communist's purportedly equally valid *"Silence,"* and he does so precisely at a point where, from the party-political perspective, a political if not moral intervention would appear imperative. In short, what happens here is between the lines—between the discourses of state-political doctrine and Fascist doctrine—and it happens in the blink of an eye: it is the coming into being of a voice denying political loyalty or accountability to anyone. In this speechlessness, or rather because of this speechlessness, a destructive potential is revealed that otherwise would be tamed or veiled by the deadening power of civilized speech.[43]

The Brothers

As the increasing clamor of an angry mob signals an uprising ("*Noise of crowds louder. Word-salad of FREEDOM GERMAN KILL THEM HANG THEM*"), the conversation between the brothers becomes more complex:

> NAZI: The Night of the Long Knives. *Do you remember.*
> I stood at your door. And I was your brother.
> *Holds out his hand. The brother doesn't take it.*
> But my brother had no hand free.
> I am your brother.
> COMMUNIST: I don't have a brother.
> NAZI: Better switch off the light, brother. The Reichstag
> Is burning bright enough. This is the Night
> Of the Long Knives. (47, 78)

---

[43]. Cf. also the interview titled "Episches Theater" between Heiner Müller and Alexander Kluge, http://muller-kluge.library.cornell.edu/en/video_record.php?f = 106v. On Müller's poetics of silence, see Nikolaus Müller-Schöll, "'...Die Wolken still / Sprachlos die Winde': Heiner Müllers Schweigen," in *AufBrüche: Theaterarbeit zwischen Text und Situation,* ed. Patrick Primavesi and Olaf A. Schmitt (Frankfurt a.M.: Theater der Zeit, 2004), 247–56.

Here Müller references the scene "The Night of the Long Knives" from his play *The Battle*,[44] involving a quarrel between two Communist brothers,[45] one of whom, after being arrested, tortured, and released by the Gestapo, is shunned by his brother and Communist comrades, who suspected him of being a traitor and possibly disclosing their identities under torture. Not long after, the Communist again is captured by the Gestapo, again tortured; but this time, already an outcast, he submits himself to the enemy (see 48, 78). If one follows the reference in *Germania* (1956/1971) to *The Battle* (1951/1974)—"Do you remember"—an ineluctable discrepancy evolves: in *The Battle* the brother who allegedly defected to the Nazis asks his Communist brother to kill him ("Give me what I ask for: To be dead"), and it appears that the fratricide does indeed follow: "I killed the traitor who's my brother, him" (*S* 473, 142). Yet in *Germania,* which seems to resume where the scene in *The Battle* leaves off, the murder never transpires:

NAZI: When I left your door and went into the
Night of the Long Knives and the revolver
Fell from your hand onto the floorboards
Louder than any shot I've heard before
Or since, and the bullet for the traitor
For whom your brother begged on his knees
Stayed in the barrel. (49, 80)

If, only provisionally, we extend the dialogue between the two brothers into a dialogue between the two scenes, the question that arises is what to make of the Communist's statement "I don't have a brother" (47, 78). Notably, the brother does *not* suggest that once he had a brother whom he murdered and therefore has one *no longer.* That is to say, the sentence does not read, "I don't have a brother *anymore,*" but rather, "I don't have a brother." It thus seems to allude to a moment and a time

---

44. "A: And when the Reichstag burned, the night turned day / In the door my brother stood, I look away. / B: I am your brother. / A: Are you sure. / And if you are, why are you coming here / Before my face, your hands all red / Of our comrades' blood. If three times you were dead. / B: That's what I want, brother, that's why I came. / A: You call me brother. I won't listen to that name. / Between us there's a knife, they call it treason / And it is you who forged it. / B: And if it's me and if my hand is red / Give me what I ask for: To be dead" (471, 141). Quotations from Heiner Müller's *Die Schlacht* are followed by two sets of page numbers. The first set refers to Heiner Müller, *Die Schlacht,* in *Die Stücke,* vol. 4 (Frankfurt a.M.: Suhrkamp, 2001); hereafter abbreviated as *S.* The second set refers to *The Battle: Plays, Prose, Poems by Heiner Müller,* ed. Carl Weber (New York: PAJ Publications, 1989). On *The Battle,* see also Frank-Michael Raddatz, "Die Schlacht," in *Heiner Müller-Handbuch,* 274–77.

45. The grotesque encounter between the two brothers as worked out in *The Battle* ("The Night of the Long Knives") as well as *Germania Death in Berlin* ("The Brothers 2") found a model in Brecht's *Vorspiel* to his *Antigone* adaptation, set during the last days of the fighting in Berlin in April 1945. Here the diametrically oppositional reactions of two sisters in response to the death of their brother, murdered by the SS, are examined in light of their own lives, which are suddenly at stake should they be identified as the sisters of the presumed deserter—a situation, as in Müller, of tragic antinomies and equivocal moralities propelled by the confusions of war.

"when the Reichstag burned, and the night turned day" (*S* 471, 141), a time when the Communist *inwardly* deprived himself of his brother, and in consequence never actually had and never actually killed a brother. Beyond this intertextual reference—this ruptured reference—an abundance of political complexities comes into being. "Twenty years ago" the Communist forsook his brother after he had been tortured by the Gestapo and—*presumably,* yet not *actually*—committed treachery; and it was precisely the resulting ostracism that rendered the brother, in the course of his second "interrogation" by the Gestapo, an easy prey to the Nazis and victim to himself:

> B: I bought—where there's a dog there is a skin—
> The brownshirt, carousels turn always right
> You swing the truncheon and the victims groan.
> That's past. I looked deep down into myself.
> The night of the long knives is asking who
> Eats whom. *I am the one and I'm the other.*
> There's one too many. Who'll cross out the other.
> Take the revolver, do what I can't do
> So I'm a dog no longer but a corpse. (*S* 472f., 143)

The Communist reduces his brother's "*I am the one and I'm the other*" to a narrative of friends and foes, thereby stigmatizing the brother as "traitor":

> A: While our comrades in the basements screamed
> And long knives cut their swath across Berlin
> I killed the traitor who's my brother, him. (*S* 472f., 143)

The fatal implication of this all-too-simple designation of his brother as "traitor" now turns against the Communist: under the impression that the uprising has been quelled by Russian tanks (*"Noise of crowd decreases and is quickly fading in the distance. Noise of moving tanks,"* 51, 82), the other inmates unite against the Communist in order to kill him. It is only at this moment of extreme danger that he seems to conjure a "truth" he had denied to his brother (*S* 472, 142):

> COMMUNIST: Those are the tanks. The ghost has vanished [Der Spuk ist vorbei].
> NAZI: One of them should at least perish today [Wenigstens einer soll dran glauben heute].
> GANDHI: He doesn't want it any different. He won't
> See Communism anyway.
> COMMUNIST: Who am I.
> *The three attack him.* (43, 82)

Expressed at a moment when he fears his own death, the Nazi brother's comment "*I am the one and I'm the other*" corresponds with the Communist's "Who am I," a comment also uttered in a moment of existential peril. The phrase "Who am I" is succeeded by a period rather than a question mark, since at this moment of imminent danger, certain power-political circumstances, beyond psychological motivation, concretize to an ineffaceable "truth" concerning his very own condition: for the inmates attacking the Communist, he is the suppressing state-socialist, a "traitor" (*Vaterlandsverräter*) and "Russian stooge" (*Russenknecht*). In that role, hearing the crowds outside getting louder, he screams to the prison guards: "Why don't they shoot at them. This can't be true. *Hammers against the door.* Comrades, defend the prison. Shoot now, shoot" (50, 81; 49, 79). In contrast to the state-Socialists who imprison him—people with whom in odd ways he keeps faith—he is a dissident and thus considered, like his Nazi brother, an "enemy" of the Socialist state (see 46, 77). Only now, at the moment of crisis, an understanding evolves according to which the question "Who am I?" very much amounts to conceptions of being-referred-to-as and being-described-as in the sense of "Who'll cross out the other" (*S* 472f., 143). In Müller's theater, the term "enemy" proves to be a vagrant constant, an unreliable signifier, not bound to any stable semantic content. The image of the enemy finds an "actual" (rather than "symbolic") materialization on the Nazi's back: engrained as scars resulting from the wounds inflicted by the Gestapo's henchmen, later "freshened up" by the state-Socialists:

Tears his jacket off, shows his back, covered with old scars.
Do you recognize their handwriting. It's
Still legible. It was a little faded
After twenty years, but your friends
Freshened them up, from the old maketh the new
So that my brother has something to read. (48, 78f.)

The scars inflicted by the Gestapo on the brother's back are freshened up by the state-Socialists, yet in both cases these scars are "true,"[46] signifying a violent "truth" about Nazism in one case, a violent "truth" about state-socialism in another, the latter restoring the violent truth of the former, refreshing it by means of yet another *process of inscription*. The Communist's brother, tortured by the Nazis as "Communist," and stigmatized by his comrades as "Nazi," again, is beaten by the state-Socialists as "Nazi." This persistent conflation of the seemingly established dichotomies of friends and foes—the ongoing moments of description and inscription—amounts to a certain indistinguishability between guilt and innocence, between traitors and betrayed. Political discourses begin to falter, and the bases for moral judgments evaporate. This, however, essentially correlates with

---

46. The corresponding scene in *The Battle* reads: "A: Your shirt is brown, that is the truth today. / B: The truth today. You want to read it, brother. / Three weeks long I have been the paper he / Wrote his truth on, your enemy and mine. / *Takes off the brownshirt. On his chest a swastika formed by / fresh scars.* / And what was left of him who was your brother / Is the traitor" (*S* 472, 142).

Müller's dramaturgy. If bourgeois drama was specific with respect to variants of intersubjective confrontation, Müller's subject is deprived of the enemy. That is to say, instead of the presentation of a dialectically or oppositionally evolving *action*, the front lines are rendered diffuse and eviscerated—as typified by the Nibelungs, whose struggle follows no logic other than the programming of the very monstrous machine into which they themselves ultimately transform.[47]

The politics of enmity, seemingly instituting historical trajectories reaching from the mythical time of the Nibelungs over Tacitus's *Germania* to the divided German workers' movement and divided postwar Germany, comes to a halt in the scene "Night Piece," where the temptation of a continuous, teleological conception of history is subjected to a surreal experiment.

The Human, Who Is Perhaps a Puppet

"Night Piece," inspired by Brecht's *Badener Lehrstück vom Einverständnis* and Beckett's *Actes sans paroles*,[48] negotiates the grotesque situation of a *struggle without a definable enemy*:

> A human stands on stage. He is larger than life-sized, perhaps a puppet. He is dressed in posters. His face is without a mouth. He regards his hands, moves the arms, tests his legs. A bicycle, from which the handlebars or pedals or both or handlebars, pedals and seat have been removed, rides quickly from right to left over the stage. The human, who is perhaps a puppet, runs after the bicycle. *A threshold rises from the stage floor. He stumbles over it and falls. Lying on his stomach he sees the bicycle disappear. The threshold disappears unseen by him. When he stands up and looks around for the cause of his fall, the stage-floor is flat again. His suspicion falls on his legs. He tries to tear them out in a seated position, on his back, standing. The heel against buttocks, holding the foot with both hands, he tears the left foot off, then, falling on his face, lying on his belly, the right leg.* He is still lying on his belly, when the bicycle slowly moves past him from left to right over the stage. He notices it too late and cannot crawl fast enough to catch it. Pulling himself up and supporting his swaying trunk with his hands, he makes the discovery that he can use his arms for locomotion, if he swings his trunk, pushes forward, following with his hands, etc. He practices the new mode of walking. He

---

47. The violence immanent in the German revolutionary workers' movement, including its intrinsic paradoxes, lies at the center of "The Brothers 2" and appears within *Germania*'s narrative topography as a *revenant*, a ghost already flitting through Tacitus's *Annales*. The fight between brothers here takes shape as that between two Cheruscan brothers yelling at each other across the waters of the Weser River. Flavus, "serving the Roman army," shouts from one bank of the river, and Arminius, putatively more patriotic than his brother and certainly more confident about his moral superiority, stands on the other bank. Yet in truth it seems as if Arminius accuses Flavus of being a "deserter" and "betrayer" (45, 76) as a way of coping with his own feelings of distress. The last sentence mentions only in passing that "Arminius was to be seen, threatening and challenging to combat: *he used the Latin tongue freely in his discourse, having once commanded a force of his countrymen in [the Roman] army*" (45, 76).
48. Cf. also Kalb, *Theater of Heiner Müller*, 166.

waits for the bicycle, first stage left, then stage right, at the gates. *The bicycle doesn't appear. The human, who is perhaps a puppet, tears off his left arm with his right and his right with his left, simultaneously.* Behind him the threshold rises from the stage floor to the level of his head, this time so that he doesn't fall over. From the gridiron comes the bicycle and remains standing before him. *Leaning against the head-high threshold, the human, who is perhaps a puppet, watches legs and arms, which lie widely scattered all over the stage, and the bicycle that he cannot use anymore.* He cries one tear with each eye. (52f., 82f.)

Much can be observed in this short passage. With respect to our question about the politics of enmity, it is striking that the dismemberment takes place in the absence of a visible enemy. The "human, who is perhaps a puppet," seeks to attain the bicycle, yet like the Nibelungs in their struggle, he merely fights what could be described as his alter ego, a person within himself, on the one hand, and the battlefield, in particular the ominous "threshold," on the other. While from our reader's perspective we can follow the first rising of the threshold and its disappearance, the human, who is perhaps a puppet, *cannot* see it, given that his perspective appears limited at that moment. Of course, what perpetuates the autodestructive procedure is the chase after or striving for the bicycle, an undertaking bringing about warlike consequences: that is, the loss of the limbs. And yet, what is missing is *a definable external enemy,* an ostensible condition once again precipitating fundamental correlatives on the performative level. A whole series of theatrical moments, showlike and playful, thwart the dramatic and thrust it aside: the motive of the puppet, the grotesque humor and clownish elements (such as the mechanical autodestruction), the crawling, the locomotive walking, moments of astonishment, perplexity, surprise, the irritation, the "suspicion," most of all, the horror or fright (*Schrecken*):

> Two Beckett-spikes are moved in at eye level from left and right. They stop at the face of the human, who is perhaps a puppet; he need only turn his head once to the right, once left, the spikes take care of the rest. The spikes are withdrawn, each with an eye on the tip. Out of the empty eye cavities of the human, who is perhaps a puppet, lice crawl, spreading themselves black across his face. He screams. The mouth originates with the scream. (53, 83)

What is to be fathomed here—as was the case with the "screaming," "larger than life-sized" Nibelungs (24, 59)—is that the condition of the "larger than life-sized" (52, 82) human who is perhaps a puppet amounts to an experience of *crisis.* Asked about his understanding of the term *Schrecken,* Heiner Müller responded: "The instance of truth, *when the enemy appears in the mirror.*"[49] Yet even the image

---

49. "Ein Gespräch zwischen Wolfgang Heise und Heiner Müller," 194.

172 Inconceivable Effects

of the "enemy" appearing in the mirror describes an ostensible dimension that proves untenable under close scrutiny: for what emerges beyond the militaristic terminology of "friends" and "enemies," beyond any political discursiveness, is the *horror,* the *screaming,*[50] the experience of an in-between, between awareness and sorrow, consciousness and suffering.[51] The specificity of the existential experience of the "human, who is *perhaps* a puppet," is rooted in the "*perhaps,*" for in spite of the "human's" likely aspiration toward autonomy, he remains "puppet," shrinking in the shadows of its own angst. The creaturely position of the human, who is perhaps a puppet, resonates, as we shall see, with Heiner Müller's paradoxical authorial role.

Hilse's Cancer

The last variant of a politics of enmity discussed here brings the final scene of *Germania,* "Death in Berlin 2," into focus. The scene takes place in a Berlin hospital, where, somewhat reminiscent of the Garbe figure in *The Scab (Der Lohndrücker),* Hilse, a bricklayer, has been hospitalized; his injuries appear to be the result of his refusal to participate in the workers' strike of June 17, 1953—a stance that had provoked skinhead youths to throw rocks at him. The incident occurs in an earlier scene, "The Workers' Monument":

>*[HILSE] works. Youth, skinheads, with bicycles....*
>THIRD YOUTH: Hey. *Sudden idea.* Can you dance, Grandpa?
>*Improvises a rock tune, throws in rhythm. The others join in.*
>*All three throw stones in Rock-Rhythm at the Bricklayer.*
>ALL THREE: Yeah—
>THIRD: You are learning, pop.
>FIRST: And faster, pop.
>SECOND: Don't fall asleep, pop.
>THIRD: No quitting on us now....
>*Hail of stones and finale. The Bricklayer collapses.*
>SECOND: Looks like a workers' monument [Arbeiterdenkmal].
>FIRST *walks up to the Bricklayer:* Man. The guy is gone.
>SECOND: Did you see anything?

---

50. The "scream" or "shout" is gesture, in that, in the words of Jacques Derrida, it has not yet been entirely frozen by "the articulation of language and logic"; as such it relates to "the aspect of oppressed gesture which remains in all speech, the unique and irreplaceable movement which the generalities of concept and repetition have never finished rejecting" (Derrida, "The Theater of Cruelty and the Closure of Representation," in *Writing and Difference,* trans. Alan Bass [Chicago: University of Chicago Press, 1978], 240).

51. On the pivotal notion of the "creature," see Rainer Nägele, "Klassische Moderne," in *Heiner Müller-Handbuch,* 152–54; cf. Klaus Teichmann, *Der verwundete Körper: Zu Texten Heiner Müllers* (Freiburg: Burg-Verlag, 1989), esp. 91–93.

THIRD: A work place accident.
SECOND: Yeah, piecework is murder.
The Three exit quickly. (42–44; 74–76)

The Bricklayer Hilse (an allusion to Gerhart Hauptmann's *The Weavers*)[52] is stoned into a "workers' monument," tragically embodying the contradictions of the Socialist system. He keeps faith with the Socialist mission as putatively manifested by the state and, in this sense, disparages the striking workers as "traitors to the working-class" (*Arbeiterverräter,* 28, 63); but ironically it is precisely this kind of thinking in terms of friends and foes that fails to do justice to the "Young Bricklayer." Hilse never wonders why the Young Bricklayer takes part in the strike, although he seems sympathetic to the Socialist state and leaves no doubt about his return to work ("Here, hold my trowel until I'm back," 42, 74). It is this kind of ambiguity Hilse appears incapable of grasping, an ambiguity, in fact, implied in the scene's title, "Arbeiterdenkmal" ("Workers' Monument"): the word, of course, proleptically refers to the fossil *monument* "Hilse," made, it seems, for eternity but not for today's problems. On the other hand, "Arbeiterdenkmal" entails the imperative "Arbeiter, denk mal!," an imperative Hilse cannot hear or will not hear.

Surprisingly, then, Hilse is hospitalized ("Death in Berlin 2") *not* because of the rocks thrown at him but because of a hidden tumor indicative perhaps of a malignant tumor intrinsic to the revolutionary movement:

Cancer Ward. Hilse. The Young Bricklayer.
YOUNG BRICKLAYER: How are you, Old Man.
HILSE: I am not well. But I'm only one half
Of me, the cancer ate the other half.
And if you ask my cancer, he is fine.
YOUNG BRICKLAYER: I didn't know that. I was thinking
It was the bricks they had piled on your bones
At our building site two weeks ago
Because you didn't want to strike.
HILSE: That's what I thought, too. I know better now. (54, 84)

While Hilse and the Young Bricklayer first assume that *exterior class enemies,* the adolescent provocateurs, had injured Hilse, it is, in fact, an externally invisible

---

52. Hauptmann's play thematizes the uprising of the Silesian weavers of 1844, a historic date for the German proletarian movement's self-conception and a precursor as part of the official history of the GDR. Müller's Hilse figure implicitly refers to Hauptmann's Hilse, a Silesian weaver who, based on his religious understanding, refuses to participate in the weavers' uprising and, hit by a stray Prussian (that is, reactionary) bullet, ultimately dies, like Müller's Hilse, by the end of the play. For a Faustian reading of Müller's Hilse figure, see Karl Heinz Götze, "'Und keiner will der Kapitalist sein': Faust als Maurer in Heiner Müller's Stück *Germania Tod in Berlin,*" *Cahiers d'Études Germaniques* 42 (2002): 319–37.

tumor that is the real threat to the proletarian icon. Ironically, the external attack provides the occasion for the discovery of the internal malady. The rocks thrown at Hilse constituted a mere *occasion* for the carcinoma to be discovered by the doctors. Not by chance, "cancer" is a conventional metaphor for a societal state of *enmity* (erupting in riots, turmoil and insurgencies),[53] such as the People's Uprising of June 17, 1953, an event *without a visible external enemy.* "Cancer was never viewed other than...metaphorically, *the barbarian within,*" Susan Sontag writes in her study of disease as metaphor (*Illness as Metaphor,* 61). "The disease itself is conceived as...*enemy*" (66).[54] It is precisely the internalization that allows for a conceptualization of the invisible enemy, thereby bestowing meaning on what seems to defy understanding. What, to hasten this line of thought, impedes the mission of the Socialist state are *not* the "skinheaded" teenage troublemakers "with bicycles" (42, 74); they merely precipitate an understanding of the violent aspects inherent in the revolutionary movement—its tragic paradoxes as epitomized by the Russian tanks putting down the uprising of June 17, tanks sent for the protection of the "republic of workers" against its workers (see 51f., 82). Given this background, the metaphor of cancer adds yet another point in Müller's theatrology of the *unascertainability of an external adversary,* displacing identifiable conflicts with a more ambiguous, figurative dimension. Seconds before his death, Hilse conjures up "the red banners...over Rhine and Ruhr," envisioning the idea of a proletarian revolution throughout Germany (57, 86). But ultimately this merely remains the hallucinatory dream of an old man on his deathbed, a dream dying with him.

In contrast to the fossilized and terminally ill "workers' monument" Hilse, the Young Bricklayer has come to terms with real socialism (*Realsozialismus*). He allows himself to unmask his beloved, "Whore 1," the "Holy Virgin," metaleptically figuring as the Communist Party (55f., 84f.): "What shall I do. She's a whore,

---

53. The figurative definition of *cancer* reads, according to the *OED:* "Anything that frets, corrodes, corrupts, or consumes slowly and secretly." By contrast, "the earliest literal definition of cancer," Susan Sontag writes, "is a growth, lump, or protuberance, and the disease's name—from the Greek *karkínos* and the Latin *cancer,* both meaning crab—was inspired...by the resemblance of an external tumor's swollen veins to a crab's legs; not as many people think, because a metastatic disease crawls or creeps like a crab" (Sontag, *Illness as Metaphor* [New York: Farrar, Straus and Giroux, 1978], 10).

54. Needless to say, "modern totalitarian movements, whether of the right or of the left, have been peculiarly—and revealingly—inclined to use disease imagery....Stalinism was called...a cancer....As was said in speeches about 'the Jewish problem' throughout the 1930s, to treat cancer, one must cut out much of the healthy tissue around it....To describe a phenomenon as a cancer is an incitement to violence. The use of cancer in political discourse encourages fatalism and justifies 'severe' measures" (Sontag, *Illness as Metaphor,* 82–84). Conversely, the metaphors employed in descriptions of cancer as a disease are frequently drawn from military terminology: "Cancer cells do not simply multiply: they are 'invasive.'" "With the patient's body considered to be under attack ('invasion'), the only treatment is counterattack." "Cancer cells 'colonize' from the original tumor to far sites in the body....Rarely are the body's 'defenses' vigorous enough to obliterate a tumor that has established its own blood supply and consists of billions of destructive cells." "Treatment," Sontag writes, also "has a military flavor. Radiotherapy uses the metaphors of aerial warfare; patients are 'bombarded' with toxic rays. And chemotherapy is chemical warfare, using poisons. Treatment aims to 'kill' cancer cells (without, it is hoped, killing the patient)" (64f.).

you know" (54, 84). Notwithstanding this insight, the whore "Party" inhabiting real socialism does not forfeit any of her utopian beauty, the beauty of an "angel" indeed: "And now the crazy part: / It's just the way it was before. I'm drunk / The moment I catch sight of her" (55, 85). While old Hilse's conjured apparition, "Red Rosa [Luxemburg]" (56, 85), seems to come from the past, the specters invoked by the Young Bricklayer arrive from the future: "She is pregnant. She says it's mine" (56, 85). Ghosts do not differentiate between past and future, and so the legacy of Red Rosa seems unscathed; she may turn up any moment, but not as part of a vestal communism, like that which the cancer-ridden Hilse seeks to uphold irrespective of blatant contradictions. As it emerges in a "dialogue with the dead" and the unborn,[55] Red Rosa's role can only be that of a *potentiality:* as an event of novelty, an uncanny potentiality for the new.[56]

Malfunction of the Müller-Machine, or the Drama of Surgery

What thus far has emerged as a politics of enmity in *Germania Death in Berlin* frequently appeared threatened, dramaturgically decelerated, and performatively undermined: undermined in the form of volatile attributions of "the" enemy, as with the seemingly cloned Nibelungs; vexed by confrontations of indistinguishable friends and foes ("The Brothers 2"); unsettled in the autodestructive struggle of a subject without a definable enemy ("Night Piece"); internalized as "metastatic" enemy ("Death in Berlin 2"), and so forth. What permeates all of these cases is *a discursive undefinability of "the" enemy* and a concurrent emphasis on the performative. For all the explicitly manifested strains of violence in *Germania* that are rhetorically eroded, one cannot help but get the impression of a certain fascination on Müller's part with the presented violence. Not by chance, the German Rotbuch edition of *Germania Death in Berlin* depicts on its cover a *New York Times* front page featuring articles on the convicted murderer Gary Gilmore and Japanese emperor Hirohito.[57] Müller dissipates all doubt as to his disinterest in any sort of moralizing critique of the slaughter, the gore, the brutality; indeed, he feeds it, and he colludes in it. "You must be complicit with the violence [Du mußt einverstanden sein mit der Gewalt], with the atrocity, so that you can describe it," runs the already-cited statement Müller made in an interview with Alexander Kluge. According to Müller the repeated incision in the scar is necessary, for "scars...of ancient wounds" are

---

55. Müller, *Jenseits der Nation,* 31. On Müller's incessant invocation of specters, see Hans-Thies Lehmann, "Heiner Müller's Spectres," in *Heiner Müller: ConTEXTS and HISTORY,* 87–96.
56. "An uncanny sentence from Brecht's Fatzer-fragment, which I cannot get out of my head these days: JUST AS GHOSTS CAME BEFORE OUT OF THE PAST / SO NOW LIKEWISE OUT OF THE FUTURE" (Müller, *Jenseits der Nation,* 62).
57. See Kalb, *Theater of Heiner Müller,* 144.

also "scars that cry for wounds [Narben die nach Wunden schrein]."[58] What suggests itself here is a predicament according to which Müller propels and perpetuates the bloodshed he poetically seeks to probe. Given this precarious double bind, what then, one may ask, are the implications of Müller's *Einverständnis* with this violence under scrutiny? And what is the efficacy of Müller's deliberate abstention from any moral commitment?

In a somewhat uncanny television interview with Kluge, which was televised in 1995 under the title "My Rendezvous with Death,"[59] Heiner Müller recounts a recent experience of undergoing surgery as a treatment for his throat cancer: Müller elaborates on what was removed from his esophagus and on the nature and intricacy of the seven-hour-long operation. He describes how he learned to make certain sounds again, to eat and swallow, and so on. What adds to the uncanniness of the interview is the sound of Müller's still-debilitated voice, a condition not preventing him from smoking a Montecristo cigar. "Heiner Müller describes a *dramatic intervention [dramatischen Eingriff]* in his life: the removal of the esophagus," an incipient intertitle reads. There is a certain correspondence between Müller's experience as cancer patient and his performance as a writer, a correspondence between the surgical intervention (*Eingriff*) on Müller's body and his own *Einverständnis* with the barbarism of history. Müller's flesh is subjected to the hands of the surgeon, in German *Chirurg* (*cheirourgos,* in Greek *cheir,* "hand," and *ergon,* "occupation, work"), the one who "works" with his "hands," a *Handwerker*.[60] Similarly, an intervention takes place under the typing hands of the dramatist Müller, a "surgical" intervention in the cultural text of history. Müller is concerned with what it means to "to open up / mankind's arteries like a book / to leaf through the bloodstream [Der Menschheit / Die Adern aufschlagen wie ein Buch / Im Blutstrom blättern]."[61] To leaf through the bloodstream, however, is possible only from a clinical, "immune," perspective, that of a machine, as it were (32, 66). In his autobiography, he writes: "Art holds and requires a bloody root. Complicity with the horror, with the terror is part of the description [Das Einverständnis mit dem Schrecken, mit dem Terror gehört zur Beschreibung]."[62] *Ein-verständnis* implies a certain readiness for complicity, for to read violence always inevitably means to write violence, to perpetuate violence, in some cases with the professional fascination that a surgeon may feel about the idiosyncrasies of a tumor.

Given this backdrop, the position of the writer is a tenuous one. In fact, Müller himself alludes to the aporetic situation in retrospective comments about his

---

58. Heiner Müller, *Wolokolamsker Chaussee II: Wald bei Moskau,* in *Werke* (Frankfurt a.M.: Suhrkamp, 1998), 5:202.
59. http://muller-kluge.library.cornell.edu/en/video_record.php?f = 116.
60. *Das Herkunftswörterbuch,* 110.
61. Heiner Müller, *Anatomie Titus Fall of Rome: Ein Shakespearkommentar,* in *Werke* (Frankfurt a.M.: Suhrkamp, 1998), 5:99.
62. Müller, *Krieg ohne Schlacht,* 227.

surgery: "The truly interesting question is to what extent one becomes an *instrument, a vehicle* [Interessant ist eigentlich, wie sehr man Instrument wird, ein Vehikel]." During the removal of his esophagus, Müller became a "vehicle" under the hands of the surgeon—a mere instrument. His body becomes the "text" of a surgical dissection. Yet the surgeon himself only acts in response to the tumor, a violence beyond his reach, and from this perspective the surgeon also is a mere vehicle of a violence "assigned" to him in his professional role. This *medial position* is one pertinent to Müller in his professional role as a dramatist. On the one hand, he presents violence, instumentalizes it according to his theatrically motivated working strategy, operating *einverständig* on the corpus of the German history of violence. On the other hand, Müller himself is only a vehicle seeking to diagnose the tumors of German history. Even though the politics of enmity pervading *Germania* are frequently left in suspense, Müller still beckons and bequeaths violence, irrespective of discursive boundaries, regardless of history's perpetrators or its victims.

This paradox, innate to Müller's conception of *Einverständnis* (i.e., his readiness to put forth the very violence he seeks to explore), finds an oblique explication in his use of the *surgical* term *darstellen:*

> I asked one of the doctors present about the course of the operation. And he responded: Well, there are at first [a cross section through the body and then a vertical transaction, and then there is...another transaction by the neck], and then we display the stomach [und dann stellen wir den Magen dar]. This vocabulary is interesting, the display of the stomach [die Darstellung des Magens]. That is to say, everything that constricts the view of the stomach is being cut away. That is the meaning of display [Das heißt darstellen].

The "display of the stomach" *(die Darstellung des Magens)* during the course of the removal of the esophagus signifies an act of cutting away tissue around the stomach, for the purpose of display as well as—Müller doesn't go on to explain this—for the purpose of the "mobilization" of the stomach (*die Mobilisierung des Magens*), that is, the flexibility of the stomach in order to pull it up and stitch it to the remaining esophagus.[63] What matters in our context is that the surgical term *darstellen* denotes a destructive momentum, inherent in any surgical intervention, in the removal of a tumor and in the recovery of a patient. The surgeon extracts and displays (*stellt dar*) Müller's stomach, he violently intervenes in the body's texture with the ultimate goal of curing Müller; similarly, Müller's art of *Darstellung,* bloody as it may be, ultimately serves to analyze a possible transgression or at least an understanding of the atrocity, the massacres, and the internecine struggles. Needless to say, the surgeon's craft is an ensanguined one, yet *moral* considerations

---

63. Cf. A. F. Chernousov, P. M. Bogopolski, Y. I. Gallinger, et al., eds., *Chirurgie des Ösophagus: Operationsatlas* (Steinkopff: Darmstadt, 2003), 57, 209.

regarding the destructive nature of his performance appear—within the professional boundaries—as mistaken as the application of moral standards to Müller's ferocious dissections of the cultural text of violence. To be sure, Müller might take the effectiveness of his proclaimed "war against the audience" into consideration,[64] or perhaps he doesn't; in contrast, the surgeon very much has to reckon with the necessity of an aggressive intervention such as that of surgery.[65] The point is that *moral* concerns address neither the work of the surgeon nor that of the dramatist Heiner Müller; they would be entirely obtrusive during an operation or the writing of a play, and at times they would be fatal.

Heiner Müller: Death in Berlin, or Conversation with a Ghost

My dialogue with Heiner Müller, who died of cancer on December 30, 1995, ten months after the eerily romantic elaboration in "My Rendezvous with Death," continues a series of "resurrections" (*Auferstehung*, 31, 66) that run through *Germania*. "I am not well. But I'm only one half / Of me, the cancer ate the other half," Hilse says to the Young Bricklayer in the cancer ward. Similarly, Müller describes his condition after the removal of his esophagus as "life with half of the machine." Whether as preoperative whole machine or postoperative half a machine, *being-machine* appears to be the *sine qua non* for Müller's poetic operations, his *Eingriffe*, surgical interventions in the cultural text: reading as machine, writing as machine. It is in this sense that Müller is interested in the "experience" of being operated on: "When you know, there is a date on which you either die or live, then that is a new situation, a new experience. And I was by all means interested in it as an experience."[66] Müller publicized his conversation with Kluge, sharing his elaborations on the expectation of death (a death that indeed was to take place some months after) as a kind of interview performance,[67] spoken from the stylized perspective of the author, including pictures from the intensive care unit. And by publicizing his "Rendezvous with Death," Müller seems to have added yet another scene to *Germania Death in Berlin*. Following those killed during the November Revolution (see 7, 45), "Germania" slain by Hitler (see 35, 67), the Communist's death

---

64. *Gesammelte Irrtümer* 2:20.

65. While *moral* concerns get to the core of neither the surgeon's nor the dramatist's work, doctors around the world, not without controversy, to be sure, still take the Hippocratic Oath pertaining to the ethical practice of medicine.

66. The very "command of one's own life" is what interests Müller in the death of Seneca, on which he also wrote a poem. In the face of governmental control over death, Müller remarks with regard to Seneca's suicide: "The only possibility to administer death oneself was to kill oneself, before one is being killed" (*Ich schulde der Welt einen Toten*, 17, 22).

67. Müller deemed interviews "performances," which is why he allegedly did not edit them. See Müller, *Gesammelte Irrtümer*, 2:155. See also Christian Schulte, "Wahrnehmungen am Nullpunkt der Sprache: Notizen zu Heiner Müller und Alexander Kluge," in *Der Text ist der Coyote*, 189–96; Olaf Schmitt, "Verausgabung, Opfer, Tod," in *Heiner Müller-Handbuch*, 62–69, here 68.

in the Berlin prison (see 52, 77), those killed during the People's Uprising on June 17, 1953 (see 51f., 82), the death of Hilse in the cancer ward, and the death of Red Rosa (whom he hallucinates rising from the Berlin Landwehrkanal [see 56, 86])—following all these *deaths* in *Berlin,* the play, begun in 1956 and published in 1971, seems to be continued by Heiner Müller's death in 1995. Müller, dead in Berlin, alive in his text, continues to haunt the pages, and with his spectral voice from the interview we can hear him shouting: "One must accept the presence of the dead as dialogue partners or dialogue disruptors—*the future emerges solely from the dialogue with the dead.*"[68] But if we are to accept Müller as "dialogue partner or dialogue disruptor," then we might do so not in the sense of a past connected to the future, not in the sense of a future re-presenting ideas and projections, but in the sense of a potentiality inscribed in *Germania,* one perhaps not less uncanny than the many specters hovering throughout Müller's play. That is to say, we may accept the dead Müller as interlocutor, but with a full understanding of the radical uncertainty of the unrepresentable as the most genuine of presentations, including dialogical presentation. That alone may be all that is possible, though perhaps entirely natural when in conversation with a ghost.

---

68. "Necrophilia is the love of the future," Müller writes (*Jenseits der Nation,* 31).

Index

Page numbers in *italics* refer to figures.

Actes sans paroles (Beckett, 1956), 170
aesthetics and ethics. *See* literary ethics
After Virtue (MacIntyre, 1981), xi, xxiii
Agamben, Giorgio, 4n8, 73n24
Albert, Claudia, 76n32
Alexander I Karadjordjevic, King of Serbia, assassination of, 134–35, *134*
Allen, Danielle, 67n16
anarchistic, Benjamin's description of political general strikes as, 95–96, 99
anarchy, Fassbinder on, 127n13
animals: in Müller's *Germania Death in Berlin,* 161–64; zoological metaphors, Arendt's use of, 24
Annales (Tacitus), 157n15, 170n47
Antigone (Sophocles): Benjamin's "Toward a Critique of Violence" and, 7, 84–86, 108, 110–12, 118–19; etymology of Antigone's name, 85n5; *Germany in Autumn* and, 7–8, 125, 136, 138–39, 143, 146, 147–49; Hegel and Derrida on, 108; Hölderlin's translation of, 110–11n12, 149n50; Müller's plays and Brecht's adaptation of, 167n45; Vernant on, 111n12
Arcades Project, The (Benjamin, 1927–40), 20
Arendt, Hannah: on "banality of evil," 62n10; Benjamin and, 19–21, 23n20, 33, 38, 43n9; *Denktagebuch* (*Thought Journal,* 2002), 3, 16, 21, 29, 38, 39, 49; *Eichmann in Jerusalem* (1994), 28, 62n10; "The Image of Hell" (1946), 24n22; interpretation and citation, art of, 37–38; Kafka and, 56; *The Life of the Mind* (1978), 20, 22, 23n18, 32, 38n51; literary qualities of writing of, xxx; on Marx, 98; "On the Nature of Totalitarianism" (1953/1954), 18n5, 31n34; on philosophy, 21n12; RAF and, 141n35; on style and understanding, 16; "Truth and Politics" (1967), 22n17, 26, 28, 40, 43, 55; "Understanding and Politics" (1954), 4n7, 18n5, 48nn15–17, 50n21, 52n25, 54n30, 54n32, 55n33; "What Is Authority?" (1961), 28. *See also* lying and politics, Arendt on; *Origins of Totalitarianism*
Aristotle: on ethics and aesthetics, x; on human beings, 57–58, 59, 67; literary criticism's interest in ethics and, xix; narrative, philosophical turn to, xiii, xiv–xv, xvii, xvin35; Neo-Aristotelianism, xxxi; *Nicomachean Ethics,* xvin35; *Politics,* 4n10, 13, 59
Arnim (in Fassbinder segment of *Germany in Autumn*), 127, 130, 131, 132–33
Arthurian German literature referenced in Müller's *Germania Death in Berlin,* 157
Attridge, Derek, xxii, xxv–xxix
Augustine of Hippo, 38
Austin, John, 100
Autorenkino (cinema of *auteurs*), 8

Baader, Andreas, 123, 124–25, 128, 129, 136, 139, 142, 144, 145n43, 147, *148,* 149. *See also Germany in Autumn*
Baader-Meinhof group (Red Army Faction), 122–23, 132, 139n31, 140–43. *See also Germany in Autumn*
Bacon, Francis, 40
Badener Lehrstück vom Einverständnis (Brecht), 157n17, 170
Baez, Joan, 149
"banality of evil," Arendt on, 62n10
Basic Law (*Grundgesetz*) of Germany, 129n19, 130n21, 140
Battle, The (Müller, 1951/1974), 151, 158, 167, 169n46
Baudelaire, Charles, 37
Beckett, Samuel, 157, 170
Beilhack, Hans, 13n29

Benjamin, Walter: *The Arcades Project* (1927–40), 20; Arendt and, 19–21, 23n20, 33, 38, 43n9; imagelessness in thought of, 104, 121; on Kafka, 60n8, 68, 163, 164; "Karl Kraus" (1931), 81, 101; literary qualities of writing of, xxx; "Notes on a Project on the Category of Justice" (posthumously published fragment), 6n19; on objective mendacity, 26n24; "On Language as Such and on the Language of Man" (1916), 82, 93, 105, 107n6; *Origin of the German Mourning Play* (1925/1928), 20; "Outline of the Psychophysical Problem" (ca. 1922/23), 117n18; on state of *flâneur* in Baudelaire, 37; "Storyteller" essay, 109n11; "Theologico-Political Fragment" (1921), 99n26; "Theses on the Philosophy of History" (1940), 19. *See also* "Toward a Critique of Violence"
Berlin, Isaiah, 20n11
Between Facts and Norms (Habermas, 2001), 45
Bible: commandment not to kill, 117–18; imagelessness in Benjamin's thought, 104, 121; Korah story, 112–15
Biermann, Wolf, 137
biopolitical logic, 4, 18, 24n22, 116
birth, in Kafka's "In the Penal Colony," 74–76
Black Book, The (1946), Arendt's review of, 50
Blumenberg, Hans, 32
body and law in Kafka's "In the Penal Colony," 58–59, 61–64, 66–67, 73–75
Böll, Heinrich, 127–28
Booth, Wayne, xi, xviii–xix, xx, xxiv, xxxi
Bosch, Robert, 144
Brauchitsch, Eberhard von, 146
Brecht, Bertolt, 35–36, 38, 157, 167n45, 170, 175n56
Brothers Karamazov, The (Dostoevsky, 1880), 54
Buber, Martin, 114n16
Bucolica (Virgil), 157n15
Butler, Judith, xxx, 85n5, 139n32

Catholic Church, Schmitt on power of representation of, 70n22
Cavarero, Adriana, 143n42
Cavell, Stanley, xviii
Caven, Ingrid, 127, 128, 129
Chernozemski, Vlado, 134
citizenship and nationality: in *Germany in Autumn*, 139; in Kafka's "In the Penal Colony," 76–77

Clemenceau, George, 28
Cohen, Hermann, 112n14
collective mendacity, 26
colonialism and totalitarianism, Arendt on link between, 62n10
Company We Keep, The (Booth, 1988), xviii
complicity between writing and ethical violations described, 1–2, 175–78
concentration camps. See *Origins of Totalitarianism*
Contingency, Irony, and Solidarity (Rorty, 1989), xiii, xxiii–xxiv
Corngold, Stanley, 74n27
Critchley, Simon, xxiin72
Critique of Judgment (third *Critique*; Kant, 1790), 145
Critique of Pure Reason (Kant, 1781), 30

De Man, Paul, xvii, 27n26, 30n31, 99n26
democracy: Arendt's *Origins of Totalitarianism* and, 52; Benjamin's "Toward a Critique of Violence" and, 82, 89n11; *Germany in Autumn* on, 127–33, 138, 145n43; Kafka's "In the Penal Colony" and, 61, 63, 67, 74n26
Denktagebuch (*Thought Journal*; Arendt, 2002), 3, 16, 21, 29, 38, 39, 49
Derrida, Jacques, xxx, 42n5, 88n8, 108, 172n50
Dickens, Charles, xiii
Dinesen, Isak, 38, 53
diplomatic action and Benjamin's "Toward a Critique of Violence," 97–98n24, 98
Disselnkötter, Andreas, 76n32
divine violence in Benjamin's "Toward a Critique of Violence," 82, 102, 103, 104, 106, 112–15, 117, 120–21
dogs and other animals, in Müller's *Germania Death in Berlin*, 161–64
Dostoevsky, Feodor, 54
"Double 'Turn' to Ethics and Literature, The" (Eskin, 2004), xi
doubtfulness, Arendt, on odium of, 23–25
Duel, The (Müller, 1993), 151

Eaglestone, Robert, xxiv, xxiiin74
Eichmann in Jerusalem (Arendt, 1994), 28, 62n10
elite and mob, totalitarian alliance between, 51–52
Emden, Christian J., 45n11, 90n14
enmity, politics of, in Müller's *Germania Death in Berlin*, 151, 155, 161, 165, 170, 171, 172, 175, 177

Ensslin, Christiane (sister of Gudrun), 125, 144, 147
Ensslin, Gudrun, 123, 124–25, 128, 136, 139, 142, 144, 145n43, 147, *148,* 149. See also *Germany in Autumn*
Ensslin, Gudrun, son of, 149
Ensslin, Pastor (father of Gudrun), 124, 139, 147
Eskin, Michael, xi, xvii
Ethics and Infinity (Levinas), 122
ethics and literature. *See* literary ethics
Ethics of Criticism (Siebers, 1988), xix
Ethics of Reading (Miller, 1987), xx, xxiv
etymological issues: anarchy, 96n21; Antigone's name, 85n5; authoritative and authoritarian, 100n30; cancer, 174n53; concept, conceive, and conception, xxxin114; *Egge* (Harrow), 66; law and justice, 107; mediality and medium, 3n3; nation derived from *nascere* (to be born), 75; performative and performatory, 100; *Übereinkunft/Einigung* (agreement) and *Kompromiss* (compromise), 92n20; *verantwürten* (to respond) and *Verantwortung* (responsibility), 6n19; *Vernunft* (reason) and *vernehmen* (to perceive, to hear), 24n20; *Volk,* 79; *Vorstellung* (representation) and *Darstellung* (presentation), 96n21

Fassbinder, Rainer Werner, 7, 123, 125n8, 126–33, 136n28, 137, 144, 145n43
Flimm, Jürgen, 158
form/medium, significance of, xxv–xxix, 2–3, 13–15
Foucault, Michel, 4n8, 57–58, 67n16, 74, 75–76
Foundations of the Metaphysics of Morals (Kant, 1785), xxi
Fragility of Goodness, The (Nussbaum, 2001), xvn28
France, Anatole, 5n11, 110
fraud/lying, violence introduced by, 93–94
Freud, Sigmund, 28n29, 58n5
Frisch, Max, 130, 138
Frye, Northrop, xix

general strikes, Benjamin on, 94–99
genre: Arendt's *Origins of Totalitarianism* and, 3–4, 10; Benjamin's "Toward a Critique of Violence" and, 5, 7, 10, 101–3; *Germany in Autumn* and, 8–9; Kafka's "In the Penal Colony" and, 12–13; medium and, x, 2; Müller's *Germania Death in Berlin* and, 10, 157
Germania (Tacitus), 10, 11, 170

Germania 3 Ghosts at the Dead Man (Müller, 1995), 151, 158
Germania Death in Berlin (Müller, 1956/1971), 151–79; *Antigone,* Brecht's adaptation of, 167n45; "Brandenburg Concerto 1" scene, 157; "The Brothers 2" scene, 157n16, 165–70, 175, 178–79; cauldron (Stalingrad) in, 152–55, 159–60; complicity of writer with violence described, 2, 175–78; "Death in Berlin 2" scene (Hilse's cancer), 157, 162, 172–75, 178, 179; dogs and other animals in, 161–64; genre and, 10, 157; ghosts in, 152–53, 156–61, 170n47, 178–79; "The Holy Family" scene and slaying of "Germania" by Hitler, 161–64, 178; "Hommage à Stalin 1" scene, 151–56, 157n15, 158, 159, 178; "Hommage à Stalin 2" scene, 156–61; on humanism, 156, 163; Kafka compared, 12; link between ethics and poetics in, 10–11; Müller's death as continuation of, 178–79; Nibelungs in, 153–55, 157, 158, 170, 171, 175; "Night Piece" scene, 157n15, 170–72, 175; People's Uprising of June 17, 1953, and, 157, 165, 170–71, 174, 179; poetic moments and literary ethics in, xxx; poetics of pure means and, 11; politics of enmity in, 151, 155, 161, 165, 170, 171, 172, 175, 177; Skull-Seller in, 157–60; on violence, 151, 153, 160–61, 169, 170n47, 174–78; "Workers' Monument" scene, 157n15, 172–73, 179
Germany in Autumn (film, 1977–78), 122–50; assassination of King of Serbia in 1938 and, 134–35, *134;* border checkpoint episode, 137; cinematic presentation of, 125–26, 145n43; complicity between writing and ethical violations described, 2; on democracy, 127–33, 138, 145n43; dualisms in, 143; faces of friends and foes in, 133–38, *134–36 figs. 3–5;* Fassbinder segment, 127–33, 136n28, 137, 144, 145n43; female pianist asked for medical help by alleged terrorist, 135–37; funerals (of Schleyer and RAF suicides) at center of, 123–27, 133–36, 138, 139–40, 144, 145n43; genre and, 8–9; on humanization and dehumanization, 124–25, 135, 136, 137–42, 145–50; on justice and law, 132, 141–42, 145–46; Nazi past in, 124, 128, 133, 143–45, 146, 149–50; poetic moments and literary ethics, xxx; Rommel segment, 143–45; Sophocles' *Antigone* and, 7–8, 125, 136, 138–39, 143, 146, 147–49; space of poetic ambiguities between political positions in, 7–8,

Index

Germany in Autumn (continued)
9–10; on violence of RAF in Mahler interview, 132, 140–43
"*Germany in Autumn:* What Is the Film's Bias?" (Brustellin et al., 1978), 8n20, 125–26
ghosts in Müller's *Germania Death in Berlin,* 152–53, 156–61, 170n47, 178–79
Gilmore, Gary, 175
"Girl from Stuttgart, The" (Biermann, 1978), 137
Göbbels, Joseph, 161, 163
Göring, Hermann, 155, 161
Gourgouris, Stathis, 85n5
Grundgesetz (Basic Law) of Germany, 129n19, 130n21, 140

Habermas, Jürgen, 45
Hamlet, Müller's translation of, 158n20
Harpham, Geoffrey Galt, xiv–xv
Hasidic tale on tradition, 18–19
Hauptmann, Gerhart, 173
Hebbel's *The Nibelungs,* 158
Hegel, Georg Wilhelm Friedrich, 9n22, 53, 60, 108, 142n38
Heidegger, Martin, xix, 21n12, 38, 75, 143n42
Hell/Hades/Purgatory, as metaphor for concentration camps, 17
Herzog, Werner, 7, 123
Heuss, Theodore, 144
He Who Says Yes / He Who Says No (Brecht, 1930–31), 35–36
Heym, Georg, 157
Hiller, Kurt, 116
Hirohito (Japanese emperor), 175
History of Sexuality, The (Foucault, 1978), 58n3, 74
Hitler, Adolf, 26, 33–34, 52n24, 144, 152, 156, 161–64, 178
Hobbes, Thomas, 36, 38, 132n24
Hölderlin, Friedrich, 110–11n12, 149n50
Holocaust. See *Origins of Totalitarianism*
How to Do Things with Words (Austin, 1962), 100
humanism in Müller's *Germania Death in Berlin,* 156, 163
humanization and dehumanization in *Germany in Autumn,* 124–25, 135, 136, 137–42, 145–50
human rights, problem of, 24, 76–77
Husserl, Edmund, 117n18

ideological thinking, Arendt on, 27–29, 34
idiomatic/proverbial speech, totalitarian use of logicality of, 33–36

Illness as Metaphor (Sontag, 1978), 32n37, 174
imagelessness in Benjamin's thought, 104, 121
"Image of Hell, The" (Arendt, 1946), 24n22
imagination: as key to philosophy of history, 52–53; lying and, 42; meaning, restoration of, 53–55
inconceivable effects of literary ethics, xxxi, 3–13
"In the Penal Colony" (Kafka, 1914), 56–80; allegory of reading in, 12n20; apparatus in, 56–57; birth, execution as figurative form of, 74–76; the body and the law in, 58–59, 61–64, 66–67, 73–75; condemned man in, 57–58, 59–60; force of law in, 73–74; genre and, 12–13; geopolitical radius of, 77–79, 77; grave of old Commandant in, 79–80; link between ethics and poetics in, 11–13; Müller's *Germania Death in Berlin* compared, 12, 157; on nationality, citizenship, and human rights, 76–77; poetic moments and literary ethics in, xxx; representation, nexus between religious, juridical, and theatrical and power of, 67–72, 69; synthetic constituency of sentence in, 64–66; totalitarian politics and colonialism in, 62n10
ius necessitatis, 142n38

Jacobs, Carol, xxx
James, Henry, xiii, xv, xvii, xxiv, xxv
Jaspers, Karl, 21n12
Jayne, Richard, 67n16
Jellinek, Georg, 44–45
Johnson, Barbara, xxiii, xxx
juridical, religious, and theatrical, power of representation and nexus between, 67–72, 69
justice and law: Benjamin's "Toward a Critique of Violence" on, 81–84, 85, 103, 104–8, 117–19; *Germany in Autumn* and, 132, 141–42, 145–46

Kafka, Franz: Arendt and, 56; Benjamin on, 60n8, 68, 163, 164; Müller and, 12, 157, 162, 164; *The Trial* (1914–15/1925), 78. See also "In the Penal Colony"
Kant, Immanuel: Arendt and, 23, 25, 30, 38, 42–43n8, 54; *Critique of Pure Reason* (1781), 30; on "Eternal Peace," 88; *Foundations of the Metaphysics of Morals* (1785), xxi; literary criticism's interest in ethics and, xix, xxi–xxii; on mendacity, 42–43n8; *The Metaphysics of Morals* (1797), 142n38; third *Critique (Critique*

of Judgment; 1790), 145; universal maxims and, xii; *Universal Natural History and Theory of Heaven* (1755), 23; on "wild men," 60
"Karl Kraus" (Benjamin, 1931), 81, 101
key metaphor in Arendt's *Origins of Totalitarianism*, 50–53
Kierkegaard, Søren, 49
Kiesinger, Kurt Georg, 123, 134
Kluge, Alexander: *Germany in Autumn* and, 7, 8n21, 123, 124, 136n28, 143, 145–46, 147; Müller's *Germania Death in Berlin* and, 164, 175–76, 178
Kohl, Helmut, 134
Kontaktsperregesetz, 128–29, 133
Korah, biblical story of, 112–15
Kraus, Karl, 81, 101
Kraushaar, Wolfgang, 129n19, 130n21
Kristeva, Julia, xix, 16n1

Lacan, Jacques, 84
Laclos, Choderlos de, xiii
law: body and, in Kafka's "In the Penal Colony," 58–59, 61–64, 66–67, 73–75; force of, in Kafka's "In the Penal Colony," 73–74; *ius necessitatis* and right of resistance, 142n38; of metaphor, 31–33; natural versus positive, 85, 86–87, 132, 142n38; Schmitt on earth as mother of, 44–45n11; situational, 63, 77, 131, 132, 133; in totalitarian politics, 31–33, 51; violence, law-positing, 88; violence, law-preserving, and the police, 88–90. *See also* justice and law
Lazarus story and problem of authentic testimony, 45–47
"Lecture on Ethics" (Wittgenstein, 1929–30), x
Leibniz, Gottfried Wilhelm, 28
Leonardo da Vinci, 149
Lessing, Gotthold Ephraim, 30, 151
Leviathan (Hobbes, 1651), 36
Levinas, Emmanuel, xvii, xxii, xxvi–xxviin92, 122, 146n46
Life of Gundling Lessing's Sleep Dream Cry (Müller, 1977), 151
Life of the Mind, The (Arendt, 1978), 20, 22, 23n18, 32, 38n51
literary ethics, ix–xxxi, 1–15; Arendt on lying and politics, 40–55 (*see also* lying and politics, Arendt on); of Arendt's *Origins of Totalitarianism*, 16–39 (see also *Origins of Totalitarianism*); of Benjamin's "Toward a Critique of Violence," 81–121 (*see also* "Toward a Critique of Violence"); complicity between writing and ethical violations described, 1–2, 175–78; as ethics of the singular, xxix–xxxi; form/medium, significance of, xxv–xxix, 2–3, 13–15; of *Germany in Autumn* (film, 1977–78), 122–50 (see also *Germany in Autumn*); inconceivable effects of, xxxi, 3–13; of Kafka's "In the Penal Colony," 56–80 (*see also* "In the Penal Colony"); literary criticism's interest in ethics, xviii–xxv; of Müller's *Germania Death in Berlin*, 151–79 (see also *Germania Death in Berlin*); philosophy's use of narrative, xi–xviii; poetics of pure means and, 13–15 (*see also* poetics of pure means); problem of, ix–xi; reading, act of, xx–xxi, xxiv–xxx, 12n20; textual otherness, xxv–xxix
logicality of totalitarian ideology, 33–36, 50–53
loneliness and solitude, Arendt on, 36–39
Love's Knowledge (Nussbaum, 1990), xv
Luther, Martin, 37, 38, 113
Luxemburg, Rosa ("Red Rosa"), 38, 143, 157, 158, 175, 179
lying and politics, Arendt on, 40–55; the art of lying, 41–43; collective mendacity, 26; imagination and lying, relationship between, 42; intentionality, 26, 41; Lazarus story and problem of authentic testimony, 45–47; logicality of totalitarian ideology, subverting, 50–53; meaning, restoration of, 53–55; metaphor and truth, 29–30; metaphor as response to, 42; Nazi "discovery" of the lie and totalitarian detachment from reality, 26–29; openness of future to action and, 47–50; Pavlov's dog and normative power of the factual, 44–45; transfigurative nature of narration and, 40–41
lying and violence, Benjamin on, 93–94
Lyotard, Jean-François, 28nn28–29, 67n18, 75, 164n41

MacIntyre, Alasdair, xi–xiv, xix, xxiii, xxiv, xxxi
Mahler, Horst, 132, 140–43
Maier, Reinhold, 144
Maihofer, Werner, 130n21
marionettes/puppets: in Arendt's *Origins of Totalitarianism*, 25; condemned man in Kafka's "In the Penal Colony" as, 59; "Night Piece" scene from Müller's *Germania Death in Berlin*, 170–72
marriage, Fassbinder on, 127

Marx, Karl, 24n21, 98
mass production of living corpses, Arendt on, 24, 45
medium/form, significance of, xxv–xxix, 2–3, 13–15
Meier, Richard, 130n21
Meinhof, Ulrike, 128, 129, 137–38, 140, 142. *See also* Germany in Autumn mendacity. *See* lying and politics, Arendt on
Mensur fencing, 124
metaphor: Arendt's *Origins of Totalitarianism,* use of metaphorical thinking in, 16–18, 21–22; law of, 31–33; linguistic transference of totalitarian ideology into, 22, 23–25; lying, as response to, 42; in Müller's *Germania Death in Berlin,* 152; Sontag's *Illness as Metaphor,* 32n37, 174; truth and, 29–30
Metaphysics of Morals, The (Kant, 1797), 142n38
Miller, J. Hillis, xi, xix, xx–xxvi, xxviii, xxix
mob and elite, totalitarian alliance between, 51–52
Montesquieu, 38, 63
Moscow subway, 29
Muir, Willa and Edwin, 56–57
Müller, Beate, 74n27
Müller, Heiner: *The Battle* (1951/1974), 151, 158, 167, 169n46; on complicity of writer with horrors described, 2, 175–78; death of, as continuation of *Germania Death in Berlin,* 178–79; *The Duel* (1993), 151; *Germania 3 Ghosts at the Dead Man* (1995), 151, 158; *Hamlet,* translation of, 158n20; Kafka and, 12, 157, 162, 164; *Life of Gundling Lessing's Sleep Dream Cry* (1977), 151; *The Scab (Der Lohndrücker,* 1956/57), 172; throat cancer surgery of, 176–78. *See also* Germania Death in Berlin
Münkler, Herfried, 141n34
Muselmann, 44
mythic violence in Benjamin's "Toward a Critique of Violence," 82, 104, 107–15, 117n18, 121

Nabokov, Vladimir, xiii
Nancy, Jean-Luc, 121n21
nationality and citizenship: in *Germany in Autumn,* 139; in Kafka's "In the Penal Colony," 76–77
natural law versus positive law, 85, 86–87, 132, 142n38
Nazis: *Germany in Autumn* and, 124, 128, 133, 143–45, 146, 149–50; in Müller's *Germania Death in Berlin,* 152, 155, 161–69

Neo-Aristotelianism, xxxi
New German Cinema, 2, 7, 8n21, 123. *See also* Germany in Autumn
Nibelungs in Müller's works, 153–55, 157, 158, 170, 171, 175
Nicomachean Ethics (Aristotle), xvin35
Nietzsche, Friedrich, xix, 30n31, 67n16
Niobe, 104, 109, 111, 112, 115n16
normative power of the factual, 44–45
"Notes on a Project on the Category of Justice" (Benjamin, posthumously published fragment), 6n19
Nussbaum, Martha, xi, xv–xix, xx, xxiii, xxiv, xxv–xxvi, xxvii, xxxi

"odium of doubtfulness" in Arendt's *Origins of Totalitarianism,* 23–25
onion structure of authoritarian systems, 28
"On Language as Such and on the Language of Man" (Benjamin, 1916), 82, 93, 105, 107n6
"On the Nature of Totalitarianism" (Arendt, 1953/1954), 18n5, 31n34
Origin of the German Mourning Play (Benjamin, 1925/1928), 20
Origins of Totalitarianism (Arendt, 1951), 16–39; *The Burden of Our Times* as initial title for, 17n2, 37; on colonialism and totalitarianism, 62n10; complicity between writing and ethical violations described, 2, 3–4; fragmentary form of narration in, 18–20; genre and, 3–4, 10; Hell/Hades/Purgatory, as metaphor for camps, 17; on law in totalitarian politics, 31–33; linguistic transference of totalitarian ideology into metaphor, 22, 23–25; link between ethics and poetics in, 3–4, 9, 10; logicality of totalitarian ideology, 33–36, 50–53; on loneliness and solitude, 36–39; marionette metaphor in, 25; metaphorical thinking in, 16–18, 21–22; mob and elite, alliance between, 51–52; on "odium of doubtfulness," 23–25; onion structure of authoritarian systems, 28; Pavlov's dog, Arendt's use of metaphor of, 24–25, 33, 44–45; problem of justificatory nature of historiography and, 3–4, 16–18; proverbial/idiomatic speech, totalitarian use of logicality of, 33–36; publication history, 17n2; on truth and metaphor, 29–30; zoological metaphors, 24. *See also* lying and politics, Arendt on
otherness of the text, xxv–xxix

"Outline of the Psychophysical Problem" (Benjamin, c. 1922/23), 117n18
Ovid, 164

Paradigmen zu einer Metaphorologie (Blumenberg, 1998), 32
Pavlov's dog, Arendt's use of metaphor of, 24–25, 33, 44–45
peace, 88, 154
Pempeit, Lilo (Fassbinder's mother), 127–28, 130–33, 144
People's Uprising of June 17, 1953, and Müller's *Germania Death in Berlin,* 157, 165, 170–71, 174, 179
Phelan, James, xxn64
Plato, x, xix
Poetic Justice (Nussbaum, 1995), xvi
poetics and ethics. *See* literary ethics
poetics of pure means: Benjamin's "Toward a Critique of Violence" and, 5–7, 9, 91–100; concept of, 13–15; Müller's *Germania Death in Berlin* and, 11
police, 88–90
Political Theology (Schmitt), 68
Politics (Aristotle), 4n10
politics of enmity in Müller's *Germania Death in Berlin,* 151, 155, 161, 165, 170, 171, 172, 175, 177
positive law versus natural law, 85, 86–87, 132, 142n38
power in Benjamin's "Toward a Critique of Violence," 105–6
Prometheus, 109, 119
pronouns, 143n42
proverbial/idiomatic speech, totalitarian use of logicality of, 33–36
puppets. *See* marionettes/puppets
pure means. *See* poetics of pure means
pure violence in Benjamin's "Toward a Critique of Violence," 82, 90, 102–3, 104–5, 120–21
Putnam, Hilary, xvi

RAF. *See* Red Army Faction
Rancière, Jacques, 138n30
Raspe, Jan-Carl, 123, 124–25, 128, 136–37, *136,* 139, 142, 144, 145n43, 147, *148,* 149. See also *Germany in Autumn*
reading, act of, xx–xxi, xxiv–xxx, 12n20
recipe film (*Zutatenfilm*), 8n21
Red Army Faction (RAF), 122–23, 132, 139n31, 140–43. See also *Germany in Autumn*
"Red Rosa" (Rosa Luxemburg), 38, 143, 157, 158, 175, 179

Reitz, Edgar, 123, 137
religious, juridical, and theatrical, power of representation and nexus between, 67–72, *69*
resistance, right of, 142n38
Ricoeur, Paul, xi–xn9
Riefenstahl, Leni, 133
rights, human, problem of, 24, 76–77
Roman Catholic Church, power of representation of, 70n22
Rommel segment of *Germany in Autumn,* 143–45
Rorty, Richard, xi, xiii–xv, xvi, xvii, xxiii–xxiv, xxxi
Rousseau, Jean-Jacques, 132n24
Rutherford, Danilyn, 76n32

sanctity of life doctrine, 116–17
Scab, The (*Der Lohndrücker;* Müller, 1956/57), 172
Scheel, Walter, 134, 138
Schleyer, Hanns-Martin, 122–25, 133, 135–36, *135,* 138, 139, 144, 145n43, 146–47, *147*. See also *Germany in Autumn*
Schlöndorff, Volker, 7, 123, 125n8, 135, 143
Schmidt, Helmut, 123, 130–31n22, 133, 143
Schmitt, Carl: Benjamin's admiration for, 90; on Catholic Church's power of representation, 70n22; on earth as mother of law, 44–45n11; on situational law, 63–64n11, 131; sovereignty, theory of, 64n11, 66n14, 68; on "state of exception," 129; *Theory of the Partisan* (1975), 161–62
Scholem, Gershom, 19n6, 91
Schreiner, Olive, xiii
Shusterman, Richard, xiv
Siebers, Tobin, xi, xix–xx, xxiii, xxiv
singular, ethics of the, xxix–xxxi
Singularity of Literature, The (Attridge, 2004), xxv
Sinkel, Bernd, 126
situational law, 63, 63–64n11, 77, 131, 132, 133
Skull-Seller in Müller's *Germania Death in Berlin,* 157–60
solidarity, Rorty's concept of, xiii–xiv
solitude and loneliness, Arendt on, 36–39
Sontag, Susan, 32n37, 174
Sophocles. *See Antigone*
Sorel, Georges, 94, 96n21, 110
sovereignty, Schmitt's theory of, 64n11, 66n14, 68
Spinoza, Baruch, 116
spontaneity, Arendt on elimination of, 44–45
Springer Press, 128
Stalin, Josef, 29, 33, 52n24, 156
Stalinism, 29, 156, 174n54. See also *Origins of Totalitarianism*
"state of exception," 129–30, 133

Steiner, Uwe, 96n21
Sternstein, Malynne, 67n16
Strauß, Franz Josef, 134
strikes, general, Benjamin on, 94–99

Tacitus, 10, 11, 157, 170
terrorism in postwar West Germany. See *Germany in Autumn*
textual otherness and form, xxv–xxix
Thalidomide wolf in Müller's *Germania Death in Berlin,* 162, 163–64
theatrical, juridical, and religious, power of representation and nexus between, 67–72, 69
"Theologico-Political Fragment" (Benjamin, 1921), 99n26
Theory of the Partisan (Schmitt, 1975), 161–62
"Theses on the Philosophy of History" (Benjamin; ed. Arendt, 1940), 19
third *Critique* (*Critique of Judgment;* Kant, 1790), 145
Third Generation, The (film, 1979), 129n20
totalitarian domination. See *Origins of Totalitarianism*
"Toward a Critique of Violence" (Benjamin, 1921), 81–121; agreement as nonviolent means of regulating human interests, 92–93; authority of law maintained by threat of coercion and violence, 81–82; on biblical commandment not to kill, 117–18; complicity with ethical violations described in, 2; contradictions in, 98; diplomatic action and, 97–98n24, 98; divine violence, 82, 102, 103, 104, 106, 112–15, 117, 120–21; fraud/lying, violence introduced by, 93–94; on general strikes and politics of pure means, 94–99; genre and, 5, 7, 10, 101–3; justice and law, relationship between, 81–84, 85, 103, 104–8, 117–19; Kafka's "In the Penal Colony" and, 60n8; Korah, biblical story of, 112–15; law-positing violence, 88, 95, 96; law-preserving violence and the police, 88–90; link between ethics and poetics in, 4–7, 9, 10; on lying, 43n9; mythic violence, 82, 104, 107–15, 117n18, 121; narrative violence of, 87, 102–3; natural versus positive law, 86–87; Niobe story, 104, 109, 111, 112, 115n16; on origins of legal violence, 115–19; on peace, 88; as performative act, 98–100, 119–21; poetics of pure means and, 5–7, 9, 91–100; power, 105–6; presentation and representation in, 101–3; pure violence, 82, 90, 102–3,
104–5, 120–21; on sanctity of life doctrine, 116–17; Sophocles' *Antigone* and, 7, 84–86, 108, 110–12, 118–19; "Toward" in title, significance of, 99; violence as moral means to just ends as fundamental question of, 84, 86–87
Tractatus Logico-Philosophicus (Wittgenstein, 1921), 1
Tractatus Theologico-Politicus (Spinoza, 1670), 116
tradition, Hasidic tale on, 18–19
transfigurative nature of narration, Arendt on, 40–41
Trial, The (Kafka, 1914–15/1925), 78
truth and metaphor, Arendt on, 29–30
"Truth and Politics" (Arendt, 1967), 26, 28, 40, 43, 55. See also lying and politics, Arendt on

"Understanding and Politics" (Arendt, 1954), 4n7, 18n5, 48nn15–17, 50n21, 52n25, 54n30, 54n32, 55n33
Universal Natural History and Theory of Heaven (Kant, 1755), 23

Vernant, Jean-Pierre, 111n12
Vesper, Bernhard, 149
Vietnam War, 140
violence: Müller's *Germania Death in Berlin* on, 151, 153, 160–61, 169, 170n47, 174–78; of RAF in *Germany in Autumn,* 132, 140–43. See also "Toward a Critique of Violence"
Virgil, 157
Voegelin, Eric, 16
Vogel, Hans-Joachim, 128
Vogl, Joseph, 64n17

Waismann, Friedrich, x
Weber, Max, 132n24, 141–42n37
Wehner, Herbert, 128
"What Is Authority?" (Arendt, 1961), 28
What Maisie Knew (James, 1897), xxv
Wilde, Frau, 149–50
"wild man," 60, 66n15
Wittgenstein, Ludwig, x, 1
Wordsworth, William, 54
Wright, Richard, xiii

zoological metaphors: Arendt's use of, 24; in Müller's *Germania Death in Berlin,* 161–64
Zutatenfilm (recipe film), 8n21

CPSIA information can be obtained
at www.ICGtesting.com
Printed in the USA
LVHW08s2037201018
594274LV00008B/121/P